The Hidden America

The Hidden America
Social Problems
in Rural America
for the Twenty-First Century

Edited by
Robert M. Moore III

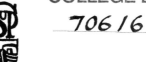

Selinsgrove: Susquehanna University Press
London: Associated University Presses

Associated University Presses
440 Forsgate Drive
Cranbury, NJ 08512

Associated University Presses
16 Barter Street
London WC1A 2AH, England

Associated University Presses
P.O. Box 338, Port Credit
Mississauga, Ontario
Canada L5G 4L8

The paper used in this publication meets the requirements of the American National Standard for Permanence of Paper for Printed Library Materials Z39.48-1984.

Library of Congress Catalogue-in-Publication Data

The hidden America : social problems in rural America for the twenty-first century / edited by Robert M. Moore.
   p.   cm.
Includes bibliographical references and index.
ISBN 1-57591-047-0 (alk. paper)
   1. United States—Rural conditions.   2. United States—Social conditions—1980–   3. Social problems—United States.   I. Moore, Robert M.

HN59.2 .H54 2001
307.72'0973—dc21
00-063523

SECOND PRINTING 2002

PRINTED IN THE UNITED STATES OF AMERICA

Contents

Part III: The People of Rural America

Preface

Having spent most of my adult life living and working in suburban or urban places, it took a couple years for me to feel comfortable in rural America. Initially I was perplexed when merchants seemed to smile too long while looking me straight in the eye for what seemed an eternity after giving me my change. I thought for sure I had done something wrong, or maybe they knew something about me I didn't. People seemed closer even in casual everyday social interaction.

Although people can be friendlier in rural America, there is often respect for privacy. Perhaps because of the cohesiveness of many communities, a sharp line is often drawn between one's public and private life. Some topics, such as money, sex, or religion, are frequently approached with caution. Being considered an insider is often impossible if you were not born in the community.

Six years ago, I was hired as a sociology professor at Susquehanna University, located in Selinsgrove, central Pennsylvania. My wife and I rented a house close to the center of town, a short walk from the university. From my office I saw outlines of hills in the distance, where once coal miners had labored beneath the earth's surface concealed from the sunlight. When the wind blew in the wrong direction, the smell of manure freshly spread on the fields seeped through our screen windows.

Local trucks laden with grain or animals regularly passed our house, and our windows rattled. Hand-sewn quilts on porches flapped in the gusts created by passing vehicles. Sometimes Confederate flags were on windshields or bumpers, more often decals of stock car racers. People drove fast in Snyder County. The distance from point to point is often great. Perhaps they thought they were in a race—tucked against the back bumper ready for the right moment to pass.

White crosses were located at different points beside the highway, usually near an intersection, indicating who had been unlucky—killed as a result of an accident. A truck might not have been able to stop at a light in time, or tried to run it, or the driver perhaps suffered from sleep deprivation. New crosses seemed to pop up each week.

At the drive-in movie theatre fifteen miles north of town, parents arrived well before dark. Children played and ran freely between parked vehicles. In addition to the drive-in there was off-track car racing. On Saturday night the roar of engines reverberated throughout the town. People usually capped off an evening with a burger and a shake at the '50s-era malt shop down the road from the mall. As they drove to get something to eat, they passed homes with glowing decorative candles on window sills.

Holidays were celebrated with zest. Front yards were frequently decorated to celebrate upcoming events. Although only a few houses had folk art on the lawn, it was not atypical to see countless houses with an abundance of plastic eggs hung from tree branches for Easter. Homemade ghosts floated above porches for Halloween, and elaborate light shows were part of the Christmas season.

One morning, the chair of the sociology department knocked on my office door. He asked if I would talk to a local reporter about rural poverty. As the newest member of the department, without tenure and desirous to see my name in print, I eagerly accepted. He transferred the call to my office. While waiting, it occurred to me that perhaps I could not speak with confidence about this subject. Although hired as an expert on social welfare-policy issues, I realized that thinking and talking about rural conditions was unfamiliar to me.

It was odd that the chair of the department preferred that I be the one to talk with the reporter. He had lived in rural America for over thirty years. A man of integrity, he probably believed that since I was hired as the expert, out of respect, I should be the one to be interviewed by the representative from the local newspaper. When the phone rang, I did the unthinkable. I passed the buck and suggested to the reporter that she talk to my colleague, an economist, across the hall.

My friend across the hall had taught me a lot about the people and places in the county—mainly in an orientation capacity, showing me where to go to get what I needed. I don't know what he and the reporter talked about, but shortly afterwards he asked me to come to his office. As if to satisfy a curiosity, we both began rummaging through textbooks systematically, first searching indexes for references to rural America. We came up empty.

I grew up in Delaware County, on the Philadelphia border, one of the most densely populated counties in the country. As a boy, late at night, hiding under the covers so my parents couldn't hear, I listened to a little transistor radio. I played a game, trying to receive stations from as far away as possible. Able to receive broadcasts in the early morning hours that originated in small towns in central Pennsylvania, I paused at each station long enough to catch the call letters and locations and then quickly moved to the next. These stations were located in towns that all seemed to end in "burg": Chambersburg, Shippensburg, Lewisburg, and more. I tried to imagine what it would be like living in those places. Their broadcasts seemed so different from the ones I listened to each day.

As a graduate student at Temple, a large university located in North Philadelphia with a very big sociology department, I gave little attention to rural America. Fellow graduate students did not discuss that part of the country and the department placed heavy emphasis on urban conditions. I knew that rural America was being neglected in my studies, but I did not compensate by reading about it. My fellow graduate students and I dreamed of teaching positions in or near big cities where the pay was usually better. Urban America was felt to be a better research laboratory as well.

Two years before completing my doctorate, I was offered a teaching position at Susquehanna. Getting a job before completing my degree was an offer I couldn't refuse. I was hooked. It was ironic that my first teaching position was not in or near a city, but near all those towns that ended in "burg" in central Pennsylvania—the very same places I had heard on the radio as a boy.

After the call from the reporter, I decided I would not be caught off guard again. I thought I could serve my students better by understanding the people and places near the university. Students have better learning experiences when there is a merging of the classroom with the real world. I needed to know about rural America if I was going to be a good teacher.

This book is geared toward people who know little about rural America as well as those who are already very familiar with it and who may even consider rural America their area of expertise. It is my hope that by reading these chapters, the reader will have a deeper understanding of a very neglected area of the country.

Acknowledgments

THIS BOOK IS DEDICATED TO MARY BETH, PAUL, AND HARRY. They understand better than I do what rural America has to offer the people who live there—its beauty, charm, and complexity.

Introduction

THEORETICAL ORIENTATION

The authors of the studies in this book use a conflict-oriented perspective to examine the dynamic qualities of a modern-day economy characterized by inter-regional differences and varied rates of development (McMichael 1996). Emphasis is placed on what people do, given their particular circumstances, to survive. Less emphasis is placed on a strong work ethic or a "good" family to explain the success or failure of people in rural America. Social problems are seen as having their origin in political and economic structures beyond the control of most people who live in rural America (Steinberg 1989).

The presence of a work ethic or belief in "positive" family values is thus seen as a by-product of those efforts rather than a predictive or causal variable, often found in a functionalist perspective. The romantic view many people have of rural America is replaced by a deeper, more structural, analysis of the variables that perpetuate social problems in rural America.

THE ORIGINS OF SOCIAL PROBLEMS

The characteristics that attract companies to rural America, such as lower taxes, lower overhead, and a dispersed population, make it more difficult for rural people to combat the social problems that accompany economic development and change. These social problems are homelessness, domestic abuse, juvenile delinquency, crime, drug abuse, and more. Regional rather than local social services compound the difficulty of providing immediate help to communities (Castle 1993). Underdeveloped rural economies make it more difficult to produce environments that foster the positive socialization of younger generations (Castle 1993; Cooper 1993; Fisher 1993; Bradshaw 1993). DeHaan and Deal's chapter, "Effects of Economic Hardship on Rural Children and Adolescents," examines the relationship

13

between a family's attainment of resources and the well being of their offspring. Levine et al. and Susan Murty in their respective chapters, "Faces on the Data: Access to Health Care for People with Disabilities Living in Rural Communities" and "Regionalization of Rural Service Delivery," look closely at the availability of health and social services.

The protection against poverty is not as great in rural America as it is in urban America. More rigid employee-employer relations depress wages and provide less protection against losing a job (Duncan 1996; Kwong 1987). Financial instability can adversely affect marital stability and parental-child relationships. College attendance by rural teenagers is lower than among suburban or urban teenagers. The lack of readily accessible social services may push some families to break up (Brown and Hirschl 1995).

Wilson believes that as middle-class families leave urban America, not only is financial capital withdrawn but also social capital, that is, role models and community leaders. The loss of "good" values often accompanies economic instability; emphasis on marriage decreases and more children are born to non-married parents (Wilson 1980, 1987, 1996; Anderson 1990). The lack of well-paying jobs in rural America can have an effect similar to what occurs in many urban areas. Kearns and Rosenthal, in their chapter "Drugs and Violence in Rural America," show that illegal drugs and violence do exist in rural America.

Given the isolation of many areas, increasing pockets of need in rural America can cause social problems to be more acute than those found in urban America. Unlike urban Americans, many rural people are without a political voice. Medicare reimbursement to rural hospitals is 40 percent less than to urban hospitals (Simons et al. 1997).

POPULATION CHANGES

Few rural Americans depend on agriculture or on the extraction of resources, compared to a few generations ago, to make a living. The majority of rural Americans are employed in service-related businesses. Because so many depend on employment in service-related businesses, as do people living in urban America, social problems in rural America often resemble those found in cities.

Karen Anijar's chapter, "Reframing Rural Education—Through Slippage and Memory," examines the role of education in the lives of the youth of rural America. Erik R. Stewart et al., in "Parenting Practices of Rural Families and Their Relationship to Adolescent Educational and Emotional Outcomes," look at the complex relationship between parenting practices and educational achievement. In most rural areas, college-educated people continue to leave (Mayer 1993; White 1998). On the other hand, some mountain areas, particularly in the west, have seen the arrival of a more educated and affluent population—fulfilling the three Rs of recreation, retirement, and a rural residence (Castle 1993). People can now set up businesses and live in remote areas, because of communication advances, without fear of losing contact with people elsewhere.

More and more high-tech firms are moving to non-metro areas, particularly in the West. High-tech industries often require post-high school training. Although "FIRE" industries (finance, investment, and real estate) have brought many new jobs to rural America, they often do not require a college degree for employment. To guard against economic fluctuations that may lead to the exacerbation of social problems, some feel that land-grant universities should be used to foster the use of non-agricultural expertise already present in rural America to attract and retain non-agricultural businesses (ibid).

Although many people do not depend on farming, the voices that are heard in the nation's capital are those that reflect agricultural interests (ibid). The need for a broad-based coalition in rural America is great (Flora and Flora 1993). The '90s produced a net in-migration to rural America (Shumway and Davis 1996). Federal policymakers need to be more aware of rural economic diversity.

DEVELOPMENT

Over thirty-five new metropolitan areas have developed in rural America since 1970 (Elliott and Perry 1996). Their formation was caused primarily by migration from other already established metro areas. This replaced an older pattern of development based on internal migration from rural area to rural area. There was some non-metro migration to the new metro areas but not as much as migration from already established metro areas. Local employment in FIRE played a significant role in the migration (ibid).

The development of metropolitan areas in rural America presents theoretical problems for researchers. It is hard to tell if parts of rural America recovered from the '80s on their own or if the migration of people from metro areas is responsible for the recovery (Elliott and Perry 1996; Castle 1993).

RURAL CULTURE

Less than 10 percent of the rural population, and less than 2 percent of the United States population, lives on farms (Castle 1993; Bird and Ikerd 1993). About 27 percent of the United States population lives in rural America (Fisher 1993; Albrecht 1998).

Farm productivity increased dramatically after World War II, and the industrialization of agriculture became the norm (Bird and Ikerd 1993). As a result, farm consolidations rose, population was lost, and there was an increase in environmental misuse of the land (ibid.). A growing sustainable-agriculture movement is trying to solve these problems by placing emphasis on organic growing, rotational grazing to better manage land, and promoting a sense of empowerment among farmers. A more educated farm population is needed (ibid.).

Even on sustainable farms, the expected duties of a man and a woman are often different. Men are more farm-centered and involved in the ideals of the movement, whereas women are more community-oriented. Agricultural communities have emphasized more traditional male and female roles (Meares 1997).

Bartering and trading of services between families is extensive (Jensen, Cornwell, and Findeis 1995). Bartering is the exchange of *different* goods or services and is often done by men. Trading is the exchange of goods and services that are similar and is often done by women, for example, babysitting. A great deal of money is saved through barter and trade. Often seen as a cultural characteristic unique to rural America, these activities are out of economic necessity. People who move to a community may feel like outsiders because access to bartering and trading may not be immediate. Barter and trading increase social contact and interaction in rural communities.

Rural cultures have been romanticized as having a slower pace and more respect for one's neighbors, as great places to raise kids and having respect for older people. Low population density produces a "high density of acquaintanceship" in many areas (Flora and Flora 1993). People know each other well and place more meaning on casual social interaction. Perhaps the minimal presence of formal helping systems, for example social services, can explain the extensive development of informal relationships among many rural Americans.

Ironically, the heightened interconnectedness in many rural communities exacerbates social problems. Women who experience domestic abuse may feel more reluctant to call for help. Tight-knit communities produce greater feelings of shame, self-blame, and feelings of "don't rock the boat." Local police, who should be called on to intervene in domestic-abuse situations, are often friends of the family. Carol Feyen's chapter, "Isolated Acts: Domestic Violence in a Rural Community," takes a close look at domestic problems in one Wisconsin community. Linda Cummins, in her chapter, "Homelessness Among Rural Women," looks at homelessness and women.

Men can also feel reluctant to call for help if they have experienced personal problems, for example, depression or excessive alcohol use. Masculinity and femininity are often more clearly delineated in many rural areas. More men work a second job for a wage in rural America than in metro areas (Nelson 1999).

Stereotypes associated with rural America include the idea that people have a stronger emphasis on family and a work ethic than in urban areas. Appearances can be deceiving. In agricultural areas farm consolidation continues to occur, and the less financially well-off leave. Agricultural communities thus have lower unemployment rates than other areas of rural America. Divorce rates are also lower, since those who remain are more economically stable. Economic stability often fosters marital stability. But service-dominated areas in rural America have experienced social problems similar to those found in metro areas (Albrecht 1998).

MINORITY POPULATIONS

The use of a conflict perspective enables researchers to examine populations in rural America that are ignored using other perspectives. For example, recent findings indicate that being part of a minority group, that is, controlling for other variables such as income and education, indicates a greater likelihood of living in poverty (Brown and Hirschl 1995). Chapters by Sandra Faiman-Silva and Bonnie Jean Adams, "Corporations and Native Americans in Rural America: Who Wins?" and "American Indians in Rural America— Conditions and Concerns," respectively, examine the situation of Native Americans in two different parts of the country.

Although few African Americans remain in rural America, 15 percent, the majority live in the South (Snippy 1996; Steinberg 1995). Most live in isolated pockets close to where their ancestors might have been slaves (Snippy 1996). African Americans reflect a broader movement that has occurred during much of this century from farm to town (Mayer 1993).

Social networks tend to be intra-racial rather than interracial. African Americans who are poor have fewer life chances compared to rural whites and African Americans in urban areas. Fewer social services are available (Albrecht, Clarke, and Miller 1998; Jones 1995;

Jensen 1995; Gates 1995). Other perspectives may ignore the considerable complexities of race in parts of rural America and how issues related to race are often interwoven with the development of a local economic infrastructure.

The income of all Black families in the South is only 60 percent that of white families (Brown, Christy and Gebremedhin 1995). African American farmers receive less help from the government than white farmers and the number of Black farmers has declined at a steeper rate (Jones 1995). African American communities exist as the direct result of Jim Crow laws (ibid). Wilburn Hayden's chapter, "African Americans in Appalachia: A Different Experience," looks at the location of African American communities in rural America.

A continued need for labor in some rural counties has attracted workers from third-world countries. In California and some midwestern states, the middle class is leaving because of a perceived change in the quality of life brought about as a result of people arriving from other countries to work (Allensworth and Rochin 1998).

A cycle is created. As the middle class leaves, more housing becomes available and more people with less money are attracted to the area. Although the middle class may leave their houses, many continue to work in the community. They commute from nearby bedroom communities (ibid.). Rochelle L. Dalla and Shirley L. Baugher in their chapter "Immigration and the Rural Midwest" examine the changes that take place in a community when workers from another country arrive.

Perhaps this is what happened in urban America in the '50s and '60s when African Americans came to urban America after living on the land. Scholars debate whether people moved first to the suburbs or to jobs. In parts of rural America, people are moving first. Jobs for the middle class may soon follow.

Flora and Flora point out that broad-based citizen involvement is important in decision-making processes. They cite the inclusion of minorities, including women, to be important to enable people in rural America to depend more on local people and resources than on outsiders (Flora and Flora 1993).

Given the nature of rural economies, that is, a strong reliance on service-oriented businesses, some solutions to social problems may be similar to those emphasized in suburban and urban areas (Bradshaw 1993). Scholars now use perspectives and concepts formerly applied primarily to suburban and urban analyses, such as feminist theory, "spatial" conceptions of work, and household divisions of labor (Tickamyer 1996). Still the stereotypes, for example, "all is well," linger about rural America.

Making a Living

The livelihood of people in rural America often depends on decisions made by those who live elsewhere. Rural policy should foster the steady development of a more permanent economic infrastructure in local communities. Economic strategies should be planned with the people they are intended to help. This allows people in rural America to feel a sense of empowerment and control over their lives (Flora and Flora 1993).

Because of its economic diversity, policies designed to apply to all of rural America are unrealistic (Cooper 1993; Bradshaw 1993). Few regions in rural America depend on each other. Those that do, called "ruralplexes," exist because of specialization. Production of a single product can take place in several plants in different locations (ibid.). Independence from region to region in rural America is more the norm than interdependence.

The needs of companies in a post-industrial economy can quickly change. An emphasis on product innovation means that companies may want to move to new locations more often than in the past (Cooper 1993). More companies seek contractual over permanent labor, lowering wages, decreasing benefits, and increasing job insecurity. Katherine Cason and Terry F. Buss, in their respective chapters "Poverty in Rural America" and "Economic Development in Rural America," examine the economic complexities of non-metro areas.

Organization of the Book

Social problems are often caused by the structure of a regional or local economy. The first and last chapters of the book deal specifically with topics related to a rural economy, such as poverty and economic opportunity. In the first section of the book, "Jobs, Tradition, and Social Behavior," three serious issues are examined: the effect of poverty on children and adolescents, homelessness among women, and domestic violence. The second section, "Taking Care of Our Own," looks at what can be done to help people lead better lives in rural America. Several key areas are presented: parenting practices, drugs and violence, health care for people with disabilities, and the availability of social services. The final section, "People of Rural America," examines people and institutions scholars often neglect: immigrants from third-world countries, education, Native Americans and African Americans.

Almost all of the twenty-four contributors have worked or been affiliated with a university or college. Their institutional affiliations are listed on the contributors' page. Many more social problems could have been included. But the chapters that follow address the ones the editor feels are most important.

REFERENCES

Albrecht, D. E. 1998. "The Industrial Transformation of Farm Communities: Implications for Family Structure and Socioeconomic Conditions." *Rural Sociology* 63 (1): 51–64.

Allensworth, E. M., and R. I. Rochin. 1998. "Ethnic Transformations in Rural California: Looking Beyond the Immigrant Farmworker." *Rural Sociology* 63 (1): 26–50.

Anderson, E. 1990. *Streetwise: Race, Class, and Change in an Urban Community.* Chicago:. University of Chicago Press.

Bird, G. W. and J. Ikerd. 1993. "Sustainable Agriculture: A Twenty-First-Century System." *The Annals of the American Academy of Political and Social Science* 529 (Sept.): 92–102.

Bradshaw, T. K. 1993. "Multicommunity Networks: A Rural Transition." *The Annals of the American Academy of Political and Social Science* 529 (Sept.): 164–75.

Brown, A., Jr., R. D. Christy, and T. G. Gebremedhin. 1995. In *Blacks in Rural America*, ed. J. B. Stewart and J. E. Allen-Smith. New Brunswick, N.J.: Transaction Publishers.

Brown, D. L. and T. A. Hirschl. 1995. "Household Poverty in Rural and Metropolitan-Core Areas of the United States." *Rural Sociology* 60 (1): 44–66.

Castle, E. N. 1993. "Rural Diversity: An American Asset." *The Annals of the American Academy of Political and Social Science* 529 (Sept.): 12–21.

Clarke, L. L., and M. K. Miller. 1998. "Community, Family, and Race/Ethnic Differences in Health Status in Rural Areas." *Rural Sociology* 63 (2): 235–252.

Cooper, R. S. 1993. "The New Economic Regionalism: A Rural Policy Framework." *The Annals of the American Academy of Political and Social Science* 529 (Sept.): 34–47.

Duncan, C. M. 1996. "Understanding Persistent Poverty: Social Class Context in Rural Communities." *Rural Sociology* 61 (1): 103–24.

Elliott, J. R. and M. J. Perry. 1996. "Metropolitanizing Nonmetro Space: Population Redistribution and Emergent Metropolitan Areas, 1965–1990." *Rural Sociology* 61 (3): 497–512.

Fisher, D. U. 1993. "Agriculture's Role in a New Rural Coalition." *The Annals of the American Academy of Political and Social Science* 529 (Sept.): 103–112.

Flora, C. B., and J. L. Flora. 1993. "Entrepreneurial Social Infrastructure: A Necessary Ingredient." *The Annals of the American Academy of Political and Social Science* 529 (Sept.): 48–58.

Gates, H. L. Jr. 1995. *Colored People: A Memoir.* New York: Vintage Books.

Jensen, L. 1995. "Employment Hardship and Rural Minorities: Theory, Research, and Policy." In *Blacks in Rural America*, ed. J. B. Stewart and J. E. Allen-Smith. New Brunswick, N.J.: Transaction Publishers.

Jensen, L., G. T. Cornwell, and J. L. Findeis. 1995. "Informal Work in Nonmetropolitan Pennsylvania." *Rural Sociology* 60 (1): 91–107.

Jones, H. S. 1995. "Federal Agricultural Policies: Do Black Farm Operators Benefit?" In *Blacks in Rural America*, ed. J. B. Stewart and J. E. Allen-Smith. New Brunswick, N.J.: Transaction Publishers.

Kwong, Peter. 1987. *The New Chinatown*, New York: Noonday Press.

Mayer, L. V. 1993. "Agricultural Change and Rural America." *The Annals of the American Academy of Political and Social Science* 529 (Sept.): 80–91.

McMichael, Philip. 1996. "Globalization: Myths and Realities." *Rural Sociology* 61 (1): 25–55.

Meares, A. C. 1997. "Making the Transition from Conventional to Sustainable Agriculture: Gender, Social Movement Participation, and Quality of Life on the Family Farm." *Rural Sociology* 62 (1): 21–47.

Nelson, M. K. 1999. "Economic Restructuring, Gender, and Informal Work: A Case Study of a Rural County." *Rural Sociology* 64 (1): 18–43.

Shumway, J. M., and J. A. Davis. 1996. "Nonmetropolitan Population Change in the Mountain West: 1970–1995." *Rural Sociology* 61 (3): 513–29.

Simons, R. L., C. Johnson, R. D. Conger, and F. O. Lorenz. 1997. "Linking Community Context to Quality of Parenting: A Study of Rural Families." *Rural Sociology* 62 (2): 207–30.

Snippy, C. M. 1996. "Understanding Race and Ethnicity in Rural America." *Rural Sociology* 61 (1):125–42.

Steinberg, Stephen. 1989. *The Ethnic Myth: Race, Ethnicity, and Class in America*. Boston: Beacon Press.

___. 1995. *The Retreat From Racial Justice in American Thought and Policy: Turning Back*. Boston: Beacon Press.

Tickamyer, A. R. 1996. "Sex, Lies, and Statistics: Can Rural Sociology Survive Restructing? (or) What Is Right with Rural Sociology and How Can We Fix It?" *Rural Sociology* 61 (1): 5–24.

White, S. E. 1998. "Migration Trends in the Kansas Ogallala Region and the Internal Colonial Dependency Model." *Rural Sociology* 63 (2): 253–71.

Wilson, W. J. 1980. *The Declining Significance of Race*. Chicago:. University of Chicago Press.

___. 1987. *The Truly Disadvantaged: The Inner City, The Underclass, and Public Policy*. Chicago: University of Chicago Press.

___. 1996. *When Work Disappears: The New World of the Urban Poor*. New York: Alfred A. Knopf.

The Hidden America

I
Jobs, Tradition, and Social Behavior

Poverty in Rural America

KATHERINE CASON

WHEN ADDRESSING THE ISSUE OF POVERTY, IT IS IMPORTANT to include some discussion about cost of living and earnings. Since the beginning of the century, there have been efforts to determine the minimum costs of meeting a family's monthly needs. Known as a living wage, this is the amount of earnings necessary for a family to meet its most basic costs. To date, most of the attempts to calculate a living wage have been based on estimates of the cost of living in urban areas.

Differences in the local cost of living by rural and urban residence limit the ability to generalize from urban-based approaches. For example, public transportation is available in urban areas for going to and from work, for shopping, for health care, as well as for other purposes. But in rural areas, public transportation is rare. The only way for an individual to get around in most rural communities is by personal transportation such as a vehicle or by sharing a ride with a friend.

Researchers have estimated cost of living for a single mother with two children in rural Kentucky to be $394 per week, $1,642 per month, or $19,709 per year (Zimmerman 1998). In order to meet the minimum budget and pay taxes, this would require an hourly wage of $10.61. According to the 1996 *Current Population Survey,* the average weekly earnings for all non-metro women aged 16 to 24 average earnings were even lower at 55 cents of the metro dollar. When calculated based on a 40 hour work week, non-metro women earned on average $8.33 per hour. This means that non-metro women are earning an average of $4556 less per year than the benchmark identified by Zimmerman (1998). For non-metro women aged 16 to 24, the gap is even larger. Non-metro women of this age group earned an average of $5.55 an hour when calculated for a 40 hour work week. This is $10,116 less per year than the benchmark, and $2,230 a year below the current poverty threshold for a family of three.

According to the 1996 Current Population Survey, the rural South has the lowest average earnings ($406 a week) compared to other rural regions. This is 81 cents for every dollar earned by metro Southern workers. The rural South is also home to the lowest proportion of college-educated workers, the largest percentage of high school graduates who do not plan to attend college, and the largest percentage of persons who have never even completed high school. Yet, employment growth has been in jobs that require ever higher levels of education and training. As a result, unemployment remains highest for those with the least amount of formal education.

While employment growth has been strong generally, rural areas have continued to lag behind urban areas. The rural job market tends to have a high proportion of low-wage jobs; 10.7 percent of rural workers earned between $4.25 and $5.14 an hour in 1995–96, compared to 7 percent of metro workers (Parker 1997). The high concentration of workers in low-wage jobs, large minority populations, and high levels of unemployment have produced high welfare dependency for rural areas of the country, especially in the South.

DIFFERENCES IN AVERAGE EARNINGS BY SEX

Data has shown that of the women aged 25 to 54 who accessed jobs, 43.1 percent entered low-paying service-producing industries. The majority of these women (82.9 percent) were paid by the hour at an average rate of $4.84. The remaining women were paid weekly and had an average pay of $196 (U.S. Bureau of the Census 1992). In contrast, only 28.8 percent of men aged 25 to 54 who accessed jobs entered the low-paying service-producing industries. Most of these men (64.7 percent) were paid hourly, with an average wage rate of $6.62. The men who were paid weekly had an average salary of $374, significantly more than women entering the same industry (U.S. Bureau of the Census 1992).

The decline in real wages has greatly affected many single mothers who shoulder the full financial burden of their households and who have disproportionately experienced a drop in level of income and an increase in the rate of poverty. As real wages have declined and incomes have become more unequal, low wages, discrimination, and a reliance on wage income have caused women's real wages to drop more than men's wages, and have caused women's poverty rates to increase at a rate much faster than men's.

RACIAL DISPARITIES IN EARNINGS

Minorities, with the exception of many Asian groups, are disadvantaged in rural labor markets. Compared with Caucasians, they are more likely to have been jobless in the previous year or, if they worked, to have worked part-time or part-year. Minority earnings are lower than average in rural areas and this gap increased between 1979 and 1989. Native American men have extremely high rates of joblessness (21 percent) and little full-time work. Hispanic men are hampered by poor English ability and a concentration in agriculture much more than that of Hispanic women. African American men appear to face pay discrimination not encountered by other groups or African American women. All of these problems tended to be more pronounced at the end of the 1980s and early 1990s than in previous decades.

Neither African American men nor African American women in the rural South, where more than 90 percent of all rural African Americans live, enjoyed significant improvement in occupational status during the 1980s, a marked contrast to earlier periods. African Americans were half as likely to work in white-collar jobs as Caucasians and twice as likely to work in service occupations. Racial differences in educational attainment and industry type explain only part of the occupational structure.

Despite some increases in education among rural minority groups during the 1980s and 1990s, they remain overrepresented among those lacking a high school diploma. They are less likely than other rural workers to have the education necessary to yield stable or increasing earnings. College completion rose only among Hispanic and Native American women, and then only slightly.

Unemployment rates were higher in 1990 than in 1980 for African Americans, especially those with lower levels of education. Due to limited job opportunities at lower skill levels, young adults who did not graduate from high school had the highest unemployment rates.

Concentrated largely in the Southwest, Hispanics had the greatest numerical growth of all minority groups in rural areas in the last decade. Poverty increased for rural Hispanics, a trend partly related to the combined effect of continuing immigration, lack of English-language proficiency, and concentration in agricultural employment.

NEGATIVE CONSEQUENCES OF BEING POOR: EFFECT OF POVERTY ON CHILD OUTCOMES

The physical, psychological, social, and economic tolls of poverty are both interconnected and interdependent. It is not difficult to document that poor children suffer a disproportionate share of deprivation, hardship, and negative outcomes as a result of living in poverty. Not only do poor children have access to fewer material goods than wealthy or middle-class children, but they are also more likely to experience poor health and to die during childhood. Poor children suffer from emotional and behavioral problems more frequently than do non-poor children. In school, they score lower on standardized tests and are more likely to be retained in grade and to drop out. Poor teens are more likely to have out-of-wedlock births and to experience violent crimes. Persistently poor children are more likely to end up as poor adults. Public concern for poor children has focused both on their material well-being and on the relationship between poverty and important child outcomes that the public values such as success in school. However, accurately measuring the effects of poverty on many important child outcomes is a challenge.

Researchers studying child poverty in the 1960s developed and tested interventions designed to ameliorate the negative effects of poverty. Much of this research examined children's intellectual development measured by I.Q. tests and school achievement. Increases in child poverty in the early 1980s spurred a subsequent wave of research, with a focus on children's overall poverty. More recent studies continue to investigate how children are affected by low income, but they use a broader range of analytical frameworks and research methods than earlier research. These studies have explored contextual influences such as school, neighborhood, and community, as well as implications of poverty for children's socioeconomic behavior.

Research consistently reports that economically deprived children are at high risk of mental health problems. Social maladaptation and psychological problems such as depression, low self-confidence, peer conflict, and conduct disorders are more prevalent among poor children than among economically advantaged children (Gibbs 1986; Kellam et al. 1977; Langner et al. 1969; Langner et al. 1970; Levinson 1969; Myers 1983). Children in families receiving Aid to Families with Dependent Children (AFDC) have significantly more emotional and behavioral problems than children in families that have never received nor applied for AFDC (Levinson 1969). Compared to children living in nonpoor, two-parent households, children in poor, female-headed households have an admission rate to psychiatric outpatient services that is two to four times higher (Belle 1980). There is also evidence that poor children in both AFDC and non-AFDC families suffer greater impairment of self-confidence, school functioning, and relationships with their peers than children from higher-income families although, in general, impairment tends to be greatest among poor children in AFDC families (Levinson 1969). Undoubtedly, poor children's struggle with ongoing negative physical conditions and with circumstances such as those described earlier contributes to the psychological problems they experience.

A large body of research documents that children raised in families with socioeconomic status do worse than children raised in families with high socioeconomic status in terms of intellectual and social development, behavioral problems, and delinquency (Hutson et al. 1994). Income loss appears to affect the well-being of children indirectly through negative impact on family relations and parenting. Single parents experience a variety of stressors related to poverty such as financial, social, and emotional stress. The link between economic stress and mental health has been documented in various studies. Financial strain is one of the strongest predictors of depression in single parents. Higher levels of depression are predictive of more punitive disciplinary practices and decreased parental nurturance, support, and satisfaction with the parenting role (McLoyd 1994). The chronic strains of poverty combined with task overload significantly increase vulnerability to new life stressors. Poor single mothers often experience a cycle of hopelessness and despair which is detrimental to both themselves and their children.

Chronic stressors, in combination with a continuous succession of negative life events, militate against positive mental health in children who are poor (Belle 1984). Poverty, especially if it is persistent, is a pervasive crisis distinguished by a high contagion of stressors that erode and deplete emotional reserves. The most blatant stressors derive from the ecological context—inadequate housing and environmental instability (Makosky 1982; Ray 1986). There is ongoing debate, however, over what factors explain the differences in children's outcomes.

Despite the evidence that poor children experience undesirable outcomes across a wide variety of indicators, many studies lack the precision needed to separate the effects on children of the array of factors other than low income associated with poverty. For example, poor families are more likely to be headed by a parent who is young, single, has low educational attainment, is unemployed, and has low earnings potential. These parental attributes, separately or in combination, may account for some of the observed negative consequences of poverty for children. In addition, the population of poor families is a mix of families who are temporarily poor and families who have experienced chronic hardship. Although the majority of poor families are only temporarily poor, the experiences of the chronically poor fit better the stereotype of underclass trapped in concentrated poverty neighborhoods, beset by high crime rates, poor schools, substance abuse, and other social pathologies. Failure to take account of the differences in the duration of poverty children experience may lead to either an under- or overestimate of the effects of poverty.

Understanding the relationships among income, other parental characteristics, community factors, and environmental hazards and child outcomes is key to designing effective policies to ameliorate the problems of the poor. Programs that only alter family income may not be the most appropriate for the reduction of poverty and its effects. Many believe that children would be better off if both parents worked rather than depending upon public assistance, even if the withdrawal of welfare support led to a reduction in their material well-being. Mayer (1997) concludes that increasing family income above the minimum required to meet children's basic material needs is not likely to correct the problems associated with child poverty, and significantly improve a child's chances for success.

Brooks-Gunn and Duncan (1997) have examined the effects of family income on a number of child outcomes, reaching different conclusions. They have reviewed studies based on large longitudinal surveys that attempt to measure the effects of income on children independent of the effects of other conditions that might be related to being raised in a low-income household. They find that family income can substantially affect child and adolescent outcomes but that the negative effects of poverty are more pronounced for some outcomes than for others and vary depending on the depth and duration of a child's exposure to poverty. Income seems to be strongly related to children's physical health, cognitive ability, and school achievement in the early grades, even after controlling for a number of other parental characteristics. These effects are most pronounced for children who experience persistent and extreme poverty. Brooks-Gunn and Duncan (1997) also suggest that the timing of poverty is important: low income during the preschool and early elementary school years is more predictive of low rates of high school completion than poverty during later childhood and adolescence. The researchers also report that much of the beneficial effect of family income on the cognitive outcomes in young children is mediated by improvements in the home environment associated with higher income.

Montgomery (1996) investigated the independent and relative effects of family structure, race, and poverty on the health of children under twenty years of age at two time periods, 1978 through 1980 and 1989 through 1991. Montgomery found that children in families headed by single mothers, African American children, and those living below 150 percent of the poverty index were much more likely to be in poor or fair health than children in two-parent families, Caucasian children, or those in more affluent families. Poverty had the strongest effect on child health in both time periods. The researcher concluded that the association between children's health and living below 150 percent of the poverty index is not explained by race or family structure. The disparity in child health is instead related directly to family income.

Educational attainment is well recognized as a powerful predictor of experiences in later life. A comprehensive review of the relationship between parental income and school attainment concluded that poverty limited school achievement but that the effect of income on the number of school years completed was small (U.S. House of Representatives 1996). In general, the studies suggested that a 10 percent increase in family income is associated with a 0.2 percent to 2 percent increase in the number of school years completed.

Several other studies using different longitudinal data sets also find that poverty status has a small negative impact on high school graduation and years of schooling obtained. Much of the observed relationship between income and schooling appears to be related to a number of confounding factors such as parental education, family structure, and neighborhood characteristics (Haveman 1995). All of the studies suggest that, after controlling for many appropriate confounding variables, the effects of poverty on school achievement are likely to be statistically significant, yet minimal. Based on the results of one study, the authors estimated that if poverty were eliminated for all children, mean years of schooling for all children would increase by 0.3 percent, or less than half a month (Haveman 1994).

Few researchers who have examined the effects of family income on child outcomes believe that material resources money can provide do not matter to children. Food, housing, health care, and other necessities are crucial for children's well-being, and extra income can make life more enjoyable. The question is whether the extra money, above subsistence level of income, would make a difference in child outcomes. Much research on income effects has attempted to separate the effects of low income from the effects of single motherhood, minority status, low levels of education, and adolescent parenting—all of which are correlated with poverty. The research indicates that income seems to have a larger, more consistent independent effect on some outcomes such as school achievement than others such as adolescent childbearing. The timing and persistence of poverty are important factors in the magnitude of the impact. However, the web of conditions contributing to the problems of children in poverty has not been completely disentangled.

POVERTY, HUNGER, AND FOOD INSECURITY

Living in poverty often means individuals are victims of hunger (Clancy and Bowering 1992). The likelihood of experiencing food insecurity is directly related to income (Uvin 1994). Living below the poverty line puts tremendous strains on a household budget, adversely affecting the ability to purchase a nutritionally adequate diet (Clancy and Bowering 1992). Hunger and the broader issue of food security have been a public concern in the United States since our nation's inception. One of the earliest underlying goals of public policy still in effect is to assure an adequate supply of safe, nutritious food at reasonable cost (Voichick and Drake 1994). Recent studies suggest at least 30 million Americans, including 11 million children, currently experience food insecurity (Wehler 1996).

Food security can be defined as access by all people at all times to enough food for an active, healthy life. Food security includes at a minimum the ready availability of nutritionally adequate and safe foods, and an assured ability to acquire acceptable foods in socially acceptable ways (Hamilton 1997). The consequences of food insecurity on the individual, the family, and society are enormous. The complex issues surrounding food insecurity encompass physiological, social, and economic dimensions. Food, or lack of it, is a determinant of human development, health, and behavior. Its absence affects a community's economy, taxes its resources, and influences its social policies (Breglio 1992).

Food security has been described as including four components. First is the quantitative aspect, which addresses whether the household has access to a sufficient quantity of food—enough to eat, not going to bed hungry. Second is a qualitative component, which is concerned with the nutritional adequacy of the available food as well as its suitability for the family. Suitability includes consideration of cultural factors and capacity for food storage and preparation, which may be affected by skills and access to usable cooking utensils and appliances. Food must also be nutritionally balanced and acceptable. The third component of food security is psychological. This has to do with anxiety, lack of choice, and feelings of deprivation when hunger and food insecurity are experienced. A social component completes the definition of food insecurity. When food security is threatened, food acquisition methods and eating patterns may deviate from what is socially acceptable, and descend to stealing, eating from dumps, and eating pet foods (Splett 1994).

Those who experience food insecurity may try to avoid hunger, the uneasy or painful sensation caused by a lack of food, by decreasing the size of meals, skipping meals, or not eating any food for one or more days. When food is severely limited, these methods for avoiding hunger are ineffective (Klein 1996). Lack of food, and subsequent under-nutrition, affects physiological function in every stage of the life cycle. Most adversely affected, however, are the fetus, pregnant and lactating women, children, and older adults. According to the Community Childhood Hunger Identification Project (CCHIP), hungry children suffer from two to four times as many individual health problems as low-income children whose families do not experience food shortages. Only 44 percent of low income children consumed at or above 100 percent of the Recommended Dietary Allowance (RDA) for calories (USDA 1989).

Failure to grow is one consequence of under-nutrition. In addition, inadequate food intake limits the ability of children to learn about the world around them (Center on Hunger, Poverty and Nutrition Policy 1993). Before growth is affected, other subtle changes occur. When children are chronically undernourished, their bodies attempt to conserve energy by shutting down "non-essential" bodily functions, leaving energy available for vital organs and growth. If any energy remains, it can be used for social activity and cognitive development. When the body conserves energy, decreased activity levels and increased apathy soon follow. This in turn affects social interactions, inquisitiveness, and overall cognitive functioning. In comparison to non-hungry children, hungry children are more than four times as likely to suffer from fatigue; almost three times as likely to suffer from irritability; more than twelve times as likely to report dizziness; and almost three times as likely to suffer from concentration problems (FRAC 1991).

In the United States, iron-deficiency anemia is still common in infants and young children between six months and three years of age, and again during adolescence. About twice as many four- to five-year-old African American children have iron deficiency as Mexican American or Caucasian children. The most common causes of anemia in childhood are inadequate intakes of iron, infection, and lead poisoning. Among children 12 to 36 months of age with iron-deficiency anemia, 20.6 percent were from low-income families (Fomon 1993).

Lead poisoning in young children is frequently, but not exclusively, associated with poverty (Needleman 1994). Exposure to lead, in paint chips or paint dust, is increased in older homes in which lead paint was used. Risk of lead poisoning increases in those children who are consuming inadequate amounts of iron and calcium, a nutritional likelihood related to poverty. The primary consequences of lead poisoning are iron-deficiency anemia, impaired I.Q., speech and language function scores, and hyperactivity (Bellinger et al. 1978).

Pregnant women who are undernourished are more likely to have low-birth-weight babies. These infants are more likely to suffer delays in their development and are more likely to have behavioral and learning problems later in life. The infant mortality rate is closely linked to inadequate quantity or quality in the diet of the infant's mother (USDHHS 1994).

Older adults are also at increased risk of suffering health consequences as a result of food insecurity and hunger. Older adults have a number of risk factors contributing to food insecurity which place them at an increased risk for developing malnutrition. Among these risk factors are diseases such as chronic lung disease, heart disease, neurological diseases; disabilities, functional impairments; sensory losses; poor dental health; multiple medication use; therapeutic diets; and social isolation. Malnutrition in older adults can result in loss of muscle mass, which can lead to disabilities that affect levels of independence. Malnutrition can also compromise immune function, increasing susceptibility to infections (Codispoti 1994).

Hunger, and insecurity about whether a family will be able to obtain enough food to avoid hunger, also have an emotional impact on children and their parents. Anxiety, negative feelings about self worth, and hostility toward the outside world can result from chronic hunger and food insecurity (World Hunger Year 1994).

WELFARE REFORM — THE PERSONAL RESPONSIBILITY AND WORK OPPORTUNITY RECONCILIATION ACT OF 1996

The Personal Responsibility And Work Opportunity Reconciliation Act of 1996 (PRWORA) is the most comprehensive welfare reform since the Social Security Act of the 1930s (Handler and Hasenfeld 1991). The PRWORA has far-reaching implications in a number of programs. The act fundamentally reforms the Food Stamp program, Supplemental Security Income (SSI) for children, the Child Support Enforcement Program, and benefits for legal immigrants. The act modifies the child nutrition programs and provides cuts in the Social Service Block Grants (SSBG) (Sawhill 1995).

The act features decreases in funding for programs for low-income children and families and requires structural changes in the Aid To Family With Dependent Children (AFDC) program. The act converts AFDC and Job Opportunities and Basic Skills (JOBS) into the Temporary Assistance to Needy Families (TANF) block grant. The act limits family assistance to five years, while granting states the option to limit assistance to a shorter time period.

The PRWORA significantly reduced funding for food assistance programs, and represented a sharp reversal from the trends of the early 1990s. This 1996 legislation contains numerous significant benefit and structural changes to the Food Stamp Program, public assistance programs in general, and to the Summer Food Program and the Child and Adult Care Food Program. Start-up and expansion funds for the School Breakfast and Summer Food Programs were eliminated by this legislation. Entire classes of people have been eliminated from eligibility for the Food Stamp Program. For example, unemployed, childless individuals aged 18 to 50 can only receive food for three months every 36 months.

SUMMARY

Despite all of the programs implemented and legislation designed to reduce poverty and its consequences, poverty and its related effects will continue to be critical issues in the next century. Policies should encompass actions that would prove beneficial in the short as well as long term. Strengthening the safety net can provide benefits that can ameliorate the consequences of poverty in the short term. Programs for social and economic assistance at the federal, state, and local levels, such as job training, child care, housing assistance, adequate minimum wage, medical care, and food assistance benefits should be strengthened. In solving the poverty equation, it is critical that policy makers provide economic initiatives for sustaining long-term economic growth and viability. Public issues education has the potential to improve circumstances across a set of conditions for both low-income children and low-income adults. More can be done over a longer time horizon for poor families, and to address the conditions that lead to poverty. Clearly, new approaches are necessary to eliminate poverty in our communities.

REFERENCES

Belle, D. 1980. "Who uses mental health facilities?" In *The mental health of women*, ed. M. Guttentag, S. Salasin, and D. Belle. New York: Wiley, 1980.

———. 1984. "Inequality and mental health: low income and minority women." In *Women and mental health policy*, ed. L. Walker, 135–50. Beverly Hills, Calif.: Sage.

Bergmann, B. 1996. "Childcare: The key to ending child poverty." In *Social policies for children*, ed. J. L. Garfinkel, A. Hochschild, and S. S. McLanahan, 112–35. Washington, D.C.: Brookings Institution.

Bianchi, S. M. 1993. "Children of poverty: why are they poor?" In *Child Poverty and Public Policy*, ed. J. Chafel. Washington, D.C.: The Urban Institute Press.

Blank, S., and B. Blum. 1997. "A brief history of work expectations for welfare mothers." *The Future of Children* 7 (1): 28–38.

Brayfield, A. A., S. G. Deich, and S. L. Hofferth. 1993. *Caring for children in low-income families: a substudy of the national child care survey, 1990.* Washington D.C.: The Urban Institute Press.

Breglio, V. J. 1992. *Hunger in America: the voter's perspective.* Lanham, Md.: Research/Strategy/Management (RMS), Inc.

Brooks-Gunn, J., and G. J. Duncan. 1997. "The Effects of Poverty on Children." *The Future of Children* 7 (2): 55—71.

Burkhauser, R. V., K. A. Couch, and D. C. Wittenburg. 1996. "Who gets what from minimum wages hikes: a re-estimation of Card and Krueger's distributional analysis in Myth and measurement: the new economics of the minimum wage." *Industrial and labor relations review* 49 (3): 547–52.

Card, D., and A. Krueger. 1995. *Myth and Measurement: The new economics of the minimum wage.* Princeton: Princeton University Press.

Center for Hunger, Poverty and Nutrition Policy. 1993. *The link between nutrition and cognitive development in children.* Medford, Mass.: Tufts University.

Clancy, K. L., and J. Bowering. 1992. "The need for emergency food: poverty problems and policy responses." *Journal of Nutrition Education* 24:12S—17S.

Codispoti, C. L., and B. J. Bartlett. 1994. *Food and nutrition for life: malnutrition and older Americans.* Washington, D.C.: National Aging Information Center. Publication No. NAIC-12.

Davis, C. G. 1977. "Poverty and Rural Underdevelopment in the United States: Where Do We Stand?" In *Rural Poverty and the Policy Crisis*, ed. R. O. Coppedge and C. G. Davis, 11-34. Ames, Iowa: Iowa State University Press.

Dignan, M. B. 1995. *Measurement and evaluation of health education.* Springfield, Ill.: C. C. Thomas Publisher.

Egan, M. 1980. "Public Health Nutrition Services: Issues Today and Tomorrow." *Journal of the American Dietetic Association* 77:423—27.

Eggebeen, D. J., and D. T. Lichter. 1991. "Race, family structure, and changing poverty among American children." *American Sociological Review* 56 (6): 801–17.

Federation of American Societies for Experiment Biology, Life Sciences Research Office. 1995. *Third Report on Nutrition Monitoring in the United States.* Washington, D.C.: U.S. Government Printing Office.

Fisher, G. M. 1992. *The Development and History of the Poverty Thresholds.* Social Security Bulletin 55 (4): 3–14.

Food Research and Action Center (FRAC). 1991. *Community Childhood Hunger Identification Project: a survey of childhood hunger in the United States.* Washington D.C.

———. 1997. *Community Childhood Hunger Identification Project: a survey of childhood hunger in the United States.* Washington D.C.

Fomon, S. J. 1993. *Normal Nutrition of Infants.* St. Louis, MO: Mosby.

Gibbs, J. 1986. "Assessment of depression in urban adolescent females: Implications for early intervention strategies," *American Journal of Social Psychiatry* 6:50–56.

Green, L. W., and M. W. Kreuter. 1991. *Health promotion planning: an educational and environmental approach.* Second Edition. Mountain View, CA: Mayfield Publishing Co.

Hamilton, W. L., J. T. Cook, W. W. Thompson, L. F. Buron, E. A. Frongillo, D. M. Olson, and C. A. Wehler. 1997. *Household Food Security in the United States in 1995.* Washington, D.C.: U.S. Department of Agriculture Food and Consumer Service.

Haveman, R., and B. Wolfe. 1994. *Succeeding generations: On the effect of investments in children.* New York: Russell Sage Foundation.

————. 1995. "The determinants of children's attainments: A review of methods and findings." *Journal of Economic Literature* 33 (3): 1829–78.

Housing Assistance Council. 1991. *Information About Poverty and Housing of Rural Women.* Housing Assistance Council under Cooperative Agreement H-5971 CA with the U.S. Department of Housing and Urban Development.

Hutson, A. C., V. C. McLoyd, and C. G. Coll. 1994. "Children and poverty: Issues in contemporary research." *Child Development* 65 (2) (April): 275—82.

Jensen, L. 1994. "Employment hardship and rural minorities: Theory, research and policy." *The Review of Black Political Economy* (Spring): 125–43.

Joy, A. B., and C. Doisy. 1996. "Food stamp nutrition education program: assisting food stamp recipients to become self-sufficient." *Journal of Nutrition Education* 28: 123–26.

Kellam, S. M. E. Ensminger, and R. Turner. 1977. "Family structure and the mental health of children." *Archives of general psychiatry* 34:1012–22.

Kirby, J. J. 1995. "Single-parent families in poverty." *Human Development Bulletin.* Department of Family Relations and Human Development: The Ohio State University Extension 1 (1): 1–2.

Klein, B. W. 1996. "Food security and hunger measures: promising future for state and local household surveys." *Family Economics and Nutrition Review* 9:31–37.

Lamison-White, L. 1997. "U.S. Bureau of the Census, Current Population Reports." Series P60-198, *Poverty in the United States: 1996.* Washington, D.C.: U.S. Government Printing Office.

Langner, R., E. Greene, J. Herson, J. Jameson, J. Goff, J. Rostowski, and D. Zykorie. 1969. "Psychiatric impairment in welfare and nonwelfare children." *Welfare in review* 7:10–21.

Langner, R., J. Herson, E. Greene, J. Jameson, and J. Goff. 1970. "Children of the city: Affluence, poverty, and mental health." In *Psychological factors in poverty,* ed. V. Allen 185–209. Chicago, IL: Markham.

Levinson, P. 1969. "The next generation: A study of children in AFDC families." *Welfare in Review* 7:1–9.

Levy, F., and R. J. Murnane. 1992. "U.S. earnings levels and earnings inequality: A review of recent trends and proposed explanation." *Journal of Economic Literature* 30 (3): 1333–81.

Lewit, E., and N. Kerrebrock. 1997. "Child Indicators: Childhood hunger." *The Future of Children* 7 (1): 128–37.

Lyson, T. A. 1991. "Real incomes of rural Black and Hispanic workers fell further behind in the 1980's." *Rural Development Perspectives* 7 (2): 7–11.

Makosky, V. P. 1982. "Sources of stress: Events or conditions?" In *Lives in Stress: Women and Depression,* ed. D. Belle, 163–76. Beverly Hills, CA: Sage.

Mayer, S. 1997. *What Money Can't Buy: Family Income and Children's Life Chances.* Cambridge, MA: Harvard University Press.

McLoyd, V. C., T. E. Jayaratne, R. Ceballo, and J. Borquez. 1994. "Unemployment and work interruption among African American single mothers: Effects on parenting and adolescent socioemotional functioning." *Child Development* 65:562–89.

Myers, H. F., and L. King. 1983. "Mental health issues in the development of the black American children." In *The psychological development of minority group children,* edited by G. Powell, A. Yamamoto, and A. Morales, 275–306. New York: Brunner/Mazel.

Needleman, H. K. 1994. "The current status of childhood lead toxicity." *Advances in Pediatrics* 40: 125–39.

Nord, M. 1997. "Overcoming persistent poverty—and sinking into it: income trends in persistent-poverty and other high poverty rural counties, 1989–94." *Rural Development Perspectives* 12, no. 3: 2–10.

Olson, S. L., and V. Banyard. 1993. "Stop the world so I can get off for awhile: Sources of daily stress in the lives of low income single mothers of young children." *Family Relations* 42:50–56.

Parker, T. S., and L. A. Whitener. 1993. "Rural workers will benefit more than urban workers from increase in minimum wage." *Rural Conditions and Trends* 8 (1): 38–47.

Phillips, D. A. 1994. "With a little help: Children in poverty and childcare." *Children in Poverty*. New York: Cambridge University Press.

Ray, S. A., and V. C. McLoyd. 1986. "Fathers in hard times: The impact of unemployment and poverty on paternal and marital relations." In *The father's role*, edited by M. Lamb, 339–83. New York: Wiley.

Splett, P. L. 1994. "Federal Food Assistance Programs. A Step to Food Security for Many." *Nutrition Today* (March/April): 6–13.

Swanson, L. 1994. "Rural poverty rate remains higher than urban rate." *Rural Conditions and Trends* 5 (1): 12–13.

Swanson, L., and L. Dacquel. 1991. "Rural families headed by women are on the rise." *Rural Conditions and Trends* 2 (1): 20–21.

———. 1992. "The effect of economic stress on family structure." *Proceedings of Agriculture Outlook 1993*. YCON-3:532–544. U.S. Department of Agriculture, Economic Research Service.

U.S. Bureau of the Census. Census data. 1992. Washington, D.C.: U.S. Bureau of the Census.

U.S. Department of Agriculture. 1996. *A Citizen's Guide to Food Recovery*. Washington D.C.: U.S. Government Printing Office.

———. 1989. *Nationwide Food Consumption Survey, Continuing Survey of Food Intakes by Individuals, Low Income Women 19—50 Years and their Children, 1–5 Years, 4 Days*. NFCF, CSFII Report 85-4. Washington, D.C.: U.S. Government Printing Office.

U.S. Department of Health and Human Services. 1994. *Healthy People 2000 Review 1993*. DHHS Publication No. PHS 94-1232-1. Washington, D.C.: U.S. Government Printing Office.

U.S. House of Representatives, Ways and Means Committee. 1996. *Overview of entitlement programs: 1996 green book*. Washington, D.C.: U.S. Government Printing Office.

Uvin, P. 1994. 8DThe state of world hunger.8C Nutrition Review 52:1151–61.

Voichick, J., and L. T. Drake. 1994. "Major stages of U.S. Food and Nutrition Policy Development Related to Food Security." *Food Security in the United States: A Guidebook for Public Issues Education*. Washington D.C.: USDA Cooperative Extension System.

Wehler, C. A., R. I. Scott, and J. J. Anderson. 1996. *The community childhood hunger identification project: a survey of childhood hunger in the United States*. Washington, D.C.: Food Research and Action Center.

Whitener, L. A., and T. S. Parker. 1998. *The proposed fair minimum wage act of 1998: Implications for rural areas*. WWW Slide Show. Economic Research Service, U.S. Department of Agriculture. http://www.econ.ag.gov. Summer 1998.

Wilson, W. J. 1987. "Long term poor African American children are also much more likely than long term poor white children to live in underclass neighborhoods." *The truly disadvantaged: The inner city, the underclass, and public policy.* Chicago: University of Chicago Press.

World Hunger Year. 1994. *Reinvesting in America: A program of world hunger year.* New York: World Hunger Year.

Zimmerman, J. N., and L. Garkovich. 1998. The bottom line: Welfare reform, the cost of living, and earnings in the rural South. Information Brief. Southern Rural Development Center, 2.

Effects of Economic Hardship
on Rural Children and Adolescents

LAURA DEHAAN AND JAMES DEAL

THE JOHNSON ADMINISTRATION'S WAR ON POVERTY IN THE 1960s focused national attention on poverty in the United States. The image of poverty facing the nation during this period was largely that of a white, rural family. In the more than thirty years since this initiative, however, the face of poverty in this country has increasingly become an urban one, due at least partly to the greater visibility of urban poor compared to rural poor (Lichter and Eggebeen 1992). Anti-poverty programs, political rhetoric, and media outlets continue to focus on the urban poor, often relegating the rural poor to a national back burner. National statistics from this time period, however, point to a continuing but overlooked problem with poverty in the non-urban areas (Fitchen 1995). This problem is exacerbated by economic crises and weather-related disasters impacting rural businesses, significant differences in characteristics of rural and urban dwellers, and a national focus which attends to urban dwellers more than rural in a variety of ways. This chapter will present an overview of rural poverty, focusing on the unique challenges facing rural children and adolescents, as well as effects of rural poverty on family interaction, risk-taking behaviors, and psychological adjustment.

POVERTY AND RURAL AMERICA

Since 1967, the rate of non-metropolitan poverty has exceeded that of metropolitan poverty in every year reported (Lichter and Eggebeen 1992; U.S. Department of Commerce 1997a). Non-metropolitan poverty is consistently higher than poverty in metropolitan areas. When metropolitan area rates are broken down into center city and non-center city rates, non-metropolitan poverty rates remain higher than non-center city (i.e., suburban) rates. It is only in the center cities that metropolitan poverty exceeds that of non-metropolitan

42

poverty, and it is only recently (i.e., 1990) that this difference has become meaningful.

When one looks beyond official poverty rates, and instead examines "ratio of income to poverty" estimates for 1997, center city and non-metropolitan areas are strikingly similar. At .50 of poverty level (i.e., earning only half of the income identified as poverty level for a particular familial configuration), the figures are 7.8 percent for center cities and 6.2 percent for non-metropolitan areas. At the 1.00 of poverty level, these figures are 18.8 percent and 15.9 percent, respectively; at 1.25 of poverty level, they are 24.4 percent and 21.9 percent, while at 1.50, they are 29.4 percent and 27.9 percent (U.S. Department of Commerce 1997b). In addition, non-metropolitan poverty rates are increasing; rates in 1990 were higher than at any other time since 1960 (Lichter & Eggebeen 1992). Clearly, even when comparing inner cities and non-metropolitan areas, rural poverty remains a significant problem.

RURAL CHILDREN AND POVERTY

Similarly, although the quite serious plight of poor inner city children has dominated the media, rural children may be at similar or even greater levels of risk (Jensen and Eggebeen 1994), although research in this area is limited (Garrett, Ng'andu, and Ferron 1994). The rate of poverty for rural children increased 47 percent from the late 1970s to the early 1990s (NCCP), and the poverty rate for these children, always higher than that for metropolitan children, is increasing (Lichter and Eggebeen 1992). In 1997, 9.8 percent of non-metropolitan children lived in households with incomes just 50 percent of the poverty level; another 22.7 percent lived in families whose incomes met the poverty level, while 29.9 percent and 36.2 percent lived at 125 percent and 150 percent of the poverty level, respectively. Similarly, the non-metropolitan poverty rate is higher than the metropolitan poverty rate for most family types (Lichter and Eggebeen 1992).

Substantial differences exist between the rural and urban poor, however. Poor children in rural areas are more likely to live in intact families than are poor children in metropolitan areas; and they are also more likely to have at least one parent working (Garrett, Ng'andu, and Ferron 1994). Single-parenthood in rural areas is increasing, however, and it carries with it effects that are of more consequence in rural areas than in urban areas. Rural kids in single-parent homes are more likely to be poor, to be poor longer, and to be in deeper poverty than metropolitan children in single-parent homes (Fitchen 1995). Non-metropolitan poor families are also less likely to receive public assistance (Jensen and Eggebeen 1994; Hirschl and Randk 1991), with those who do receive it getting less aid than metropolitan poor (Jensen and Eggebeen 1994). Rodgers and Weiher (1986) found the rural poor less likely to live in mother-headed families, more likely to have the head-of-the-household employed, less likely to be African-American, and less well-educated than the metropolitan poor. They also reported higher levels of malnutrition, hunger, and health problems among the rural poor.

Garrett et al. (1994) found that, for children born in rural areas, the odds of their spending their entire lives in poverty were 1.27 times higher than for other children. In addition, if children lived half their lives or more in rural areas, they were 1.32 times more likely to spend the majority of their lives in poverty than children who lived the majority of their lives in urban areas. Children born in rural areas were also more likely to have inadequate family incomes, which was also related to the amount of time spent in a rural environment. Dorsey (1991) noted that rural children are less likely to pursue education past high school than were urban children.

Unique Challenges Facing Rural Children and Adolescents

Urban and rural environments differ in other substantial ways besides concentration and duration of poverty. Urban environments undoubtedly present unique challenges for adolescents, with higher concentrations of poverty and single-parent families, as well as gangs and high crime rates (Thompson 1992). But it is also true that aspects of rural life, such as fewer curricula choices and structured activities in schools, lack of job opportunities, and geographic isolation, may also represent stressful contexts for adolescents (Rojewski 1995). Some have suggested that rural environments, due to rising crime rates, drug use, and gang involvement, may be even more stressful for adolescents than urban areas (Helge 1990). Helge argued that "[t]he image of rural children living wholesome, trouble-free lives compared with youth in more crowded settings [is] in need of revision" (3). This may explain why many adolescents do not intend to remain in rural areas as adults, as Elder, King, and Conger (1996) found that half of their rural sample of high school seniors did not desire to remain in rural communities after graduation.

Even though several studies have examined the contribution of rural or urban environments to child and adolescent development, few have examined differential effects of poverty within the two contexts. A study comparing urban and rural eighth graders from the Midwest found that while the two groups did not differ in levels of drug use, delinquent behavior, self-esteem, or depression, different factors were associated with these outcomes within the two environments. Gender and poverty were more significantly related to behavioral outcomes in urban adolescents, while decreased parental involvement was more closely linked to substance use, loneliness, and depression for rural students (De Haan, Gunvalson, and Ritter 1996).

After reviewing existing research on substance use, Donnermeyer (1992) found that alcohol use was virtually the same for both rural and urban youth, and rural marijuana use also was catching up to urban use, even though hard drug use remained more frequent among urban youth. Patterns for delinquent behavior based on rural or urban status also appear remarkably similar. Rural and urban differences were not found in teachers' reports of delinquent behavior in a study of school-aged children (Zahner, Jacobs, Freeman, and Trainor 1993). Parental reports of children's delinquent behavior for rural and urban boys were also similar, although parents of urban girls reported more delinquent behavior than did parents of rural girls. A study of adolescent boys indicated that although caucasian males began violent behavior later than African Americans in urban environments, age of onset for violent behavior was similar for both groups in rural contexts (Salts, Lindhom, Goddard, and Duncan 1995).

Hope and Bierman (1998) compared how kindergarten children from rural and urban areas differed in behavioral problems both at home and at school. After surveying both parents and teachers, they found that while there were no differences in reports of behavioral problems at home, urban teachers were more likely to report behavioral problems at school, even after SES, gender, and minority status were controlled. They argue that while rural schools, with their smaller size and lower confidentiality may be more effective in curtailing behavior problems within social settings, many rural children do exhibit problem behaviors at home. In both groups, children in poverty were more likely to exhibit behavioral problems.

Children from rural environments may also suffer from elevated feelings of loneliness and depression. Even though urban girls (aged six through eleven years of age) were found to exhibit higher levels of social withdrawal than rural girls, urban boys showed higher levels of emotional disturbances than rural boys (Zahner, et al. 1993). In the previously mentioned study by Hope and Bierman (1998) teachers were more likely to report internalizing symptoms, such as depression, for rural than for urban kindergarteners.

Rural adolescents may also struggle with depression. One study found that over one-half of a sample of rural adolescents were highly depressed, with family financial stress strongly related to depression for rural sixth, seventh, and eighth graders (Clark-Lempers, Lempers, and Netusil 1990). A large-scale adolescent study found that rural youth were slightly more likely to report feeling lonely or depressed than were urban adolescents (Blum and Rinehart 1997).

Although few studies have examined differences between rural and urban poverty per se, it becomes evident that rural environments contain elements of high risk for children and adolescents. Risk behaviors in rural areas are accelerating concurrently with, and in many cases faster than, national levels. This fact, coupled with increasing economic hardship and uncertainty, may create a climate of limited future prospects as well as limited current resources to deal with the future.

FAMILY INTERACTION AND POVERTY

Although economic deprivation has been associated with several psychological and behavioral outcomes for children and adolescents (Gad, Treadwell, and Johnson 1980; Lempers, Clark-Lempers, and Simons 1989), these effects are usually *indirect*. This indicates that it is not so much poverty itself, but factors affected by economic hardship, that shape developmental outcomes. One of these critical mediating factors is family interaction.

An important examination of the effects of poverty on family interaction has taken advantage of a comprehensive study begun in 1929 in California. This yearly longitudinal study was administered from 1929 to 1945, covering the years of the Great Depression. This allowed an examination of family dynamics before and during the time that many families experienced heavy economic loss and pronounced economic change. In analyses of parent and child data, Elder, Liker, and Cross (1984) concluded that economic deprivation was associated with poorer behavioral adjustment in children. This occurred as an indirect effect, mediated by increased arbitrary and inconsistent disciplining by fathers. Fathers who increased arbitrary discipline after economic loss were also more likely to have had less marital satisfaction and poorer relationships with their children *before* the Great Depression, with economic loss further straining family relationships for these fathers.

Another analysis of these data (collected from parents, children, and clinical observations), found that economic hardship increased fathers' rejecting behaviors, which damaged peer relationships for girls, but increased peer identification for boys (Elder, Nguyen, and Caspi 1985). Physical attractiveness was related to less rejecting behavior of fathers towards their daughters, but had no effects on the father-son relationship.

The importance of families in mediating the effects of poverty has been shown in other studies. One of the best examples of the study of economic stress among rural families is the Iowa Youth and Families Project (Conger and Elder 1994). Based on Elder's research on the effects of the Great Depression, Conger and colleagues utilized a sample of rural Iowa families to test a series of models linking economic pressure to marital conflict, emotional distress, disrupted parenting, and adolescent adjustment.

In general, economic pressure was positively related to depressed mood. For wives, this depression influenced hostile behaviors (positively), which negatively impacted spouses' marital quality. For husbands, a similar pattern was found, with the addition of a negative relation between husbands' depression and the wife's marital quality (Conger, Ge, and Lorenz 1994). For both husbands and wives, economic pressure and hostility toward the spouse were related to negative parenting practices (Simons, Whitbeck, Melby, and Wu 1994). Economic pressure and negative parenting practices were then positively related to anti-social behavior for boys and psychological well-being for girls (Simons, Whitbeck, and Wu 1994), completing the model.

Brody and colleagues (Brody, Stoneman, Flor, McCrary, Hastings, and Conyers 1994) have attempted to apply Conger and Elder's model to rural African American families. While Brody et al.'s methodology makes interpretation and comparisons somewhat difficult, the results generally tended to confirm Conger and Elder's findings.

Lempers, Clark-Lempers, and Simons (1989) examined both the direct and indirect effects of economic deprivation on rural midwestern families in the 1980s. Path analyses indicated that economic hardship had a direct effect on loneliness and depression for both male and female adolescents, but only an indirect effect on delinquency or drug use, moderated by consistency of perceived parental discipline. There was also an indirect effect of hardship on loneliness and depression, moderated by parental nurturance.

McLaughlin and Sachs (1988) argued that rural environments are especially difficult for rural mothers, in that the traditional values of rural communities may make it more difficult to find outside employment. Rural women also tend to be less educated, have larger families, earn less, and have fewer childcare options than do urban women, which results in longer and more stressful periods of poverty.

RISK-TAKING BEHAVIORS

Incidence of three risk-taking behaviors in rural environments will be examined: substance use, delinquent behavior, and academic achievement.

Substance Use

There are very few differences between rural and urban alcohol use, and some studies have indicated that rural use may be among the highest in the nation (Donnermeyer 1992). Belyea and Zingraff (1985), examining drug arrests and marijuana use, found that although rural drug use was lower than urban use, the rate of increase in substance use was parallel for rural and urban youth. Stevens, Youells, Whaley, and Linsey (1995) also found levels of rural adolescent use of alcohol, marijuana, and tobacco to be similar to and sometimes higher than national averages.

Several studies have found differing rates for substance use based on the degree of rurality, with very small towns (populations less than 2500) reporting significantly less substance use. Larger rural towns reported similar levels of use to urban areas (Edwards 1997). Edwards also noted that among rural towns similar in size, vast differences often existed in alcohol consumption, indicating the presence of other community factors. Factors behind these differences were not examined, but regionality, community norms, and religious involvement have been suggested as possible influences (Harrell and Cisin, 1980; Leukefeld, Clayton, and Meyers 1992).

Webb, Baer, and McKelvey (1994), in a study of primarily Caucasian, rural school-aged children, found that for fifth graders, the biggest predictor of use of alcohol was the reported influence of older peers. Parental attitudes about alcohol and sensation-seeking were also significant factors. For sixth graders, attitudes about alcohol were the most significant predictor, followed by influence of older peers, tolerance of deviance, and rejection of parental authority. Peer influence was again the most predictive variable in determining drug usage in a study of rural high school students (Pruitt et al. 1991), especially perceptions of how often their friends used drugs.

In a study of rural elementary schoolchildren who were followed until the beginning of junior high, it was found that children's beliefs about alcohol, low self-esteem, and negative school attitudes in third and fourth grades were significantly related to use of alcohol later on (Long and Boik 1993). Girls were less likely to use alcohol (54 percent) than boys (61 percent) were.

Farrell, Anchors, Danish, Howard (1992), in a study of rural seventh graders, found that attitudes towards drug use, delinquency, and lack of expectation to graduate predicted drug and alcohol use. Boys were significantly more likely to use alcohol or smoke cigarettes than girls, but were not significantly more likely to use other illicit drugs.

In a study of rural fifth-grade students, it was found that 26 percent of males and 16 percent of females had tried cigarette smoking, with whites more likely to experiment with cigarettes than African Americans. Males were more likely to have tried smoking if they had experimented with alcohol and had friends who smoked, while for females, having a father who smoked and having tried alcohol were more predictive.

Delinquent Behavior

Juvenile delinquency rates are rising faster in rural areas than in urban ones. One study found that half of a rural sample of teens had committed acts of vandalism or another type of property crime (Helge 1990). As the following studies demonstrate, delinquent behavior may be more heavily influenced by economic hardship than substance use.

Dubrow and Ippolito, 1994, in a longitudinal study of 473 children followed from five to nine years of age, found that number of years living in poverty predicted antisocial behavior, as chronic poverty remained a significant predictor, even when the presence of two parents and maternal education were controlled for.

Most research on the relationship between poverty (regardless of context) and delinquent behavior, however, has found that this relationship is mediated by other factors. Noting that impoverished adolescents were more often arrested for delinquent offenses, but that those differences disappeared when self-report measures were used, Larzelere and Patterson (1990) examined the role of family management in moderating the relationship between hardship and delinquent behavior. In their longitudinal study, parental management entirely mediated the effects of poverty, indicating that parental discipline was a stronger predictor of delinquency than economic deprivation.

The relationship between rural poverty and adolescent aggression has been found to be influenced by other family factors as well. In a longitudinal study of rural youth, the relationship between hardship and aggression was mediated by the parents' (particularly fathers') ability to adjust to increased financial hardship. Increased aggression among adolescents tended to appear when fathers became more hostile to their children and less supportive to their wives (Skinner, Elder, and Conger 1992). Marital relations were the most important intervening factor in the relationship between rural hardship and aggression. Economic pressure may also lead to increased hostility in rural parents' reactions to their adolescent children, which in turn can lead to more aggressive behavior (Conger et al. 1994).

Academic Achievement

Adolescents living in poverty have very different educational experiences than do middle and upper class youth. In a comprehensive review of research on educational aspirations and attainment for impoverished adolescents, Sum and Fogg (1991) concluded that poor adolescents have weaker math and reading skills and scored considerably lower on standardized tests than middle- and upper-class adolescents (18 percent versus 53 percent for non-poor adolescents).

Poor adolescents were also less likely to see themselves going on to college (32 percent versus 63 percent for middle and upper class adolescents). They were also half as likely to be involved in college preparatory programs, which are associated not only with less college attendance but with lower rates of completing high school as well.

A study of 14,700 adolescents (aged 14–21) found that family background variables, such as parental education and poverty, were most strongly associated with dropping out (Rumberger 1983). Poor females were more likely to leave school because of pregnancy, and males for work-related reasons. High career aspirations decreased the likelihood of dropping out.

In a study of 90 African American rural families, financial hardship was directly related to academic achievement. The level of involvement the mother had with the school, and observations of positive family relationships, were related to higher economic resources as well as to higher levels of achievement (Brody, Stoneman, and Flor 1995). Maternal involvement in schooling was more directly linked to childrens' performance than was paternal involvement, in fact, maternal education was negatively related to paternal involvement.

After examining 1990 Current Population Survey data, Lichter, Cornwell, and Eggebeen (1993) found that living in a single-parent family and having a child were related to dropping out of high school. The statistical significance of these effects, however, disappeared when the financial resources of adolescents were entered in the equation, particularly among rural youth. In other words, poverty played a more important role than family structure for rural adolescents.

In a study of farm and non-farm families in the rural Midwest, Russell and Elder (1997) found that youth living in farm families were more likely to do well in school, in part because these families tended to be more closely tied to the community, and their parents were more involved in school, religious, and community organizations.

When county-to-county comparisons were made of impoverished counties in rural West Virginia, Bickel and McDonough (1997) found that as post-high school economic opportunities increased, the rates of dropping out of school decreased. Youth placed in a lower curriculum track, or attending high schools with a high student/teacher ratio were also more likely to drop out.

PSYCHOLOGICAL ADJUSTMENT

Despite widespread concern about adolescent risk-taking, it should not be assumed that the mere absence of behavioral problems is indicative of positive adjustment, given that many rural adolescents who report few or no behavioral difficulties do report higher levels of anxiety and depression (Luthar and Zigler 1991). Psychological problems may also serve as a precursor to later behavioral difficulties. In a study of adolescents living in rural poverty, junior high school students were more likely to report problems with loneliness and depression, while senior high students reported higher levels of negative behavioral outcomes (Lempers, Clark-Lempers, and Simons 1989).

Even though many argue that depression and anxiety are the normal by-products of adolescence (Hall 1904; Erikson 1968), research has not substantiated this idea. Self-esteem appears to be relatively stable during the junior and senior high-school years in longitudinal studies (Alsaker 1989; Simmons and Blyth 1987), as do feelings of loneliness and social dissatisfaction (Asher, Hymel, and Renshaw 1984).

Although adolescence itself does not appear to cause marked changes in psychological well being, contextual influences are associated with differing levels of adjustment. In a large-scale study of junior and senior high-school students, minority students reported lower levels of self-esteem (Martinez and Dukes 1991), suggesting that the effects of racism may lower self-esteem levels. Another study that examined race, gender, and class influences on self-esteem (Kohr et al. 1988) found that higher economic resources were associated with higher self-esteem. Racial differences were present only in impoverished environments.

In general, females have been found to report higher depression levels than males, and black adolescents are more likely to be depressed than whites (Comstock and Helsing 1976). A study of junior high students found that low-income adolescents reported higher depression scores than those in middle and upper classes (Schoenbach et al. 1982).

Living in a rural environment may also place adolescents at risk, as depression is a serious problem facing many rural communities. Many changes in rural life have been argued to account for the increase in depression, such as a greater increase in two-income families, and, consequently, latchkey children. Churches are no longer the center of community life, and since many individuals have to travel considerable miles to work, this leaves less time for close-knit communities. (National Mental Health Association 1988). Beeson and Johnson (1987) found that rural Americans went from being the least psychologically distressed in 1981 to the most distressed in 1986. This corresponded to farmland values peaking and plummeting during those years.

Garfinckel and Hoberman (1986) found that teenage suicide in rural areas was 15 times higher than the national average. Thirty four percent of their adolescent sample reporting being depressed in the last three months. On average these teens reported higher levels of depression than a group of New York adolescents who were hospitalized for depression, although the rural youth were living at home and receiving no treatment.

In a national sample of urban and rural adults, those in urban poverty reported higher levels of physical health than those in rural poverty, but the two groups did not differ in levels of depression (Amato and Zuo, 1992). Whites reported higher levels of depression in rural areas, while African Americans reported higher depression in urban areas.

After comparing rural farm and non-farm families, Clark-Lempers, Lempers, and Netusil (1990) found that parents from farm families reported higher levels of stress and depression, but adolescent farm children were not necessarily more likely to report higher stress or depression. When parents perceived themselves to be more highly stressed, however, their adolescent children were also more likely to report higher levels of depression.

Felner et al. (1995), in a study of rural middle adolescents, found that experiencing hardship did not influence all adolescents equally. Youth of poorly educated parents reported much lower levels of adjustment and well being than did youth from poor but more highly educated parents. School experiences and exposure to other negative life events also mediated the relationship between hardship and socioemotional functioning.

It is not just economic hardship that has the potential to disrupt the parenting relationship. In a study of rural families, both experiencing hardship and the father's feelings of job autonomy and occupational status were related to harsher parenting and less inductive parenting techniques (Whitbeck et al. 1997). These harsher parenting techniques were significantly related to adolescents' feelings of self-efficacy.

Brody and Flor (1997) found, in a study of rural African American parents and their school-age children, that financial hardship was associated with mothers having lower levels of self-esteem and feeling more depressed. The mother's self-esteem was related to her ability to maintain family routines and maintain a higher-quality relationship with her children. Interestingly, the links between these family variables and children's psychological adjustment were mediated by the child's ability to engage in self-regulation (i.e., make plans before acting a particular way, or work towards goals).

The effects of hardship on rural youth's psychological well being have been found to be mediated by marital quality (Ge et al. 1992). This indicates that couples who were able to maintain a positive marriage were also more likely to have children reporting lower levels of psychological distress.

SUMMARY

Rural poverty remains a compelling, if somewhat under-explored, problem in society. Most poor children reside in rural areas, and children and adolescents living in rural poverty are more likely to remain in poverty for longer periods of time, be less well educated, and report greater levels of hunger and health problems than other poor children. Even though rural children appeared to have "caught up" to urban children in terms of substance use and delinquency, some evidence has suggested that depression and loneliness may be higher for rural children and adolescents.

The effects of rural economic hardship on child outcomes, however, although potentially serious, are not uniform. Many of the effects of poverty are indirect, mediated through the parental relationship. Experiencing poverty is often associated with decreased marital satisfaction, harsher parenting practices, and depressed mood. These behaviors relate to poorer child outcomes both behaviorally and psychologically. A few direct effects of poverty have been found, with somewhat weak links between hardship and substance use and delinquency, and a more robust association between poverty and loneliness and depression.

It is clear that the majority of children living in poverty will continue to live in rural areas. As rural areas continue to face economic crises in farming, and rural towns continue to grow smaller due to outmigration, rural children will face uncertainty both in terms of family finances and future prospects. It is therefore essential to examine how rural children and adolescents cope with both family and community hardship. Future study would also benefit from exploring the considerable community differences in child and adolescent outcomes in order to identify which factors facilitate positive development in these uncertain times.

REFERENCES

Asher, S. R., Hymel, S., and P. D. Renshaw. 1984. "Loneliness in children." *Child Development* 55: 1456–64.

Belyea, M., and M. Zingraff. 1985. "Monitoring rural-urban drug trends: An analysis of drug arrest statistics 1976–1980." *The International Journal of the Addictions* 20: 369–80.

Bickel, R., and M. McDonough. 1997. "Opportunity, community, and reckless lives: Social distress among adolescents in West Virginia." *Journal of Social Distress and the Homeless* 6: 29–44.

Blum, R. W., and P. M. Rinehart. 1997. *Reducing the risk: Connections that make a difference in the lives of youth.* Minneapolis: University of Minnesota.

Brody, G. H., and D. L. Flor. 1997. "Maternal psychological functioning, family processes, and child adjustment in rural, single-parent, African American families." *Developmental Psychology* 33: 1000-1011.

Brody, G. H., Z. Stoneman, and D. Flor. 1995. "Linking family processes and academic competence among rural African American youths." *Journal of Marriage and the Family* 57: 567–79.

Brody, G., Z. Stoneman, D. Flor, C. McCrary, L. Hastings, and O. Conyers. 1994. "Financial resources, parent psychological functioning, parent co-caregiving, and early adolescent competence in rural two-parent African-American families." *Child Development* 65: 590–605.

Bronfenbrenner, U. 1986. "Ecology of the family as a context for human development." *Developmental Psychology* 22: 723–42.

Clark-Lempers, D., J. Lempers, and A. Netusil. 1990. "Family financial stress, parental support, and young adolescents' academic achievement and depressive symptoms." *Journal of Early Adolescence* 10: 21–36.

Comstock, G. W., and K. J. Helsing. 1976. "Symptoms of depression in two communities." *Psychological Medicine* 6: 551–63.

Conger, R. D., X. Ge, G. H. Elder, F. O. Lorenz, and R. L. Simons. 1994. "Economic stress, coercive family process, and developmental problems of adolescents." *Child Development* 65: 541–61.

Conger, R., X. Ge, and F. Lorenz. 1994. "Economic stress and marital relations." In *Families in troubled times*, ed. R. Conger and G. Elder, 187–206. New York: Aldine de Gruyter.

Conger, R., and G. Elder. 1994. *Families in troubled times.* New York: Aldine de Gruyter.

De Haan, L. G., D. Gunvalson, and T. Ritter. "Contributing factors to risk-taking and well being in early adolescence: Rural and urban differences." Presented at the biannual meeting of the Society for Research on Adolescence, Boston, March 1996.

Donnermeyer, J. 1992. "The use of alcohol, marijuana, and hard drugs by rural adolescents: A review of recent research." In *Drug use in rural American communities*, ed. R. Edwards, 31–75. Binghamton, N.Y.: Harrington Park.

Dorsey, L. 1991. "The rural child." *Journal of Health Care for the Poor and Underserved* 2: 76–84.

Edwards, R. W. 1997. "Drug and alcohol use among youth in rural communities." In *Rural substance abuse: State of knowledge and issues*, ed. E. B. Robertson, Z. Sloboda, G. M. Boyd, L. Beatty, and N. J. Kozel. Rockville, Md.: U.S. Dept. of Health and Human Services, National Instutes of Health, National Institute on Drug Abuse.

Elder, G. H., V. King, and R. D. Conger. 1996. "Attachment to place and migration prospects: A developmental perspective." *Journal of Research on Adolescence* 6: 397–425.

Elder, G. H., Liker, and C. E. Cross. 1984. "Parent-Child behavior in the great depression: Life course and intergenerational influences." *Life Span Development and Behavior* 6: 109–58.

Elder, G. H., T. V. Nguyen, and A. Caspi. 1985. "Linking family hardship to children's lives." *Child Development* 56: 361–75.

Erikson, E. H. 1968. *Identity: Youth and crisis*. New York: Norton.

Felner, R. D., S. Brand, D. L. DuBois, A. M. Adan, P. F. Mulhall, and E. G. Evans. 1995. "Socioeconomic disadvantage, proximal environmental experiences, and socioemotional and academic adjustment in early adolescence: Investigation of a mediated effects model." *Child Development* 66: 774–92.

Fitchen, J. 1995. "'The single-parent family,' child poverty, and welfare reform." *Human Organization* 54: 355–62.

Gad, M. T., and J. H. Johnson. 1980. "Correlates of adolescent life stress as related to race, SES, and levels of perceived social support." *Journal of Clinical Child Psychology* 9: 13-16.

Garrett, P., N. Ng'andu, and J. Ferron. 1994. "Is rural residency a risk factor for childhood poverty?" *Rural Sociology* 59: 66–83.

Ge, X., R. D. Conger, F. O. Lorenz, G. H. Elder, R. B. Montague, and R. L. Simons. 1992. "Linking family economic hardship to adolescent distress." *Journal of Research on Adolescence* 2: 351–78.

Hall, G. S. 1904. *Adolescence*. New York: Appleton-Century-Crofts.

Harrell, A. V., and I. H. Cisin. 1980. *Drugs in rural America: A special report from the 1979 national survey on drug abuse*. Washington D.C.: George Washington University, Social Research Group.

Helge, D. 1990. *A national study regarding at-risk students*. Washington D.C.: National Rural Development Institute.

Hirschl, T., and M. Rank. 1991. "The effect of population density on welfare participation." *Social Forces* 70: 225–35.

Jensen, L., and D. Eggebeen. 1994. "Nonmetropolitan poor children and reliance on public assistance." *Rural Sociology* 59: 45–65.

Larzelere, R. E., and G. R. Patterson, G. R. 1990. "Parental management: Mediator of effect of socioeconomic status on early delinquency." *Criminology* 28: 301–23.

Lempers, J. D., D. S. Clark-Lempers, and R. L. Simons. 1989. "Economic hardship, parenting, and distress in adolescence." *Child Development* 60: 25–39.

Leukefeld, C. G., R. R. Clayton, and J. A. Meyers. 1992. "Rural drug and alcohol treatment." *Drugs and Society* 7: 95–116.

Lewin, K. (1951). *Field theory in social science.* New York: Harper and Row.

Lichter, D.T., and D.J. Eggebeen. 1992. "Child poverty and the changing rural family." *Rural Sociology* 57: 151–72.

Lichter, D. T., G. T. Cornwell, and D. J. Eggebeen. 1995. "Harvesting human capital: Family structure and education among rural youth." *Rural Sociology* 58: 53–75.

Luthar, S. S., and E. Zigler. 1991. "Vulnerability and competence: A review of research on resilience in childhood." *American Journal of Orthopsychiatry* 61 (1): 6–22.

Rodgers, H., and G. Weiher. 1986. :"The rural poor in America: A statistical overview." *Policy Studies Journal* 15: 279–89.

Rojewski, J. W. 1995. "Impact of at-risk behavior on the occupational aspirations and expectations of male and female adolescents in rural settings." *Journal of Career Development.*

Rumberger, R. W. 1983. "Dropping out of high school: The influence of race, sex, and family background." *American Educational Research Journal* 20 (2): 199–220.

Russell, S., and G. H. Elder. 1997. "Academic success in rural America: Family background and community integration." *Childhood* 4: 169–81.

Salts, C. J., B. W. Lindholm, H. W. Goddard, and S. Duncan. 1995. "Predictive variables of violent behavior in adolescent males." *Youth and Society* 26: 377–99.

Simons, R., L. Whitbeck, and C. Wu. 1994. "Resilient and vulnerable adolescents." In *Families in troubled times,* ed. R. Conger and G. Elder, 223–34. New York: Aldine de Gruyter.

Simons, R., L. Whitbeck, J. Melby, and C. Wu. 1994. "Economic pressure and harsh parenting." In *Families in troubled times,* ed. R. Conger and G. Elder, 207–22. New York: Aldine de Gruyter.

Simmons, R. G., and D. A. Blyth. 1987. *Moving into adolescence.* New York: Aldine De Gruyter.

Skinner, M. L., G. H. Elder, R. D. Conger. 1992. "Linking economic hardship to adolescent aggression." *Journal of Youth and Adolescence* 21: 259–76.

Stevens, M., F. Youells, F. Whaley, and S. Linsey. 1995. "Drug use prevalence in a rural school-age population: The New Hampshire survey." *American Journal of Preventative Medicine* 11: 105–13.

Sum, A. M., and W. N. Fogg. 1991. "The adolescent poor and the transition to early adulthood." In *Adolescence and poverty: Challenges for the 1990s,* ed. P. Edelman and J. Ladner. Washington, D.C.: Center for National Policy Press.

Thompson, T. 1992. "For the sake of the children: Poverty and disabilities." In *Saving children at risk: Poverty and disabilities,* ed. T. Thompson and S. C. Hupp, 3–12. London: Sage.

U.S. Department of Commerce. 1997a. *Historical Poverty Tables—People.*

U.S. Department of Commerce. 1997b. *Poverty in the United States: 1997.*

Whitbeck, L. B., R. L. Simons, R. D. Conger, K. A. S. Wickrama, K. A. Ackley, and G. H. Elder. 1997. "The effects of parents' working conditions and family economic hardship on parenting behaviors and children's self-efficacy." *Social Psychology Quarterly* 60: 291–303.

Zahner, G. E. P., J. H. Jacobs, D. H. Freeman, and K. F. Trainor. 1993. "Rural-urban child psychopathology in a northeastern U.S. state: 1986—1989." *Journal of American Academy of Child and Psychiatry* 32: 378–87.

Homelessness Among Rural Women

LINDA K. CUMMINS

INTRODUCTION

Homelessness among women has been a significant problem since the early 1980s (Anderson, Boe, and Smith 1988; Bassuk 1993; Bassuk, Rubin, and Lauriat 1984, 1986; Browne 1990, 1993; Burt and Cohen 1989; Calsyn and Morse 1990; Crystal 1984; Hagen and Ivanoff 1988; Johnson and Kreuger 1989; McChesney 1995; Mills and Ota 1989). Today, women are estimated to represent as much as 50 percent of the homeless population, with the most rapidly growing segment being female-headed families (Bassuk, Rubin, and Lauriat 1986; Brown and Ziefert 1990; Hagen 1990; Hagen and Ivanoff 1988; Hertzberg 1992; Mills and Ota 1989). In some regions in the country it is believed that 70 to 85 percent of all homeless families are headed by women (Bassuk, Carman, Weinreb, and Herzig 1990; First, Rife, and Toomey 1995; U.S. Department of Housing and Urban Development [HUD] 1994).

Homelessness among women has been attributed to personal difficulties, such as mental illness (Buckner, Bassuk, and Zima 1993; D'Ercole and Struening 1990; Fischer 1991), alcohol and drug dependency (Anderson et al. 1988; Bassuk 1990; Stovall and Flaherty 1994; Weinreb and Bassuk 1990), disaffiliation (Rossi, 1990; Solarz and Bogat 1990; Stovall and Flaherty 1994), and domestic violence (Anderson et al. 1988; Cummins, 1996; Cummins, First, and Toomey 1998; D'Ercole and Struening 1990; Hagen and Ivanoff 1988; Homeless Information Exchange, 1994; Zorza 1991). However, larger structural factors also contribute to homelessness among women. The inability to secure affordable low income housing, inadequate welfare benefits, low-paying jobs (primarily in the service industry), unemployment, and barriers to employment, such as child care and transportation (Bassuk, 1993; Burt, 1991; Housing Assistance Council [HAC] 1995; Karger and Stoesz 1994) are some of the barriers women face in securing safe and stable homes.

The problems of poverty and homelessness among women can also be understood as an outcome of inadequate and inappropriate policy and program initiatives (Abramovitz 1994; Bassuk 1993). The rise in the number of homeless women that began in the 1980s coincided with the country's entrance into a conservative era in politics (Abramovitz 1994; Bassuk 1993). Social policies over the past two decades have led to cuts in social spending, increased eligibility requirements for welfare and food stamp benefits, and reduced availability of public housing (Abramovitz 1994; Bassuk 1993; Gorham 1992; Karger and Stoesz 1994). Policy changes, compounded with institutionalized sexism in the labor market reflected in wage inequalities and job segregation, suggests that women and children have borne the heaviest burden of conservative policies and the economic recessions of the 1980s and 1990s (Eisenstein 1984, 1988; Gorham 1992; Karger and Stoesz 1994).

HISTORY OF HOMELESS WOMEN

Prior to the 1980s, the last big surge of homelessness occurred during the Great Depression of the 1930s. At the peak of the Depression, the homeless count was estimated between 200,000 and 1.5 million, and was primarily comprised of men moving from town to town seeking employment (Rossi 1990). A small portion of the homeless population during this period was women; however, little is known about them. Homelessness declined dramatically with the country's entry into World War II and remained low during the post-war economic boom of the 1950s and 1960s. Most homeless people during this period have been described as disaffiliated and alcoholic men (Bahr 1970; Bogue 1963; Rossi 1990).

Reports of homeless "skid row women" and "bag ladies" began to appear in the 1970s (Garrett and Bahr 1973; Strasser 1978). The number of homeless women has escalated in the late 1970s, and women were estimated to comprise 25 percent of the homeless population (Slavensky and Cousins 1982). By the early 1980s, women were identified as a substantial portion of the growing homeless population (Crystal 1984; Hagen 1987; Stoner 1983). More recently, homeless women's conditions and individual characteristics are most often described as heterogeneous (Buckner et al. 1993; Burt and Cohen 1989; Johnson and Kreuger 1989; Mills and Ota 1989; Cummins 1996). Currently, female-headed families and young single women constitute the fastest-growing segment of the homeless population in the United States (Bassuk et al. 1990; Bassuk 1993; Cummins 1996; Cummins et al. 1998; First et al. 1995).

HOMELESSNESS IN RURAL PLACES

Research on rural homelessness is limited, but early assessments suggest that homelessness in rural areas is growing (Cummins et al. 1998; Cummins 1996; First, Toomey, and Rife 1990; First, Rife and Toomey 1995; Fitchen 1991; Patton 1988; Roth, Bean, Lust, and Saveanu; Roth, Toomey and First 1985; 1987; Segal 1989). Still less is known about rural homeless women and the complexity of causal factors that contribute to their homeless state. Rural poverty and homelessness have been linked to economic causes. Barriers to accessing the limited services and resources, such as the lack of public transportation, negative attitudes toward public social services, and the geographic dispersion of services prevent many rural people from using needed services. The extremely high poverty rates among female-headed families in rural areas make rural women particularly vulnerable to homelessness (Duncan 1992; Gorham 1992; HAC 1995; Tickamyer and Tickamyer 1988).

THE RURAL CONTEXT

Geographically, most of the United States remains rural and is home to 62 million Americans (Rural Community Assistance Program 1995). Historically, rural areas have lagged behind urban areas in wages and economic development (Deavers and Hoppe 1992; Hobbs 1988), and, in recent decades, rural poverty rates have exceeded those of inner cities (Gorham 1992; Rural Community Assistance Program 1995). Traditionally, rural economies have lacked diversity and have concentrated on one means of supporting their communities (Deavers and Hoppe 1992; Gorham 1992), usually by the production of goods through farming, mining, timber, and manufacturing. Changes in federal policies in agriculture, tax laws, relaxation of antitrust laws, increased deregulation, and the shift from formula funding to competitive grant funding for social services have further disadvantaged rural communities (Flora and Flora 1989). With the restructuring of public policies and the national economy from an agricultural and industrial economy to a service, financial, and technology economy, businesses in rural areas have closed up, leaving unemployment, poverty, and homelessness in their wake (Deavers and Hoppe 1992; Gorham 1992; Housing Assistance Council 1995; Hobbs, 1988; Lichter, Johnston, and McLaughlin 1994).

With the movement of manufacturing and the extraction of natural resources overseas, the United States has become a resource center for knowledge and financial control—areas where rural communities are disadvantaged due to lack expertise and an infrastructure for the development of such services (Deavers and Hoppe 1992; Gaventa and Lewis 1989). Since 1981, over half a million rural manufacturing jobs have been lost, 650,000 farms have been foreclosed, and energy-related production in timber, mining, and petroleum has suffered severe cutbacks (Duncan and Lamborghini 1994; Gorham 1992; Patton 1987). During this same period, high-technology industries grew at an unprecedented rate, creating 1.2 million jobs, 85 percent of which were located in metropolitan areas (Glasmeier and Kay-Teran 1989). Historically, urban unemployment rates have exceeded those in rural areas, but, by 1988, rural unemployment rates were 135 percent of urban rates (Deavers and Hoppe 1992). By the end of the 1980s, 91 percent of the nation's rural counties were experiencing or had experienced unemployment rates at least double the national average (Glasmeier and Kay-Teran 1989; Patton 1987). The rural poverty rate reached 17.3 percent in 1993 (Rural Community Assistance Program 1995).

Poverty and inequality have been persistent features of rural communities (Duncan and Sweet 1992). Since the late 1970s, rural areas have been marked by low and declining wages, and, by 1989, the poverty rate among rural workers heading families was 100 percent higher than metro workers heading families (Lichter et al. 1994). The percentage of American workers in rural areas whose hourly wages could not lift a family of four out of poverty increased significantly between 1979 and 1987 from 31.9 percent to 42.1 percent (compared to 25.7 percent and 31.5 percent in urban areas) (Gorham 1992). For every job available in rural areas, six people are seeking to fill it (Deavers and Hoppe 1992). Those hit hardest by this economic downturn have been minorities, the young, and women. In 1979, 43.7 percent of rural women earned poverty-level wages (for a family of four). By 1987, this increased to 53.9 percent compared to an increase from 32.2 percent (1979) to 36.0 percent (1987) for urban women (Gorham 1992). Rural women face harsher economic realities than do urban women, and this trend appears to be growing.

The downturn in the economic conditions of rural America in the 1980s contributed to a growing inability to afford decent housing (Housing Assistance Council 1995). The decline in the number of affordable housing units has added further hardship to economically depressed rural areas. In 1983, it was estimated that 840,000 very low-income rural households were living in "severely inadequate" housing (Patton 1987). In 1990, 20 percent of all non-metro households were paying more than 30 percent of their income for housing (Housing Assistance Council 1995). Many low-income families are forced to live in substandard housing. This is almost twice as likely for rural renters (most often women) compared to homeowners (Housing Assistance Council 1995). The scarcity of affordable housing coupled with the decline in job opportunities and wage rates has left many rural people in a state of "shelter poverty" (Stoner 1989).

Rural female-headed families are more likely to be living in housing with severe physical problems (Housing Assistance Council 1995). In some areas, even for those who can afford to pay rent, adequate housing is not available (Housing Assistance Council 1995; Isenhart 1988). The waiting lists for subsidized housing can be two to five years long, and many people fall into homelessness while waiting for subsidized housing (Housing Assistance Council 1995; Interagency Council on the Homeless 1989).

Federal cuts in the construction and subsidized housing and income-maintenance programs have imposed added hardships in rural areas that are already at an economic disadvantage compared to their metropolitan counterparts. In the past fifteen years, the federal government has eradicated all but minimal housing aid, cut several income-maintenance programs through changes in eligibility and payment standards, and eliminated significant numbers of the rural poor from the welfare rolls (Deavers and Hoppe 1992; Housing Assistance Council 1995; Karger and Stoesz 1994; Stoner 1989).

The extent to which urban conditions of homelessness among women mirror those of rural homeless women remains unclear; however, recent studies on rural homelessness suggests that it has unique features distinct from urban homelessness (Cummins 1996; Cummins et al. 1998; First, Rife, and Toomey, 1995; Fitchen, 1991).

WOMEN IN THE RURAL CONTEXT

Researchers on women's development have consistently observed that women's identities are formed in the context of social relationships with others (Belenky, Clinchy, Goldberger, and Tarule 1986; Berzoff 1989; Gilligan 1982; Miller 1976; Surrey 1991a). This is especially true for rural women who have traditionally defined self through the nurturing roles of mother and wife (Fiene 1991; Fitchen 1981). However, in response to the economic downturns of recent years, rural women have increasingly entered the labor force and constitute nearly half of rural workers (Gorham 1992). In addition, the number of female-headed households increased 22 percent between 1980 and 1990. Increasingly, rural women are finding themselves supporting their children alone in low-wage jobs (Housing

Assistance Council, 1995; Morris, 1986). The most rapidly growing portion of the rural poor population is female-headed households (Lichter et al. 1994).

The growing poverty in rural areas combined with the multiple roles women fill and conflicts with traditional roles and values contribute to what Fried (cited in Olson 1988) referred to as "endemic stress." Fried describes endemic stress:

> [A] condition of continuous and manifold changes, threats or deprivations . . . embedded in daily life events. . . . They may be widespread and affect much of the population or be discrete and personal. . . . They have diverse origins in economic, social, physical-environmental, psychological or physiological conditions and events. (9)

Endemic stress may include poverty, powerlessness, gender inequality, chronic deprivation, and other conditions (Olson 1988). Women in rural communities experience many of these conditions on a daily basis. Olson (1988) cited primary examples of endemic stress of rural women, including "the feminization of poverty, superwoman expectations, and domestic violence" (9).

While women in all locales may struggle with these conditions, the isolation of rural women and rigid gender roles and cultural values intensify these endemic stresses (Olson 1988). Gagné's (1992) study of women in an Appalachian community concluded that the normative attitudes and behaviors toward women, the geographic isolation and social isolation imposed by male partners, and the high rate of domestic violence produced a wide range of social controls over women and promoted the dominance of men as the cultural norm. Fiene (1995) found that battered Appalachian women who left their abusive partners were stigmatized and ostracized by family and community members for violating the cultural norms.

HOMELESSNESS AMONG RURAL WOMEN

Rural women are renowned for making do with very little (Fink 1992; Geissinger, Lazzari, Porter, and Tungate 1993; McInnis-Dittrich 1995; Olson 1988; Tickamyer and Tickamyer 1988). Rural researchers consistently describe rural women as resourceful and resilient (Butler 1993; Cummins 1996, Cummins et al. 1998; Liebow 1993). Using informal, formal and temporary resources, rural women skillfully weave safety nets for themselves and their families during homeless periods that may range from one day to ten years. Rural women most often find temporary housing with friends or relatives. Homeless shelters are scarce in many rural communities, but about a third report using them. Approximately ten percent of rural homeless women report living with limited or no shelter for some period of time (Cummins 1996; Cummins et al. 1998; First et al. 1995; Fitchen 1991; Toomey and First 1987).

Dependence on community and family networks is a common source of food for rural homeless women. Most often, rural homeless women report purchasing food and preparing it in the home of a family member or friend. Fewer report eating regular meals prepared by family and friends. However, the use of public formal social services appears to be critical to surviving in homelessness for rural women. The services most often reported being used include welfare grants; homeless shelters; emergency rooms; community kitchens; Community Mental Health Centers (CMHC); and battered women's shelters, respectively (Cummins 1996; Cummins et al. 1998; First et al. 1995; Fitchen 1991; Toomey and First 1987).

PRECURSORS TO HOMELESSNESS

Family conflict: Family conflict and domestic violence can be the deciding factor that leads women into homelessness in urban as well as rural areas. (Anderson et al. 1988; Browne 1993; Cummins 1996; Cummins et al. 1998; First et al., 1990; Goodman 1991; Hagen and Ivanoff 1988; Roth et al. 1987; Stoner 1983). The nature of the conflicts in rural areas has been tied to a rural patriarchy in which social control of women escalates to domestic violence that eventually pushes women into homelessness (Cummins 1996).

Economic hardship: Poverty and inequality have been persistent features of rural communities (Duncan and Sweet 1992). Contrary to traditional images of rural women, rural homeless women frequently have ties to the formal labor market. The primary sources of incomes for rural homeless women in Ohio included AFDC grants; earnings; other income maintenance grants such as SSI, SSDI, SS, unemployment benefits, and workmen's compensation; donations from family, friends or charities; and child support, respectively (Cummins et al. 1998).

Economic hardships are major factors contributing to homelessness among rural women. Problems with paying the rent and eviction, and unemployment, are prominent factors contributing to homelessness among rural women. Over half (50.8 percent) of rural female-headed families with children live in poverty compared to 40.1 percent of their urban counterparts (HAC 1995). In recent years, rents have escalated and the number of renting households has increased by 50 percent while federal housing assistance has declined sharply and the number of low-income units has dropped off (HAC, 1995; Karger and Stoesz 1994). The appropriations for the U.S. Department of Housing and Urban Development (HUD) were reduced from $32.2 billion in 1978 to $11.7 billion in 1991, and by 1990 there were 3.8 million more low-income renters than there were available units (HAC 1995; Karger and Stoesz 1994). High unemployment rates, depressed wages, and escalating rents have exacerbated the housing problem in rural areas and left rural female-headed families in an economically precarious position.

Lack of Social Networks: For women raising children alone, social networks are essential to survival, often keeping them afloat in economically desperate times (Bassuk 1993). Homelessness in urban areas has been linked to the exhaustion of social supports and it has been suggested that disruptions in support networks often precipitate homelessness (Calsyn and Morse 1990; Rossi 1990; Shinn, Knickman, and Weitzman 1991). Yet social networks among the rural homeless women are reportedly strong. Most maintain contact with friends and/or relatives, and have a friend or relative they can count on for help (Cummins et al. 1998; First et al. 1995). The tight-knit communities of rural areas may be experiencing strain. Fitchen's (1991a) report on homelessness in rural New York communities indicated that the traditional support networks of rural communities and families have been weakened by persistent and increasing poverty, limited housing options, growing instability of rural families, and increasing numbers of single-parent families. These factors contributed to the risk of homelessness for rural women.

Mental Illness: Factors commonly associated with homelessness in the urban setting, such as drug, alcohol, and health-related problems, are less common among the homeless in rural areas (Cummins 1996; Cummins et al. 1998; First et al. 1995; Rife, Toomey, First, and Royalty 1992; Roth et al. 1985). Compared to urban homeless women, rural homeless women have fewer serious psychiatric or behavioral disorders, and fewer episodes of psychiatric hospitalizations. Only about 5 percent of rural homeless women in Ohio were assessed as having serious psychiatric or behavioral symptomology (Cummins et al. 1998).

Substance Abuse: Fischer's (1991) review of the epistemological studies of the homeless found that one-third of the women had problems with alcohol and substance abuse. McChesney (1995) reviewed the empirical literature on urban homeless families and reported that alcohol and/or drug abuse among homeless women ranged from 6 percent to 50 percent across studies. Compared to incidence among homeless women in urban studies, alcohol and drug use among rural homeless women tends to be low. Only 8 percent of 473 rural homeless women in Ohio (Cummins et al 1998) indicated a serious alcohol problem, and fewer (7 percent) reported having been hospitalized for alcohol problems at some time in their lives. Drug use appears to be even less of a problem. Only 4.4 percent indicated a serious drug problem and 5.2 percent said that they had been hospitalized for drug treatment at some point in their lives.

Few methodologically sound studies have been done on rural homeless people. An exemplary state-wide study in 1990 from the Ohio State University reported that the primary reasons for homelessness among the 473 women included in the sample were family conflict and dissolution, eviction and problems paying the rent, and unemployment, respectively (First, Toomey, and Rife 1990; Cummins et. al 1998). Factors commonly reported to be major contributors to homelessness in urban studies were not supported in this rural study.

STAGES OF HOMELESSNESS

The stages of homelessness depicted in the following section emerged out of an ethnographic study of six rural homeless women in Southern Ohio from 1990 to 1996, and builds on the rural homelessness work of First, Toomey, and Rife (First, Rife, and Toomey 1994, 1995; First, Toomey, and Rife 1990; Toomey, First, Greenlee, and Cummins 1993) and Fitchen (1991a, 1991b, 1992); women's development as discussed by Gilligan (1982), Belenky et al. (1986), Flax (1981), Surrey (1985, 1991a, 1991b), and Berzhoff (1989); and, pat-

Table 1
Factors Contributing to Homelessness (N = 473)

Reason for Homelessness	N	Percent
Family conflict/dissolution	179	37.9
Eviction/problem paying rent	133	28.1
Unemployment	67	14.2
Disaster	36	7.6
Drugs/alcohol	13	2.7
Deinstitutionalized	4	0.8
Pregnancy/poor health	10	2.1
Other	29	6.1
Missing	2	0.4
Total	473	99.9

terns of domestic violence by Gagné (1992), Feine (1990, 1991, 1995), and Ulrich (1991). The stage theory of homelessness presented below is considered by the author to be a work in progress.

Common themes of the rural homeless women's stories emerged into a chronology of life stages that were propelled and shaped by personal perceptions, cultural norms, and structural barriers. The life stages can best be described as (a) the road to homelessness—cultural engendered dependency, (b) stepping into homelessness—"no way to stay and nowhere to go," (c) surviving in homelessness—"making it on my own," and (d) the journey back—"my own place." The women's journeys through homelessness were intertwined with their development of self. Each stage reflects a tenacious determination to redefine self outside cultural norms, and a willingness to pay the cost in terms of personal loss, community snubbing, and institutional discrimination.

STAGE 1: THE ROAD TO HOMELESSNESS

Culturally Engendered Dependency

The road to homelessness began long before literal homelessness occurred, and encompassed the majority of the women's rural lived experiences. Socialization into a dependent perception of women's roles, expectations, and place in rural society was the backdrop for setting the stage for homelessness. A dependent attitude that defined rural women's realities in social, economic, and political life best describes the outcomes of growing up female in rural society. The rural women arrived at young adulthood with an imposed identity, and were often unable to define themselves except in relation to their home cultures' expectations of rural women (Cummins, 1996). Feine (1991) concluded that the dynamic social processes in Appalachian communities leave women vulnerable.

Several authors have discussed the enduring traditional values of rural communities (Brown and Schwarzeller 1974; Naples 1994; Peterson and Peters 1985). Rural culture continues to enforce the traditional gender roles of mother, caregiver, and wife in the subservient position within the male-dominant family (Egan 1993; Fiene 1991), leaving women in economically and politically dependent positions. In her study of cultural identity among Appalachian women, McCoy (1993) identified cultural identity as a powerful tool for ensuring that community members participate in roles supported by the local culture. Naples (1994) and others believed that pre-existing patterns of family, community, ethnic solidarity, and identity are determinants in community members' selection of survival strategies (Mingione 1991). Gagné (1992) observed that the normative order of social control used in Appalachian communities ensures the maintenance of female dependency. Traditional norms of female dependency were transferred from the family patriarch in families of origin to husbands as women followed the traditional path to early marriage and traditional roles within the marriage (Cummins 1996). Zalk (1986) was explicit in her claim that the institution of family, as it has been traditionally constructed, has been a primary obstacle to change, and limits real options for women. For rural women, time, money, and movement outside the home may be closely monitored (Cummins 1996; Feine 1995; Gagné 1992). Silent and isolated women experience social (relationships with others), psychological (relationship with Self), and material (access to resources) deprivation (Cummins 1996; Nesto 1994).

Marriage Patterns and Expectations

Rural women most often began early adult life with expectations of fulfilling prescribed traditional gender roles of wife and mother. Marrying soon after high school before having established financial independence or emotional emancipation was a common phenomenon for rural women who rarely questioned the shift of dependence from their parents to their male partner. Expectations to stay home and care for the house, children, and husband dictated their life choices.

Cecilly

I got right out of high school and got married and then, you know, left him and got married again. . . . Because my mom was always there. When I worked, she was always there to take care of my kids. So I really didn't have a big responsibility because Mom was always there. . . . I've never had to do it for myself.

Karen

I went from being the daughter of my mom and dad to the wife of my husband to the mother of my kids and I forgot who Karen was. I was 16 [when I got married]. I was three months pregnant at the time and I was happy about it. I wanted a baby.

A subservient position requires a silencing of one's ideas and desires in order for the dominant person to be in control. In traditional rural marriages, women experience little control over the rules of the home, family decision-making, and access to money. Positions of silence secure the positions of wife and caretaker within the patriarchal home (Belenky et al. 1986; Cummins 1996; Feine 1995; Gagné 1992)

Silent Rural Women

Silence in women is not just a culturally engendered attribute, but is specific to certain types of women who have grown up knowing words as things that separate and degrade people (Belenky, Clinchy, Goldberger, and Tarule 1986). Living in homes where words were used as weapons and methods to control others, women learn early on to use silence as a strategy for safety and security. To speak is to invite punishment. In a patriarchal family structure, subservient members are socialized to understand that punishment is deserved if the rules of silence are broken. In such households, family discussions are discouraged and communications are unidirectional from the power head downward in the family structure (Belenky et al. 1986). In rural culture, this may represent extreme enforcement of the cultural values that women should be seen and not heard, and encourage submission to male authority (Cummins 1996). Outcomes of such an environment include a distrust of words, isolation from others and self, and a passive, unquestioning acceptance of one's circumstances in life. Silent women most often come from backgrounds that are economically, socially, and educationally deprived (Belenky et al. 1986), characteristics that mirror those of poor and homeless rural women (Cummins 1996).

Self-Concept

Silent women unconsciously give total control to external authorities, including the defining of who they are. Rural women who later became homeless were unable to describe themselves except as they had heard others describe them, and were usually in relationships where social control escalated from the normative behaviors in traditional marriages to brutal physical violence.

Lana

'Cause I had no feeling about me at all, you know. No self-es—you know, no self-esteem. No nothing. I mean he took all that. When I was married, like I said, I was, really nothing. 'Cause he'd done took everything from me that makes a person a person.

Beth

It [self-esteem] was very low . . . I felt bad . . . the way they [men] put you down . . . they have you believing . . . you're not worth nothing . . . [three and a half years ago] I was no good.

Silence Through Social Control

Control over the lives of women has historically been used by men and the larger society to keep them silent and politically and economically disengaged. For many women, silence is a survival strategy to avoid punishment (Belenky et al. 1986; Cummins 1996). A coming to consciousness of the extent to which partners control their lives signals women's movement out of silence and into reconsidering dependency as a way of being. An awakening to the constraints on freedom of movement, limitations in decision-making, or the pervasiveness of external control in intimate relationships begin stirrings of discontentment. Expanding consciousness brings to the fore the extent to which social controls are sanctioned by family and community members and social structures. Areas of limited control encompass finances, decision-making, freedom of movement, and physical control through abuse (Cummins 1996).

Gagné (1992) demonstrated the breadth of social-control methods used by men against women in an Appalachian community, and constructed a continuum of social-control methods that ranged from nonviolent to violent. Her classification system included: a) normative order methods; b) persuasive methods; and, c) violent methods of social control.

Normative order methods of control are "nonactive, nonviolent forms of social control . . . a product of cultural norms, values, and beliefs as well as the social structure" (392), and included employment norms for men and women, domestic responsibilities as to what men and women "should do," objectification of women, and other accepted standards of behavior in coupled life such as power of decision-making and financial management (Gagné 1992). Persuasive methods of control are nonviolent ways in which people persuade others to act against their will or prevent them from acting of their own free will. Such methods include withholding transportation, monitoring and controlling another's behavior by verbal persuasion, playing "mental games," sexual divisiveness (e.g., infidelities in the partnered relationship), verbal complaints, and emotional distancing within intimate relationships (Gagné 1992). Physical violence against women constituted the third category of social control in rural culture. Rural women who eventually became homeless experienced social control in their partnered relationships across all three categories, and reached a point where they began to reject the rural cultural norms of gender relationships. Social controls escalated over time from normative to life-threatening physical violence. Fear for one's life often pushed rural women into homelessness (Cummins 1996).

NORMATIVE SOCIAL CONTROLS:

Diana

I went from one boss to another boss. . . . That's just the way I look at it. You go from one house [parents] to another [husband]. You got one boss then you got another one. . . . You still got somebody over, ya tellin' ya what to do. . . . He [husband] made most of the decisions.

Karen

. . . and since we got married, it was like now I was his . . . a possession . . . his little playtoy that he told when to walk and when to talk and what to do and when to do it.

PERSUASIVE SOCIAL CONTROLS:

Lana

I had no say-so [in the marriage]. . . . I reported in. . . . [Decisions were limited to] what to have for supper! . . . I mean, there was none. He done them all [decisions]. He had the money. He's the one that worked.

Cecilly

I really didn't have a lot of friends—he didn't like for me to have friends. He had friends and he ran around and I was not to say nothing. We had nobody coming around, nobody come and saw us. The friends of mine that did, he questioned me, like I was doing something wrong, and I really wasn't. They [friends] just kinda went away and I was just kinda on my own. I never saw any of the checks [husband's income].

Karen

He'd be jealous and so [he said] he wasn't jealous. I mean, I couldn't win, no matter what I did. His money went to his girlfriends . . . about fifteen that I knew of . . . and to the bars. It was cause I wasn't woman enough for him . . . my husband said, I was too ugly, and too unsexy, and too skinny and nobody would have me.

VIOLENT SOCIAL CONTROLS:

Lana

He like to hit around [on me]. . . . [Things] just turned around [from thinking I had someone to take care of me] and I was worrying about everything. About how drunk he was going to be; how bad I'd be hurt toward the morning, and—when will he start beating on her [daughter]?

Beth

He'd come home drinking and he started arguing about me always being over there with the kids. And he knew I wasn't always over there and I wouldn't argue with him and it seems like that would, I don't know, really tick him off. And he'd get in my face and start hollering, wanting me to, begging me to hit him. And I wouldn't hit him. And I think that night he threw me down and held me down and really worked me over real good. I think that was the worst there was.

Cecilly

When we went to the WSYN fireworks and he got very drunk, very obnoxious, and it's very crowded down there. It's like wall-to-wall people. His sister and her boyfriend had went with us and we were all pretty sober but he was just terrible. So we hooked on each other's jackets. We had Levi jackets on. We like hooked on each other's jackets and Kurt led the way through the crowds 'Cause we was wanting to get as close to [the river] as we could. And I was hooked onto Bryan's jacket and he just, he got mad about that and slammed me into the wall, busted my head open. . . . I was bleeding really bad and they was holding my head.

Karen

I was abused physically and mentally from my husband. When we first got married, we moved in with his family. He had like eight brothers and sisters, and here was me and due with one baby, and then I had another baby and another baby, and—and he was from a violent home. The police come to the house once a week . . . and me going away in an ambulance. [He] threatened that he was going to kill me. . . . I have had my nose replaced four times. . . . He busted me in the head one time. My head got cut pretty bad. [I started having] seizures after that.

STAGE 2: STEPPING INTO HOMELESSNESS

"No Way to Stay and Nowhere to Go"

To ponder leaving traditional roles of wife and mother forces a redefinition of self outside the cultural norms, and may represent a rejection of the imposed identity adopted and lived throughout rural women's adult lives. A recognition of the possibility of "making it on my own" marked the women's beginning definition of self outside their cultural norms. In the context of an emerging self and life-threatening circumstances of partner abuse, women were often faced with a realization that "there was no way to stay." Moreover, on a very practical level for rural women who later became homeless, "there was nowhere to go." Stepping into homelessness was the outcome of intensified violent and persuasive social controls within the women's intimate relationships and an emerging self that demanded more than a controlled, silenced existence.

Coming to consciousness about one's position and choices in life shifts women's movement from passivity to action (Belenky et al. 1986; Cummins 1996). This coming to consciousness about one's self is marked by a rejection of external authorities and what others dictate as "right" or "wrong." Chopra (1995) called this shift of value orientation a process of moving from object-referral, where individuals respond to external cues to govern their behaviors, to self-referral, where one looks within to one's own value system to influence one's thoughts and actions. Ulrich (1991) defined leaving abusive relationships in rural and metropolitan Midwest women as a decision process signaling a change of consciousness, with the final exit tied to a concrete event.

A consistent theme among rural homeless women was a fear of "making it on my own." However, times away from their partnered relationships often provided safe periods when they nurtured their small inner voices and fortified social relations with significant supportive others. As fragile women with little sense of self or worth, brief periods away from their partnered relationships prior to entering homelessness may have been critical times for building the inner strength that eventually facilitates moving out of controlled abusive relationships and into homelessness and reconnection with self and others (Cummins 1996).

A growing confidence in self-knowledge provides women with the conviction and strength to make changes in their lives, based on what seems right to them. Women often leave their pasts behind and step out of the old defined roles of wife and mother, and retreat from old responsibilities and old relationships. Decisions were made with little forethought. The rural women often took the first opportunity to escape and chart their life courses on their own. Impulsive responses had serious consequences for the women's social arrangements, relationships, self-concepts, and behaviors (Belenky et al. 1986; Cummins 1996).

Reconsidering Dependency

In the beginning stage of defining self, women often experience an unstable and fluctuating self-concept. While they struggle to hear the small emerging inner voice, they are pulled back to the embedded self-concept imposed by male authorities. Past images of self may have a tyrannical hold on women as they struggle to break free from their socially controlled and yet familiar relationships of the past, and move into contexts that provide a space for the developing self to emerge (Belenky et al. 1986; Cummins 1996). The rural women's uncertainty about whether to stay or leave was manifested by testing waters of independence for brief periods of time, followed by a return to an abusive partner. Ambivalence about leaving and staying, and about relinquishing the traditional role of caring for mate and children, was common. A decision to stay or leave may constitute a moral dilemma as described by Gilligan (1982). Much like the women in Gilligan's (1982) study on the moral development of women, rural women became more concerned with the moral responsibilities to themselves as they nurtured their small inner voices and less concerned with the culturally defined duties and obligations of women in rural society (Cummins 1996; Zalk 1986). Eventually, these women chose freedom and homelessness over security and abuse (Cummins 1996).

Stepping into Homelessness

The women's exits from abusive relationships may have been instinctive responses to abuse and self-protection. The decision to sever relationships with abusive intimates represented a turning point in their lives, and a commitment to a life free of abuse even if it is on the street. For women beginning to define themselves otherwise, leaving abusive relationships may represent a self-advocating action that rejects male authorities' definitions of women within a cultural norm. This phenomenon is akin to what Erikson (1968) called 'negative identity,' that is, the defining of self in opposition to others, such as male authorities (Belenky et al. 1986; Cummins 1996). Nesto's (1994) study of use of psychological, social, and material resources among low-income separated and divorced women, many of whom suffered physical and sexual abuse in their marriages, reported on their abilities to draw upon their inner psychological resourcefulness to withstand threats in their environment. Similarly, Geissinger et al. (1993) observed that strategies to relieve isolation among the rural women in their study emerged as self-advocating actions that precipitated a change in their relational disconnection. From a developmental perspective, abruptly leaving dangerous relationships may symbolize a commitment to self as authority over one's own life. However, failure to think through decisions and plan their exits placed rural women in precarious and unstable circumstances. It was this abrupt shift from passivity to action that propelled rural women into homelessness (Cummins 1996).

Beth

And the morning I left he had raped me. And [pause] I had bought a car off his sister 'cause I had wrecked mine. And he wouldn't let me have the car so I walked to Holler Run . . . about four miles.

Lana

Well, I went at night. . . . We ran out. Me and my daughter. We just ran out. 'Cause he was hittin' on us . . . ran out with nothin'. . . . I had two dollars. Two dollars, and that was it. That's all I had on me, you know. 'Cause . . . I left everything there. . . . To get away was the main thing. You know, it was like—deal with the rest of it later. I just got to get out. You know. And I did it. I couldn't take any more. . . . Oh, I knew it— 'cause I didn't—I guess I'd been just waiting for it to happen. You know? Give me a reason to get out. I was just waiting for it. That way, he couldn't say, you're the one, you know? We just walked out. I wanted to make him feel like it was his fault . . . there wasn't nowhere else to go 'cause he liked to hit around. And then I just took and—there was no way I was staying there. . . . 'Cause I had a daughter, when will he start beating on her? It was awful. 'Cause I couldn't take it. And I'd rather done without. I'd rather been on the street . . . and that's where I went.

STAGE 3: SURVIVING IN HOMELESSNESS

"Making It on My Own"

Following an impulsive exit from controlled and abusive relationships, women often found themselves homeless, alone, and with few resources for surviving. Stepping into homelessness forced women to test their assumptions about their abilities to care for themselves. In such dire circumstances, women are compelled to pull upon their internal resources and adaptability in order to fashion strategies for surviving in homelessness. Survival strategies were often diverse and usually included informal and formal supports (Cummins 1996; First, Toomey, and Rife 1995; Fitchen 1991a, 1991b).

Significant Supportive Others

Women's competencies develop in the context of relationships with significant supportive others, and concurrently, so does their sense of Self. Researchers and theorists on women's development underscore the importance of attachment in the psychological development of women (Belenky et al. 1986; Chodorow 1978; Gilligan 1982; Miller 1976; Surrey 1985, 1991a, 1991b). The Self-in-relations theory holds that attachment and connectedness are central organizing principles for women's development of Self (Surrey 1991a). Building on Surrey's work, Geissinger et al. (1993) studied isolation among rural women and suggested that isolation and disconnectedness may represent an "amputation of a core aspect of one's self" (294) and noted that cutting off supportive relationships, as through physical abuse, is a potent method for disempowering women. They further suggested that physical violence endangered a woman's sense of self and competency (Geissinger et al. 1993). Women's friendships with other women contribute to self-knowledge and self-identity by clarifying issues and affirming strengths (Berzoff 1989). "Through relationships with other women, women heal the hurts of their psychological development" (Flax 1981, 60). For rural homeless women, psychological resources, such as self-esteem, were developed in the context of social relationships, the medium for the development of Self. Through the enrichment of social and psychological resources, women were able to reclaim self as the authority in their life. Moving through homelessness became a process of working out rules and values to live by that reflected an expanding definition of Self (Cummins 1996).

Significant supportive others provided care and assistance unconditionally, and proved to be critical to survival in the early stages of homelessness. Relying on truth grounded in firsthand experience of the women most like themselves provided a foundation for relationships that, over time, grew in trust and dependability. Reassurances and affirmations from significant supportive others led women to believe that they could also learn to think and know and be a woman (Belenky et al. 1986; Cummins 1996).

Beth

If it wasn't for her [cousin], I don't know what I would have done. I was with my cousin. [Pause] And I lived with her for probably, probably a year.

Diana

She's [Sarah] really helped me out a bunch. I don't know what I'd done without her. . . . Sarah found me the trailer. . . . Sarah told me about it [apartment.]. I'm working with ABCAP with the highly functioning in a group home. Sarah got me this job, too.

Lana

And I had told her [Sarah] a lot. She always told me 'cause she knew how he was and she was always—"When it gets too much, you know, you can come stay with me. Don't worry about it." So, you know, that was—the first thing that went through my head, you know, I can go to Sarah's. So that's where I went and that's where I stayed until she helped me get this place. At the time she was, she was my best friend. I wouldn't be where I'm at, that's for sure [if it wasn't for her].

Survival Strategies

As time in homelessness progressed, women adapted and implemented a variety of strategies for surviving including: (a) trading services with friends; (b) developing new social networks; (c) employment; (d) use of formal social services including AFDC, food stamps,
Medicaid, and subsidized housing; (e) reliance on significant supportive others; (f) retooling for the marketplace through college and
vocational education; (g) moving frequently from friend to friend or
to different and more affordable housing; (h) entering relationships
with men; (i) relying on family members; (j) redefining the role of
motherhood; (k) taking on new and multiple roles; and (l) living in
a car (Cummins 1996).

Community and Family Supports

While homeless, rural women's families and community members
offered little support. Some refused to ask family members for help,
viewing it as living by the old traditional rules of male dominance.
Others refused help from family members when it was offered con-
ditionally. In some cases, family and community members refused to
give help because they disapproved of the women breaking a cultural
value, "stand by your man." Some women negotiated services with
friends, such as exchanging meals for car repairs. Help was rejected
if it forced women into unwanted roles and/or conditions.

Beth

There's five of us girls. . . . They don't [live in this community] now but
they did then [when I was homeless. I asked] all my sisters [for help].
. . . [They] weren't helpful at all. . . . I never expected that 'cause I was
always there for them [sisters], I just wondered why. It sort of hurt my
feelings that they wouldn't help me. . . . They said that I couldn't stay
there. Or if I could, they didn't want the kids there. . . . It did [surprise
me] . . . 'cause I always helped them, you know, whenever they were
having problems and I don't know. . . . I figured they'd be there for
me. But they weren't.

Karen

None of my family would take me in. . . . They [children] helped me
with, you know, things I'll need.

Lana

No [I didn't asked them for help]. None. I just didn't want to. I just
felt that I'd done this. I'm doing it myself. You know. They're not the
ones that got me into this, and I can't keep running to them to get me

out. Kristi [daughter] stayed with them, you know, and to me that was enough help.

For women getting in touch with who they are, making it on their own was an important part of surviving in homelessness and finding their way out of homelessness; a rite of passage that gained them the right to govern their own lives. Investment in relationships was the foundation of new social networks the women developed throughout their homeless episode (Belenky et al. 1986; Cummins 1996).

Redefining Motherhood

Mothering had been at the center of the rural women's lives prior to becoming homeless, and was closely linked to their identity. Mothering has been and continues to be "a central and defining feature of the social organization of gender" (9) and in the construction and reproduction of male dominance (Chodorow 1978). For rural homeless women determined to break out from under the control of male authorities, redefining mothering was a necessary step toward independence; however, even as the women's parenting roles changed, of primary importance was a continued connection with their children. The shift in the mothering role was central to successfully navigating homelessness and assuring that their children were well cared for. The women employed several strategies in order to provide for the well-being of their children. Some relinquished the role of primary parent. Others kept their children with them and sought help in fulfilling this role. Still others used a combination of these strategies.

Cecilly

My mom usually does [watch the children]. . . . She comes over here [apartment] or I'll take then down there and . . . she'll get them [children] ready for me in the morning and I'll go get them and drop them off at school and it depends on how she's feeling [and] who's at home. . . . Or my mom will come down and like help them with their homework.

Diana

I told him [ex-husband] I can't deal with it no more. You take care of the kids. . . . I couldn't afford to keep the house, there was no way, I'd have needed to have a job that paid $20 an hour to even make it, paying the insurance and everything like that. It's been hard on the girls though. I got one, she'll be 12 next month and the oldest one, she'll be 16 in September. It's been real rough on them . . . because we had joint custody . . . whenever they could come and stay with me, [mostly] they'd stay with their dad. He's [ex-husband] had a lot more responsibility of makin' sure they get here and get there in the last 3 years.

Lana

I took my daughter to my mom and dad's the next day. So she lives with Mom and Dad, and then I get her whenever. . . .

Heather

Me and my daughter . . . well, she stayed mostly with relatives [when we were homeless]. She was seven [then].

Multiple Roles

Surviving in homelessness requires changes in the type and/or number of roles for women. Women most often choose to remain active and involved as mothers. Many grappled with learning how to manage their meager finances effectively and being solely responsible for securing and caring for adequate housing. Working multiple jobs and attending vocational or college programs were common strategies for managing life in and out of homelessness.

Lana

. . . 'cause after I got—you know, got started there [work], well, then I guess I needed to learn how to manage my money, pay the bills, you know. So I started by helping Sarah, paying half of everything, you know. And then just worked my way up to where, you know, I could do it on my own, 'cause I had no—when I was married . . . as far as managing the money, I had no idea how to do it.

Cecilly

I have like my school and my kids. We have football three nights a week. We have football games on Saturdays. I work third shift. I have no time. . . . [But] it's got to be done. . . . It's just got to be done . . . and I work at Riggs. . . . They've got me on six nights right now. Last week I had four and it kind of varies. I only wanted four to start with. . . . I [also] work third shift—up here at this truck stop and fuel mart on the corner [second job]. Usually I don't go into school until—I go to school at 10 on Tuesdays and Thursdays, and so I get all them kids off and I have my last one gets off at 9:15 and I might lay down then or I'll come home and I'll lay down. I got straight sleep [for two hours] and I felt pretty good when I get—straight sleep like that, I feel really better than the chop sleep that I get. . . . The boys will come in [after school] and they'll get their homework done and then I try to get up like 4:30 or 5 to cook them dinner. Then we'll eat our dinner and then we'll do their hard homework or study spelling words or reading, whatever we got to do. And then by 8:00, they got to get baths and, hopefully, by 8:30 they're in bed. I lay back down with them until 10:00 p.m.

and then I get up and get ready for work. [I sleep] between three and five [hours a day].

Diana

There for a while, I was working two jobs, plus going to school. I'd get home at 12 midnight and have to get up at 5 a.m. to go to the nursing home and get off at 4 and go back to work at 6 at the bar. I'm working with ABCAP with the highly functioning group I started that [group home resident manager] part-time in February and then they needed somebody for 30 days to basically live there . . . work like 120 hours a week and only have 48 hours a week off. [I also started part-time with] So, I basically lived in Georgetown for a month and worked for Passport, cleaning senior citizen's houses, and then I started school for a nurse's aide . . . all this in one month.

Formal Support Services

Formal supports were essential survival strategies for most women while homeless, and included social welfare services, such as AFDC, Medicaid, food stamps, subsidized housing, vocational and college education, and counseling. Some used subsidize housing as a means to getting their own place. Others used AFDC and food stamp and Medicaid benefits to support themselves and their children, in spite of their negative attitudes toward "welfare." Rural communities have a more negative attitude toward welfare than their urban counterparts, while at the same time favoring government assistance to the poor (Davis 1988; Duncan and Lamborghini 1994; McInnis-Dittrich 1995). Some women harbored ambivalence toward welfare, saying that welfare was for those who really needed it, but that they could make it on their own. Being homeless, in and of itself, was not interpreted as being "truly needy." Even the women who applied for and benefited from the use of public assistance related feeling ashamed for having done so and sought to conceal its use from others outside the immediate family. Others viewed public assistance as symbolic of males who sought to control their lives (Cummins 1996).

Cecilly

I went and applied for assistance and I had to use my mom and dad's address. . . . I was ashamed. . . . I didn't want—I would have my mom go pick up my food stamps for the longest time 'cause I was afraid of who I would see in the food stamp line.

Lana

I could never bring myself to do that [welfare. Someone] might need it more than me, right. That's why I've never really messed with it, you know. I hope it's for the people that really need it that's unable to do for theirselves. To help people that's unable . . . you know, it's like a family. . . . It's not that I'm against it or it's like—you know, it would feel like I was depending on someone else again, but then I would also feel that I was taking from someone that [needed it]. You know, 'cause that'd be like depending on someone else again . . . you know, and that's what I was trying to get away from. I just—I don't know—me and welfare, I just don't think on it. If I can't make it on my own, then you know, that would be the very last resort.

Heather

Well, actually, I had to lie to welfare and tell them that I was staying at my mom's 'cause I didn't have an address. In order to receive help, you had to have an address. . . . But I was actually living in my car. . . . 'Cause I couldn't write down, Ford Mustang Avenue, Holler Run [laugh]. . . . After I lied about having a place to stay [they let me submit my application]. . . . [It took] something like . . . five months. . . . Well, I didn't like it [being on welfare]. . . . Most of the county's on welfare, so it's no real big deal, but . . . it's just . . . I like to support myself.

Surviving in homelessness required women to discover and draw upon inner resources, as well as manipulate informal and formal support systems in ways that were congruent with their evolving sense of Self and value system. Building new social networks through friends, co-workers, and even clients affirmed the women's growing commitment to Self and broadened their repertoire of resources. Informal relationships were also useful in trading services and learning new skills, especially from significant supportive others. Subsidized housing provided avenues out of homelessness for many women, and while some rely on AFDC, food stamps, and Medicaid for one to two years, eventually they moved toward self-sufficiency and off public assistance. Contrary to most of the professional literature that depicts homeless women as deficient or plagued with personal problems, rural homeless women demonstrated extraordinary resourcefulness and resolve (Cummins 1996).

Barriers to Stability

Homeless women encounter many personal, cultural, and structural barriers to residential stability including harassment and physical abuse from ex-partners, shunning by family and community members, and institutional practices that deny women protection from abuse, and/or access to needed resources. Personal problems such as chemical dependency and mental illness were rare (Cummins et al., 1998; Cummins 1996; Roth et al. 1987). Many of the barriers to stability of rural homeless women replicate Gagné's (1992) episte-mological categories of social control within the extended family, community, and local and federal institutions (Cummins 1996). As women moved beyond male authorities' definition of Self to an exploration of a larger world, family and spouses often responded with anger and erected obstacles to their success (Belenky et al. 1986; Cummins 1996). Family and community barriers contribute to home-less women's isolation from family and others (Cummins 1996). Women who resist returning to the social conventions and defini-tions of Self are characteristic of women on the move toward greater autonomy and independence (Belenky et al.. 1986).

Family Barriers

Rural women described being rejected by family members and denied help when they were homeless, and attribute the lack of fam-ily support to breaking the community norm of "stand by your man." Homeless women found themselves isolated outside the supportive structure of family when they took on roles and values that are con-trary to the cultural norm. Disapproving attitudes of family members were represented by refusal to help at points of the women's greatest need. A prevalent rural attitude appears to be "you made your bed, now lie in it." Some women shared this attitude toward themselves as well, and refused to ask family members for help.

Harassment and Abuse from Estranged Partners

Violent social control and harassment continued for months and some-times years after the women left their abusive partners. Women described being run off the road in their cars, having their tires slashed, verbal intimidation at their places of work, and repeated beatings as methods used by ex-partners to persuade them to return to their tradi-tional subservient roles in the marital relationship (Cummins 1996).

> *Diana*
>
> He threatened me a couple of times, and finally I just told him, I said
> . . . I caught him at the truck stop one day and I told him, I said, "ya
> know," I said, "you've flattened my tires three times, you've run me off
> the road, you've threatened me," I said, "I'm tired of it." I mean, I was
> at the truck stop eatin' one evening and he flattened my tires. I told
> him [ex-husband] . . . and I said, "From now on all I have to do, if you
> bother me one more time, all I have to do is make one phone call . . .
> and I will do it." It was just a real good friend that told me, ya know, if
> he comes around and bothers you again, let me know.

Lana

He shoved around on me a couple times but he'd never hit me after I left . . . but I think the worse—him cutting my tires was probably the worse 'cause then he knew I didn't have no money for new tires, you know. It was always something behind everything he done. There was a reason, well not a reason, but a motive or something. You know, just trying I guess to bring me down, all the way.

Cecilly

'Cause he climbs in these windows 'cause these locks are all broke. And he doesn't think a thing about climbing in a window. If I'm gone for the week-end, he'll leave notes "where the heck are you this weekend? You know, you're supposed to be home." He does not spend any time in the house in the evening and the nighttime. When I go, I lock the place. He has no visitation rights for his children, but he is at the house every day. He has no place of his own . . . he sleeps in the parking lot of my apartment in his truck every night. . . . Well one night he came in and he was mad about something. I don't even remember what and he pulled a gun on me and we fought over the gun and he hit me in the jaw with the gun and broke my jaw.

Community Barriers

Sanctions from community members contributed to the women's social isolation while homeless. Most often, rural homeless women described being shunned and made to feel that they "just weren't good enough . . . like trash." Some women expressed a similar view of themselves as homeless and poor women, and experienced a sense of shame and failure as community members. Community responses to the women's homelessness erected an invisible barrier that placed the women outside the supportive structures of their home culture (Cummins 1996).

Diana

You hear people say, "well, look at her, she's on food stamps and she dresses better than I do." or "they got things better than we do." I've heard that a lot.

Cecilly

Just the way they [community members] look at you. They kind of leave you out. Like when the boys were on the ball team, the parents—all the mothers would sit together, and you go up there but they don't talk to you . . . they just don't make you feel welcome at all. . . . You just wanted to like just sink in a far area, in a corner of the wall, you know, or anything. It just was bad, just was real embarrassing. [Their attitude was] I wasn't as good as they were—just like I was trash.

Karen

My kids did not eat lunch. 'Cause my kids were too embarrassed to use their free lunch cards. . . . Like on the free lunch program, they [schoolmates] made fun of them. [The] kids wouldn't take food stamps in [the store]. You know, it's like, "Mom, go get me some juice or something," and I'd say, "Well, you go up." [They'd say] "I ain't taking no food stamps in there." Which I understand their point. You know, they were growing up and they were embarrassed. . . . It's people make fun of them. . . . Oh, you're a food stamp recipient, you know, your mom and dad don't work. You're bums.

Homeless women compensated for the loss of community by spending much of their social time with their significant supportive others, their children, and by building new relationships. Using Gagné's (1992) epistemological categories of social control, the family and community responses to homeless women could be defined as forms of normative, persuasive, and for some, violent social control. It was, on a mezzo level, a social response based in the cultural norms, values, and beliefs of the community toward women who had violated community standards. Gagné (1992) clarified normative social control as the result of patriarchal social structure and male-biased cultural beliefs. Community shunning may also represent silent support of male dominance in the family home (Cummins 1996).

Belenky et al. (1986) observed that when women were faced with demands from family and community to remain in their silent and conforming positions, many chose to walk away from their past, symbolizing an affirmation of their new emerging Self. In some sense, the isolation imposed by family and community provided an opportunity for the rural women to establish new social networks based on their value of Self, instead of how well they fulfilled their prescribed roles in rural society.

Structural Barriers

Institutional barriers to resources also contributed to homelessness among rural women, and may have prolonged homeless episodes. Barriers such as normative attitudes of social service personnel became verbal coercion by social service personnel that thwarted the women's efforts to access public resources. Rural homeless women describe negative interactions with social welfare personnel and believed that the workers acted as though the money they were applying for was "coming out of their own pockets." Due to the low population density it is common for social service workers to have personal knowledge about local clients prior to their arrival at the welfare office for assistance. Some rural women reported that personal knowledge was used inappropriately to deny them services.

Heather

When I first went up to apply for welfare, they made me feel so bad, I went out crying. . . . Well, I went in to ask them to help us find a place to stay. All they would say was well, "what are you going to do about this" . . . "what are you going to do about this". . . . I said, I don't know, 'cause I'm here to find out what I can do to do about it. "Well, we can't help you, what are you going to do about it." You know, it was just useless. . . . Basically, they just badgered me. . . . Oh, I had to go back again. . . . After I lied about having a place to stay [they let me submit my application]. . . . [It took] something like . . . five months. . . . [After I got on welfare] I don't know, they [attitudes] just changed. It was like I paid, now "I can help you now" . . . which really pissed me off [laugh].

Diana

A lot of 'em acted like it was comin' out of their own pocket. . . . Now there's a few of 'em over there that were really nice, but there's a couple of 'em [act like] they were feedin' ya. . . . It just seemed like they give you the runaround . . . make ya gather up all kinds of papers and birth certificates and everything, ya know. Here's my two kids, ya know, they're mine. It was like they didn't believe ya. A lot of red tape.

Rural homeless women reported difficulty in getting support and protection from local police and court systems when dealing with abusive ex-partners. Passive policing practices of rural officers in domestic violence cases support the traditional gender roles and patriarchal ideology of rural society, and produce a form of sociocultural isolation that makes rural women particularly vulnerable to domestic violence (Websdale 1995). Police were likely to resist "sticking their nose in where it doesn't belong" (111), tended to side with the batterers and their right to exercise control over their wives, and to believe that "a good man might beat his wife" (112). Websdale (1995) concluded that the attitudes of rural police mirrored the patriarchal construction of women's social position in rural society and established institutional social control of rural women.

Cecilly

[Paraphrased] He went to high school with the police officers. . . . his history with this community and with the law enforcement officers prevent me from being protected. . . . I pressed charges against him. . . . Three [times]. I mean, like millions of times, I'm going to be away for the weekend, [I will ask the police] "will you make sure he's not going to come around my apartment and break in. Will you just kind of patrol this area?" . . . I've tried that millions of times and then I'll find a note inside my house [from ex-husband]. Well, how did he get in here? [I've] had a restraining order placed on him which the police do not enforce. They take him out, and then they release him. . . . The police came, picked him up, released him, and on the way out one of the policemen stopped him on the road and asked him if he wanted his gun back, and immediately returned the gun to him.

Beth

Well, I went to an attorney, and he started telling me I had to go for everything, and I didn't want to take everything, I just wanted my fair share . . . then he started telling me these high rates which I didn't have the money to pay, so when I went to court, I went by myself . . . I had no attorney. And so, when I got to court, I was just shocked and surprised that my husband had gotten neighbors and friends to testify against me. They had made up stories about terrible things I had done in terms of mothering and leaving my kids and not caring for them, and none of it was true and I was just shocked and I basically said nothing throughout the hearing . . . and the judge didn't get me a public defender. I ended up losing everything. I got nothing. The children went with their father.

The most common housing problem reported by rural women was the unavailability of affordable housing and the long waiting list to access public and subsidized housing units. Some women were refused rental housing when applying without a male partner, or when they had more than two children.

The normative value that the male controls the home and finances was reflected in the institutional practices of banks that held the mortgage on the marital property. Bank foreclosures occurred without notification to female mortgage holders, which severely limited their housing options.

Some women encountered discriminatory actions by the I.R.S., which refused refund payments because back taxes were due from ex-spouses, even when ex-spouses were court-ordered to pay the back taxes. Often poor and homeless women spend more on legal fees to collect what is rightfully theirs than the actual amount of money due them.

Diana

He [ex-husband] agreed to give me my money from my half of the house. . . . He still hasn't paid me. It's been, what, 3 years. We're getting ready to go back to court again. He's running around saying he ain't got no money, but yet he's got money to go on vacations . . . [and] finally, I had to get another lawyer and take him back to court for my money, and he started making payments last fall. And they kept this year's refund, too, and he told me when I filed that, instead of going back to court, he would pay me. Well, I haven't got it yet. Just before we went back to court ... here I hired another lawyer to get my income tax money back from him, I tried to talk to him about givin' me my income tax money back. . . . He hem hawed around about it. I said, "you don't leave me no choice." He said, "what do you mean by that." I said, "well, I'm gonna hire me another lawyer." I said, "you signed the divorce papers. You agreed to pay those back taxes. You're not payin' 'em, and they're keepin' my refund."

Rural women have traditionally been tied to the domestic sphere, but in recent years have entered the labor market in increasing numbers. When this occurs, women face gender bias in the employment structure. Employed rural homeless women reported that the common practice was for women to earn half the wages of men for the same job responsibilities. Bushy (1993) noted that, on average, rural women earn only 50 percent of rural men's wages for comparable work. Discrimination in hiring practices also exists, with male workers being hired over female workers (Cummins 1996). Such practices represent forms of institutionalized normative values and result in limited resources for rural homeless women.

The patriarchal value base that dominates the lives of rural women creates structural barriers to women's pursuits of stability and self, and infuses social and cultural subsystems with traditional values of what it means to be female in rural society. Normative male values and priorities permeated the personal lives, the cultural norms, and local institutions of their public and private lives, and thus perpetuated and naturalized patriarchal culture and legitimized male hegemony (Przybylowicz 1989–1990).

Walby's (1990) understanding of the term "patriarchy" included the processes of domination, oppression, and exploitation of women by men. She noted that these processes are manifested in society when the patriarchal state resists confronting violence against women and in the gendering of a capitalist economy. For rural homeless women, the inability to gain protection against abusive ex-partners from local authorities, and inequities in wages and employment opportunities, demonstrated the patriarchal features described by Walby (1990). The impact of these complex and pervasive patriarchal values is represented in the struggles of rural homeless women. The oppressive interplay of the social control dynamics left homeless women in a state of socio-cultural isolation that limits their access to resources.

Heather

A lot of places I would sit like say maybe . . . the park . . . or old school lots . . . you know, where schools use to be . . . sit there and read the paper or try to find a place to go just to sit and think about things . . . the police would run you off . . . "you can't sit there." At the time, I saw a lot of people sittin' there when I was sittin' there, and they'd just go on by them . . . but these people were like waiting for a bus to pick them up or something. . . . The police had pushed or ran me to another county. That was their solution, push them [homeless] somewhere. Well, I was staying in Greene County at a place . . . in my car . . . and they asked me to leave, and I kept driving around, and they kept following me, and when I got to the county line, they quit following me. When they left, I went back. I went through a lot of gas that night.

STAGE 4: THE JOURNEY BACK

Supportive Contexts for Leaving Homelessness

The contexts for moving out of homelessness encompassed new social networks, social welfare services, education and training, stable employment, child support, and the enduring presence and guidance of significant supportive others. Movement into supportive structures and their own residences created spaces of safety and a sense of control over the women's lives that facilitated a reconnection with self (Cummins, 1996). Surrey (1991b) illustrated that "capacities such as competence, agency, and initiative are developed for women in the context of important relationships" (37), and Berzoff (1989) described how female friendships enhanced self-worth and self-esteem. Much like the therapy groups described by Berzoff and Bayes (cited in Berzoff 1989), the relationships with significant supportive others created "holding environments of safety and nurturance" (275). Nesto (1994) and Geissinger et al. (1993) encountered comparable dynamics among the women in their studies and concluded that, through work, school, and other accomplishments, women developed a dynamic relationship with self and, over time, women become less dependent on significant others, and improve their self-esteem.

New social networks affirmed the women's life choices and provided both material and psychological resources. Affirmations from significant supportive others, friends, and fellow workers promoted the rural women's self-esteem and provided help in meeting daily needs. Formal social services were critical supports for ending homelessness. Education and training opened opportunities for stable jobs. Success in learning validated the women's competence and boosted their self-worth. Stable employment was a primary support for leaving welfare and homelessness, and was also a place where competencies and belief in self developed.

Meaning of Home

Having escaped the violent, persuasive, and normative forms of social control experienced in their partnered relationships and home communities, the women identified having their own place with autonomy and control over Self. Often, they described home as what it was not—"no one bossin' me" or "no one to answer to," but also, what is was—a place of safety and a "sanctuary" where they made the rules. Home was a place where they had control over who stayed and who didn't. If there was any throwing out to do, *they* would be the ones doing it. The women felt a strong attachment to their own place that represented control over their lives. In Gowdy and Pearlmutter's (1993) study of AFDC women, their meaning of economic self-sufficiency (ESS) encompassed being both economically independent and having a sense of freedom and control over their lives. Gowdy and Pearlmutter (1993) suggested that, when subjective and objective aspects of ESS are both considered, the meaning of ESS can be understood as a process along a continuum through stages of personal and economic growth.

Reclaiming Self

The journey through homelessness and back to Self was a process of women claiming their own values and rejecting the prescribed gender roles and norms of their rural home culture. They spoke of "getting back to themselves," which was similar to Belenky et al.'s (1986) concept of reclaiming Self. Journeys were characterized by personal growth, a discovery of self-worth and competence, and establishing economic and housing stability. Homeless women reclaimed their personal power through accomplishments, competent decision-making, and paying their own way. Having their own place embodied their understanding of claiming their own space and achieving independence. It meant "it's mine and no one can take it" and "I'm my own boss." The reclaiming of Self paralleled the women's growing stability in the material world.

Reclaiming self was a critical task for achieving emotional emancipation, coming to terms with old conflicts, and reconnecting with family and community members. In coming to terms with the conflict between Self as authority and the male dominance of their home communities, the women developed an understanding of Self separate from others but also in connection with others. Berzoff (1989) asserted that the psychological task for women is differentiation from others through relationships and not autonomy. With this understanding came empathy and genuine caring for family and community members who had "wronged" them in the past. Many were drawn to heal conflicts with family members and gained a sense of peace after working out a caring relationship that did not violate Self but instead, provided them with a new way of understanding and accepting family members. Bridging the distances by forgiving old hurts, acknowledging their own failures, and striving to understand others' perspectives on the course of events in their lives, the women were able to extend themselves in a selfless way. Empathy and mutuality have been delineated as core aspects of women's experiences with Self and others (Belenky et al. 1986; Berzoff 1989; Surrey 1991a). Jordan (1991) defined empathy as "the process through which one's experienced sense of basic connection and similarity to other humans is established" (69). Self and culture converged when differentiated self-defined rural women made their way back to family and community, speaking in their own voices

Lana

I'm more self-assured, I think. Stronger. Well, I didn't have to worry about him [ex-husband]. I could just be me—instead of being what he wanted me to be. [I'm] a happy person [laughter] . . . that I like. . . . I just feel like—that I've worked for everything I've got and it just makes me feel better. You know, not degraded. It's been a long three years. It's been the happiest three years since I got back but it's been rough, but I haven't really let nothing get me down, you know, at all. Hasn't been nothing to get me down. You know, I guess I'm finally getting it the way I always wanted it to be. It's slow, but I think it's coming.

Beth

I just prefer myself back to where I was. I got control. It's [self-esteem] better. I mean, I think it gets better. You know, each day I feel better, you know, about myself. I just prefer myself back to where I was. You know, I'm not a bad person, and it took me a long time to see that. And even sometimes now I'll get a-thinking about things and I just got to forget about the things in the past. Cause I'm not a bad person and I do love myself and my kids. [On a scale of one to ten, my spirits are] . . . oh, probably an eight, seven or eight. I can improve myself so I wouldn't rate myself as a ten.

Diana

I was to the point where I wasn't gonna let nobody use me again. . . . [My self-esteem] is better . . . a lot better. In the last year or so . . . [I've been] just wisenin' up and not payin' no 'tention to it [gossip]. . . . I don't care what the gossip is around this town. I was not going to let people use me for anything. . . . I feel like a person again.

CONCLUSIONS

The journeys out of homelessness and into stability were complex intertwining paths of self-discovery, and testing abilities in new roles and responsibilities outside the culturally defined domestic sphere. The interplay of these two developing paths of Self—those of financial independence and emotional emancipation—was reflected in the women's growing self-esteem and confidence in their abilities to make it on their own. As their self-confidence grew, so did their willingness to engage opportunities for self-growth and material stability. Moving from part-time jobs to permanent employment, embarking on vocational and college careers, and transitioning from shared temporary housing to their own places demonstrated in concrete ways their growing emotional and financial independence and a belief that they could make it on their own. The women's movements from homelessness to economic and residential self-sufficiency was driven by a commitment to self and a reevaluation of their worth according to internal standards (Chopra 1995).

SUMMARY AND DISCUSSION

Rural patriarchy was a dominant force in the lives of the rural homeless women and magnified their struggles toward economic self-sufficiency. Male preferences in hiring and 50 percent wage differentials between men and women in rural jobs hampered women in finding stable employment with adequate wages. Many worked multiple part-time jobs, and others worked in situations where men were paid double what women earned for the same work. Cultural values that support male dominance were reflected in institutional practices that limited women's access to financial supports and protection from abusing ex-partners. To the extent that rural society is defined and operates from a male-dominant model, women may be at a greater risk for homelessness when they define themselves outside their traditional family roles within rural society. The rural women's stories described active and conscious processes of domination, oppression, and exploitation by men within their intimate relationships, and at the family, community and institutional levels of functioning as well (Eisenstein 1988; Lengermann and Niebrugge-Brantley 1992; Taylor 1989; Tong 1989; Walby 1990). Normative, persuasive, and violent social controls within their intimate relationships were major factors leading to homelessness. Once homeless, social controls were exerted by family and community members and economic, social welfare, and judicial institutions.

Feminist scholars have situated violence against women within the patriarchal structures of society and interpreted it as a manifestation of the larger society's male-dominated ideology played out within the micro institution of marriage and personal gender relations (Bograd 1988; Gagné 1992; Przybylowicz 1989–90; Walby 1990; Websdale 1995). Walby (1990) defined patriarchy as "a system of social structures and practices in which men dominate, oppress, and exploit women" (20). She contended that the patriarchal household replicates and is supported by the larger patriarchal structures in society. Cultural beliefs promote and support men's use of violence against women (Gagné 1992). Traditional gender ideology in rural communities fashions community practices that perpetuate gender inequalities (Naples 1994). The women in this study experienced normative, persuasive, and violent forms of social controls across varying levels of social structures while in and out of homelessness, within a cultural context that upheld the dominance of men in the community and rebuked women who left abusive mates.

The rural women demonstrated a passive acceptance of normative controls embedded in rural culture as they entered intimate relationships in their early adult lives and took on the traditional gender roles. The understanding of what it means to be partnered women reflected the patterns of living experienced in their families of origin. Przybylowicz (1989–90) explicated the process of perpetuating male hegemony within the family and culture and noted that the traditional family structure justifies male dominance through cultural acceptance. Biological, ideological, and social reproduction of gender norms occurs through the socialization of children within the family, thus naturalizing the male dominant and female subordinate gender relations and strengthening the position of men, and producing an unconscious consent of the oppressed to oppression (Przybylowicz 1989–90; Ritzer 1992). The dominant group's values are internalized by subordinate group members through day-to-day experiences and legitimized in group rules and laws.

Leaving abusive relationships led rural women into homelessness. The socio-cultural isolation imposed by family and community members supported male dominance as the cultural norm. Freudenberg (1986) described rural culture as having "density of acquaintanceships," signifying that people within the community had close personal relationships. Weisheit and Wells (1996) contended that the close interpersonal connections among rural residents contributed to the group identity and provided a sense of solidarity. Bly (1981) concluded from her observations on connectedness in rural Midwest communities that rural residents had strong desires to be perceived as pleasant, but, in actuality, relationships were marked by superficiality and insecurity. Everyone knowing everyone's business (as Freudenberg [1986] suggested), needing to appear normal (as Bly [1981] believed), and a strong bond to the group identity (as Weisheit and Wells [1996] described), constructed a context where it may be difficult, at best, to ask for or offer support to members violating cultural norms (Feyen 1989). Rural women described feeling "ashamed" and "embarrassed" at being homeless. Community and family members were reluctant to provide assistance, and women were blamed for their homeless situation. The women and their children bore the brunt of shunning, ridicule, verbal harassment, and malicious gossip in public places within the community. When denied access to basic survival needs, such as food, housing, and protection from abusive partners, women are left in vulnerable positions that threaten their very existence. Community acts that deny access to basic needs for survival constitute mezzo forms of violence against women.

Feminist literature is replete with the discussions on the role of institutions in maintaining the dominance of men and subordination of women. Rules are designed and practices implemented with normative male values as referents (Eisenstein 1988). And while institutions may appear to operate autonomously, they are mutually supporting in their male ideological orientation and collectively constitute patriarchy (Walby 1990). Given little relief from family members, rural homeless women sought resources in the public domain through the economic, social welfare, and judicial systems. Within these public institutions, they were often met with punitive attitudes, verbal harassment, or a non-response. In the labor market, the women commonly worked for half the wages paid to men, forcing them to work multiple jobs and long hours, leaving little time to care for Self and their children or to carefully plan for their recovery from homelessness. Banks foreclosed on mortgages without notifying the women, and the Internal Revenue Service withheld essential funds for payment of back taxes owed by ex-partners. Within the social welfare institutions, women described denial of benefits based on the service workers' personal knowledge of their family problems, and long delays in receiving benefits once their applications were taken. Many waited six to nine months for housing while on preferential waiting lists. Courts ruled in favor of men and/or neglected to enforce their own ruling against men. Police officers failed to file charges on behalf of abused women and failed to protect them from further abuse. Rural families, communities, and institutions were mutually supportive subsystems that maintained the oppressive normative attitudes and behaviors toward rural women and as a whole constituted rural patriarchy.

IMPLICATIONS

Violent social control of women is a consistent theme that dominates the lives of the rural and urban homeless women (Anderson et al. 1988; Cummins 1996; Cummins et al. 1998; D'Ercole and Struening 1990; Hagen and Ivanoff 1988; Homeless Information Exchange 1994; Zorza 1991). Responsible and self-advocating decisions to leave dangerous and destructive relationships may result in homelessness. For some women, homelessness may represent their only avenues to safe environs when leaving abusive relationships. Defining domestic violence as a causative agent of homelessness expands the meaning of homelessness beyond the deficiency model that currently dominates the professional literature and popular media, to a survival strategy for exiting abusive relationships within non-supportive contexts.

Cultural contexts that support male dominance and the social control of women impede women's efforts to escape violent relationships. The lack of emotional and material supports from family and community members while in homelessness bring into question the nature of helping relationships within rural communities, and sheds new light on the conditions for receiving help in some sub-cultures. The socio-cultural isolation imposed by family and community members reinforced a sense of shame and low self-esteem among the women who defined self outside cultural norms, and made basic survival needs, such as shelter, inaccessible for some. Traditional norms may represent unique barriers to stability. Diminished social and psychological resources may limit women's abilities to successfully negotiate homelessness, may prolong homeless episodes, or may force women back into violent relationships.

Subscribing to culturally defined roles of women within a context that supports and perpetuates male dominance puts women and their children at risk for homelessness, because it engenders dependency, isolates women from social supports necessary for women's development of self, limits women's opportunities for acquiring personal skills, work histories, and education, and on the whole restricts women's options for successfully maintaining themselves outside the traditional family structure.

Cultural and structural problems over which women have little power are major contributors to women becoming and remaining homeless. Homeless women have demonstrated remarkable resourcefulness, resiliency, self-reflexivity, and abilities to construct safe and supportive realities (Butler 1993; Cummins 1996; Cummins et al. 1998; Liebow 1993). Rural women's aptitudes for manipulating both informal and formal support systems in ways that provide for their material, social, and psychological well-being challenges professionals and others to see beyond the limitations of homeless women to the strengths that are their potentials for erecting self-sustaining lives. The importance of connectedness with self and significant support-ive others, and of the qualities of relationships that enhance the women's efforts in providing for their material well-being is momen-tous. Supportive relationships are characterized by unconditional caring, validation of women's strengths, assisting women in develop-ing latent skills, providing safe environments, and connecting women to new social networks. These dimensions of women's social supports are critical to building psychological, social, and material resources. The women's commitments to self and inner value systems eventually led them to stability, and speaks to the importance of con-necting with inner knowledge for navigating one's life course.

Rethinking the causes of homelessness necessitates a rethinking of the approaches to the problem. For rural women, homelessness is a complex phenomenon rooted in multiple factors within the family, culture, and structure of their lives. Approaches to homelessness must extend beyond treating personal pathologies to addressing cul-tural values and structural factors that limit rural women's options for securing stable lives. Policy interventions that build on the resource-fulness and strengths of women and consider the context of their homeless conditions are fundamental to effective and meaningful responses to the problem of homelessness. Broad and flexible social welfare policies that recognize the complexity of homelessness among women and the context of homelessness may facilitate the implementation of creative and contextually appropriate approaches to the problem of homelessness.

The most acute needs of single homeless women are money, hous-ing, employment, and obtaining welfare benefits (Cummins 1996; Cummins et al. 1998; Dail 1990). Rural women who contend with gender barriers in the private sector in geographic locales where low-wage jobs dominate may be at a higher risk for homelessness than their urban counterparts (Cummins 1996; Cummins et al. 1998; Deavers and Hoppe 1992; Duncan and Lamborghini 1994; Gorham 1992). Current social welfare policies that limit women's access to public assistance under Temporary Assistance to Needy Families (TANF), reduce availability of public and subsidized housing, and reduce the value of cash assistance and food stamps may be particu-larly difficult barriers to stable housing. Entitlement programs and social welfare policies that have assisted women and families for sixty years appear to be essential components of creating pathways out of homelessness. Cuts in public social supports through the Personal Responsibility and Work Opportunities Reconciliation Act of 1996 may push more rural women into homelessness.

REFERENCES

Abramovitz, M. 1994. "Challenging the myths of welfare reform from a woman's perspective." *Social Justice* 21 (1): 17–21.

Anderson, S. C., T. Boe, and S. Smith. 1988. "Homeless Women". *Affilia* 3 (2): 62–70.

Bahr, H. 1970. *Disaffiliated man.* Toronto: University of Toronto Press.

Bassuk, E. L. 1990. "The problem of family homelessness: A program design." In *Community care for homeless families manual* ed. E. L. Bassuk, R. W. Carman, L. F. Weinreb, and M. M. Herzig, 7–11. Washington, D.C.: Interagency Council on the Homeless.

Bassuk, E. L. 1993. "Social and economic hardships of homeless and other poor women." *American Journal of Orthopsychiatry* 63 (3): 340–47.

Bassuk, E. L., R. W. Carman, L. F. Weinreb, and M. M. Herzig. 1990. Preface. *Community care for homeless families: A program design manual.* Washington, D.C.: Interagency Council on the Homeless.

Bassuk, E. L., L. Rubin, and A. S. Lauriat. 1984. "Is homelessness a mental health problem?" *American Journal of Psychiatry* 141: 1546–50.

Bassuk, E. L., L. Rubin, and A. S. Lauriat. 1986. "Characteristics of sheltered homeless families." *American Journal of Public Health* 76 (9): 1097–1101.

Belenky, M. F., B. M. Clinchy, N. R. Goldberger, and J. M. Tarule. 1986. *Women's ways of knowing: The development of self, voice and mind.* New York: Basic Books.

Berzoff, J. 1989. "The therapeutic value of women's adult friendships." *Smith College Studies in Social Work* 59 (3): 267–79.

Bly, C. 1981. *Letters from the country.* New York: Penguin.

Bograd, M. 1988. "Feminist perspectives on wife abuse: An introduction." In *Feminist perspectives on wife abuse,* ed. K. Yllo and M. Bograd, 11–26. Newbury Park, CA: Sage.

Bogue, D. 1963. *Skid row in American cities.* Chicago: University of Chicago.

Brown, J. S., and H. K. Schwarzeller. 1974. "The Appalachian family." In *Appalachia: Its people, heritage, and problems,* ed. F. S. Ruddel, 63–75. Dubuque, Iowa: Kendall/Hunt.

Brown, K., and M. Ziefert. 1990. "A feminist approach to working with homeless women." *Affilia* 5 (1): 6–20.

Browne, A. 1990. "Family violence and homelessness." In *Community care for homeless families: A program design manual,* ed. E. L. Bassuk, R. W. Carman, L. F. Weinreb, and M. M. Herzig, 119–25. Washington, D.C.: Interagency Council on the Homeless.

Browne, A. 1993. "Family violence and homelessness: The relevance of trauma histories in the lives of homeless women." *American Journal of Orthopsychiatry* 63 (3): 370–82.

Buckner, J. C., E. L. Bassuk, and B. T. Zima. 1993. "Mental health issues affecting homeless women: Implications for intervention." *American Journal of Orthopsychiatry* 63 (3): 385–98.

Burt, M. 1991 (April). *Causes of the growth of homelessness during the 1980s.* (Report). Washington, D.C.: The Urban Institute.

Burt, M., and B. Cohen. 1989. "Differences among homeless single women, women with children, and single men." *Social Problems* 36 (5): 508–24.

Bushy, A. 1993. "Rural women: Lifestyle and health status." *Rural Nursing* 28: 187–97.

Butler, S. S. 1993. "Listening to middle-aged homeless women talk about their lives." *Affilia* 8 (4): 388–409.

Calsyn, R. J., and G. Morse. 1990. "Homeless men and women: Commonalties and a service gender gap." *American journal of community psychology* 18 (4): 597–608.

Chodorow, N. 1978. *Reproduction of mothering.* Berkeley: University of California Press.

Chopra, 1995. *Ageless body, timeless mind: The quantum alternative to growing old.* New York: Harmony Books.

Crystal, S. 1984. "Homeless men and homeless women: The gender gap." *Urban and Social Change Review* 17: 2–6.

Cummins, L. 1996. "In and out of homelessness and 'makin' it on my own." Dissertation. The Ohio State University, Columbus, Ohio.

Cummins, L., First, R. J., and Toomey, B. G. 1998. "Comparisons of rural and urban homeless women." *Affilia* 13 (4): 435–53.

Dail, P. W. 1990. "The psychosocial context of homeless mothers with young children: Program and policy implications." Child Welfare 69: 291–308.

Davis, L. F. 1988. "Rural attitudes toward public welfare allocation." *Human Services in the Rural Environment* 12 (2): 11–19.

Deavers, K. L., and R. A. Hoppe. 1992. "Overview of the rural poor in the 1980s." In *Rural poverty in America,* ed. C. M. Duncan, 3–20. New York: Auburn House.

D'Ercole, A., and E. Struening. 1990. "Victimization among homeless women: Implications for service delivery." *Journal of community psychology* 18: 141–52.

Duncan, C. M. 1992. "Persistent poverty in Appalachia: Scarce work and rigid stratification." In *Rural poverty in America,* ed. C. M. Duncan, 111–34. New York: Auburn House.

Duncan, C. M., and N. Lamborghini. 1994. "Poverty and social context in remote rural communities." *Rural Sociology* 59 (3): 437–61.

Duncan, C. M., and S. Sweet. 1992. "Introduction: Poverty in Rural America." In *Rural poverty in America* ed. C. M. Duncan, xix–xxvii. New York: Auburn House.

Egan. 1993. "Appalachian Women: The path from the 'hollows' to higher education." *Affilia* 8 (3): 265–76.

Eisenstein, Z. 1984. *Feminism and sexual equality: Crisis in liberal America.* New York: Monthly Review Press.

Eisenstein, Z. 1988. *The female body and the law.* Berkeley: University of California Press.

Erikson, E. H. 1968. *Identity: Youth and crisis.* New York: Norton.

Feyen, C. 1989. "Battered rural women: An exploratory study of domestic violence in a Wisconsin county." *Wisconsin Sociologist* 25 (1): 17–32.

Fiene, J. I. 1990. "Snobby people and just plain folks: Social stratification and rural low-status Appalachian women." *Sociological Spectrum* 10 (4): 527–39.

Fiene, J. I. (1991). "The construction of self by rural low-status Appalachian women." *Affilia* 6 (2): 45–60.

Fiene, J. I. 1995. "Battered women: Keeping the secret." *Affilia* 10 (2): 179–93.

First, R. J., J. C. Rife, and B. G. Toomey. 1994. "Homelessness in rural areas: Causes, patterns, and trends." *Social Work* 39 (1): 97–108.

First, R. J., J. C. Rife, and B. G. Toomey. 1995. "Homeless families." In *Encyclopedia of Social Work,* ed. R. Edwards. Washington, D.C.: National Association of Social Workers.

First, R. J., B. G. Toomey, and J. C. Rife. 1990. *Preliminary findings on rural homelessness in Ohio.* Columbus: The Ohio State University College of Social Work.

Fischer, P. J. 1991. *Alcohol, drug abuse, and mental health problems among homeless persons: A review of the literature, 1980–1990.* Rockville, Md.: National Institute on Alcohol Abuse and Alcoholism.

Fitchen, J. M. 1981. *Poverty in Rural America: A case study.* Boulder, Colo.: Westview Press.

Fitchen, J. M. 1991a. "Homelessness in rural places: Perspectives from upstate New York." *Urban Anthropology* 20 (2): 177–210.

———. 1991b. "Residential mobility as a form of homelessness in rural New York." Paper presented at the Rural Sociological Society, Columbus, Ohio.

———. 1992. "On the edge of homelessness: Rural poverty and housing insecurity." *Rural Sociology* 57 (2): 173–95.

Flax, J. 1981. "The conflict between nurturance and autonomy in mother-daughter relationships." In *Women and mental health,* ed. E. Howell and M. Bayes, 51–70. New York: Basic Books.

Flora, C., and J. Flora. 1989. "Rural area development: The impact of change." *Forum for Applied Research and Public Policy* 4 (3): 50–52.

Freudenberg, W. R. 1986. "The density of acquaintanceship: An overlooked variable in community research." *American Journal of Sociology* 92: 27–63.

Gagné, P. L. 1992. "Appalachian women: Violence and social control." *Journal of Contemporary Ethnography* 20 (4): 387–415.

Garrett, G. R., and H. M. Bahr. 1973. "Women on skid row." *Quarterly Journal of Studies on Alcohol* 34: 1228–43.

Gaventa, J., and H. Lewis. 1989. "Rural area development: Involvement by the people." *Forum for Applied Research and Public Policy* 4 (3): 58–62.

Geissinger, C. J., M. M. Lazzari, M. J. Porter, and S. L. Tungate. 1993. "Rural women and isolation: Pathways to reconnection." *Affilia* 8 (3): 277–99.

Gilligan, C. 1982. *In a different voice.* Cambridge: Harvard University Press.

Glasmeier, A., and A. Kays-Teran. 1989. "Rural area development: Competing for the chips." *Forum for Applied Research and Public Policy* 4 (3): 53–57.

Goodman, L. A. 1991. "The relationship between social support and family homelessness: A comparison study of homeless and housed mothers." *Journal of Community Psychology* 19: 321–32.

Gorham, L. 1992. "The growing problem of low earnings in rural areas." In *Rural poverty in America,* ed. C. M. Duncan, 21–40. New York: Auburn House.

Gowdy, E. A., and S. Pearlmutter. 1993. "Economic self-sufficiency: It's not just money." *Affilia* 8 (4): 368–87.

Hagen, J. L. 1987. "Gender and homelessness." *Social Work* 4: 312–16.

Hagen, J. L. 1990. "Designing services for homeless women." *Journal of Health and Social Policy* 1 (3): 1–16.

Hagen, J. L., and A. M. Ivanoff. 1988. "Homeless women: A high-risk population." *Affilia* 3 (1): 19–33.

Hertzberg, E. L. 1992. "The homeless in the United States: Conditions, typology and interventions." *International Social Work* 35: 149–61.

Hobbs, D. 1988. "Factors influencing the demand for rural infrastructure." In *Local infrastructure investment in rural America*, ed. T. G. Johnson, B. J. Deaton, and E. Segarra, 51–63. Boulder, Colo.: Westview Press.

Homeless Information Exchange. 1994 March. *Domestic violence: A leading cause of homelessness.* Fact Sheet No. 10. Washington, D.C.

Housing Assistance Council. 1995 September. *The poorest of the poor: Female-headed households in nonmetro America.* Washington, D.C.

Interagency Council on the Homeless. 1989. "Rural homeless find shelter." *Council Communiqué* 2 (1): 4–5.

Isenhart, C. 1988. "The death of hope: Profiles of the rural homeless." *Earth Matters: A Journal of Faith, Community and Resources* 37 (4): 4–6.

Johnson, A. K., and L. W. Kreuger. 1989. "Toward a better understanding of homeless women." *Social Work* 34 (6): 537–40.

Jordan, J. V. 1991. "Empathy and self boundaries." In *Women's growth in connection: Writings from the Stone Center*, ed. J. V. Jordan, A. G. Kaplan, J. B. Miller, I. Stiver, and J. L. Surrey, 67–70. New York: Guilford.

Karger, H. J., and D. Stoesz. 1994. *American social welfare policy: A pluralist approach.* New York: Longman.

Lengermann, P. M., and J. Niebrugge-Brantley. 1992. "Contemporary Feminist Theory." In *Contemporary Sociological Theory*, ed. George Ritzer. New York: McGraw-Hill.

Lichter, D. T., G. M. Johnston, and D. K. McLaughlin. 1994. "Changing linkages between work and poverty in Rural America." *Rural Sociology* 59 (3): 395–415.

Liebow, E. 1993. *Tell them who I am: The lives of homeless women.* New York: The Free Press.

McChesney, K. Y. 1995. "A review of the empirical literature on contemporary urban homeless families." *Social Service Review* 69 (3): 429–60.

McCoy, V. H. 1993. "Appalachian women: Change in gender role expectations and ethnic identity." *International Journal of Group Tensions* 23 (2): 101–13.

McInnis-Dittrich, K. 1995. "Women of the shadows: Appalachian women's participation in the informal economy." *Affilia* 10 (4): 398–412.

Miller, J. B. 1976. *Toward a new psychology of women.* Boston: Beacon.

Mills, C., and H. Ota. 1989. "Homeless women with minor children in the Detroit metropolitan area." *Social Work* 34 (6): 485–89.

Mingione, E. 1991. *Fragmented societies: A sociology of economic life beyond the market paradigm.* Cambridge, Mass.: Basil Blackwell.

Morris, L. C. 1986. "The changing and unchanging status of rural women in the workplace." *Affilia* 1 (2): 20–29.

Morriss, P. 1987. *Power: A philosophical analysis.* Manchester, U.K.: Manchester University Press.

Naples, N. A. 1994. "Contradictions in agrarian ideology: Restructuring gender, race-ethnicity, and class." *Rural Sociology* 59 (1): 110–35.

Nesto, B. 1994. "Low-income single mothers: Myths and realities." *Affilia* 9 (3): 232–46.

Olson, C. S. 1988. "Blue ridge blues: The problems and strengths of rural women." *Affilia* 3 (1): 5–17.

Patton, L. 1987. *The rural homeless.* Washington, D.C.: Health Resources and Services Administration, U.S. Department of Health and Human Services.

____. 1988. "The rural homeless." In *Homelessness, Health, and Human Needs.* Institute of Medicine, Committee on Health Care for Homeless People. Washington, D.C.: National Academy Press.

Peterson, G. W., and D. F. Peters. 1985. "The socialization of values of low-income Appalachian white and rural black mothers: A comparative study." *Journal of Comparative Family Studies* 16 (1): 75–91.

Przybylowicz, D. 1989–90. "Toward a feminist cultural criticism: Hegemony and modes of social division." *Cultural Critique* 14: 259–301.

Ritzer, G. 1992. *Contemporary Sociological Theory.* New York: McGraw-Hill.

Rossi, P. H. 1990. "The old homeless and the new homelessness in historical perspective." *American Psychologist* 45 (8): 954–59.

Roth, D., J. Bean, N. Lust, and T. Saveanu. 1985. *Homelessness in Ohio: A study of people in need.* Columbus: Ohio Department of Mental Health.

Roth, D., B. G. Toomey, and R. J. First. 1985. "Homeless women: Characteristics and service needs of one of society's most vulnerable populations." Mimeographed. Columbus: Ohio Department of Mental Health.

Roth, D. B., G. Toomey, and R. J. First. 1987. "Homeless women: Characteristics and service needs of one of society's most vulnerable populations." *Affilia* 2 (4): 6–19.

Rural Community Assistance Program. 1995. *Still living without the basics, A report on the lack of complete plumbing that still exists in Rural America.* Leesburg, VA.

Segal, E. A. 1989. "Homelessness in a small community: A demographic profile." *Social Work Research and Abstracts* 25 (4): 27–30.

Shinn, M., J. R. Knickman, and B. C. Weitzman. 1991. "Social Relationships and vulnerability to becoming homeless among poor families." *American Psychologist* 46: 1180–87.

Slavensky, A. T., and A. Cousins. 1982. "Homeless women." *Nursing Outlook* 30: 358–62.

Solarz, A., and G. A. Bogat. 1990. "When social support fails: The homeless." *Journal of Community Psychology* 18: 79–96.

Stoner, M. R. 1983. "The plight of homeless women." *Social Service Review* 57: 565–81.

———. 1989. "Beyond shelter: Policy directions for the prevention of Homelessness." *Social Work Research and Abstracts* 57 (4): 7–11.

Stovall, J., and Flaherty, J. 1994. "Homeless women, disaffiliation and social services." *International Journal of Social Psychiatry* 40 (2): 135–40.

Strasser, J. A. 1978. "Urban transient women." *American Journal of Nursing* 73: 2076–79.

Surrey, J. L. 1991a. "The 'self-in-relation': A theory of women's development." In *Women's growth and connection: Writings from the Stone Center,* ed. J. V. Jordan, A. G. Kaplan, J. B. Miller, I. P. Stiver, and J. L. Surrey, 51–66. New York: Guilford.

———. 1991b. "The relational self in women: Clinical implications." In *Women's growth and connection: Writings from the Stone Center,* ed. J. V. Jordan, A. G. Kaplan, J. B. Miller, I. P. Stiver, and J. L. Surrey, 35–43. New York: Guilford.

Taylor, V. 1989. "The future of feminism: A social movement analysis." In *Feminist frontiers II: Rethinking sex, gender and society,* ed. L. Richardson and V. Taylor. New York: Random House.

Tickamyer, A. R., and C. H. Tickamyer. 1988. "Gender and poverty in Central Appalachia." *Social Science Quarterly* 69 (4): 874–91.

Tong, R. 1989. *Feminist thought.* Boulder Colo.: Westview Press.

Toomey, B. G., R. J. First, R. Greenlee, and L. K. Cummins. 1993. "Counting the rural homeless: Methodological dilemmas." *Social Work Research and Abstracts* 29 (4): 23–27.

Ulrich, Y. C. 1991. "Women's reason's for leaving abusive spouses." *Health Care For Women International* 12: 465–73.

U.S. Department of Housing and Urban Development. 1994, May. *Priority: Home! The federal plan to break the cycle of homelessness.* (HUD-1454-CPD(1)). Washington, D.C.

Walby, S. 1990. *Theorizing patriarchy.* Cambridge, Mass.: Basil Blackwell.

Websdale, N. 1995. "An ethnographic assessment of the policing of domestic violence in Rural Eastern Kentucky." *Social Justice* 22 (1): 102–21.

Weinreb, L. F., and E. L. Bassuk. (1990). "Substance abuse in homeless families." In *Community care for homeless families: A program design manual,* ed. E. L. Bassuk, R. W. Carman, L. F. Weinreb, and M. M. Herzig, 129–46. Washington, D.C.: Interagency Council on the Homeless.

Weisheit, R. A., and L. E. Wells. 1996. "Rural crime and justice: Implications for theory and research." *Crime and Delinquency* 42 (3): 379–97.

Zalk, R. R. 1986. "Evolving gender roles and the paradox of choice: Options or illusions." *Frontiers* 9 (1): 17–21.

Zorza, J. 1991. "Woman battering: A major cause of homelessness." *Clearinghouse Review* 24 (4): 421–29.

Isolated Acts: Domestic Violence in a Rural Community

CAROL K. FEYEN

INTRODUCTION

The physical abuse of women is a serious social problem that does not lend itself to easy resolution. Family-disturbance calls have be labeled the "common cold" of policing (Merder and Gelles 1989). Brutality by a spouse or a partner "is the greatest cause of injury to women, and cuts across lines of race, ethnicity, class and sexual orientation," (Rhode 1994) and geographic location. Americans continue to hold close to their hearts that "gemeinschaft" characterization of rural communities made of close-knit families and friendly neighborhoods where " the women are strong, the men good-looking, and all the children are above average."[1] In spite of the tenacity of such images, research shows that incidences of rural wife abuse are comparable to incidences in urban centers and battered women's shelters in rural areas have a constant flow of clients.

The purpose of this study is to examine domestic violence as it is manifest in a rural community. I examine the characteristics of one rural community as a constellation of factors affecting the lives of rural battered women.[2] I add to the literature on domestic violence insofar as much of the current data has been gathered only at the national, state, or statistical metropolitan level. In addition, little qualitative research has been done to examine how a battered woman's experiences and life-chances are affected by the social fabric of her rural community. This research attempts to fill in some of the missing data on rural domestic abuse by focusing on one rural Wisconsin county. I examine how the discourse on domestic violence and the micropractices of a rural community can form barriers to legal remedies for domestic violence. Micropractices include the rural labor market, the local welfare system, rural churches, and the intergenerational complexities of the family-run farm within the dynamics of a patriarchal agrarian system. Using both quantitative

101

and qualitative data, I examine the local responses to domestic violence as well as the victims' experiences.

River County[3] has a population base of 17,895 and is identified as a non-contiguous, non-metropolitan county. The nearest urban area is approximately 65 miles away. According to the 1990 United States Census, more than 75 percent of the population lives outside the county seat in rural places as farm owners, renters, or wage laborers. Others reside in rural hamlets, or in isolated settings, or "open country."

In 1979, one of the state's first women's domestic violence programs serving primarily rural Wisconsin women was established in this county. Information from shelter data and interviews with clients and staff, with service providers and members of the county criminal justice system, provide data to examine actual experiences of abused rural women in River County. Analysis of the process of establishing this program provides insights into the county's power structure and the conflicts faced by battered-women's advocates working in a rural area.[4]

DOMESTIC VIOLENCE: THE STATE AND LOCAL SCENE

In Wisconsin, between 1984 and 1987, 41 percent of the 145 women murdered were victims of husbands, former husbands, or male "friends" (Wisconsin Dept of Justice 1992). Of the 176 murders in Wisconsin in 1989, eighty (45 percent) were domestic-related. Thirty-two of the thirty-five women murdered in domestic homicides that year were killed by men. Seventy percent of victims were between the ages of 20 and 39 and almost forty percent were married at the time to their abusers. Data from the 1996 Wisconsin Department Of Justice report show 43 adult, domestic homicides. Of these, 24 (55.8 percent) were adult women killed by their partner or estranged partner. Eleven of these women resided in a rural county at the time of their deaths. The weapon of choice was a firearm (Wisconsin Department of Justice 1996). In spite of the prevalence of this form of violence in the state, it was not until the implementation of the Wisconsin Mandatory Arrest Act[5] in 1989 that there was any coordinated account of this form of criminal behavior by county in Wisconsin.[6]

The first comprehensive county-by-county statistics on reported cases of domestic abuse in Wisconsin were published in 1991 and the latest data were published for the years 1994 and 1995. The number of reports in River County varied between a low of forty-nine in 1990 and a high of eighty-one in 1995. The average number of reports of domestic violence during the five-year period was 79.8, or 4.5 reports per 1,000 residents in River County (United States Census 1990). In order to make comparisons with other rural Wisconsin counties, I selected only those counties with population statistics similar to those of River County. Using the 1990 Census of Population and Housing, I found seventeen rural, Wisconsin counties had populations between 13,000 and 20,000.[7] Seven of these counties showed a decline in reported incidences between 1990 and 1995. Two counties had no change in incident reports and the remaining nine, including River County, had an increase in the number of reported incidences between these years. In none of these counties were the patterns linear. Most counties experienced pronounced fluctuations in incidences within this time frame. Calculating the rate of reported violence per 1,000 in each of these seventeen rural counties for 1990, I found the data ranged from a high of 9 to a low of 1.4. The average rate for these rural counties was 3.7/1,000. River County's rate of 3.1 falls well within the range of rural counties of comparable population size.

SHELTERING WOMEN IN RIVER COUNTY

Statistical and anecdotal data were collected from the files of women who contacted the battered women's shelter between 1979 and 1992.[8] Table 1 identifies characteristics of victims and their abusers. The self-reported data were collected during intake interviews by volunteers. Seventy-three percent of the victims were between the ages of twenty and thirty-nine at the time of their first contact with the program. Seventy-five percent of the victims were married. Although thirty-two percent of the victims reported to have been in a relationship with their abuser for four years or less, fully one quarter had been with their abusers for eleven years or more.

Fifty-three percent of the women had only two children or fewer. Fifty percent had high school diplomas yet sixty-three percent reported incomes of less than $1,000 while thirty-eight percent reported AFDC as their sole source of income. Forty-three percent of these women reported working at some kind of job. The most common jobs reported were waitress and factory work. The median age of the perpetrators was slightly older than that of the victims. Thirty-four percent of the abusers had high school diplomas. Twelve percent of the abusers were employed as farm laborers with draftsman and farmer as the next most reported employment categories.

The literature on intergenerational abuse suggests that a child who observed or experienced abusive/violent behavior in the natal family is likely to copy that behavior as an adult (Strauss and Steinmetz 1980; Finkelhor et al. 1983). Table 2 shows data on family history of

Table 1
Characteristics of 147 Domestic Abuse Victims and
their Abusers from Shelter Files in One Rural County*

Characteristics of Victims		
Age	Number	Percent
18–19	13	8
20–24	43	29
25–29	33	22
30–39	32	22
40–49	11	7
50–65	4	2
No Info.	11	7
Marital Status		
Married	111	75
Never-Married	16	11
Divorced	16	11
No Info.	4	3
Length of Relationship		
4 years or less	47	32
5–10	44	29
11 or more	38	26
No Info.	18	12
Number of Children		
0	24	16
1	35	23
2	44	30
3	22	15
4 or more	6	10
No Info.	16	10
Educational Attainment		
10 years or less	36	24
H.S. Diploma	74	50
Some college or +	18	12
No Info.	19	13
Monthly Family Income		
AFDC	56	38
500–599	15	10
600–999	19	13
1000–1999	4	2
2000 or more	8	4
No Info.	45	30
Characteristics of Abusers		
18–19	5	3
20–24	30	20
25–29	30	20
30–34	21	14

Table 1 (*continued*)

Characteristics of Victims		
Age	*Number*	*Percent*
35–39	18	12
40–49	15	10
50–65	6	4
No Info.	22	15
Educational Attainment		
10 years or less	28	21
H.S. diploma	50	34
Some college or +	11	7
No Info.	59	40
Employment Status		
Employed	44	29
Unemployed	15	10
No Info.	88	60

*Data from shelter are self-reports collected from shelter clients through in-take interviews and self-administered questionnaires.

abuse. Data collected on this question is incomplete as about fifty percent of the data consisted of "no information." While the extent of abuse experienced in the natal families of the abusers or their victims is unclear, eighteen percent of the victims reported experiencing or observing abuse within their families. Victim reports indicated that forty percent of the perpetrators were abused in childhood, or observed abuse of some kind in their natal family. In both groups, the type of abuse most frequently reported was observed to have occurred between parents.

The woods and fields of Wisconsin's rural counties are full of game animals. It is not uncommon to find many households that contain, even display, an assortment of hunting weaponry. Table 2 displays the incidence of use of weapons in domestic assaults. Thirty-five percent of the victims reported that some kind of weapon was used or its use was threatened during incidences of domestic abuse. Fifty-four percent of the victims reported that alcohol or drugs were implicated in the abuse.

Twenty-two percent of the victims lived within two miles of the shelter. That is, they lived in the county seat and the service area of the city police department. Sixty-three percent lived from five to twenty-five miles from the center within the jurisdiction of the county sheriff's department. Thirty percent of the victims reported having no phone. This is in great contrast to the general population in which it

Table 2
Characteristics and History of Abuse*

History of Abuse: Victim	Number	Percent
Experience in Family of Origin		
Yes	33	22
between parents	(11)	7
between siblings	(8)	5
abused by parent	(14)	9
No	34	23
No Information	80	54
History of Abuse: Abuser		
Experience in Family of Origin		
Yes	56	38
between parents	(20)	34
between siblings	(3)	2
abused by parent	(27)	18
No	17	11
No Information	76	45
Reported (by victim) Use of Weapons During Abuse		
Yes	52	35
No	28	19
No Information	67	45
Alcohol/Drugs Used by Abuser During Attacks		
Yes	79	54
No	32	21
No Information	36	24

*Data are self-reports by victims

was reported that only four percent were without a phone (United States Census 1990). Forty-seven percent of the victims reported having no access to a vehicle.[9] The impact of this dilemma on women fleeing violence is reflected in the number of times police transported victims to the shelter. Approximately twenty percent of the women who come to the shelter were transported by sheriff's patrol. Forty-five percent of the victims reported no family nearby and thirty-five reported no supportive neighbors.

Narratives offered by the women who used the shelter or crisis line included their self-description of the effects of the abuse. Many of these women reported some form of isolation from friends or family due to the violent and controlling behavior of the partner. About one third reported low levels of self-esteem and self-confidence while others reported that they could not leave home either for lack of transportation or fear of angering their abuser. This form of isolation, that is, as a result of the behavior of the batterer, is found in urban as well as rural cases. The problem is compounded for rural women by the increased geographical distance from most forms of help. The most often cited reasons given by these women for remaining in an abusive relationship were consistent with research summarized by Pagelow (1984). They included self-blame, the desire to make the marriage work, no job or money of their own, and the inability to cope with the welfare system. Interviews conducted with shelter staff highlighted several dilemmas faced by abused wives in this rural county over the years. These include social isolation, unresponsive clergy, unsupportive police and judges, difficulty in accessing new housing situations,[10] and discomfort with the welfare and court systems. Additionally, employment options and educational opportunities for job training are limited. In the following pages I address these issues, showing how the rural setting has detrimental effects for women facing domestic violence.

LIFE ON THE EDGE: GEOGRAPHIC ISOLATION AND COMMUNITY RESPONSES

The literature on domestic violence almost universally mentions isolation as a factor in the severity of violence and in the inability of women to leave abusive relationships (Dobash and Dobash 1979; Gells 1972; Pagelow 1984; Murray and Gelles 1990; Wharton 1987). Battered women tend to be disconnected from their social networks, typically because of the behavior of the batterer. Because physical abuse is a source of shame and not one of a strong self-identity, battered women typically are isolated from each other and not likely to organize themselves into a social movement. They often believe as individuals, they alone are victims of abuse (Wharton 1987).

Isolation in an urban area may also be compounded by anonymity within a mobile and heterogeneous population. In rural areas, isolation is typically associated with geographic distance between neighbors, from police protection, and from safe havens. Even though modern American farm families have become more like urbanites in some ways—for example smaller family size, and urban consumption patterns (Fitdhen 1992)—they now seem more like their rural forebears in other ways:

> The continual decline in farm numbers has returned modern farm families to some of the physical isolation of their pioneering ancestors, albeit moderated by telephone, television, and the car. Farm families now see fewer neighbors in the countryside and have to travel further for services than even their parents did. (Salamon 1992, 40)

Because of the isolation of farm families across the countryside, geography and proximity to neighbors can be an important factor in the outcome of a violent episode. There are no neighbors to hear screams and no doors to knock upon for immediate help.

Isolation also comes from the humiliation associated with small-town gossip and widespread knowledge of the intimate details of family discord (Bly 1982). In a small rural community, gossip is a form of ritual discourse which can act as a source of social control. The effect of this ritual discourse can be the silencing of abuse victims due to this potential for humiliation (Salamon 1992, 162). Isolation is also associated with public disclosure of welfare dependency following divorce, particularly in a rural community where self-sufficiency is considered a paramount virtue (Cassamo and Moore 1985; Davidson 1990; Fitchen 1992; Salamon 1992).

Human/social service needs have reached a level of citizen awareness, public discourse, and public agenda more slowly in rural areas than in urban and suburban areas. Fitchen offers four reasons for this slowness:

> The presumed adequacy of rural social systems to take care of their own people through informal means rather than through formal institutions and programs; an almost legendary rural commitment to "independence" rather than "dependence" on government programs; the small and dispersed [and hard to see] number of people with similar service needs; and the belief that most of the problems that human services address hardly exist in rural areas because they are "urban" problems. (Fitchen 1992, 160)

A conceptual lag, that is, a lag in perceiving, understanding, and diagnosis, as well as under-commitment to addressing social problems, divide the problems into "old familiar problems that we've had all along" and "new problems that have come in recently from the cities (ibid, 162)." In addition, this method of seeing social problems as the *old* vs. the *new*, may actually impede public willingness to support programs which address the problems.

> The old ones [problems] are simply "just there," "always with us," "part of the rural landscape" not requiring attention or money. The new ones are seen as unwanted and unwelcome intrusions from the city, which, it is hoped, might go away if ignored. (ibid)

This dilemma was manifest in the difficulty faced by the first women who attempted to organize a battered women's shelter in River County. Strauss et al. found the incidence of wife abuse in rural areas to be as high as the incidence in cities and considerably higher than the national yearly average of 3.8 percent (Strauss and Steinmetz

1983, 131). Nevertheless, prior to the establishment of the county shelter in 1979, leading officials and other local citizens including physicians and social workers, when confronted with battered women's advocates, repeatedly denied the presence of such a problem in their community.[11] Start-up funds for the shelter program initially came from state grants, not local funds.

THE RURAL ECONOMY

The extent of poverty, the lack of employment experience, and limited access to technical training which is so common among rural women also prevents some women from leaving abusive relationships (Martinez-Brawley and Durbin 1987; Tickamyer et al. 1993).[12] Rural America has long been home to a disproportionate share of the nation's poor. In 1990, populations living outside Standard Metropolitan Statistical Areas have only one-fifth of the nation's population, but one-third of its poor (Tickamyer and Duncan 1990; Lichter et al. 1993; Morris 1986). Compared with urban and suburban areas, economic opportunities for rural women are more limited in quantity and quality (Cautley and Slesinger 1988), and often require traveling great distances in geographic areas where public transportation is almost non-existent. Low wage scales contribute to rural women having the highest poverty rates of all women working full-time across the country (ibid, 804). Some rural counties currently have a ratio as high as two adult welfare recipients to every available job. Overwhelmingly, these recipients, soon to be forced into the rural labor market, are women with children (Howell 1997).[13] The new welfare program in Wisconsin, called W2 (Welfare Works) which went into affect in April of 1998, is expected to have a profound impact on battered women who could once depend on AFDC as an alternative to remaining with an abusive spouse. Unskilled, and poorly educated, battered rural women are likely to find themselves pushed into an extremely poor rural job market.[14]

AGRARIAN IDEOLOGY AND THE STATUS
OF FARM WOMEN

Rural women are not only disadvantaged in the contemporary labor force. Over the decades women have faced barriers to their independent participation in modern agriculture, and may spend their married lives within a nexus of social relationships that comprise the "family farm." Feminist scholars have re-examined the role of farm women in the United States.[15] They provide evidence that policy affecting the structure of American agriculture coupled with patriarchal social norms fostering female subordination and a gendered division of labor, tended to force Midwestern and prairie states farm women out of their historical roles as direct producers in the agricultural commodity market.[16]

Since World War II, farm women have increasingly been unable to earn their own cash from on-farm production of such commodities as eggs, butter, and cream (Fink 1986) and are not likely to own farms or productive capital unless they are widows (Salamon and Keim 1979). In many a rural locale, female off-farm employment may be scarce, or where available, low-wage (Tickamyer and Duncan 1990). Overlay this with a history of male control of the income from farm operations, and we have a setting laden with important implications for the power arrangements within rural families and for the *range of choices* open to farm women who need to leave abusive relationships. Interviews with formerly battered farm women bring to light the intricate dynamics of life within a community dominated by remnants of this agrarian ideology. First, I will provide a brief history of the discourse on domestic violence as it was transformed within the county over the span of almost ninety years.

THE INSTITUTIONAL RESPONSE:
DOMINATING THE DISCOURSE

The way domestic violence has been defined and addressed in River County has changed greatly over the decades. Historical documents show that battered women were typically ignored or treated as criminals, particularly when their children were victims of paternal abuse. During the 1920s and 1930s, "friendly visitors"—early 20th century social workers and well-to-do women who took on the overseeing of the poor—were likely to remove children from "abusive" homes and leave the mother to defend herself against the husband. Women who left abusive husbands often had their children taken from them and were expected to find work even if it meant migrating out of the county and leaving their children behind in foster care or with relatives.[17]

I interviewed six River County farm women whose childhood memories went back to the 1930s. They recalled that farm families seldom responded to evidence of domestic abuse. It was "a man's world," they recalled, and few dared to interfere in the concerns of other family members. "Divorce was almost unheard of and few neighbors or family members could afford to take in an abused woman and her children." They all agreed that intervention prior to critical injury or spousal death would have been useless. Each of the six women interviewed could recall hearing her parents and neighbors discuss in hushed tones the plight of some nearby abused wife. None could recall any form of intervention in any of these cases.[18]

Much of the literature on family violence that predates the battered women's movement was hostile towards women. According to Susan Schechter, psychiatrists, and family counselors, criminologists and sociologists, saw women as culpable in their own battery if not outright masochistic in their needs to be beaten. Families where husbands beat or killed their wives were seen as

> problematic or exceptional. . . . Victim provocation theories leave sexist behavior and ideology unquestioned. They leave us scrutinizing the victim's behavior, as a result, remove responsibility from the man the community, and social structures that maintain male violence. (Schechter 1990)

Schechter's research suggests that police, courts, hospitals, and social service agencies cooperated, although not conspiratorially, in defining the abusers' behavior as legitimate or insignificant and the victims' behavior as crazy, provocative, or reformable—"a few sessions with a psychologist and she will understand what she is doing wrong" (ibid, 24–27).

River County's response to battered women was consistent with Schechter's analysis. Prior to 1976, when the county's mental health clinic was established, the primary non-legal resources available to an abused woman in this county were her family, her personal physician, or a minister.[19] The clinic was designated to serve the mentally ill and addicted of the region. R is a certified counselor with a master's degree. She worked at the clinic between the late 1970s and the mid-1980s and became one of the core group of women who organized the first battered women's crisis line and shelter in the county. According to R, many women refused to come to the clinic for help with an abusive husband because the common attitude among locals was that "only 'crazy people'go to the clinic." In addition, the dominant treatment for family violence was couples-counseling. According to R, this method of counseling has been shown to be highly correlated with renewed and increased violence between the partners. She lamented:

> We had nothing to offer these women except advice on how to deflect or minimize the violence. There were no safe places for the women to go. We had no money in our budgets to pay for hotel or motel rooms for these women and their children. The county was not willing to budget for such services.

In addition the clergy of the county were not happy with the clinic's efforts to counsel couples. Dr. M. came to River County in 1949 to practice family medicine. He sat on the board of directors of the clinic when it first opened. He recalled that several ministers demanded the client files of persons who were members of their congregations and who were receiving family counseling. These clergymen felt only they could provide a "Christian foundation" to marriage counseling, a foundation missing from the secular clinic. According to Dr. M, and R, the clergymen were not successful in their demands. Nevertheless, this additional conflict made the clinic even less attractive to abused women.

MEMBERSHIP IN THE RURAL CHURCH:
THE PRICE OF PEACE

The rural church is one of the cornerstones of identity and community. It is the basis of female networks even more so than for men who have the opportunity to engage in networking at the feed mill or the implement dealer.

> Female solidarity groups assure a better status for women by providing social support where other female contacts are restricted. When no land on the couple's farm is derived from the woman's relatives and when the woman has little contact with her kin, her network is limited. The availability of solidarity groups through the church is thus particularly important when a woman is prevented from regularly socializing with women other than her kin. (Salamon 1992, 181)

Church affiliation, while serving as a locus of religious training and social gathering, also reinforces gender and social hierarchies and echoes community social structure and divisions (ibid 182). The rural church tends to be more fundamentalist than its urban counterpart, more literalist in the reading of Biblical texts. Members tend to support the male-dominated family. Woman's role is to be long-suffering and patient with an errant or backsliding (abusive) husband.[20] I interviewed W, a 48-year-old farm woman who had been married for over twenty years before she left her farm home because of physical abuse. She expressed total amazement at the response of her neighbors (all of whom attended her church) when learning of her actions. After decades of silent suffering, she revealed to these neighbors that her husband had been physically and emotionally abusing her and their daughters.

> People whom I had known all my life, people whose children I baby sat for as a teenager refused to speak to me. They crossed the street

when they saw me coming. They brought cookies to K [her husband] and thought of him as a poor guy whose wife deserted him. I was accused of not doing my job and all of a sudden I was 'bad.' In the church K and I attended all our married life, he continued to be accepted while I was the outcast.

Neighbors helped K with the chores, never fully appreciating the reason he needed help. As part of his abuse of his family, K required W and the children to do all the chores. According to W, she and the children ran the farm. W's pastor and congregation turned their backs on her and the children, surrounding K with sympathy. W went to three different churches seeking help and comfort. None of the pastors believed her except the last one who responded to the bruises on W's face. His counsel consisted of telling her to try harder to keep the family together.

Thirty-three-year-old N, another farm woman, left her abusive husband in 1987. She also left the church she had attended due to a prohibition regarding divorce. She went to several different churches in the region looking for a sense of community. "Most of the churches were quite fundamentalist and didn't believe in divorce. I was very uncomfortable. I was being asked to pay too high a price for membership in these churches."

Shelter staff have had their own problems with rural pastors. Often pastors will call the shelter to speak to women who belong to their congregation. Many women reported that their pastors took the side of their abusive husbands and tried to convince the women to return home. One victim was encouraged by her physician to commit herself to a local mental health facility for in-patient care. She had suffered a nervous breakdown due to the extent of her abuse. The minister from her church contacted her *in the hospital* saying he would help the victim's husband gain legal custody of their children if she did not check herself out of the facility and return home. Fearful of losing her children, and against her doctor's suggestions, the woman left the facility.

According to one Methodist minister I interviewed, the typical rural pastor does not know about, and is not trained to deal with, the dynamics of domestic violence nor the issues of power and control which surround and shape such a relationship. "They think the woman needs therapy rather than safety. . . . Ministers who sincerely think they can save a violent marriage through counseling . . . in doing so endanger the woman."

The Lutheran minister I interviewed was on the shelter board in the mid-1980s and did a great deal of outreach to other religious congregations. She said the issue of domestic abuse was part of the agenda at the national level of the Lutheran Church, but the local congregations had to be "dragged into the twentieth century on this issue." She also felt the presence of a conservative attitude toward welfare in the county was linked to religious groups. Fundamentalist churches, which dominate this county in number, tend to socially separate a battered woman from the congregation if she attempts to leave her husband. Since these churches tend to be very exclusive groups, this means effectively that she loses her community, her whole social support group. These churches have a strong effect upon their members, many of whom are county board members who control local funding sources. They may be encouraged by their pastors and fellow congregants to limit local discretionary funds for social programs that would help women escape their abusers.[21]

These stories, as told by formerly battered women and their advocates, indicate that many rural churches are a crucial cultural component of community life, one that wields substantial power to define certain women as "deviant." Women who might lose their social support network if they are forced to leave their church may remain in abusive relationships until critically injured or emotionally destroyed.

THE LEGAL RESPONSE:
PROTECTION OR MALE PRIVILEGE?

The police, even more than professional social workers or marriage counselors, provide immediate services to families experiencing violence (Finklehor et al. 1983; Roy 1977; Strauss and Steinmetz 1980). As indicated above, the sheriff's department provided transportation to about twenty percent of the River County women who came to the shelter. These women depended upon this transportation as their sole means of escape from an abusive situation. Responding officers are also called upon to mediate disputes and, as of 1989, are required by law to arrest anyone suspected of committing an act of violence in a private residence. The attitude of the officers providing these services and their willingness to respond rapidly can make the difference between life and death for rural women. Therefore, it was anticipated that an interview with a senior officer in the sheriff's department would shed light on the professional conduct of law enforcement officers and their attitudes toward domestic abuse calls. The interview was conducted in 1988. The official continues to hold the same job within the department.

This officer indicated the new, younger officers on the force have brought with them more progressive attitudes toward family violence than the older patrolmen and were less likely to refuse to make an arrest.[22] He was quite proud of the progress he claims the department had made in dealing with domestic violence calls. Yet, the shelter staff reported a pattern of reluctance by police officers to arrest a man if the *woman* in question had a known history of drinking or was drunk at the time of the abuse or had called for help on previous occasions but refused to prosecute. They also felt that a decision to arrest may be colored by an officer's personal opinion of the abuser and whether the abuser is wanted for any other criminal activity or if the abuser was a childhood friend or schoolmate.[23]

Time and distance are critical to police protection in a sparsely populated county, and can make a difference in a potentially life-threatening situation. Therefore, the speed at which officers respond to crisis calls, and the number of patrolmen on duty each shift, are of vital concern to victims and shelter staff. This is especially so concern on weekends and evenings when domestic violence is most likely to occur (Roy 1977). Insufficient staffing in the sheriff's department could lead to situations where the only officer on duty had to respond to an emergency call for assistance at the opposite end of the county. This was the case on several occasions when I was staffing the shelter in the mid-1980s, and the officers responding to particular calls took almost an hour to reach the victims' homes.

The officer I interviewed said that cutbacks in county funding together with conditions specified in the patrolmen's union contract have made it impossible to fill a vacancy whenever one of the two scheduled officers for any shift called in sick. According to this officer, there were dozens of weekends in that fiscal year when there was only one officer covering the entire county.[24] This is consistent with Salamon's findings:

> The demise of the rural community life is not necessarily bad for farm families. Yet, when the community dies (from loss of population and tax base) families are deprived of intangible supports that they are unaware of until a crisis arises. Once social networks are weakened and little social capital exists, it is difficult to suddenly generate them when needs materialize. (Salamon 1992, 246)

A major concern of abuse victims and their advocates is enforcement of the Domestic Abuse Injunction (DAI). A legal tool which was designed to provide a woman protection from her abuser, the DAI is issued by a judge and enforced by the police. It requires arrest if the abuser violates its terms of "no contact" with the victim. This officer felt that his patrolmen were strict in enforcing DAIs. Any exceptions would occur, according to this officer, only when it was determined that the petitioner, the victim, had willingly broken the terms of the contract by allowing the abuser to enter her home or speak to her in person.

In 1988, I interviewed the personnel at the women's shelter. Contrary to the assessment of the officer I interviewed, the shelter staff's overall appraisal was that local law enforcement officers frequently did not take the DAIs seriously and refused to enforce an injunction if the officers felt the woman was in little danger or she did not deserve protection. "The old idea of 'woman as the property of her husband' is still strongly embedded in the minds of the local male population, including the patrolmen" was the way one staff member explained it. Shelter staff have also known women who had their Domestic Abuse Injunctions unofficially revoked by sheriff's officers without the victim's knowledge.[25] According to one staff member;

> Not until a woman happened to call for help and the officers refused to respond would she find out she had no protection. . . . In one case in 1986, a woman was refused protection even though she had a DAI in place and it was common knowledge among the sheriff's department that the abuser was often and seriously "out of control." When an arrest warrant was finally issued for the abuser (in conjunction with a felony), it took a week for the officers to locate him.

The woman in this case indicated that the officers charged with making the arrest were high school and drinking buddies of her abuser. She and the long-time shelter staff felt strongly that this was a factor in the length of time which elapsed before this abuser was finally arrested. Shelter staff reported this problem was not a rare occurrence in the county.

Officers who were specially trained in dealing effectively with domestic disputes were unquestionably successful in controlling violence and providing mediation at the scene of a domestic disturbance call. Training in domestic abuse includes sensitization to the problems victims face when asked to participate in sending their husband or partner to jail (Bard and Zaker 1971).[26] According to the shelter staff, both the training they provided to the sheriff's department, pressure from the Mandatory Arrest Act, and the presence of a new District Attorney, finally made domestic abuse a "crime" worthy of arrest in their county. One shelter advocate explained it this way:

> None of the men [in control of the legal/justice system in the county] have ever been in situations of absolute powerlessness which resembles the situations in which battered women find themselves. The psychological pressures from abusers who threaten to take or injure the children or who may wine and dine a woman and promise to seek help if only she will return; from a society which says you're supposed to live

happily ever after; and from a welfare system which humiliates women and leaves them in poverty—these psychological pressures are often more than a woman can withstand. I have seen many women return to an abuser because she felt she could better tolerate his physical abuse than the emotional abuse she received from the "system" . . . and for this the police criticize and refuse to support the victim when again she needs their intervention.

In 1992, I requested second interviews with shelter staff to see what kinds of changes, if any, have occurred in the county. One staff member responded:

The biggest improvement I have seen for women in abusive situations is in the area of choices. These women now have the choice of using several types of legal action against their abusers; they can choose to come to the shelter or they can have the abuser removed from the home. They receive help from us in dealing with the legal and welfare system, and they will find a network of women in similar situations who will be supportive.

Yet, all these services were provided by the women's shelter program or through the efforts of the staff who lobbied for changes in services to women. One victim's advocate who had been associated for more than eight years with the program expressed relief with the way the court was accepting accounts of abuse from women and children.

I have helped battered women coming into the court today who are facing the same judge they encountered as children in divorce cases maybe 15 or 20 years ago. They remember being returned to custody of abusive fathers against their wishes. Because their mothers had no means of support and the fathers tended to be employed [as farmers] the children were placed in their father's custody. Today, this same judge takes a strong stand against abuse and tends to look very closely at any indications of potential threat to children. He is also quite willing to grant DAIs upon request.

She felt strongly that the presence of the shelter and the willingness of the staff to provide in-service training to the judge made the critical difference in his attitude toward battered women and abused children.

THE VOICES OF ABUSED FARM WOMEN

I have attempted to bring to life the historical pattern of discourse on domestic violence in this rural community through an examination of social and cultural factors shaping the life chances of rural and farm women who experienced this form of abuse. I conclude my presentation of data with highlights from my interview with contemporary farm women. In each case these women made the decision to leave the farm because of the physical, sexual, and or emotional abuse they suffered at the hands of their male partners. The interview focused on factors which they felt affected their decision to leave their relationships.

Thirty-five-year-old G and her husband were the third generation on his family's farm. Her in-laws lived down the road and several other of her husband's relatives farmed in the immediate area. When G first was married, some of her neighbors told her never to learn how to milk or her husband would take advantage of her. "They were speaking from years of experience." She took their advice and refused to learn although she did substantial field work. G felt compelled to remain in her abusive relationship longer than she otherwise might have because of her two sons.

> I really wanted the boys to have a sense of "belonging" to the farm to feel they had roots and a future on the farm if they choose to. But [her husband] did not own the farm, it's still in his father's name. Only the machinery and half the cattle were his. His mother got half the milk check each month. If I divorced [her husband] and asked for a cash settlement I know he would have to leave the farm as well, sell all his machinery and stuff. The boys would be locked out of farming for good, too. The farm might have been sold out of the family if I had pressed for alimony or my fair share of the equity I put into it over the years. Finances weren't my first concern. I felt I could manage financially because I've worked in town since I was a teenager and continued to work throughout our marriage.

When asked about the community, whether she felt it affected her decision to leave, she said there was pressure to stay for the sake of the family farm. Her in-laws' family had farmed on their ridge a long time and the neighbors tended to be supportive of her husband. Farm families tended to keep their personal problems to themselves, she said, and divorce was seen as an unacceptable public display of family problems for which she was criticized. Eventually, her husband's temper became public knowledge and the neighbors believed her stories. According to G, abuse was not new in her ridge-top neighborhood:

> One neighbor woman tried for years to leave her husband. She was treated like a hired hand and her husband was a drunk who left the chores to her and beat her. Her in-laws were desperate to keep the farm in the family and pressured her to stay by making her feel responsible for their future well being.

The first time G attempted to leave her husband was before the passage of Wisconsin's Mandatory Arrest Act. Her angry husband broke into her apartment in town twice and once when she was staying at a friend's house. This is another case in which police officers who responded to her calls were drinking and high school buddies of her husband. According to G,

> They took him aside, talked to him and made him promise not to do it again. Then they pressured me not to press charges against him. A few months after we were divorced he got drunk and broke into my place again. The police took him away but charges were never filed.

Twenty-nine-year-old E expressed similar feelings about the farming community in her part of the county. Her divorce settlement required the sale of the farm and the machinery. The neighbors who attended the auction were hostile towards her, resentful that *she* had forced their friend and neighbor out of farming. These neighbors were buying the things she had worked over ten years to accumulate. "I felt abandoned by all my neighbors."

"Your life is everybody's business in a small community. Gossip is the major source of entertainment even for men." K left her farming husband twice before she had the courage to make it permanent. Married for 18 years to a farmer who "hated cows," she found herself doing heavy manual chores even when pregnant, and never knowing when her husband would come home with a new scheme to "make the farm work." She finally complained about the physical and emotional abuse she was receiving to her mother-in-law who lived in a second house on the farm. The mother-in-law was not sympathetic, since she had been abused all her married life and merely accepted it.

Each of these women said that while she was responsible for the bookkeeping, she was never allowed to participate in decisions about how the money was spent. In spite of her experience with farm record-keeping, when 49-year-old F applied for jobs as an accountant she was told she didn't have "proper training," that is, "I didn't have formal schooling in accounting." All of these farm women who spent their lives working at various jobs on the farm were faced with the dilemma of being officially "unskilled." According to F,

> The longer you stay in the relationship, the less strength you have to recover emotionally from the abuse. You can't think straight any more . . . the loss of your support network, your community of neighbors who abandon you is terrible and the older you get the less chance you have of getting a decent job.

These women expressed distress at the lack of job opportunities in the rural sector for farm women who married right out of high school as all but one of these women did. One finally got a job as a cook; another managed to obtain an associate degree in accounting. G struggled (successfully) with social services when they threatened to cut her off halfway through her four-year degree program; and F eventually became a bookkeeper at the local hospital.

Rural women, particularly farm women, are often reluctant to leave an abusive relationship because of concern over and emotional attachments to farm animals. Several women told me in interviews that they knew their husbands would abuse or neglect the animals as a way to get back at them personally, even if it was detrimental to the farm income. F expressed anxiety over leaving her farm when the abuse was at its height in a particularly poignant fashion:

> A farm woman tends to include the animals on the farm in her "circle of caring." What happens to the cows she has raised from little calves is almost of as much concern to her as the care of her children, particularly when she know her alcoholic or violent husband will neglect them and make them suffer. It is a compelling reason to hang on just a little longer.

A New Issue: Mandatory Arrest

Since 1989, state law requires officers responding to domestic violence calls to arrest the *primary aggressor.* On the surface, Wisconsin's Mandatory Arrest Act 346[27] appears to benefit battered women by physically removing and detaining a batterer. More generally, the community is thought to benefit from the actions of police. Arrests reinforce the notion that wife abuse is a punishable crime. The goal of this pro-arrest policy was to eliminate one of the main concerns of battered women's advocates; the discretionary power of responding officers who choose not to arrest an abuser.[28]

Not all battered women's advocates were happy with the final version of this legislation. Notified only towards the end of the legislative process and with little time to respond, women's advocates were torn between getting *some legislation passed* or getting the *best possible* legislation enacted. The primary sponsor of the state's mandatory arrest law did not include funding for training or implementation, and advocates were not sure the law, as passed, would provide favorable outcomes for Wisconsin women (1996 interview). A follow-up study was done in western Wisconsin six months into the new policy. This non-random phone survey in a nineteen-county region of the state which included mainly rural counties can be summarized as follows: sixty eight percent of respondents who had contact with law enforcement personnel following the implementation of the mandatory arrest law said they *would not call* law enforcement again. "Battered women are indicating via surveys that they fear future violence as a direct result of calling the police on the batterer and subsequent arrests being made" (Stafne 1989). "While this study was not a scientific random sample, it was alarming to find large numbers of women alienated by what was intended to be a law to help them" (ibid).

This study was done within six months of the implementation of the new arrest law. It might be expected that the lack of knowledge about the dynamics of domestic abuse, about the most effective methods of training officers, and possible confusion over the interpretation of this new law would pose some problems early into the implementation process. Indeed this was the case, and still problems exist across jurisdictions. As of 1995, the Wisconsin Office of Justice Assistance was advised to study the ongoing problems with implementation of the law. "Time has not cured Wisconsin's problems with mandatory arrest . . . the law has been implemented with serious backlash problems against women" (Zorza 1992). Backlash includes dual arrests where the officers decide not to determine who is the *primary aggressor* but instead arrest both parties. These women would be placed in jail, to be released later with no charges filed against them. Few women were found to be culpable of the crime of domestic violence.

There may be some evidence that dual arrests were instigated by officers unsympathetic to the victims, so as to intimidate and prevent women from ever calling for help again (ibid.). A particularly unexpected outcome of the mandatory arrest law happened in southwest Wisconsin in 1997. The husband was arrested, found guilty, and fined for physically abusing his wife. Because of the economic situation of this family, the husband was unable to pay his fine. The county attempted to repossess the family's furniture to recover the fine. Here is a case where the wife almost lost her furniture because of her husband's arrest. That is not the outcome she had in mind when she called 911 for assistance in dealing with her husband's behavior. Only through in-depth interviews with victims can we learn how this new legislation affects rural women's experiences of domestic violence. Future research should include an analysis of both the long- and short-term impact of Wisconsin's Mandatory Arrest Act on rural women.

Feminists and victims' advocates have worked through the decades to make changes in laws to protect and to promote the interests of women. Law is *one of the many* venues for the exercise of power and, as such, appears as an appropriate venue for feminist social reform. Yet, appearances can be deceiving. Carol Smart argues:

> [Because] experience has shown that hard-won legal reforms have actually achieved little in transforming the social order . . . [it becomes

necessary] . . . to look more critically at the law to establish how radical demands are transformed into occasions for *niggardly benevolence* and to raise questions of whether criticisms of the content of law or the constitution of the judiciary and legal profession are really enough (Carol 1989).

Indeed, Smart argues for a "full, complex, and nuanced analysis" of state powers and their relationship to male dominance (ibid. 7). To ignore the social context within which the expression of legal power is most fully experienced by women is to perform an incomplete analysis of women's oppression. In this sense, it is necessary both to examine the role of the state and the social milieus as factors shaping the life-chances of rural battered women.

CONCLUSION

Data collected in River County, Wisconsin show that rural women's experience of domestic violence is often shaped by community gossip, the agrarian ideology of self-sufficiency, rejection by local church and farming communities, and by limited access to social and economic resources. The attitude that family violence was not a local problem or a community problem remained dominant in River County until the women's shelter was established and a more profeminist ideology reshaped the discourse. Oral histories and interviews with local residents illustrate a variety of community responses to domestic violence. These responses from neighbors, police, ministers, physicians, social welfare providers, and government officials varied from a lack of understanding and sympathy to helplessness. While the presence and persistence of shelter staff over the years has paid off in the amount and type of services offered to battered women,[29] the problem remains a critical issue from the perspective of funding for victims' programs and prevention. In addition, it is clear that additional research is needed to track the impact of Wisconsin's Mandatory Arrest Act on rural battered women. The lack of economic opportunities in River County and current changes in Wisconsin's welfare system may well keep some of the poorest and least-educated women trapped in violent relationships.

The findings of this research may not be generalizable to all rural communities since every community has its own ethnic, social, and economic history. Nevertheless, the quantitative data and personal stories presented here may be useful for feminists and domestic violence activists interested in working within rural or non-metropolitan areas that have characteristics similar to those of River County.

NOTES

1. Part of Garrison Keillor's monologue from his radio show *A Prairie Home Companion* aired on Saturdays over Minnesota Public Radio.

2. Throughout this paper, the terms "domestic violence" and "domestic abuse" will be used interchangeably to refer to behaviors of domestic partners who are married, were married, or are cohabiting. These actions include sexual, physical violence, as well as emotional abuse designed to harm or intimidate the victim. Only heterosexual couples are included in this study. "Battered women" and "abused women" will also be used interchangeably to describe women who are survivors of these kinds of crimes.

3. Because of the racial make-up of this county, and its overwhelmingly white population, I will not deal with race or ethnicity within the context of domestic violence. I would like to acknowledge that there are geographic areas of the rural Midwest where race relations may play a large role in women's experiences of abuse.

4. This paper focuses on contemporary experiences of domestic violence/abuse but is part of a larger work that includes an historical analysis of the county's treatment of legally dependent and often-abused women from the turn of the century.

5. Wisconsin State Statues 939.621 and 968.075 Sections B and C and Wisconsin Act 346 specify conditions under which officers must arrest a suspected "primary aggressor" at the scene of a domestic dispute. Implemented in 1989.

6. Counties kept domestic abuse records according to their independently established criteria, not coordinated by the state Department of Justice. In addition, the way data were collected and collated has changed through the years, so data are difficult to compare across counties.

7. I felt it was methodologically sound to compare only those counties with populations within 25 percent of that of River County in order to minimize population density as a mitigating variable in domestic violence rates.

8. Women who used the services of the River County women's shelter were disproportionately from the lowest economic strata of the county and thus are not representative of River County families. All quantitative data are aggregated to protect the identities of clients who sought help from this shelter program.

9. According to reports from victims who were interviewed, this is more a reflection of cases where the abuser had control of the only available vehicle at the time of the abuse rather than complete lack of transportation.

10. Rural areas are consistently short of affordable housing and often, as is the case with River County, the rural housing stock is older and dangerously in need of new wiring and mechanicals. United States Census of Housing and Population 1990 and interviews with River County housing contractors.

11. From interviews conducted with founders of River County's battered women's shelter program.

12. Martinez-Brawley, Emilia, and Nancy Durbin, "Women in the Rural Occupational Structure: The Poverty Connection." *Human Services in the Rural Environment,* vol. 10, no. 4 (1987); Tickamyer, Ann, Janet Bokemeier, Shelly Feldman, John P. Jones, DeeAnn Wenk, and Rosalind Harris, 1993. "Women and Persistent Rural Poverty" in Gene Summers, ed., *Persistent Poverty in Rural America.* Boulder, Colo.: Westview Press.

13. Frank M. Howell. "Challenges to Welfare Reform in the South." *Southern Perspectives.* Southern Rural Development Center, Mississippi State University. 1997. http://www.msresource.com/mental/ms-map.html

14. Division of Employment and Training, State of Wisconsin. Survey of Wage

Rates for Selected Occupations in Southwestern Wisconsin Service Delivery Area 1990. I selected the occupations typically filled by women (as identified by Martinez-Brawley and Durbin, cited in note 32). Data show that slightly more than half of these gender-specific jobs paid enough to bring a woman and one child up to the poverty level as established by the federal government.

15. The following is a sampling of feminist literature dealing with the status of farm women in the United States during the nineteenth and twentieth centuries. Fink, Deborah. 1986. *Open Country Iowa: Rural Women, Tradition and Change.* New York: State University of New York Press; Fink, Deborah. 1992. *Agrarian Women: Wives and Mothers in Rural Nebraska, 1880–1940.* Chapel Hill: University of North Carolina Press; Fink, Virginia S. 1988. "The Impact of Changing Technologies on the Roles of Farm and Ranch Wives in Southeastern Ohio." In Wava Haney and Jane Knowles, eds., *Women and Farming,* op. cit. here. Haney, Wava and Gene Wilkening, "From Ker-chifs and Pails to Plaid Collars and Record Books: The Impact of Technology and Policy on Wisconsin Dairy Farm Women in the 20th Century" paper presented at the American Farm Women in Historical Perspective Conference, New Mexico State University, Las Cruces, February, 1984; Haney, Wava and Jane Knowles. 1988. "Intro-duction" in Haney and Knowles (eds.) *Women and Farming: Changing Roles, Changing Structures.* Boulder, Colo: Westview Press; Osterude, Nancy Grey, "The Valuation of Women's Work: Gender and the Market in a Dairy Farming Community During the Late Nineteenth Century" in Frontiers, vol. 10, no. 2 (1984): 18–24; Sachs, Carolyn. 1983. The Invisible Farmers: Women in Agricultural Production. New Jersey: Row-man and Allanheld; Salamon, Sonya and A. M. Keim, "Land Ownership and Power in a Midwestern Farming Community" in *Journal of Marriage and the Family,* vol. 41, no. 1 (1979): 109–14; Salamon and Karen Davis-Brown. 1988. "Farm Continuity and Female Land Inheritance: A Family Dilemma" pp. 195–210 in Haney and Knowles, eds., *Women and Farming: Changing Roles, Changing Structures.*

16. Producer is defined as the individual who produces a commodity and obtains cash from its sale. It is contrasted with the status of "helper" or "adjunct" to some-one else's (typically the husband of father's) agricultural production.

17. Diaries of Ada James, State Historical Society Archives, Madison Wisconsin. Restricted documents from the Child Welfare Board of River County 1920s–1930s. University of Wisconsin-Platteville Historical Documents Collection.

18. Interview with six River County farm women who were in their late seventies at the time of the interview.

19. One 48-year-old former farm wife explained the only help she received dur-ing the decades of physical abuse she endured came from her physician. After see-ing her battered and terribly bruised, he offered to treat her husband for a minor back ailment. This "treatment" was actually a psychotropic drug designed to reduce the husband's energy levels and calm him. The "treatment" worked for a while until the husband decided the pills weren't helping his back. He stopped taking the pills and the abuse resumed soon after.

20. Interview with a River County Lutheran minister.

21. Interview with female, River County Lutheran minister. In an attempt to pro-vide gender-balance and broaden the religious foundation of these interviews, I ini-tiated an interview with a priest who is now serving in a different community. I began with questions about his church's participation in the annual *Stop Domestic Abuse Week* during which church bulletins carry information on domestic violence and sources of help. This minister's first response was that he had a problem with the program because "some of the women who used the shelter were not married to men who they are *running away from.*" The interview deteriorated further into a diatribe against women living in sin and the abuses, allegedly perpetrated by social workers and angry women, against innocent men who are accused of "molesting children."

I ended the interview at that point.

22. During an interview with a resident of the shelter, I was told the following story. This woman had summoned the sheriff's department to remove her abusive husband from her home in 1988. Her husband was under the limitations of a domestic abuse injunction and she had the right to have him removed. The officer I interviewed responded to her call. According to this woman, he called her "a stupid bitch" in the presence of the junior patrolmen and the woman's husband. He also tried to convince her to allow the abuser to remain on the premises against her wishes and in spite of the abuser's history of violent behavior towards her.

23. These observations are only of specific individual officers. The author's experience as a volunteer in the program included at least three occasions where emergency assistance was required. During these situations the individual law enforcement officer displayed professional behavior and courtesy.

24. One local resident told me that her son's house was burglarized one weekend in January of 1992. Because officers were so busy responding to domestic disturbance calls, he had to wait almost two days before an officer was free to make the report.

25. Only the judge who authorized the injunction can revoke it legally.

26. Bard, Morton, and Joseph Zaker. 1971. "The Prevention of Family Violence: Dilemmas of Community Intervention," The Graduate Center, CUNY.

27. Wisconsin State Statute 968.621 and 968.075 passed in 1989. Sections B and C Relating to Arrest, Domestic Abuse and Providing Penalties: Section 1 of B. "If probable cause exists to believe that a crime is being committed, a Deputy Sheriff shall arrest and take a person into custody if either or both of the following circumstances are present: The Deputy has a reasonable basis for believing that there is a possibility of continued violence against the alleged victim; there is evidence of physical injury to the alleged victim. Section D. A Deputy who has reasonable grounds to believe that both parties committed domestic abuse against each other should arrest the person whom the deputy believes to be the primary physical aggressor. A Deputy should consider the intent of this policy to protect victims of domestic violence, the relative degree of injury inflicted on the persons involved experienced by each party, the relative degree of fear and any history of domestic abuse between these persons.

28. The most famous court case leading to mandatory or pro-arrest legislation occurred in 1984 (Thurman vs City of Torrington). Tracey Thurman was nearly killed by her abusive partner after several attempts to secure protection from Torrington, Connecticut police. Her successful law suit (2.3 million) was based on the city's "failure to protect" Thurman from a known violent abuser (National Center on Women and Family Law, 1994). For competing arguments over mandatory arrest policies see Buzawa, Carl and Buzawa. "Domestic Violence: The Criminal Justice Response" and David Ford and Mary J. Regoli. "The Criminal Prosecution of Wife Assaulters: Processes, Problems, and Effects" in N. Zoe Hilton (ed.), *Legal Responses to Wife Assault: Current Trends and Evaluations,* 1993.

29. The most recent service provided to battered women who are income-eligible is called transitional housing. Leases are offered at reduced rent in a complex that provides child-care, job counseling and support group. The complex was completed in 1996 in spite of strong objections of the local home owners in the county seat and a lack of funding sources.

REFERENCES

1996. Interview with Kathleen Krenic, Director of Wisconsin Coalition Against Domestic Violence.

Bard, Morton and J. Zaker. 1971. "The Prevention of Family Violence: Dilemmas of Community Intervention." The Graduate Center, CUNY.

Bly, Carol. 1981. *Letters From The Country.* New York: Harper and Row.

Cassamo, Michael J., and D. E. Moore. 1985. "Rurality and The Residualist Social Welfare Response" in Rural Sociology 50 (3): 397–408.

Cautley, Elanore and D. P. Slesinger. 1988. "Labor Force Participation and Poverty Status Among Rural and Urban Women Who Head Families." *Policy Studies Review* 7 (4): 795–809.

Davidson, Osha Grey. 1990. *Broken Heartland: The Making of The Rural Ghetto.* New York: Maxwell Maxmillan.

Diaries of Ada James, State Historical Society Archives, Madison Wisconsin. Restricted documents from the Child Welfare Board of River County 1920s-1930s. University of Wisconsin-Platteville Historical Documents Collection.

Division of Employment and Training, State of Wisconsin. 1990. "Survey of Wage Rates for Selected Occupations in Southwestern Wisconsin Service Delivery Area 1990."

Dobash, R., and E. Dobash. 1979. *Violence Against Wives: A Case Against Patriarchy.* New York: Free Press.

Fink, Deborah. 1986. *Open Country Iowa: Rural Women, Tradition and Change.* New York: State University of New York Press.

Finkelhor, David, R. J. Gelles, G. Hotaling, and M. A. Strauss. 1983. *The Dark Side Of Families.* Beverly Hills: Sage.

Fitchen, Janet. 1992. *Endangered Spaces, Enduring Places: Change, Identity, and Survival in Rural America.* Boulder, Colo.: Westview Press.

Frank M. Howell. 1997. "Challenges To Welfare Reform In The South." *Southern Perspectives.* Southern Rural Development Center, Mississippi State University. http://www.msresource.com/mental/ms-map.html. December, Vol. 1, pages 10–12.

Gells, Richard J. 1972. *The Violent Home: A Study of Physical Aggression Between Husbands and Wives.* Newbury Park, Calif.: Sage.

Lichter, Daniel T, L. J. Beaulieu, J. L. Findeis, and R. Teixeria. 1993. "Human Capital, Labor Supply, and Poverty in Rural America." In *Persistent Poverty in Rural America,* ed Gene Summers. Boulder, Colo.: Westview Press.

Martinez-Brawley, Emilia, and N. Durbin. 1987. "Women in The Rural Occupational Structure: The Poverty Connection." *Human Services in the Rural Environment* 10 (4).

Merder, Helen J., and R. J. Gelles. 1989. "Compassion or Control: Intervention in Cases of Wife Abuse." *Journal of Interpersonal Violence.* 4 (1): 25-43.

Morris, Lynn C. 1986. "The Changing and Unchanging Status of Rural Women in The Work Place." *Affilia, Summer* 20–29.

Pagelow, Mildred. 1984. *Family Violence.* New York: Prager.

__, Murray A. Strauss, and Richard J. Gelles. 1990. *Physical Violence in American Families.* New Brunswick, N.J.: Transition Books.

Rhode, Deborah L. 1994. "Feminism and the State." *Harvard Law Review* 107: 1173, 1179–1210.

Roy, Maria. 1977. *Battered Women: A Psychological Study of Domestic Violence.* New York: Van Nostrand.

Salamon, Sonya. 1992. *Prairie Patrimony: Family, Farming, and Community in The Midwest.* Chapel Hill: University of North Carolina Press.

Salamon, Sonya, and A. M. Keim. 1979. "Land Ownership and Power in A Midwestern Farming Community." *Journal of Marriage and Family* 41 (1): 109–14.

Schechter, Susan. 1990. *Women and Violence: The Visions and Struggles of The Battered Women's Movement*. Boston: South End Press.

Smart Carol. 1989. *Feminism and The Power of Law*. New York: Routledge.

Stafne, Gigi. 1989. "The Wisconsin Mandatory Arrest Monitoring Project: Final Report." Madison, Wisc.: Wisconsin Coalition Against Domestic Violence.

Strauss, Murray A., and S. Steinmetz. 1980. *Behind Closed Doors: Violence In The American Family*. New York: Anchor.

Tickamyer, Ann, J. Bokemeier, S. Feldman, J. P. Jones, D. Wenk, and R. Harris. 1993. "Women and Persistent Rural Poverty." In *Persistent Poverty in Rural America*, ed. Gene Summers. Boulder, Colo: Westview Press.

Tickamyer, Ann, and Cynthia Duncan. 1990. "Poverty and Opportunity Structure in Rural America." *Annual Review of Sociology* 6: 67–86.

United States Census of Population and Housing. 1990. Statistical Tape File 3.

Wharton, Carol. 1987. "Establishing Shelters for Battered Women: Local Manifestations of A Social Movement." *Qualitative Sociology* 10, no. 2: 71-76.

Wisconsin Department of Justice. 1992. *Domestic Abuse Incident Report, 1990–1991*. Madison, Wisc.: Office of Crime Victim Services.

Wisconsin Department of Justice. 1996. *Domestic Abuse Incident Report, 1994–1995*. Madison, Wisc.: Office of Crime Victim Services.

Zorza, Joan. 1992. "Mandatory Arrest: Problems and Possibilities." Washington, D.C.: National Center on Women and Family Law.

II
Taking Care of Our Own

Parenting Practices of Rural Families and Their Relationship to Adolescent Educational and Emotional Outcomes

ERIK R. STEWART, STEPHEN M. GAVAZZI,
PATRICK C. MCKENRY, TAMMY H. SHEIDEGGER

INTRODUCTION

American youth today are often considered to be in a state of crisis (McKenry and Gavazzi 1994). Approximately half of all adolescents are at moderate to high risk of engaging in one or more self-destructive behaviors, including unsafe sex, teenage pregnancy, and child-bearing; drug and alcohol abuse; delinquent or criminal behaviors; and school underachievement, failure, or dropping out (Dryfoos 1990, 1992; Lerner, Entwisle, and Hauser 1994). Another important concern is that too many adolescents today will not reach their full potential because of inadequate support (Santrock 1996). Adolescents are not a homogeneous group of individuals. Most adolescents negotiate the path to adulthood successfully, but too large a group do not. Cultural, socioeconomic, gender, and lifestyle differences influence the actual life trajectory of each adolescent, and membership in such groups may restrict adulthood options (Santrock 1996).

As we proceed into the new millenium, we take with us the concerns that have developed related to the adjustment, integration, and success of children and adolescents growing up in rural environments (Wilson 1994). These children and adolescents are subject to a unique set of circumstances and dynamics that we believe have a significant impact on their futures (Rural and Appalachian Youth and Families Consortium 1996). This chapter will focus on some of these issues and the manner and extent that a child's family may impact them.

THE FAMILIES OF RURAL YOUTH

Unfortunately, to date the knowledge base on families with adolescents has been largely focused on urban subjects. There has been an assumption that rural families with adolescents have been insulated from the developmental and situational stressors associated with the adolescent stage of development. However, research is increasingly indicating that rural families are experiencing problems usually associated with urban populations, such as divorce, economic hardships, drug abuse, and violence (Brown 1981; Coward and Smith 1982; Jurich and Russell 1987). In addition, research suggests that rural youth per se are evidencing more symptoms of hypersensitivity, tension, and depression (Lindholm 1986; Wall 1985).

While rural families bestow upon children certain strengths which enhance their ability to cope, for example, a greater sense of responsibility, stronger work ethic, higher levels of cooperativeness, and generally closer family ties compared to urban families, there are features of rural family life that may act to intensify the impact of normative and situational stressor events (Rosenblatt and Anderson 1981). For example, parents in rural settings exert more influence on their children, and thus rural youth are more likely to subordinate their own goals to those of their parents. Thus, they are likely to identify very closely with their parents' concerns at a time when developmentally they should be relieved of excessive stress so that they can develop their adult identities and coping mechanisms (Larson 1978).

Similarly, when rural families are experiencing stress, research has indicated that rural youth, as compared to their urban counterparts under similar conditions, display lower futuristic aspirations, as well as significantly reduced self-images and educational plans (Zimbleman 1987). Research findings also suggest that rural parents may emphasize intellectual and emotional development within their children to the neglect of social development, thus placing them at greater risk for negative emotional consequences (Coleman et al. 1989; French and Berlin 1979). Van Hook (1990) reports that the strong sense of individualism and pride associated with the rural lifestyle serves to inhibit the pursuit of assistance from the extended family or community; thus, rural youth suffer greater loneliness and may be less likely to obtain the social support needed to mediate the impact of stressor events (Woodward and Frank 1988).

THE "RURAL YOUTH IN A CHANGING ECONOMY" PROJECT

This study sample involved 108 rural adolescents and their parents from four rural counties in Ohio. Approximately two-thirds of the families involved resided on farms or in very small towns, with the majority of the rest residing in slightly larger towns with populations between 1000 and 5000. The sample of adolescents were sophomores, juniors, and seniors in high school, with an average age of 17. The sample disproportionately represented adolescent females (two-thirds of the sample). Parents of the involved youth were relatively well educated, with approximately two-thirds of the mothers and fathers reporting a vocational or trade school degree or completion of some college. Adolescents academically were doing well, with about one-third of the sample indicating mostly As in school and only 12 percent indicating mostly Cs or below. With regard to income, 78 percent of respondents reported incomes below $50,000, with 32 percent of the sample indicating household incomes of less than $25,000. Approximately 40 percent of respondents reported their incomes had remained the same during the past five years, with 42 percent reporting an increase and approximately nineteen percent indicating a decrease.

The "Rural Youth in a Changing Economy" project utilized a variety of standardized instruments chosen for their psychometric properties and their relevance to the study of rural families and the adolescent adjustment under stress. Additionally, various fixed-choice questions were used to obtain salient demographic information. The sample was obtained through solicitation of families by letters sent home with students either at school or through 4-H club meetings, as well as direct requests made through high school-affiliated parent groups. This method of sampling likely resulted in the disproportionate involvement of more affluent families within the rural areas investigated with this belief seemingly corroborated by the aforementioned demographics such as parent education and family income. While it has been reported that 29 percent of white and 56 percent of black household heads in rural areas lack a high school degree, only 6.4 percent of the current sample reported such a level of education (Sherman 1992). Similarly, the current sample reflected a level of poverty which appeared to be approximately 9 percent among respondent families, while Census Bureau data have revealed figures for rural areas which place it closer to 17 percent (Porter 1989).

A variety of paper-and-pencil instruments were used in the research project, including the Epidemiologic Studies Depression Scale (CES-D; Radloff 1977), the Adolescent-Family Inventory of Life Events and Change (A-FILE) (McCubbin, Patterson, Bauman, and Harris 1981), the Family Crisis Oriented Personal Evaluation Scales (F-COPES) (McCubbin, Larsen, and Olson 1995), the Parent-Adolescent Communication Scale (Barnes and Olson 1985) and the Family Adaptability and Cohesion Evaluation Scales (FACES) (Olson et al. 1985), and the Bengston's Measure of Intergenerational Relations (Bengston 1982). Following is a brief description of each of each instrument.

The Center for Epidemiologic Studies Depression Scale (Radloff 1977) measures current levels of depressive symptomatology with an emphasis on the affective component. The twenty-item scale was developed through the selection of items from previously validated depression scales. The major components identified through factor analytic studies, and therefore reflected in the scale, were depressed mood, feelings of guilt and worthlessness, feelings of helplessness and hopelessness, psychomotor retardation, loss of appetite, and sleep disturbance. Although not developed as a clinical diagnostic tool, the CES-D has been shown to discriminate moderately among severity levels within patient groups and has been shown to effectively discriminate between general population samples and psychiatric inpatient samples through the utilization of a 16-point cutoff score.

The Family Adaptability Cohesion Evaluation Scales (Olson et al. 1985) provide a measure of family cohesion and family adaptability taking into account information provided by the parents as well as the adolescent. The instrument is based upon a twenty-item questionnaire with a Likert-type response format. Scores of respondents within each family are summed and then divided by the number of respondents in order to attain the most accurate assessment of the dynamics within the family system.

The Family Crisis Oriented Personal Evaluation Scales (McCubbin, Larsen, and Olson 1985) was designed for the purpose of identifying effective problem-solving strategies used by families in difficult or problematic situations. It is believed that families operating with more coping behaviors will more readily adapt to stressful situations.

The Adolescent-Family Inventory of Life Events and Changes (McCubbin, Patterson, Bauman, and Harris 1981) was designed for the purpose of recording normative and non-normative life events and changes occurring within the previous 12-month period.

The Parent-Adolescent Communication Scale (Barnes and Olson 1985) serves to assess the perceptions of adolescents and their parents in regard to communication patterns. Three main factors have been discerned in the scale through the application of factor analysis: (a) open family communication, (b) problems in family communication, and (c) selective family communication.

Bengston's Measure of Intergenerational Relations (Bengston 1982) is a 14-item Likert-type scale designed to measure intrafamilial consensus on attitudes and opinions. Religiosity, marital norms, and political conservatism were assessed using this measure.

ADOLESCENT DEPRESSIVE SYMPTOMATOLOGY

While it has been reported that limited research attention has been given to the area of adolescent depression (Sullivan and Engin 1986; Kandel and Davies 1982), the study of depression in adolescence has persisted for many years but has often focused upon behavioral patterns which have only more recently been considered to be indicative of depression. Indeed, depression in adolescence has been referred to as "being masked" because the symptoms often differ significantly from those seen among adults. Others have referred to "depressive equivalents" to explain the different overt manifestations of depression that are seen among children and which vary markedly from those witnessed in adults (Trad 1987). Such masks or depressive equivalents may take the form of aggressive and antisocial behaviors, as well as such behaviors as school problems, school refusal, anxiety episodes, and conduct difficulties (French and Berlin 1979; Puig-Antich 1982). Additionally, such conditions may be examples of co-occurring conditions as research has indicated a significant occurrence of comorbidity for depressed children and adolescents with conditions such as conduct disorder/oppositional defiant disorder, anxiety disorders, and attention deficit disorder (Adrian, A. and Costello, E. 1993).

In addition to the discrepancies that have existed in defining depression in adolescence, prevalence rates have also been quite disparate. French and Berlin (1979) have estimated prevalence rates of depression among children to range from "less than one percent to more than 50 percent" (31). Similar levels of disparity in reports of prevalence have been reported with adults, and have been, at least partially, attributed to the criteria utilized in discerning the condition (Rutter et al. 1986).

Much of what is known about depression during adolescence has been developed through studies on urban populations, yet rural populations have been impacted greatly by factors commonly implicated as predisposing and/or exacerbatory elements in depression. Among these factors are the deteriorating financial conditions of the farm economy (Ward 1986), and the more limited social amenities which exist within rural areas (Dillmån and Hobbs 1983). Additionally, rural populations suffer from disproportionately fewer government resources as compared to urban communities. Wagenfeld (1988) reports that while rural residents receive 20 percent of government antipoverty funding, they constitute 30 percent of the nation's poor. Likewise, Bergland (1988) reports that although 25 percent of the nation's population resides in rural areas, 38 percent of the nation's poverty cases are in rural areas.

Rural youth also tend to be exposed to unique familial, interpersonal, and intrapersonal dynamics that may increase their susceptibility to depressive conditions. Previous research efforts seem to suggest that rural parents may emphasize intellectual and emotional development within their children (Coleman, Ganong, Clark, and Madison 1989) at the expense of social development. French and Berlin (1979) report that youth with fewer social and coping skills are at greater risk for depression. Van Hook (1990) has reported that although farming is an inherently high-stress occupation (which may serve to enhance the experience of depression), the strong individualism and shame associated with the rural lifestyle serves to inhibit the pursuit of assistance from extended family or community resources. Rural adolescents, as opposed to their urban counterparts, appear generally to be more independent and isolated. As a result, rural youth report extremely high levels of loneliness (Woodward and Frank 1988), and they exhibit a more internal orientation in locus of control than do urban youth (Witt 1989). An internal orientation in locus of control may result in an increase in negative self-attributions that could result in heightened levels of depression. Additionally, Marotz-Baden and Colvin (1986) found that rural youth exert more effort in attempting to control their lives. This need for control may be problematic given the necessary reliance upon external forces involved in farm and farm-related occupations.

Numerous theories have been proposed in attempts to explain adolescent depression. Given the amount of extant research indicating a relationship between depression and familial variables, it is not surprising that families have become a significant focus within this area. Research has clearly shown that such things as family environment, parenting practices, and family functioning are related to adolescent depression (Sheeber, Hops, Alpert, Davis, and Andrews 1997; Reiss, Howe, Simmens, and Bussell 1997; Martin, Rozanes, Pearce, and Allison 1996). Similarly, research exists which seems to indicate certain family characteristics and strengths can serve a protective function when it comes to the onset of depression in youth, both directly and indirectly (McFarlane, Bellissimo, Norman, and Lange, 1995; Brage and Meredith, 1994; Cumsille and Epstein 1994).

Family models of adolescent depression indicate that "adolescent depression does not develop in isolation from the individual's inner psyche, but rather emerges and is reinforced within the context of disruptive and disturbed family patterns of relating" (Oster and Caro 1990, 17). Oster and Caro describe numerous unique processes present during adolescence which are highly significant when considering depression in rural youth. Among these processes are the adolescent's individual identity transition, moving from dependence to independence, becoming involved in a larger social environment, and the assumption of increasing responsibility. Specific to parents of adolescents are the issues of decreasing influence on the child and the child's changing level of dependence upon the parent, as well as an adjustment to new roles. Oster and Caro have suggested several major dynamics within families that contribute to pathology. Among these are the quality of family boundaries and structures and the ability of the family to express and to process emotions.

Olson and colleagues (1985) have provided us with a unique means of measuring some of the dynamics within families through their circumplex model of marital and family systems. This model is based largely upon two dimensions, cohesion and adaptability. Cohesion, according to Olson and colleagues (1979), refers to "the emotional bonding members have with one another and the degree of individual autonomy a person experiences in the family system" (5). Family adaptability, on the other hand, is based upon a system's ability "to change its power structure, role relationships, and relationship rules in response to situational and developmental stress" (Olson et al. 1985, 3). It is thought that the most healthy, functional families avoid the extremes on the cohesion dimension of disengaged and enmeshed systems and on the adaptability dimension of chaotic and rigid systems.

Given that previous research has found that the family milieu may serve to mediate the effects of depression in parents (Billings and Moos 1983), it is reasonable to consider the possibility that similar dynamics might be present for adolescents. This was the basis for this first study. Measures utilized in exploring this issue included the Family Adaptability Cohesion Evaluation Scales (FACES-III), the Family Crisis Oriented Personal Evaluation Scales (F-COPES), the Center for Epidemiologic Studies Depression Scale (CES-D), the Adolescent-Family Inventory of Life Events and Changes (A-FILE), and the Parent-Adolescent Communication Scale. In addition to these instruments, a measure of family economic stability was obtained using a single item Likert-type question regarding the families' economic position, and changes therein, during the past five years.

It was hypothesized that family life events, parent-adolescent communication, family economic stability, family cohesion, family adaptability, family coping mechanisms, and a number of moderated relationships between adolescent depressive symptomatology and family life events, parent-child communication, and family economic stability would play a significant role in predicting adolescent depressive experience.

As hypothesized, bivariate analyses indicated a significant positive relationship between family life events and depressive symptomatology. The bivariate analysis also indicated a relationship between adolescent depression and family cohesion such that those families indicating higher levels of cohesion had adolescents that reported lower levels of depressive experience. Similarly, those families reporting more positive communication patterns had adolescents who indicated lower levels of depressive symptomatology. The analysis failed to indicate a relationship between adolescent symptomatology and family adaptability, family coping mechanisms and family economic stability [see Table 1]. Additionally, a linear regression analysis yielded a significant interaction effect between family economic stability and family cohesion such that as family cohesion was reduced, depressive symptomatology increased dramatically for families reporting negative economic changes.

In order to further explore the data, a series of multiple regression analyses were conducted upon three separate clusters representing life stressors, family dynamics, and family coping skills. Results for the life stressors cluster confirmed the significant relationship for family life events and family economic stability. In regard to the family dynamics cluster, father-adolescent communication practices proved to be significant, and the family coping skills cluster failed to indicate any significant factors.

Table 1
Correlations Between Adolescent Depressive Symptomatology and Study Variables (Pearson r)

Study Variable	r
Family Life Events	.276**
Family Cohesion	.230*
Family Adaptability	−.066
Father-Adolescent Communication	−.321**
Mother-Adolescent Communication	−.272**
Family Coping—Acquiring Social Support	−.095
Family Coping—Reframing Family Problems	−.039
Family Coping—Seeking Spiritual Support	−.161
Family Coping—Mobilizing Family	−.145
Family Coping—Passive Appraisal	.094
Family Economic Stability	−.199

$*p < .05$ $**p < .01$

As a last step in reviewing the data, the significant factors revealed through the three clusters were incorporated into a final stepwise multiple regression equation. Results of this analysis indicated that while family life events, communication between the adolescent and father, and the interaction effect between family cohesion and family economic stability all contributed in an approximately equal manner to the predictability of depressive symptomatology reported by the adolescent, only the family life events and adolescent-father communication proved to be statistically significant.

Additional research using a path analytic model on these data has served to further corroborate the findings, stressing the importance of family life events and their relationship to adolescent depressive symptomatology, such that those youth reporting more numerous family life events also appear to be subject to higher depressive experience. Additionally, this analysis revealed that youth experiencing higher numbers of life events report poorer communication with the mother (Stewart, McKenry, Rudd, and Gavazzi 1994). The analysis failed to reveal any statistically significant importance of family dynamics and communication as mediators of depression. This finding is not terribly surprising given previous research which found life events to be a much stronger predictor of negative outcomes, such as depression, than resources that would include family processes (Garrison et al. 1990; McKenry et al. 1990).

Other correlational analyses were conducted between reported depressive symptomatology and a series of descriptive items that are worthy of note. Findings from these analyses indicated that adolescents reporting lesser levels of depressive symptomatology were more likely to report satisfaction with where they lived, with the availability of athletic programs, reported more frequent involvement with their church, were more popular among their peers at school, expressed more positive feelings towards school, received better grades, indicated higher future academic aspirations, and reported better health. Some of these relationships would seem to indicate the importance of peer relations as a possible predictor of depressive experience.

Given the significant relationship between family life events and depressive symptomatology, it is worthwhile to note the most frequently mentioned family life events for these rural youth. Those most frequently cited were: 1) increased family living expenses; 2) increased pressure to do well in school; 3) increased arguments between parents and the adolescent over curfew or use of car; 4) a family member starting a new business; and, 5) increased arguments about completing chores at home.

ADOLESCENT EDUCATIONAL ASPIRATIONS

Analysis of the "Rural Youth in a Changing Economy" data were also conducted in an attempt to discern the impact of parenting practices and family dynamics on the educational aspirations of adolescents growing up within this rural Midwestern environment. The importance of examining the educational aspirations of youth is clear. Although it has been documented that aspirations of all youth are higher than their actual attainment (MacBrayne 1987), research has shown that early occupational attainment is defined as a function of prior education, and that the influences of significant others affect the development of status aspirations which, in turn, act directly on educational attainment (Blau and Duncan 1967; Hauser et al. 1983; Haller and Portes 1973; Jencks et al. 1983; Sewell et al. 1969; Sewell et al. 1970). Hence, the forces that may place a rural adolescent at risk for depression also are often evidenced in lower achievement aspirations and other school-related issues.

While some conflicting reports exist, certainly there is evidence that rural youth do not share the generally high aspirations towards post-secondary education exhibited by youth growing up in urban and suburban environments. Cobb, McIntire, and Pratt (1989), using longitudinal data collected from 10,416 seniors form varying geographic backgrounds in the High School and Beyond study by the National Center for Educational Statistics, reported this finding as well as, lower levels of confidence by rural youth in their ability to complete a college education. Additionally, they further confirmed the findings of others that rural students place lower value on making money and higher value on friendships than their urban and suburban counterparts. Similarly, rural adolescents as well as their parents appeared to place more emphasis on full-time jobs than on education. In a review of data published through ERIC, Haas (1992) reported that rural youth believed that parents were more supportive of their taking full-time jobs, attending trade schools, or entering the military upon completion of high school. Similarly, other researchers who have found lower aspirations among rural as opposed to urban youth have indicated that rural parents were seen as being less supportive in regard to their adolescents attaining a college education. Others (Jackson, et al. 1974; Lee 1984; Marjoribanks 1984, 1985, 1986; Wilson et al. 1993) have demonstrated the importance of parental influence upon rural adolescents' educational aspirations.

In an attempt to discern the role played by parents in the educational aspirations of their children, this study utilized the sample of 108 adolescents and their parents (Scheidegger, 1998). In addition to the fixed-choice measures of adolescent educational aspirations, information concerning parents' SES (determined by their own achieved level of education), parental values, family adaptability and cohesion, family communication, the adolescent's perceived parental emotional support for education, and the adolescent's perceived financial support from parents for continuing education beyond high school were examined. Previous research exists which would indicate that these measures and possible interactions among them would play a significant role in determining adolescent educational aspirations.

Correlational analyses were conducted separately for (a) adolescents and fathers, and (b) adolescents and mothers. For the adolescent-father analyses, results indicated a relationship between adolescents' educational aspirations and father's level of education, father-adolescent communication, perceived financial support, gender values, and perceived support for education. Similar results were discerned for adolescents and mothers with the exception that communication and perceived support for education failed to reach statistical significance.

Additional analyses utilizing covariance structure modeling were conducted for the purpose of investigating the hypothesized relationships. Separate models were developed for (a) adolescents and fathers and (b) adolescents and mothers. Covariance structure modeling using RAMONA (Browne and Mehls, 1995) and maximum likelihood estimations were conducted separately for the Fathers' Model and the Mothers' Model. In accordance with the recommendations of Hoyle and Panter (1994), the assessment of model fit was based on three indices: one absolute fit index, the Root Mean-Square Error of Approximation (RMSEA; Browne and Cudek 1993; Steiger and Lind 1980); two incremental fit indices, the Tucker-Lewis (TLI; Tucker and Lewis 1973) or Non-Normed Fit Index (NNFI; Bentler and Bonett 1980); and the Comparative Fit Index (CFI; Bentler 1989, 1990).

The Mothers' Model yielded a good fit to the data according to all three indices, but there was some disagreement among the fit measures for the Fathers' Model. The Fathers' Model provided fair fit according to the RMSEA, but poor fit according to the TLI/NNFI. The values for the CFI also indicate a poor fit. Thus, the Fathers' Model must be viewed with some caution.

FATHERS' MODEL

In the Fathers' Model, adolescent educational aspirations were hypothesized to be positively related to fathers' educational level, family gender and work values, father-adolescent communication, and perceived support for education. In addition, fathers' educational level and family gender and work values were predicted to be related to perceived financial support. Gender and work values also were anticipated to be positively related to family cohesion, which, in turn, was to be predictive of both perceived educational support and father-adolescent communication. Support for five of these nine hypothesized relationships was obtained. Fathers' educational level and father-adolescent communication were significantly related to adolescents' educational aspirations and as expected, both path coefficients were positive. Fathers' educational level and perceived financial support also were positively related, as were family cohesion and perceived support for education. Lastly, family cohesion was a positive predictor of perceived support for education.

MOTHERS' MODEL

The Mothers' Model is identical to that of the fathers' in terms of hypothesized relationships. For the mothers, support for only three of the nine hypotheses was found. Similar to the results for the fathers, family cohesion was significantly (positively) related to both perceived support for education and mother-adolescent communication, and the path between mothers' education and adolescent aspirations was significant.

IMPLICATIONS OF THE TESTED MODELS

These findings support status attainment theory (e.g., Beau and Duncan 1967; Sewell et al. 1969) in explaining the impact of the family on adolescent educational aspirations. That is, parents' educational levels were the strongest predictors of adolescent educational aspirations. According to this theory, adolescents will model the educational levels of their parents in the process of parent-child socialization and identity formation. The adolescent will model these behaviors to the extent that the parent-child relationship is positive. The qualitative nature of the relationship was indicated in this study by the significant relationship between father-adolescent communication and educational aspirations.

The measure of father-adolescent communication has been used in other studies to assess the quality of the parent-adolescent relationship. The adolescent's relationship with the father may be pivotal in the rural community in that fathers often are seen as the "gate-

keepers" to the outside world (Parke 1995), and hence their example and support are critical to a child's feelings of competency in
extrafamilial roles such as education and career (Langman 1987).
The father's role may be even more important to females (two-thirds
of the sample) as career and higher education are viewed as less normative behaviors in some rural communities. Further, the female's
relationship with their mothers at least temporarily may be less close
because of the strains of identity formation.

SUMMARY AND FUTURE TRENDS

The ability of an adolescent to reach his/her full potential is very
much related to achievement motivation. Adolescence is a critical
juncture in achievement, and the level of achievement established at
this time may well predict future adult outcomes (Henderson and
Dweck 1990). Adolescents' achievement is determined in large part
by psychological and motivational factors, far more than by their
actual intellectual ability. Adolescent achievement motivation is thus
highly related to hope for success, self-confidence, persistence, and
supportive and involved parents who have high expectations by parents (Baumrind 1991; Paulson 1994). Adolescents who are depressed
are thought to have much difficulty in setting and working toward
long-term goals. These individuals who have a cognitive schema characterized by self-devaluation and lack of confidence about the future
(Clark and Beck 1989) often have parents who are emotionally
unavailable, have their own mental health needs, and/or have economic problems (Downey and Coyne 1990; Lempers and Clark-
Lempers 1990).

Psychological well-being and development of educational and
occupational aspirations consistent with their abilities and desired
lifestyle are two major adjustment outcomes for adolescents. As mentioned, because of rural family patterns and changes in the rural
economy, rural adolescents are thought to be at greater risk for both
depression and diminished educational aspirations. The studies
reported here sought to determine the role of families, that is, parents, in influencing adolescent depression and educational aspirations in an era of rapid economic change in rural communities.

Interestingly, while many of the youth involved in this study had
reported levels of depressive experiences that were at a "concerning"
level of symptomatology (at or above the 16-point cutoff used by
Radloff), they concurrently exhibited rather high educational aspirations. In both studies, however, the role of family dynamics and
specifically the parent-adolescent relationship were instrumental in

predicting these outcomes. Both studies supported the importance of the father-adolescent relationship in terms of adjustment as measured by the two study outcomes. This finding underscores the importance of the father in the socialization of adolescents, in particular their identity formation and their anticipation of roles beyond their immediate family. The father as head of the family and "gatekeeper" in the more traditional rural family appears to service a pivotal role, apart from that of the mother, in meeting the adolescent's socioemotional needs (in addition to serving as a role model for life outside the family). Langman (1987) among others has noted that father support is essential for a child's feelings of competency in roles outside the family.

Also, the parents' socioeconomc status was predictive of both depression and achievement aspirations. The importance of the educational level of both parents to adolescent educational aspirations suggests the validity of a status attainment theory explanation, although, according to this theory, the effect of parents' education is strengthened by the quality of the parent-adolescent relationship, in this case the father-adolescent relationship. In terms of depression, family economic factors also were implicated in the relationship between family life events (many items were related to economic changes) and depression, and family economic stability and depression, suggesting that economic threats to the family could be manifest in terms of adolescent depression. When the parents' economic status was destabilized, the adolescent's sense of optimism was challenged, resulting in a more depressed outlook. However, as in the case of educational aspirations, perhaps the father, because of his role as as head of household and gatekeeper, could affect the relationship between these changes and depression.

Certain dynamics related to living in rural America are persistent and should cause us great concern as we reflect on the difficulties that rural youth will face in the new millenium. Specifically, there continues to exist a disproportionately larger percentage of new jobs being created within metropolitan areas, while those within rural areas lag behind. Compensation for these jobs also differs significantly, with rural residents receiving considerably less in both wages and benefits than those living and working in urban America. Even with the generally favorable economic times of the 1990s that have helped to stabilize economic conditions in some rural areas, there continues to be a pattern of migration among the young towards those urban centers that can offer better future prospects.

Continued migration of this form will serve to "age" the existing rural population, creating the possibility of increased dissatisfaction among the young who do remain. Additionally, the dearth of similar-age peers may reduce socialization opportunities with similar-age peers. Indeed, future work should incorporate peer-related variables in an attempt to better understand the impact and importance of this area within the adjustment issues of interest. While the current work did not directly examine this as a variable within the models presented, specific items incorporated in the larger project clearly indicated that those youth reporting more positive social contacts reported more favorable adjustment as measured by levels of depressive experience.

The economic, social, and political marginalization of rural families will continue to play a role in how parents choose strategies for raising their offspring. It has been suggested elsewhere (Rural and Appalachian Youth and Families Consortium 1996) that policy, education, and therapeutic concerns all might better address the needs of rural populations if a "family-centric" paradigm were adopted.

> Respectful of the diversity of family systems, family-centric paradigms direct attention to the processes that are used in planning, approving, implementing, and evaluating policies that are responsive to the needs and practices of real families . . . basically, family-centric policy is more responsive to the perceived needs and dynamics of families who are considered and recognized as competent codecision makers in terms of crafting policy that best works. (Rural and Appalachian Youth and Families Consortium 1996, 393)

Hence, we end this chapter with a call for continued gains to be made in our theoretical and empirical understanding of those family-related factors that most significantly impact the growth and development of rural youth, and more specifically those factors that symbolize the strengths and capabilities of rural families.

NOTE

Foundational work on this project was conducted by the Rural Appalachian Youth and Families Consortium (RAYFC). The RAYFC began as an initiative at The Ohio State University (funded in part by the North Central Regional Center on Rural Development) in order to conduct a comprehensive study of rural youth and their families. The data presented in this chapter were generated from an interdisciplinary research program funded by the Ohio Agricultural Research Development Center.

REFERENCES

Adrian, A., and E. Costello. 1993. "Depressive comorbidity in children and adolescents: Empirical, theoretical, and methodological issues." *American Journal of Psychiatry* 150 (12): 1779–91.

Angell, R. C. (1965). *The family encounters the depression*. Gloucester, Mass.: Peter Smith.

Baldwin, C. M., and T. A. Revenson. 1986. "Vulnerability to economic stress." *Journal of Community Psychology* 14: 161–75.

Barnes, H. L., and D. H. Olson. 1985. "Parent-adolescent communication and the Circumplex model." *Child Development* 56: 438–47.

Baumrind, D. 1991. "Parenting styles and adolescent development." In *Encyclopedia of adolescence*, ed. R. M. Lerner, A. C. Petersen, and J. Brooks-Gunn, 746–58. New York: Garland.

Bentler, P. M. 1989. *EQS structural equations program manual*. Los Angeles: BMDP Statistical Software.

Bentler, P. M. 1990. "Comparative fit indexes in structural models." *Psychological Bulletin* 107: 238–46.

Bentler, P. M., and D. G. Bonett. 1980. "Significance tests and goodness of fit in the analysis of covariance structures." *Psychological Bulletin* 110: 305–14.

Bergland, B. 1988. "Rural mental health: Report of the national action commission on the mental health of rural Americans." *Journal of Rural Community Psychology* 9 (2): 29–39.

Billings, A. G., and R. H. Moos. 1983. "Comparisons of children of depressed and nondepressed parents: A social-environmental perspective." *Journal of Abnormal Child Psychology* 11: 463–86.

Blau, P. M., and O. D. Duncan. 1967. *The American Occupational Structure*. New York: John Wiley and Sons.

Brage, D., and W. Meredith. 1994. "A causal model of adolescent depression." *Journal of Psychology* 128 (4): 455–68.

Browne, M. W., and R. Cudek. 1993. "Alternative ways of assessing model fit." In *Testing structural equation models*, ed. K. A. Bollen and J. S. Long, 136–62. Newbury Park, Calif.: Sage.

Browne, N. W., and G. Mehls. 1995. *RAMONA PC user's guide*. Columbus: Ohio State University, Department of Psychology.

Cavan, R. S., and K. H. Ranck. 1938. *The family and the depression: A study of 100 Chicago Families*. 1 (1): 27–32.

Clark, D. A., and A. T. Beck. 1989. "Cognitive theory and therapy of anxiety and depression." In *Anxiety and depression*, ed. P. C. Kendall and D. Watson. San Diego, Calif.: Academic.

Cobb, R. A., W. G. McIntire, and P. A. Pratt. 1989. "Vocational and educational aspirations of high school students: A problem for rural America." *Research in Rural Education*, 6 (2): 11–16.

Coleman, M., L. H. Ganong, J. M. Clark, and M. Madsen. 1989. "Parenting perceptions in rural and urban families: Is there a difference?" *Journal of Marriage and the Family* 51: 329–35.

Couto, R. 1994. *An American challenge: A report on economic trends and social issues in Appalachia*. Dubuque, Iowa: Kendall/Hunt.

Cumsille, P., and E. Norman. 1994. "Family cohesion, family adaptability, social support, and adolescent depressive symptoms in outpatient clinic families." *Journal of Family Psychology* 8 (2): 202–14.

Dillman, D. A., and D. J. Hobbs, eds. *Rural Society in the U.S.: Issues for the 1980's*. Boulder, Colo.: Westview Press.

Downey, G., and J. C. Coyne. 1990. "Children of depressed parents: An integrative review." *Psychological Bulletin* 108: 50–76.

Dryfoos, J. G. 1990. *Adolescents at risk: Prevalence and prevention.* New York: Oxford University.

Dryfoos, J. G. 1992. "Integrating services for adolescents: The community schools." Paper presented at the biennial meeting of the Society of Research on Adolescence, Washington, D.C.

Elder, G. H., Jr. 1974. *Children of the Great Depression.* Chicago: University of Chicago Press.

Fitchen, J. 1981. *Poverty in rural America: A case study.* Boulder, Colo.: Westview Press.

French, A. P., and I. N. Berlin. 1979. *Depression in children and adolescents.* New York: Human Sciences Press.

Garrison, C. Z., K. L. Jackson, F. Marsteller, R. McKeown, and C. Addy. 1990. "A longitudinal study of depressive symptomatology in young adolescents." *Journal of the American Academy of Child Psychiatry* 29: 581–85.

Heffernan, J. B., and W. D. Heffernan. 1986. "Impact of the farm crisis on rural families and communities." *The Rural Sociologist* 6: 160–70.

Hoyle, R. H., and A. T. Panter. 1995. "Writing about structural equation models." In *Structural equation modeling: Concepts, issues, and applications,* ed. R. H. Hoyle, 158–76. Thousand Oaks, Calif.: Sage.

Hughes, R., Jr. 1988. "Empowering rural families and communities." In *Families in rural American: Stress, adaptation, and revitalization,* ed. R. Morotz-Baden, C. B. Hennon, and T. H. Brubaker, 261–69. St. Paul, Minn.: National Council on Family Relations.

Haas, T. 1992. "What can I become: Educational apirations of students in rural America." ERIC document ED345931.

Haller, A.O. and A. Portes. 1973. "Status attainment processes." *Sociology of Education* 46: 51–91.

Hauser, R. M., S. L. Tsai, and W. H. Sewell. 1983. "A model of stratification with response error in social and psychological variables." *Sociology of Education* 56: 20–46.

Henderson, V. L., and C. S. Dweck. 1990. "Motivation and achievement." In *At the threshold: The developing adolescent,* ed. S. S. Feldman and G. R. Elliott. Cambridge: Harvard University.

Jackson, R. M., N. M. Meara, and M. Arora. 1974. "Father identification, achievement, and occupational behavior of rural youth." *Journal of Vocational Behavior* 4: 85–96.

Jencks, C., J. Crouse, and P. Mueser. 1983. "The Wisconsin model of status attainment: A national replication with improved measures of ability and aspiration." *Sociology of Education* 56: 3–19.

Kandel, D. B., and M. Davies. 1982. "Epidemiology of depressive mood in adolescents: An empirical study." *Archives of General Psychiatry* 39: 1205–13.

Komarovsky, M. 1940. *The unemployed man and his family.* New York: Wiley.

Langman, L. 1987. "Social stratification." In *Handbook of marriage and the family,* ed. M. B. Sussman and S. K. Steinmetz, 211–49. New York: Plenum Press.

Lee, C. 1984. "An investigation of the psychosocial variables in the occupational aspirations and expectations of rural black and white adolescents: Implications for vocational education." *Journal of Research and Development in Education* 17 (3): 28–34.

Lempers, J. D., and D. S. Clark-Lempers. 1990. "Family economic stress, maternal and paternal support, and adolescent distress." *Journal of Adolescence* 13: 217–29.

Lerner, R. M., and D. R. Entwisle, and S. Hauser. 1994. "The crisis among contemporary American adolescents: A call for the integration of research, policies, and programs." *Journal of Research on Adolescence* 4: 1–4.

Lobao, L. M. 1990. *Locality and inequality: Farm and industry structure and socioeconomic conditions.* Albany: State University of New York.

Lihler, D. T., G. T. Cornwell, and D. J. Eggebeen. 1993. "Harvesting human capital: Family structure and education among rural youth." *Rural Sociology* 58 (1): 53–75.

MacBrayne, P. S. 1987. "Educational and occupational aspirations of rural youth: A review of the literature." *Research in Rural Education* 4 (3): 135–41.

Marjoribanks, K. 1984. "Occupational status, family environments, and adolescents' aspirations: the Laosa model." *Journal of Educational Psychology* 76 (4): 690–700.

____. 1985. "Families, schools, aspirations: Ethnic group differences." *Journal of Experimental Education* 53 (3): 141–47.

____. 1986. "A longitudinal study of adolescents' aspirations as assessed by Seginer's model." *Merrill-Palmer Quarterly* 32 (3): 211–30.

Marotz-Baden, R. and P. L. Colvin. 1986. "Coping strategies: A rural-urban comparison." *Family Relations* 35: 281–88.

Martin, G., P. Rozanes, C. Pearce, and S. Allison. 1994. "Adolescent suicide, depression and family dysfunction." *Acta psychiatrica Scandinavica* 92 (5): 336–44.

McCubbin, H. I., A. Larsen, and D. H. Olson. 1985. "Family crisis oriented personal evaluation scales." In *Family inventories: Inventories used in a national survey of families across the family life cycle*, ed. D.H. Olson, 121–37. St. Paul: Family Social Science, University of Minnesota.

McCubbin, H. I., J. M. Patterson, E. Buaman, and L. H. Harris. 1981. *Adolescent-family inventory of life events and changes (A-FILE).* St. Paul, Minn.: Family Social Science.

McFarlane, A., A. Bellissimo, G. Norman, and P. Lange. 1995. "Adolescent depression in a school-based community sample: Preliminary findings on contributing social factors." *Journal of Youth and Adolescence* 23 (6): 601–20.

McKenry, P. C., and S. M. Gavazzi. 1994. *Visions 2010: Adolescents and Families.* Minneapolis, Minn.: National Council on Family Relations Publications.

McKenry, P. C., J. B. Kotch, D. H. Browne, and M. J. Symons. 1990. "Mediators of depression among low-income, adolescent mothers of infants: A longitudinal perspective." *Journal of Youth and Adolescence* 19: 327–47.

Olson, D. H., D. H. Sprenkle, and C. S. Russell. 1979. "Circumplex model of marital and family systems: I. Cohesion and adaptability dimensions, family types, and clinical applications." *Family Process* 18 (1): 3–28.

Oster, G. D., and J. E. Caro. 1990. *Understanding and Treating Depressed Adolescents and their Families.* New York: John Wiley and Sons.

Parke, R. D. 1995. "Fathers and families." In *Handbook of parenting*, vol. 3, ed. M. H. Bornstein. Mahwah, N.J.: Lawrence Erlbaum Associates.

Paulson, S. E. 1994. "Parenting style or parental involvement: Which is more important for adolescent achievement?" Paper presented at the Biennial Meeting of the Society for Research on Adolescence, San Diego, California.

Peters, D. F., S. M. Wilson, and G. W. Peterson. (1986). "Adolescents and rural Appalachian families." In *Adolescents in Families*, ed. G. K. Leigh, and G. W. Peterson, 456–69. Cincinnati: South-Western Publishing Co.

Porter, K. H. 1989. *Poverty in Rural America: A National Overview.* Washington, D.C.: Center on Budget and Policy Priorities.

Puig-Antich, J. 1982. "Major depression and conduct disorder in prepuberty." *Journal of the American Academy of Child Psychiatry* 21: 118–28.

Radloff, L. S. 1977. "The CES-D Scale: A self-report depression scale for research in the general population." *Applied Psychological Measurement* 1 (3): 385–401.

Reiss, D., G. Howe, S. Simmens, and D. Bussell. 1996. "Genetic questions for environmental studies: Differential parenting and psychopathology in adolescence." *Annual Progress in Child Psychiatry and Child Development,* 206–35.

Rudd, N. M., P. C. McKenry, G. Leigh, and M. M. Sanik. 1988. "Rural youth in a changing economy: Stress, coping, and educational and occupational decision-making." Unpublished proposal. Ohio Agricultural Research and Development Center. Columbus, Ohio.

Rural and Appalachian Youth and Families Consortium. 1996. "Parenting practices and interventions among marginalized families in Appalachia: Building on family strengths." *Family Relations* 45: 387–96.

Rutter, M., C. E. Izard, and P. B. Read. 1986. *Depression in Young People: Developmental and Clinical Perspectives.* New York: The Guilford Press.

Santrock, J. W. 1987. *Adolescence: An introduction.* Dubuque, Iowa: Wm. C. Brown.

Scheidegger, T. H. 1998. "Family structure, process, and values as influences on educational aspirations among rural youth." Doctoral dissertation, The Ohio State University.

Sewell, W. H., A. O. Haller, and A. Portes. 1969. "The educational and early occupational attainment process." *American Sociological Review* 34: 82–92.

Sewell, W. H., A. O. Haller, and G. W. Ohlendorf. 1970. "The educational and early occupational attainment process: Replication and revision." *American Sociological Review* 35: 1014–27.

Sheeber, L., H. Hops, A. Alpert, B. Davis, and J. Andrews. 1997. "Family support and conflict: Prospective relations to adolescent depression." *Journal of Abnormal Child Psychology* 25 (4): 333–44.

Sherman, A. 1992. *Falling by the Wayside: Children in Rural America.* Washington, D.C.: Children's Defense Fund.

Stewart, E. R., P. C. McKenry, N. M. Rudd, and S. M. Gavazzi. 1994. "Family processes as mediators of depressive symptomatology among rural adolescents." *Family Relations* 43: 38–45.

Sullivan, W. O., and A. W. Engin. 1986. "Adolescent depression: Its prevalence in high school students." *Journal of School Psychology* 24: 103–9.

Trad, P. V. 1987. *Infant and Childhood Depression: Developmental Factors.* New York: John Wiley and Sons.

Tucker, L. R., and C. Lewis. 1973. "A reliabiity coefficient for maximum likelihood factor analysis." *Psychometrika* 38: 1–10.

Van Hook, M. 1990. "Family response to the farm crisis: A study in coping." *Social Work* 35: 425–31.

Wagenfeld, M. O. 1988. "Rural mental health and community psychology in the post community mental health era: an overview and introduction to the special issue." *Journal of Rural Community Psychology* 9 (2): 5–12.

Wall Street Journal. 1988. Quiet crisis, p. 1. (August 4)

Ward, S. L. 1986. "Rural isolation: The need for information." *Educational Considerations* 13 (2): 32–34.

Wilson, S. M. 1994. "Rural and Appalachian youth and their families." In *Visions 2010: Adolescents and Families,* ed. P. C. McKenry and S. M. Gavazzi, 38–39. Minneapolis, Minn.: National Council on Family Relations Publications.

Wilson, S. M., G. W. Peterson, and P. Wilson. 1993. "The process of educational and occupational attainment of adolescent females from low-income, rural families." *Journal of Marriage and the Family* 55: 158–75.

Witt, L. A. 1989. "Urban-nonurban differences in social cognition: Locus of control and perceptions of a just world." *The Journal of Social Psychology* 129: 715–17.

Woodward, J. C., and B. D. Frank. 1988. "Rural adolescent loneliness and coping strategies." *Adolescence* 23: 559–65.

Zimbelman, K. 1987. "Locus of control and achievement orientation in rural and metropolitan youth." *Journal of Rural Community Psychology,* 8: 50–55.

Substance Abuse in Rural America

DAVID KEARNS AND DAVID ROSENTHAL

"In the United States there is more space where nobody is than where
anybody is. This is what makes America what it is."
—Gertrude Stein, *The Geographical History of America*

INTRODUCTION

Kathleen Norris—poet, memoirist, and former resident of Virginia,
Illinois, Hawaii, Vermont, and New York—has emerged as one of our
culture's most careful and experienced observers of rural America.
In her book *Dakota: A Spiritual Geography,* she provides a compelling
account of the move that she and her husband made from New York
City to Lemmon, South Dakota, and of the benefits and sacrifices that
can accompany rural living (Norris 1996). The messages in her text
are rich and subtle.

In a subsequent essay, one that was written as part of a multi-author
review of David Sutherland's documentary film "The Farmer's Wife,"
Norris's message, though no less riveting, is more harsh and urgent.
Undoubtedly influenced by the powerful events that unfolded in the
film, she argues that rural America is in fact a "hidden America," one
whose realities—its virtues and its problems—have become less visible with the country's progressive urbanization. Norris contends that
this diminished visibility has been fostered by the media (Norris
1998). Thoughts of rural America often make their way to the
broader (urban?) American consciousness only with the unfolding of
"newsworthy" events: a despondent Iowa farmer's murder of three
people, and his attempted murder of several others, before he took
his own life (Davidson 1996); the 81-day standoff on the plains of
Montana involving the anti-government "Freemen" and a host of FBI
agents (Norris 1998); or more recently, fatal shootings in schools in
several small towns (Sleek 1998).

These events command attention not only because of the details
that surround them, but because the images that accompany them
run counter to the view that so many people have of rural America as

151

peaceful, idyllic, and, generally, downright boring. People are forced to think, at least momentarily, that the views they have held may need to be expanded, or possibly revised entirely. To do so, however, would be a major task. At a minimum, it would require sustained thought about rural America as something other than an idealized counterbalance to the complexities than can accompany urban living (Castle 1995).

Rural America can no longer be thought of as unchanging and perpetually tranquil. These views simply don't fit the facts. In recent years, significant changes have occurred across large segments of the rural landscape: increased poverty (Fitchen 1995); the virtual decimation of the family farm (Berry 1977; Davidson 1996); population changes (Fuguitt 1995; Hart 1995; Norris 1998); and a general erosion of the infrastructure that must exist if small towns are to survive (Davidson 1986; Jackson 1996). The stresses accompanying these changes have resulted in dramatic increases in reported rates of domestic abuse, depression, anxiety, and substance abuse (Meyer 1990). And with these changes and the resulting stresses has come the harsh realization—for many who live there, and for some who don't—that it is no longer accurate or acceptable to view rural America as immune to the struggles and problems that previously seemed the exclusive province of more densely populated areas of the country.

Two questions will serve as points of organization for the information contained in this chapter. The first question is, *"How is 'rural' defined?"* Terms like "metropolitan," "nonmetropolitan," "urban," and "rural" are to a great extent defined by the population of the area in question. A widely used definition of rural first appeared in a supplementary census report in 1906 (Hart 1995). In that report, the term rural essentially attained its meaning through negation: everything not classified as urban was considered rural. According to the Bureau of the Census, "the urban population consists of all persons living in urbanized areas and in places of 2,500 or more inhabitants; all other population is considered rural" (Hart 1995; USBC 1985).

Population, however, should not be the only criterion used to demarcate rural areas. Although their populations may be similar, a rural area that primarily contains farms that provide work and residence for local inhabitants is fundamentally different from one that includes people who live on farms but don't work there. Similarly, a small town that is adjacent to a metropolitan area is different from one that is situated in a nonmetropolitan region. These distinctions are more than semantic: at the very least, major differences can result across these rural areas in terms of employment opportunities, economic stability, the availability of goods and services, and resident/community identity (Berry 1996; Davidson 1996; Jackson 1996). And although alternatives to the Census Bureau's view of what constitutes "rural" have been offered by other governmental agencies, in the end, the population threshold of 2,500 remains a frequently invoked component of these definitions (Hart 1995).

The second question is, *"How is 'substance abuse' defined?"* The answer to the question necessitates a discussion of varying patterns of substance use. The vast majority of people who use substances— alcohol, prescription drugs, and over-the-counter medications—do so in legal and responsible ways. And after starting to use a particular substance, most people can bring their use to a close without difficulty. It is also clear that a number of otherwise responsible people occasionally expand their pattern of use to include one or more illicit substances as well (Brecher 1972). Despite the accompanying illegality, many people manage to use even these substances in a manner that does not result in prolonged functional compromise or chemical dependence. But substance use can of course be very problematic.

According to the *Diagnostic and Statistical Manual* of the American Psychiatric Association (APA 1994),

Substance-Related Disorders include disorders related to the taking of a drug of abuse (including alcohol), to the side effects of a medication, and to toxin exposure. . . . [T]he term *substance* can refer to a drug of abuse, a medication, or toxin. . . . Many prescribed and over-the-counter medications can also cause Substance-Related Disorders. Symptoms are often related to the dosage of the medication and usually disappear when the dosage is lowered or the medication is stopped. However, there may sometimes be an idiosyncratic reaction to a single dose. (175)

The Substance Abuse-Related Disorders are divided into two groups: the Substance-Use Disorders (Substance Dependence and Substance Abuse) and the Substance-Induced Disorders (Substance Intoxication, Substance Withdrawal, Substance-Induced Delirium, Substance-Induced Persisting Dementia, Substance-Induced Persisting Amnestic Disorder, Substance-Induced Psychotic Disorder, Substance-Induced Mood Disorder, Substance-Induced Sleep Disorder). . . . The essential feature of Substance Dependence is a cluster of cognitive, behavioral, and physiological symptoms indicating that the individual continues use of the substance despite significant substance-related problems. There is a pattern of repeated self-administration that usually results in tolerance, withdrawal, and compulsive drug-taking behavior. (176)

The essential feature of Substance Abuse is a maladaptive pattern of substance use manifested by recurrent and significant adverse consequences related to the repeated use of substances. There may be repeated failure to fulfill major role obligations, repeated use in situations in which it is physically hazardous, multiple legal problems, and recurrent social and interpersonal problems. (182)

In this chapter, we will provide a glimpse at substance use and abuse in rural America. We will discuss: (1) the prevalence of the problem; (2) factors that appear to increase and decrease the likelihood that people will abuse substances; (3) particular consequences that result from substance abuse; (4) factors that often make the treatment of rural substance abuse especially difficult; and (5) recommendations that ultimately may decrease the substance abuse problem.

INCIDENCE OF SUBSTANCE ABUSE

Many people have at least a general idea that alcohol and drug abuse are very common in the U.S., including many segments or rural America. But it is one thing to have an intuitive sense that these are common difficulties, and quite another to come face-to-face with data that specifically highlight the extent of the problem.

One glimpse of the pervasiveness of these problems comes from a report by the Department of Health and Human Services (DHHS 1990a). According to that report, 18.5 million Americans regularly abuse alcohol; 1 to 3 million citizens use cocaine regularly; another 900,000 use I.V. drugs.

Although many of the published studies in the area of substance abuse have focused on urban and suburban populations, there is a growing literature that focuses more specifically on rural areas (Sarvella et al. 1990). The general consensus in this literature is that the prevalence rate of substance abuse in rural settings at least equals—and in some instances exceeds—that seen in contrasting urban settings (Kelleher et al. 1992; Robertson and Donnermeyer 1997). Alcohol appears to be the most commonly abused drug in rural areas (Kelleher et al. 1992). Holroyd et al. (1997) argued that alcohol problems are more prevalent among rural residents, especially those living in the South. They reported 4.2 percent and 2.8 percent prevalence rates for rural and urban residents, respectively. A companion view of the extent of alcohol problems in rural areas comes from studies that report higher rural rates of alcohol-related arrests, more hospitalizations for substance-related problems, and more unintentional injuries that are the direct result of alcohol consumption (Kelleher et al. 1992).

Multiple studies have been conducted that provide a glimpse at alcohol and drug use by rural pre-adolescents and adolescents. These studies are of interest because they provide important information about the early substance-use histories of people who may in fact become the next generation of adult substance abusers. It has been estimated that nearly 40 percent of school children have at least tried alcohol by age 10. This finding gains additional importance when it is juxtaposed with the fact that nearly 65 percent of adult problem drinkers report having taken their first drink before age 13 (Finke et al. 1996).

Based on an investigation of drug and alcohol use among a large sample (N = 4,406) of rural school-age children, Stevens et al. (1995) reported that alcohol was the preferred drug in all grades for both genders, followed by cigarettes. Girls listed marijuana as their third drug of preference; boys listed spitting tobacco, followed by marijuana. The lifetime exposure to other illicit substances (e.g., inhalants, cocaine, downers, heroin, psychedelics, etc.) was comparatively low. However, there was a steady progression of alcohol use from fourth grade (50 percent had used it) through twelfth grade (almost all had used it). Although fewer students reported marijuana use, by the twelfth grade, 50 percent of the boys in the sample had tried it. Despite the fact that the lifetime and 30-day prevalence rates of marijuana use were lower for girls, by the twelfth grade, their pattern of use approximated that of the boys.

In general, the drug preferences of some students were similar to those reported in several national surveys. Importantly, their lifetime and 30-day use rates were equal to, and in some instances slightly higher than, those reported in comparison samples of urban preadolescents and adolescents (Sarvela and McClendon 1988; Stevens et al. 1995). Others have suggested that in comparison to their urban counterparts, rural youth may consume alcohol more abusively (Sarvela et al. 1990). Given these findings, it is not surprising to learn that when rural adolescents are injured or killed, these occurrences are typically the direct result of health-compromising behaviors such as alcohol use (Kelleher et al. 1997).

It should be recognized, however, that the high incidence of alcohol abuse in rural areas also extends beyond the young. Colsher and Walace (1990) report, for example, that rural elderly report higher rates of alcohol abuse than those in comparative urban samples. Among the elderly, alcohol-related hospitalizations are in fact as common as admissions for myocardial infarction (Holroyd et al. 1997). Collectively, these findings clearly suggest that rural living in and of itself seems to afford little protection from experimental and sometimes intensifying drug use (Stevens et al. 1995).

RISK FACTORS AND PROTECTIVE FACTORS

The information presented above clearly indicates that substance abuse is a significant problem in both urban and rural settings.

Despite the prevalence of the problem, it is clear, however, that not everyone abuses substances. This fact underscores the importance of a discussion of factors that appear to increase the risk that someone may abuse substances, and those that appear to have a more protective influence. Much of this literature focuses on influences in the environments of children and adolescents that appear to increase or decrease the likelihood of substance abuse.

Demographic Variables

Certain demographic characteristics tend to be associated with an increased likelihood of substance use/abuse. In general, the risk of substance use/abuse increases with age. This is evident from studies that track the increasing use of alcohol by students as they progress through the various grades (Stevens et al. 1995). Older adolescent males tend to use alcohol more regularly than younger males. With reference to gender, older males generally use alcohol more regularly than younger or same-age females (Bloch et al. 1991; Gibbons et al. 1986; Pope et al. 1994). It has also been reported that rural, African-American males may be at particular risk for alcohol abuse (Blazer et al. 1986; Long and Boik 1993).

Family Variables

A number of protective factors have been identified at the level of the family. It has consistently been shown, for example, that children and adolescents whose parents (or parent substitutes) are nurturing, and who demonstrate responsible alcohol use themselves, are less likely to demonstrate deviance in general, or alcohol abuse in particular (Bloch, et al. 1991; Long and Boik 1993). Although there is considerable variation as to the strength of the association, there is a developing literature that supports the general contention that strong bonds to parents decrease the likelihood that adolescents will use drugs. A number of factors appear to be involved. With strong bonds, adolescents respect, listen to, and do more things to please their parents than when the reported bonds are weaker. There is also evidence that the ability of parents to monitor the behaviors of their children can powerfully influence the likelihood of adolescent substance abuse. Parents who watch and supervise the behavior of their children are often more aware of friends and situations that might encourage drug use. Armed with this information, parents can implement corrective actions that ideally will reduce the likelihood of substance use and abuse (Bahr et al. 1995).

The risk of abuse increases significantly if family members tolerate the excessive alcohol use of others or if they engage in this behavior themselves (Ary et al. 1993). These findings suggest a direct modeling- or imitation-based relationship between family drug use and adolescent drug involvement. Others have suggested a more indirect influence. Bahr et al. (1995) have speculated that adolescents from families in which other members also use substances are more likely to choose peers who use substances. In turn, again via modeling and imitation, these peers then exercise a more direct influence on drug use.

Religious Practice

Researchers have also documented the interrelatedness of drug use and religiosity (Bahr and Hawks 1995; Bloch et al. 1991; Pope et al. 1994). According to Roof (1979), religiosity refers to "an individual's beliefs and behavior in relation to the supernatural and/or high-intensity values" (18). Non-users commonly report being more religious than users. Similarly, religious involvement has consistently been shown to be negatively associated with drinking and marijuana use (Bahr et al. 1998). This information underscores the role that religious practice may play in the prevention of drug abuse.

School Behavior

The manner in which students approach their tasks at school also appears to be important. Students who have a good attitude toward school, who are focused on academic performance (Bloch et al. 1991; Long and Boik 1993; Pope et al. 1994), and who spend time studying (Gibbons et al. 1986) tend to be at lower risk for alcohol abuse. Behavior outside of school is also important. Gibbons et al. (1986) reported that students who spend more time socializing, working, and playing video games tend to report higher levels of alcohol consumption.

Self-Confidence

Although no one denies its general importance, the precise role that self-confidence plays in reducing the risk of substance abuse is not yet clear. Several researchers have reported that a positive self-concept is associated with lower levels of alcohol consumption (Finke et al. 1996). Others, however, have reported a more confusing picture regarding the potential impact of self-concept. For example, in an investigation of the antecedents of alcohol use among rural adolescents, Bloch et al. (1991) reported that self-concept was not a strong predictor of future levels of alcohol consumption. A study by Long and Boik (1993) underscored the interrelatedness of self-concept and other factors. They reported that third- and fourth-grade students who had either a positive self-concept or a positive school attitude—but not both—were less likely to use alcohol in grades six and seven. The authors hypothesized that the students with positive self-concepts and school attitudes were more likely to use alcohol in later grades because they in fact were quite secure emotionally; they tended to use alcohol in an exploratory but not necessarily abusive manner.

Beliefs About Alcohol

The beliefs that adolescents have about alcohol also appear to be quite important. Adolescents who believe that alcohol will relieve tension or enhance their performance in some way are especially likely to abuse it. Positive beliefs about the effects of alcohol have been shown to increase the current and lifetime likelihoods that people will engage in drinking and drunkenness. Importantly, however, these attitudes appear to have less influence than the family variables that were noted earlier (Long and Boik 1993).

Researchers have argued that the risk factors that are at issue in terms of substance use/abuse tend to operate in an additive fashion. Examining alcohol abuse longitudinally, Bloch et al. (1991) reported, for example, that students who regularly used alcohol in their third year of high school tended to be the students who reported the highest number of risk factors in their first year. A pivotal task for researchers will be to devise studies that more precisely explain how particular factors interrelate to increase or decrease the risk of substance use/abuse.

CONSEQUENCES OF SUBSTANCE ABUSE

Economic Consequences

The economic consequences of alcohol and drug abuse are staggering. In 1983, the costs associated with alcohol abuse in the U.S. was estimated to exceed $70 billion. Another $44 billion was spent addressing problems directly related to the use of illicit drugs (DHHS 1990a). A Department of Health and Human Services report addresses the outlay of money for medical services. In 1960, 5 percent of the Gross National Product went to medical services. The total cost of illness (including lost productivity attendant to illness and early death) equaled 18 percent of the GNP in 1980, and 12 percent in 1990 (DHHS 1990b). It is estimated that the total cost of alcohol-related deaths in the U.S. exceeds $75 billion each year.

Health Consequences

Nationally, it is estimated that there are approximately 105,000 alcohol-related deaths each year. Although many of these deaths are the result of the progressive decline in health that accompanies regular alcohol abuse, others are clearly accident-related. Excessive alcohol use resulted in 320,000 traffic-related injuries in 1987. Approximately two-thirds of the motor vehicle accidents that year occurred in rural areas (Sarvela et al. 1990). There were more than 47,000 traffic-related fatalities in 1988; nearly half of these deaths were alcohol-related (Gunby 1989). According to the National Highway Traffic Safety Administration, 57 percent of the fatal crashes in 1988 occurred in rural areas. Almost half of these crashes occurred on weekends—usually Saturdays (Gunby 1989).

Sarvela et al (1990) investigated patterns of drinking, drug use, and driving in a sample of 3,382 junior and senior high school students in 19 rural counties in Illinois. Thirty-nine percent (39 percent) of the students in the survey reported that within the previous six months, they had ridden in a car in which the driver had been drinking. Nearly eight percent of these students indicated that this occurred at least weekly. Sixteen percent reported that during the past six months, they personally had driven a car while under the influence of alcohol or drugs; 3.4 percent of these students reported doing so at least weekly. Alcohol was the most frequently abused substance. Slightly more females than males reported riding in a car with a drinking driver, while more males than females reported driving under the influence. The tendency to drive after drinking or using drugs increased with grade level, as did riding with someone who was under the influence of alcohol or drugs. Over 40 percent of the senior high students in the sample reported driving after drinking or using drugs in the previous six months. These findings are alarming because youth are at particular risk for accidents due to their inexperience as drinkers and drivers (Sarvela et al. 1990).

Alcohol is also implicated in at least half of the homicides (DHHS 1990a), and 25 percent to 50 percent of the suicides that occur in the U.S. each year (Holroyd et al. 1997). Similarly, one-third of all drowning and boating accident victims are intoxicated (DHHS 1990a). Excessive alcohol consumption is also often implicated in falls, fires, hunting accidents, and high-risk sexual behaviors (DHHS 1994).

Precise information is lacking regarding high-risk sexual practices in rural areas. A glimpse at the potential impact of excessive alcohol consumption on such practices comes, however, from national data concerning high-risk sexual behavior, and contrasting information from a sample of in-patient alcoholics. Information derived from the national sample indicated that nearly 14 percent of those surveyed reported having more than one sexual partner in the previous year, and that condoms were not consistently used during these encounters (Leigh et al. 1993). An even more startling picture emerged, however, in a study of the HIV risk of alcoholics in treatment (Scheidt and Windle 1995). In the six-month period before the survey, in contrast to the 14 percent figure reported in the survey by Leigh et al. (1993), more than three times as many alcoholics in the study by Scheidt and Windle (1995) reported unprotected sexual behavior with multiple partners. It can be argued that the urban-based study by Scheidt and Windle (1995) is irrelevant to a discussion of potential health consequences resulting from substance abuse in rural settings. These data are included, however, to make a very basic point: the high level of at-risk behavior in the sample of alcohol abusers is the likely result of a number of individual-level effects that accompany excessive consumption (e.g., disinhibition, cognitive-perceptual distortion, bad judgement, etc. (Kelleher and Robbins 1997). The bottom line is that these outcomes are determined by the amount that is consumed, not the residence of the drinker. In instances involving excessive alcohol use, the potential for at-risk behavior by rural residents may therefore be quite comparable to that seen in urban settings.

There is consistent evidence that problem drinking is strongly associated with increased morbidity and premature mortality. On average, between 9 and 22 years of life are lost when an alcoholic succumbs to liver disease, in contrast to two years for cancer, and four years for heart disease. Alcoholism is commonly associated with a host of medical conditions: hypertension, delirium/dementia, incontinence, malnutrition, myopathy, and accidental hypothermia (Fleming et al. 1997).

Colsher and Wallace (1990) investigated the health consequences associated with heavy drinking. They examined three groups of rural elderly men: those with clear histories of heavy drinking; those who drank but not heavily; and those who never drank. Compared to the other groups, the men with a history of heavy drinking experienced more major illnesses, poorer functional status, more impairment in performing daily living activities, increased utilization of medical services, more depression, lower life satisfaction, smaller social networks, and lower overall social activity.

In a study of community-dwelling alcoholic patients in the rural

South, Holroyd et al. (1997) reported that the majority of the subjects did not have a designated primary care physician. They also were significantly more likely than non-alcoholics to utilize hospital emergency rooms even for routine medical care. This tendency to utilize more costly emergency services may in fact be an artifact of not having a designated physician who would aid in more coordinated medical care.

School Consequences

Besides its obvious educational function, school plays an important role in the socialization and emotional development of children and adolescents. Donnermeyer (1997) summarizes some of the literature concerning the relationship between substance abuse and a variety of academic outcomes. Students who use substances are more likely to experience school performance problems, and to leave school before graduation (Donnermeyer 1997; Fagan and Pabon 1990; Jajoura 1993). There also is a clear association between drug use and compromised academic performance, including lower grade point averages (Bloch et al. 1991; Donnermeyer 1997), reduced participation in extracurricular activities (Donnermeyer 1997; Gibbons et al. 1986), and less time spent doing homework (Donnermeyer 1997; Wolford and Swisher 1986).

Criminal Behavior

Researchers have consistently documented a strong association between substance abuse and criminal behavior. Summarizing information from the General Accounting Office, Kelleher and Robbins (1997) report that

> Rural states and counties have arrest rates for substance abuse violations (e.g., driving under the influence, liquor law violations, drunkenness, and possession of illegal substances) equal to those of non-rural states and counties. Rural states, counties, and towns have higher arrest rates involving illegal use of alcohol than non-rural states, suburban counties, and larger cities. Most prison inmates in rural states have abused alcohol, other drugs, or both. (203)

It is also estimated that between one-third and over one-half of police-investigated episodes of spousal abuse also involve abusive drinking (Kelleher and Robbins 1997).

Workplace Consequences

Although we assume that at least some of the research findings that exist regarding substance use/abuse and the workplace may be relevant to discussions of rural settings, it should be recognized that this is an area that actually received little research attention (Kelleher and Robbins 1997). This notwithstanding, estimates from studies conducted in nonrural areas suggest as many as 10 percent of all workers may experience drinking problems that affect their job performance. Typical difficulties for the workplace include increased employee absenteeism, decreased productivity, frequent employee turnover, and increased retraining expenses; and for the worker, increased use of health care, reduced opportunity for promotion, decreased job satisfaction, and job loss due to poor performance (with accompanying economic hardship) (DHHS 1990; Kelleher and Robbins 1997). The potential interplay of these outcomes was underscored in a study by Helzer et al. (1991). They reported that for both men and women, the frequency of alcohol use in adolescence was positively associated with the number different employers they reported having had by age 25 (Helzer et al. 1991; Kelleher and Robbins 1997).

Speculating about the general impact of substance abuse in rural areas, Kelleher and Robbins (1997) commented as follows:

> To the extent that economic structures of rural areas are more tentative and fragile, rural workers are likely more vulnerable to layoffs and to dismissals with cause. Rural areas are characterized by less diversified economies with higher rates of unemployment and lower educational attainment of workers. . . . All deviant behavior, including problem drinking, is therefore likely to have stronger negative consequences for rural individuals in the workplace. (205)

Child-Focused Outcomes

The potential for adverse outcomes exists well in advance of the birth of a child. A substantial literature exists documenting the adverse developmental consequences that can result from substance use/abuse during pregnancy (Abel 1984; Conry 1990). Sloane et al. (1992) investigated the prevalence of substance abuse during early pregnancy in a sample of rural women. Information was gathered from self-report and from urine specimens collected and analyzed as part of routine prenatal care. In terms of self-reported substance abuse, 46 percent of the women in the study indicated that they currently smoked tobacco; 15 percent reported using alcohol during pregnancy; 8.3 percent reported having used illicit drugs at some point within the previous month. In general, these findings were corroborated by the urine sample data. The tobacco use of 46 percent of the women in the sample was confirmed. Marijuana was detected in the urine samples of 9.4 percent of the women; cocaine, benzodiazepines, barbiturates, and alcohol were each detected in 0.6 percent of the sample. This project also underscored the strong association between subjects' tobacco use and the increased likelihood that they would ingest other substances during pregnancy. "[S]mokers were 3.6 times more likely to use another tested substance" (Sloane et al. 1992, 246). The authors argued that given the tendency in our culture to assume that substance abuse is less prevalent in rural settings than in urban areas, many problems simply go undetected. Importantly, improved screening and intervention in early pregnancy could reduce the likelihood of substance-induced fetal damage (Sloane et al. 1992).

After birth, the abuse of substances by parents can significantly compromise their capacity to be emotionally supportive and nurturing, and to offer the encouragement and guidance that children and adolescents so obviously need. Parents who are capable of behaving in these ways are doing things that have recurrently been shown to exercise a protective influence over their children. These parental behaviors are part of a complex pattern of influences that can reduce the chances that a child will abuse substances (Oetting et al. 1997— see Risk Factors and Protective Factors above).

Family Problems

Although the direction of causality begs to be questioned (i.e., Which came first, the substance problems or the family problems?), there is a lot of information documenting the co-morbidity of substance abuse and marital and family difficulties (Oetting et al. 1997; Peterson et al. 1994; Stanton and Todd 1982; Windle 1993).

Studies have consistently shown that if children are raised in families in which there are histories of drug use, criminality, and aggression, the chances are increased that they too will abuse substances. In contrast to nonusers, adolescent drug users are more likely to report high levels of family conflict, to come from families that are not intact, to perceive their families as less caring, and to report being beaten by their parents and/or siblings (Bahr et al. 1995; Oetting et al. 1997). Kelleher and Robbins (1997) report that 60 percent of those who struggle with diagnosed alcohol use or dependence, and 30 percent of weekly heavy drinkers, report family conflict due to drinking. Very often, these conflicts escalate to a point of physical violence.

Substance abuse also greatly impacts the overall stability and viability of marital relationships. The marriages of heavy drinkers are often tension-filled (Zweben 1986). The probability of divorce increases dramatically in relationships in which one or both marital partners drink excessively. There also is evidence that alcohol abuse sets the scene for serial divorces (Kelleher and Robbins 1997).

EFFECTIVENESS OF SUBSTANCE ABUSE TREATMENT

The information presented thus far emphasizes that substance abuse is prevalent in rural areas and that a number of significant consequences can result. And despite the fact that there are a number of factors that appear to reduce the likelihood that substance abuse will occur, as the data indicate, overall, substance abuse in both urban and rural settings remains a significant health problem.

There is clear evidence that many people who experience substance abuse problems can be successfully treated (Finney and Moos 1998). Although it is beyond the scope of this chapter to summarize this literature in detail, particular features will be highlighted.

Particular treatments—cognitive-behavioral therapy (incorporating social skills training, community reinforcement, and behavioral marital treatment), and the so-called 12-step treatment model—have in general proved to be effective. It appears however, that the greatest effectiveness comes with a careful matching of patients and treatments. Interpersonally oriented treatments appear to be particularly effective with patients who are functioning better at the start of treatment. More impaired patients seem to be helped more with the use of cognitive-behavioral techniques. There also is evidence that particular therapist characteristics can powerfully influence the outcome of therapy. Specifically, therapists who are more interpersonally skilled, less confrontational, and more empathic tend to get better treatment results. It also has been reported that substance-abuse patients may get the most benefit from treatment if it occurs over a long period of time. And finally, with the possible exception of severely impaired patients, in terms of overall effectiveness, there appears to be little or no difference between inpatient versus outpatient treatment (Finney and Moos 1998).

BARRIERS TO SUBSTANCE ABUSE
TREATMENT IN RURAL AREAS

There is no reason to believe that if available (and used), substance abuse treatment would be any less effective for rural patients than for those living elsewhere. What we will argue, however, is that even though effective treatments for substance abuse do exist, a number of often overlapping factors serve to constrain formal substance abuse treatment in rural settings.

Resident Views of Problems and Treatment

The often-voiced contention that rural people have strong tendencies toward privacy and self-reliance appears to be true (Pothier

1991). Considerable stigma can also be associated with even the ideas of receiving substance abuse treatment. In combination, these factors can increase the chances that people will be reluctant to pursue treatment, even where services exist and the need is recognized.

Often, problems like substance abuse are not viewed as artifacts of heredity, stress, vulnerability, or interpersonal difficulty, but as evidence of personal weakness (Meyer 1990). This tendency was documented in a study conducted by the National Alliance for the Mentally Ill. Of the rural residents surveyed, 71 percent reported that they viewed mental illness as a personal weakness; 65 percent underscored "bad parenting" as the likely etiology of these difficulties; 43 percent expressed a belief that people themselves bring on the difficulties they experience (Meyer 1990).

A Shortage of Trained Professionals

Even if the residents of rural areas are willing to risk the stigma that can accompany treatment, one simple but critical fact remains: there is a severe shortage of professionals who are trained in mental health and/or substance abuse treatment. The majority of rural counties have few, if any, psychologists, social workers, or psychiatrists (Knesper et al. 1985; Meyer 1990). A study conducted by the National Rural Mental Health Association revealed that 1682 counties in the U.S. lacked the assistance of any core mental health professionals (Blank et al. 1995). It is estimated that 34 million rural residents (61 percent) live in designated Mental Health Professional Shortage Areas (Kenkel 1996). Many rural areas simply lack the resources that are necessary to attract trained professionals and to keep existing facilities open (Robertson and Donnermeyer 1997).

The issue regarding the shortage of trained professionals has not gone unrecognized. In recent years, the problem has been a periodic focus of attention in the U.S. Congress. A Senate Rural Health Caucus was formed during the 99th Congress, in part, out of a realization that the needs of rural America are unique. It was also recognized that the problems experienced in rural settings had not been carefully attended to by virtually every previous Administration. (A similar caucus was formed in the House of Representatives.) These congressional efforts are ongoing. Discussions thus far have centered on the impact that new reimbursement and service consolidation strategies may have in terms of reducing the service needs in rural areas (DeLeon and Wakefield 1995).

The shortage-of-professionals issue has also been taken up by the American Psychological Association (Gaddy 1995). In the mid-1980s, only 28 psychology internship programs had training experiences that specifically addressed work in rural settings. By the mid-1990s, this number had increased to 70 (Gaddy 1995). Although these efforts certainly are noteworthy, if we weigh the size of the problem against the services that have resulted from these efforts, the supply of trained professionals in rural areas is still extremely low; it is predicted to remain so (Blank et al. 1995).

Besides the shortage of psychiatrists and doctoral-level psychologists in rural areas, the same is true for master's-prepared professionals. Currently, many insurance companies will not reimburse master's-level clinicians for the services they provide. As a result, many well-trained professionals who otherwise might be available to work in rural areas simply can't afford to do so. The continuing shortage of mental health professionals assures that the caseloads of those who do work in rural settings are larger than would be the case under more ideal circumstances (Blank et al. 1995; Fox et al. 1995).

Transportation and Inconvenience

Given the shortage of professionals who may be available to provide substance abuse treatment locally, many rural residents who are in need of such services must travel to receive them (Robertson and Donnermeyer 1997). Many people who might benefit from these services do not have ready access to personal transportation (i.e., the young and the old—the predominant age groups in many rural areas (Davidson 1996; Fuguitt 1995). Others, who may in fact have their own transportation, should not be encouraged to use it given the functional impairment that accompanies their substance abuse. Transportation can be less of an issue for residents of rural settings that are adjacent to metropolitan areas: the so-called "metropolitan-rural." The problem is often sharpened, however, for the 46 million people in this country who live in recognizably remote areas, or in communities with populations of less than 10,000 (Hart 1995). If someone needing treatment must travel even moderate distances to receive them, the inconvenience is obviously increased; and so is the likelihood—particularly in the case of outpatient substance abuse treatment—that they will prematurely end their use of much-needed services.

Economic and Insurance Issues

Rural service providers often receive less money for the work they do. For example, Medicare typically pays less for services administered in rural settings than for similar services in urban locations (Meyer 1990). Medicaid coverage is less extensive in rural areas as well: 33 percent of poor rural residents receive Medicaid assistance compared to approximately 51 percent of urban poor residents (Fox et al. 1995).

The insurance status of many people in rural areas is also a critical issue. Depending on the specifics of the policy, insurance can sometimes be used to offset the cost of mental health and substance abuse treatment. A study conducted by the American Psychiatric Association revealed, however, that only 6 percent of insured employees have comparable outpatient coverage for both mental and physical health. Complicating things even more, during the economic decline of the 1980s, many rural families were forced to cancel their insurance coverage as part of a desperate strategy to make ends meet. Tragically, during times of economic hardship, medical care and health insurance are often viewed as luxuries rather than necessities (Davidson 1996; Meyer 1990; Robertson and Donnermeyer 1997). Many small companies and manufacturing firms in rural areas can't (or won't) offer insurance coverage as an employment benefit. For employer and employee alike, the premiums that must be paid are often extreme given the high-risk work that takes place in many rural settings. In 1992, the uninsured rate of nonmetropolitan residents was 15.7 percent higher than the national average. In contrast to poor residents in urban areas, rural poor residents who are uninsured tend to go longer without insurance (Fox et al. 1995).

The 1980s brought drastic reductions in funds that were available to support even bare-bones health, mental health, and social services— including substance abuse treatment. These reductions often occurred because of the depreciated value of farmland, and the out-migration of residents to find employment elsewhere. These departures further depleted the dwindling tax base of many small communities (Robertson and Donnermeyer 1997). Many hospitals in rural areas were forced to close. Of those that remain open, fewer than 10 percent offer psychiatric services (Enright 1994; Fox et al. 1996).

Physician Issues

Given the shortage of professionals who are available to treat people with mental health difficulties in general and substance abuse problems in particular, by default, much of the responsibility for assessment and treatment has shifted to physicians who practice medicine in rural areas. Many have argued that primary care medicine has in fact become the de facto mental health service delivery system in our country (Fox et al. 1995; Hankin et al. 1982; Norquist and Regier 1996; Regier et al. 1978, 1982; Schurman et al. 1985).

Residency education programs for primary care physicians are required to provide at least some training to resident physicians in the assessment and treatment of psychosocial complaints, including substance abuse (Task Force on Objectives 1979, Task Force on the Family 1989). This training mandate is driven by the fact that regardless of the location of their practices—rural, suburban, or urban—primary care physicians see a tremendous number of patients who present with stress-related psychosocial complaints. It is estimated that at least 50 percent of the patients seen by primary care physicians are there for nonmedical reasons (Doherty and Baird 1983; McDaniel et al. 1990). A survey of the mental health difficulties commonly seen by family physicians revealed that substance abuse—in addition to anxiety, depression, obesity, marital discord, and sexual difficulties—is a problem commonly encountered in office-based clinical practice (Cassata and Kirkman-Liff 1981; Philbrinck et al. 1996). Leckman et al. (1984) examined the prevalence of alcoholism among patients served in an outpatient family practice center. Based on information derived from the Michigan Alcoholism Screening Test, 42.9 percent of the patients surveyed reported being alcoholic themselves, or having an immediate or extended family member who struggled with alcohol abuse.

Despite the prevalence of these problems in their practices, physicians often express reservations about working with people experiencing problems like anxiety, depression, and substance abuse. And although there are a number of reasons for these reservations (Williamson et al. 1981), in the end, many of them are directly related to physician concerns that they have not been adequately trained to work with people who have these presenting problems.

Hendryx et al. (1994) compared the mental health practices of rural and urban physicians. They found few differences between rural and urban physicians in terms of the estimated prevalence of particular mental health difficulties (including substance abuse) seen in their practices. The physicians were also similar in the lack of confidence they expressed in their ability to treat patients who abuse substances. They reported being more confident working with patients experiencing anxiety and depression. Our hunch is that the physicians expressed greater confidence regarding these problems because a host of medications are available that make the office-based management of these difficulties easier (Frohberg and Herting Jr. 1997). There has been less success, however, in the psychopharmacologic management of drug and alcohol abuse (O'Brien and McKay 1998). Successful treatment of these problems often necessitates a willingness by patients and clinicians alike to move beyond a strict focus on substance consumption to a discussion of particular circumstances in the lives of patients—what Mishler (1988) calls the lifeworld of patients—that constrain alternative, less destructive behaviors.

Despite the reservations that physicians voice about their ability to treat patients who abuse substances, there is evidence that with the use of standardized, problem-focused treatment protocols, they can successfully reduce the substance-abusing behaviors of their patients. Fleming et al. (1997) investigated the use of a brief, workbook-based intervention protocol by physicians. The intervention specifically targeted problem alcohol drinkers who were seen for outpatient medical services. Following the use of the intervention protocol, significant reductions were reported in both alcohol intake and associated health care utilization for men and women who at the start of the study, reported drinking 14-plus and 11-plus drinks per week, respectively. These results were obtained following only two 15-minute visits (scheduled one month apart) with their physicians, and two brief follow-up telephone conversations with a nurse shortly after each physician visit. There is also evidence that as little as five minutes of physician counseling with problem drinkers can significantly reduce levels of alcohol consumption (WHO Brief Intervention Study Group 1996). Clancy (n.d.) has also devised an intervention protocol for physicians. Entitled the Rapid Introduction to Drug and Alcohol Rehabilitation (RaIDAR), the protocol uses a series of handouts and worksheets to structure the conversations that physicians have with patients who are struggling with alcohol problems. These intervention protocols offer particular promise to busy rural physicians who, regardless of the extent of their formal training in substance abuse treatment, are often the sole purveyors of treatment services for the patients they see.

Patients with Dual Diagnoses

There is growing awareness that many people who struggle with substance abuse problems also experience additional mental health difficulties. The literature consistently has revealed that the association of these problems is greater than would be expected by chance alone (Howland 1995; Regier et al. 1990). One-third of patients who receive general psychiatric care also have substance abuse problems that clearly influence their mental health status. Similarly, two-thirds of the patients who enter substance abuse treatment programs also experience accompanying psychiatric difficulties (Donnermeyer 1997). In terms of treatment, the dual-diagnosis issue presents unique challenges for professionals. The interaction of the coexisting conditions results in a clinical entity that is often difficult to assess and treat. These patients often don't respond well to standard treatments, and frequently are noncompliant with the recommendations that are made. They tend to utilize emergency and inpatient medical services frequently, and in contrast to patients with single identified problems, are at particular risk for suicide and violence (Howland 1995).

Although these patients would present a challenge wherever they reside, their treatment in rural settings is often particularly challenging. Besides the fact that there typically are not enough trained professionals to meet the service needs in rural areas, and that existing professionals already often have large caseloads, there are even fewer professionals who have been specifically trained to treat patients with dual diagnoses. Also, even in areas that are fortunate enough to have access to basic (and usually distinct) mental health and substance abuse treatment services, coordination between these service delivery systems is often quite minimal. Careful coordination is an essential component to any treatment effort that targets this treatment population (Howland 1995).

SUMMARY

In the sections above, we have presented information that at the very least suggests the following:

- Substance abuse is prevalent in both urban and rural areas
- Factors that increase and decrease the risk of substance abuse have been identified
- A number of significant consequences result from substance abuse and dependence
- Although substance abuse treatment can be effective, specialized treatment services are in short supply in rural areas, and are likely to remain so

In light of these factors, the fundamental question becomes, "*What should be done in the future to better address the problem of rural substance abuse?*"

Although there is evidence that substance abuse treatment can be effective (Finney and Moos 1998), a more panoramic view suggests that in all parts of the county, the so-called "war on drugs,"—what Duke (1994) refers to as "America's longest war"—has been characterized by few sustained victories. Efforts in this regard have included mandatory sentencing laws for substance abusers, increases in the numbers of police, the construction of more and larger prisons to house convicted offenders, and increased minimum drinking ages, etc. However, there is surprisingly little evidence that these efforts have in fact reduced the overall substance abuse problem. It therefore seems unwise to argue that the best solution would be to do more of what is already being done.

Instead, we think that the greatest successes in reducing the problem of substance abuse—in urban and rural settings alike—are likely to come after a change in the general philosophy that has guided traditional intervention efforts. Government officials and policy makers need to allocate funds differently. The focus needs to be on prevention rather than punishment, and treatment rather than interdiction. More programs need to be created that have at their core existing information concerning the influences that appear to diminish the likelihood that substance abuse will occur (see Risk Factors and Protective Factors above). Such programs will be relevant not only for rural areas that historically have been underserved, but also for those that are comparatively "service rich." Particular attention should be given to innovative programs that build on strengths that already exist in families and communities.

Reevaluating Substance Abuse

There must be a change in the mindset concerning how the problem of substance abuse can and should be addressed. Through a variety of efforts—media, community-, school-, and church-based education—rural residents must learn that there are things that can be done to prevent substance abuse. An increased sense of agency, the idea that people can play an active role in shaping their lives (White 1993), will be a critical component in this shift toward prevention. We are not arguing that formal treatment for people struggling with substance abuse is unimportant. However, although it can be effective, as has been stated, treatment is often costly, time-consuming, and hard to find. Under ideal circumstances, treatment should be available to those who need it. But ultimately, if fewer people struggle with substance abuse as a result of more carefully organized and adequately funded prevention efforts, the need for treatment services will be reduced. One particular challenge for the future will be to discover ways that prevention can be facilitated through the use of technologies like television and the Internet.

Parenting Behavior

Improved parenting must be a central component of all prevention efforts. The evidence summarized above in the section on Risk Factors and Protective Factors clearly suggests that a number of parenting practices are associated with decreases in child and adolescent substance abuse. Parents need to monitor the behavior of their children.

They must be encouraged to make efforts to know what their children are doing when the parents are not around, to learn about the behavior of their children when they are at school and with friends, and to minimize the amount of time that is spent without adult supervision. Parents also need to develop skills in limit setting. And very importantly, they need to spend time nurturing and interacting with their children.

It is important to recognize that these parenting behaviors do not necessarily come naturally—especially for parents who may not have experienced them during their own upbringing. However, these behaviors can be learned. There must be a redistribution of funds so more money is available for educational programs that aid parents in the acquisition of good parenting skills. Prevention efforts also must include better services that can aid both dual- and single-parent households that are experiencing poverty, social isolation, and, for whatever reason, an inability to engage in those parenting behaviors that exert a protective influence on their children (Biglan et al. 1997).

Better Helping Networks

At the community level, rural residents should be encouraged to become a part of informal helping networks. These networks could be built under the auspices of more formalized self-help groups, or through less-structured neighborhood collaboration. If prevention is to succeed, families need to work to come together in the service of developing a stronger psychological sense of community (Sarason 1974). They must learn to support, help, and educate one another, and to realize that requests for assistance (e.g., with parenting advice, child monitoring, etc.) are not admissions of failure but rather, essential ingredients of preventive community involvement.

Training Teachers and Administrators

Directly and indirectly, schools can play a central role in the prevention of substance abuse. Families need to understand the important role that schools can play in the prevention effort. It also needs to be recognized that teamwork and collaboration between families and schools will increase the likelihood of a successful outcome (Rosenthal and Sawyers 1996).

Following Biglan et al. (1997), we would recommend that school personnel begin or continue prevention efforts in three specific ways: (1) they can provide in-school prevention programs that encourage students not to use alcohol and drugs. At a minimum, these programs should address the consequences of drug and alcohol abuse, dispel the myths that often accompany substance use, and teach appropriate methods for tension reduction; (2) through a careful examination of instructional practice, they can identify school-based factors that ideally will minimize occurrences of school failure. Academic failure is a powerful predictor of both the initiation and continued use of substances; and (3) school personnel can learn more quickly to identify students at risk for substance abuse and initiate efforts to address the problem. With reference to student identification, the most successful efforts at prevention are typically those that are initiated sooner rather than later. There is evidence, for example, that the risk of eventual substance abuse or dependence doubles for individuals with a prior history of anxiety disorders or depressive episodes (Christie et al. 1988). At the very least, this suggests that some instances of substance abuse might be prevented with early detection and appropriate treatment for precipitating affective conditions. Anyone who has regular contact with children and adolescents—parents, teachers, doctors—should become familiar with the signs and symptoms of these conditions and knowledgeable of existing treatment options.

Physician Education

Given the indispensable role they play in providing health care to rural residents, their reticence about working with psychosocial difficulties, and the evidence that exists that clearly indicates that physicians can have an impact in terms of reducing the substance use of their patients, rural primary care physicians need to be better trained to assess and manage patients with substance abuse problems. This recommendation has clear implications for those who train physicians who plan to work in rural areas. During their training, at the very least, physicians should have opportunities to assess and treat patients who are using/abusing a variety of substances. Much like their involvement with patients suffering any number of medical complaints, physicians should have enough supervised experience in assessment and intervention that these skills ultimately can be implemented with ease. This means that these skills should not simply be learned, but overlearned. Given the service realities in many rural areas, it is very likely that primary care physicians will continue to play a crucial role in the assessment and treatment of substance abuse problems (Norris et al. 1996).

CODA

So what outcome might result from an increased emphasis on prevention? Given the extent of the substance abuse problem in the U.S., it is easy to pessimistically conclude that the factors that facilitate the problem must be easier to come by than those that would otherwise contain it. Although we think that a shift toward prevention must be an essential ingredient in future efforts to address rural substance abuse, we have no illusions that this will ever solve the problem entirely. There is every reason to believe that the words "suffering," "substance abuse," and "treatment" will remain inexorably linked. It is equally plausible, however, that a shift toward prevention will make it possible to slowly attain a better outcome; one in which there is simultaneously a reduced need for treatment, and a better appreciation of the protective influences that families, schools, neighborhoods, and churches can have on the individuals they encompass.

REFERENCES

Abel, E. 1984. *Fetal alcohol syndrome.* New York: Plenum Press.

American Psychiatric Association. 1994. *Diagnostic and statistical manual of mental disorders* (4th edition). Washington, D. C.: American Psychiatric Association.

Ary, D. V., E. Tildesley, H. Hops, and J. A. Andrews. 1993. "The influence of parent, sibling, and peer modeling and attitudes on adolescent use of alcohol." *International Journal of the Addictions* 28: 853–80.

Bahr, S. J., and R. D. Hawks, 1995. "Religious organizations." In *Handbook on drug abuse prevention: A comprehensive strategy to prevent the abuse of alcohol and other drugs,* ed. R. H. Coombs, and D. Ziedonis, 159–79. Boston: Allyn and Bacon.

Bahr, S. J., A. C. Marcos, and S. L. Maughan. 1995. "Family, educational and peer influences on the alcohol use of female and male adolescents." *Journal of Studies on Alcohol* 56: 457–69.

Bahr, S. J., S. L. Maughan, A. C. Marcos, and B. Li. 1998. "Family, religiosity, and the risk of adolescent drug use." *Journal of Marriage and the Family* 60: 979–92.

Berry, Wendell. 1977. *The unsettling of America: Culture and agriculture.* San Francisco: Sierra Club Books.

___. 1996. "Conserving communities." In *Rooted in the land: Essays on community and place,* ed. W. Vitek, and W. Jackson, 76–84. New Haven: Yale University Press.

Biglan, Anthony, T. Duncan, A. B. Irvine, D. Ary, K. Smolkowski, and L. James. 1997. "A drug abuse prevention strategy for rural America." In *Rural substance abuse: State of knowledge and issues.* National Institute on Drug Abuse Research Monograph no. 168, 364–97. Washington, D.C.: National Institute on Drug Abuse.

Blank, M. B., J. C. Fox, D. S. Hargrove, and J. T. Turner. 1995. "Critical issues in reforming rural mental health service delivery." *Community Mental Health Journal* 31: 511–24.

Blazer, Dan, B. A. Crowell Jr., and L. K. George. 1987. "Alcohol abuse and dependence in the rural south." *Archives of General Psychiatry* 44: 736–40.

Bloch, L. P., L . J. Crockett, and J. R. Vicary. 1991. "Antecedents of rural adolescent alcohol use: A risk factor approach." *Journal of Drug Education* 21: 361–77.

Brecher, Edward M. 1972. *Licit and illicit drugs.* Boston: Little, Brown.

Bureau of the Census. 1985. *Census geography: Concepts and products.* Washington, D.C.: U.S. Government Printing Office.

Cassata, D. M., and B. L. Kirkman-Liff. 1981. "Mental health activities of family physicians." *Journal of Family Practice* 12: 683–92.

Castle, Emery N. 1995. "The forgotten hinterlands." In *The changing American countryside: Rural people and place,* ed. Emery N. Castle, 3–9. Lawrence: University of Kansas Press.

Christie, Kimberly A., J. D. Burke Jr., D. A. Regier, D. S. Ray, J. H. Boyd, and B. Z. Locke. 1988. "Epidemiologic evidence for early onset of mental disorders and higher risk for drug use in young adults." *American Journal of Psychiatry* 145: 971–75.

Clancy, Gerald P. n.d. *Rapid introduction to drug and alcohol rehabilitation.* Iowa City: University of Iowa Department of Psychiatry.

Colsher, Patricia L., and R. B. Wallace. 1990. "Elderly men with histories of heavy drinking: Correlates and consequences." *Journal of Studies on Alcohol* 51: 528–35.

Conry, Julianne. 1990. "Neuropsychological deficits in fetal alcohol syndrome and fetal alcohol effects." *Alcoholism: Clinical Experimental Research* 14: 650–55.

Davidson, Osha Gray. 1986. "The rise of the rural ghetto: Small towns in trouble." *The Nation* 14 June, 820, 822.

Davidson, Osha Gray. 1996. *Broken heartland: The rise of America's rural ghetto* (second edition). Iowa City: University of Iowa Press.

DeLeon, Pat, and M. S. Wakefield. 1995. "The senate rural caucus catalyzing innovative rural health initiatives." *Rural Health Bulletin* 2: 1–2 [On-line]. Available: http://www.apa.org/rural/rbullet2.html#art2. 6/18/98.

Department of Health and Human Services. 1990a. "Alcohol and other drugs." In *Healthy people 2000: National health promotion and disease prevention objectives.* DHHS Publication no. PHS 91-50212, 164–65. Washington, D.C.: U.S. Government Printing Office.

———. 1990b. "Introduction." In *Healthy people 2000: National health promotion and disease prevention objectives.* DHHS Publication no. PHS 91-50212, 5. Washington, D.C.: U.S. Government Printing Office.

———. 1994. "Effects of alcohol on behavior and safety." In *Eighth special report to the U. S. Congress on alcohol and health.* DHHS Publication no. NIH 94-3699, 233–50. Washington, D.C.: U.S. Government Printing Office.

Doherty, William J., and M. A. Baird. 1983. *Family therapy and family medicine.* New York: The Guilford Press.

Donnermeyer, Joseph F. 1997. "The economic and social costs of drug abuse among the rural population." In *Rural substance abuse: State of knowledge and issues.* National Institute on Drug Abuse Research Monograph, No. 168, 220–45. Washington, D.C.: National Institute on Drug Abuse.

Duke, S. B. 1993. *America's longest war.* New York: Putnam's Sons.

Enright, Michael. 1994 Summer. "American Psychological Association responds." *Rural Health Bulletin* 2: 2–3 [On line]. Available: http://www.apa.org/rural/rbullet1.html.

Fagan, J., and E. Pabon. 1990. "Contributions of delinquency and substance abuse to school dropout among inner-city youths." *Youth Society* 21: 306–54.

Finke, L., J. Chorpenning, B. French, C. Leese, and M. Siegel. 1996. "Drug and alcohol use of school-age children in a rural community." *Journal of School Nursing* 12: 10–13.

Finney, John W., and R. H. Moos. 1998. "Psychosocial treatments for alcohol use disorders." In *A guide to treatments that work*, ed. Peter E. Nathan, and Jack M. Gorman, 156–66. New York: Oxford University Press.

Fitchen, Janet M. 1995. "Why rural poverty is growing worse: Similar causes in diverse settings." In *The changing American countryside: Rural people and places*, ed. Emery N. Castle, 247–67. Lawrence: University of Kansas Press.

Fleming, M. F., K. L. Barry, L. B. Manwell, K. Johnson, and R. London. 1997. "Brief physician advice for problem alcohol drinkers: A randomized controlled trial in community-based primary care." *JAMA* 277: 1039–45.

Fox, J., E. Merwin, and M. Blank. 1995. "De facto mental health services in the rural south." *Journal of Health Care for the Poor and Underserved* 6: 434–68.

Frohberg, Nora R., and R. L. Herting Jr. 1997. "Psychiatry." In *The family practice handbook* (third edition), ed. Mark A. Graber, Peter P. Toth, and Robert L. Herting Jr., 598–626. St. Louis: Mosby-Year Book, Inc.

Fuguitt, Glenn V. 1995. "Population change in nonmetropolitan America." In *The changing American countryside: Rural people and places*, ed. Emery N. Castle, 77–100. Lawrence: University of Kansas Press.

Gaddy, Catherine D. 1995 Summer. "Psychology training programs offering rural focus double in past decade." In *Rural Health Bulletin*, 2: 3–4 [On-line]. Available: http://www.apa.org/rural/rbullet2.html#art2.6/18198.

Gibbons, S., M. L. Wylie, and L. Echterling. 1986. "Situational factors related to rural adolescent alcohol use." *The International Journal of Addictions* 21: 1183–95.

Gunby, P. 1989. "Weekends, rural roads, alcohol among risk factors gleaned from traffic death data." *JAMA* 262: 2196.

Hankin, J. R., D. M. Steinwachs, D. A. Regier, B. J. Burns, I. D. Goldberg, and E. W. Hoeper. 1982. "Use of general medical services by persons with mental disorders." *Archives of General Psychiatry* 39: 225–31.

Hart, John Fraser. 1995. "'Rural' and 'farm' no longer mean the same." In *The changing American countryside: Rural people and places*, ed. Emery N. Castle, 63–76. Lawrence: University of Kansas Press.

Helzer, J. E., Burnam, A., and L. T. McEvoy. 1991. "Alcohol abuse and dependence." In *Psychiatric disorders in America: the epidemiologic catchment areas study*, ed. L. E. Robins, and D. A. Regier. New York: Free Press.

Hendryx, Michael S., B. N. Doebbeling, and D. L. Kearns. 1994. "Mental health treatment in primary care: Physician treatment choices and psychiatric admission rates." *Family Practice Research Journal* 14: 127–37.

Holroyd, S., L. Currie, A. Thompson-Heisterman, and L. Abraham. 1997. "A descriptive study of elderly community-dwelling alcoholic patients in the rural South." *The American Journal of Psychiatry* 5: 221–28.

Howland, R. H. 1995. "Treatment of persons with dual diagnoses in a rural community." *Psychiatric Quarterly* 66: 33–49.

Jackson, Wes. 1996. "Matfield Green." In *Rooted in the land: Essays on community and place*, ed. William Vitek, and Wes Jackson, 95–103. New Haven: Yale University Press.

Jajoura, G. 1993. "Does dropping out of school enhance delinquent involvement? Results from a large-scale national probability sample." *Criminology* 31: 149–72.

Kelleher, K. J., V. I. Rickert, B. H. Hardin, S. K. Pope, and F. L. Farmer. 1992. "Rurality and gender: Effects on early adolescent alcohol use." *American Journal of Diseases of Children* 146: 317–22.

Kelleher, K. J., and J. M. Robbins. 1997. "Social and economic consequences of rural alcohol use." In *Rural substance abuse: State of knowledge and issues*. National Institute on Drug Abuse Research Monograph, No. 168, 196–19. Washington, D.C.: National Institute on Drug Abuse.

Kenkel, Mary Beth. 1996 spring. "Rural women's work group meets." *Rural Health Bulletin*, 3: 1–2 [On-line]. Available: http://www.apa.org/rural/rbullet3.html.

Knesper, D. J., D. J. Pagnucco, and J. R. C. Wheeler. 1985. "Similarities and differences across mental health services providers and practice settings in the United States." *American Psychologist* 40: 1352–69.

Leckman, A. Lane, B. E. Umland, and M. Blay. 1984. "Alcoholism in the families of family practice outpatients." *Journal of Family Practice* 19: 205–7.

Leigh, B. C., M. T. Temple, and K. F. Trocki. 1993. "The sexual behavior of U. S. adults: Results from a national survey." *American Journal of Public Health* 83: 1400–8.

Long, K. A., and R. J. Boik. 1993. "Predicting alcohol use in rural children: A longitudinal study." *Nursing Research* 42: 79–86.

Meyer, H. 1990. "Rural America: Surmounting the obstacles to mental health care." *Minnesota Medicine* 73: 24–31.

Mishler, Elliott G. 1984. *The discourse of medicine: Dialectics of medical interviews*. Norwood, N.J.: Ablex Publishing Corporation.

Norris, Kathleen. 1993. *Dakota: A spiritual biography*. Boston: Houghton Mifflin.

———. 1998. On "The farmer's wife," 1–4. [On-line]. Available: http//www.pbs.org/wgbh/pages/frontline/shows/farmerswife/essays/norris.html. 9/25/98.

Norris, T. E., J. B. Coombs, and J. Carline. 1996. "An educational needs assessment of rural family physicians." *Journal of the American Board of Family Practice* 9: 86–93.

Norquist, G. S., and D. A. Regier. 1996. "The epidemiology of psychiatry disorders and the de facto mental health care system." *Annual Review of Medicine* 47: 473–79.

O'Brien, C. P., and J. R. McKay. 1998. "Psychopharmacological treatments of substance abuse disorders." In *A guide to treatments that work*, ed. Peter E. Nathan and Jack M. Gorman, 127–55. New York: Oxford University Press.

Oetting, E. R., R. W. Edwards, K. Kelly, and F Beauvais. 1997. "Risk and protective factors for drug use among rural American youth." In *Rural substance abuse: State of knowledge and issues*, National Institute on Drug Abuse Research Monograph, no. 168, 90–130. Washington, D.C.: National Institute on Drug Abuse.

Peterson, P. L., J. D. Hawkins, R. D. Abbott, and R. F. Catalano. 1994. "Disentangling the effects of parental drinking, family management, and parental norms on current drinking by black and white adolescents." *Journal of Research on Adolescence* 4: 203–27.

Philbrink, John T., J. E. Connelly, and A. B. Wofford. 1996. "The prevalence of mental disorders in rural office practice." *Journal of General Internal Medicine* 11: 9–15.

Pope, S. K., P. D. Smith, J. B. Wayne, K. J. Kelleher. 1994. "Gender differences in rural adolescent drinking patterns." *Journal of Adolescent Health* 15: 359–65.

Pothier, P. 1991. "Demythologizing rural mental health." *Archives of General Psychiatry* V: 119–20.

Regier, D. A., I. D. Goldberg, and C. A. Taube. 1978. "The de facto U. S. mental health services system: A public health perspective." *Archives of General Psychiatry* 35: 685–93.

Regier D. A., I. D. Goldberg, B. J. Burns, J. Hankin,, E. W. Hoeper, and G. R. Nycz. 1982. "Specialist/generalist division of responsibility for patients with mental disorders." *Archives of General Psychiatry* 39: 219–24.

Regier, D. A., M. E. Farmer, D. S. Rae. B. Z. Locke, S. J. Keith, L. L. Judd, and F. K. Goodwin. 1990. "Comorbidity of mental disorders with alcohol and other drug abuse: Results from the epidemiologic catchment area (ECA) study." *JAMA* 264: 2511–18.

Robertson, E. B., and J. F. Donnermeyer. 1997. "Illegal drug use among rural adults: Mental health consequences and treatment utilization." *American Journal of Drug and Alcohol Abuse* 23: 467–84.

Roof, W. C. 1979. "Concepts and indicators of religious commitment: A critical review." In *The religious dimension*, ed. R. Wuthnow, 17–45. New York: Academic Press.

Rosenthal, David M., and J. Y. Sawyers. 1996. "Building successful home/school partnerships: Strategies for parent support and involvement." *Childhood Education*, 72: 194–200.

Sarason, Seymour B. 1974. *The psychological sense of community: Prospects for a community psychology*. San Francisco: Jossey-Bass.

Sarvela, P. D., and E. J. McClendon. 1988. "Indicators of rural youth drug use." *Journal of Youth and Adolescence* 17: 335–47.

Sarvela, P. D., D. J. Pape, J. Odulana, and S. M. Bajracharya. 1990. "Drinking, drug use, and driving among rural midwestern youth." *Journal of School Health* 60: 215–19.

Scheidt, D. M., and M. Windle. 1995. "The alcoholics in treatment HIV risk (ATRISK) study: Gender, ethnic and geographic group comparisons." *Journal of Studies on Alcohol* 56: 300–8.

Schurman, R. A., P. D. Kramer, and J. B. Mitchell, 1985. "The hidden mental health network: Treatment of mental illness by nonpsychiatrist physicians." *Archives of General Psychiatry* 42: 89–94.

Sleek, Scott. 1998. "Experts scramble on school shootings." *American Psychological Association Monitor* 29: 1, 35–36.

Sloane, L. B., J. W. Gay, S. W. Snyder, and W. R. Bales. 1992. "Substance abuse during pregnancy in a rural population." *Obstetrics and Gynecology* 79: 245–48.

Task Forces on the Family in Family Medicine. 1979. *A resource of objectives for training in family medicine: An "atlas."* Kansas City, Mo.

Task Force on Objectives, Education Committee. 1989. *The family in family medicine: Graduate curriculum and teaching strategies* (2nd edition). Kansas City, Mo.

Stanton, M. Duncan, T. C. Todd, and Associates. 1982. *The family therapy of drug abuse and addiction*. New York: The Guilford Press.

Stevens, Marguerite, F. Youells, F. Whaley, and Susan Linsey. 1995. "Drug use prevalence in a rural school-age population: The New Hampshire survey." *American Journal of Preventive Medicine* 11: 105–13.

White, Michael. 1993. "Deconstruction and therapy." In *Therapeutic conversations*, ed. Stephen Gilligan and Reese Price, 22–61. New York: W. W. Norton.

Williamson, P., B. D. Beitman, and W. Katon. 1981. "Beliefs that foster physician avoidance of psychosocial aspects of medicine." *Journal of Family Practice* 13: 999–1003.

Windle, M. A. 1993. "A retrospective measure of childhood behavior problems and its use in predicting adolescent problem behaviors." *Journal of Studies on Alcohol* 54: 422–31.

Wolford, C., and J. Swisher. 1986. "Behavioral intention as an indicator of drug and alcohol use." *Journal of Drug Education* 16: 305–26.

World Health Organization Brief Intervention Study Group. 1996. "Across national trial of brief intervention with heavy drinkers." *American Journal of Public Health* 86: 948–55.

Zweben, A. 1986. "Problem drinking and marital adjustment." *Journal of Studies on Alcohol* 47: 167–72.

Faces on the Data: Access to Health Care for People with Disabilities Living in Rural Communities

PHYLLIS LEVINE, DENISE LISHNER, MARY RICHARDSON, AND ALICE PORTER

ACCESS TO ADEQUATE HEALTH CARE SERVICES AND RESOURCES is a critical problem for people living in rural communities in America. Rural Americans in general receive fewer specialized services, travel farther to obtain these services, and have fewer choices than do non-rural residents. Compared with their urban counterparts, rural Americans are more likely to contract chronic health conditions, to experience injuries, and to be in poor health. The health care that is available in rural communities is generally less specialized than in urban areas, despite the fact that rural residents, on average, pay a greater share of their incomes for health services.

For people with disabilities living in rural communities, access is even more complicated. They often face such barriers to care as communication problems, providers with little experience working with disabilities, and physical isolation. The major causes of disability throughout the life span are birth defects and developmental disabilities, injuries, and disease and chronic conditions associated with aging. Evidence indicates that, in addition to age, ethnicity, and lower socioeconomic status, rural residence is a primary risk factor for incurring disabling conditions. Approximately 54 million Americans report some level of disability, according to the latest report from the U.S. Census Bureau, and 26 million describe their disability as severe. A disproportionate share of people with disabilities in the United States live in rural areas, where access to health care is further complicated by factors of geographic distance, weak local economies, and fewer health care providers (Greenwood 1995).

BACKGROUND

Several years ago, Washington State and the federal government were considering major reform of the health services delivery system. At that time and with financing from the federal Agency for Health Care Policy and Research (AHCPR), the University of Washington Center for Disability Policy and Research (CDPR) and the Washington, Wyoming, Alaska, Montana, and Idaho (WWAMI) Rural Health Research Center (RHRC) began to research how people with disabilities living in rural communities access and obtain health and social services. This work included a comprehensive review of academic articles, reports, and other literature (Lishner, Richardson, Levine, and Patrick 1996), and a secondary analysis of national data sets. Most importantly, we visited rural areas and met with people with disabilities, their families, and those who provide them care.

WHAT THE LITERATURE SAYS

There has been little serious research about access to health care for people with disabilities in rural areas. What analysis does exist suggests that the health care system has seriously neglected the complex medical and social service needs of these individuals.

A comprehensive literature review conducted by CDPR and colleagues demonstrates that major barriers impeding access to care include difficulty in attracting and retaining qualified health care professionals, lack of training for primary care providers to treat the complex needs associated with a wide variety of disabling conditions, and a lack of population base and resources necessary to offer highly specialized services (Lishner, Richardson, Levine, and Patrick 1996). In sum:

- There are severe obstacles to using customary sources of primary care, often because physicians' offices are inaccessible or because providers tend to focus more on patients' disabilities on than their immediate health problems.
- Primary care physicians in rural areas generally lack the training and experience necessary to identify, treat and refer individuals with disabilities.
- Remote areas may lack the population base and resources needed to offer specialized services.
- Rehabilitation services are usually based in large, urban areas.

These barriers persist across different ages and circumstances:

- Rural areas have a high proportion of children and adolescents with disabilities, often living in poverty. Poor rural children experience significant problems accessing primary care, traveling to health care providers, and receiving adequate continuity of care. Centers for treatment of children with physical disabilities are usually located in centralized urban areas, and families incur crushing expense when they seek services far from home. Medically fragile children in rural areas face limited availability of qualified home care. Locally available services are offered infrequently, are usually fragmented, and are often obtained from itinerant providers (Newacheck 1989; McManus, Newacheck, and Weader 1990, Levey, Curry, and Levey 1988; Malach and Segel 1990; Fiene and Taylor 1993; Clark 1990).
- Agricultural workers show a high prevalence of respiratory disorders, cancer, neurological problems, injuries and traumatic deaths, exposure to chemicals, hearing loss, and stress. However, rural hospitals may lack the technological advances and other resources to handle severe injuries and address other disability-related needs. Access to adequate health care is constrained by lack of practitioners within a reasonable distance, limited access to technological advances, hospital closures, and lower health care funding in rural areas (Donham and Thu 1993; Wright 1993; Zejda, McDuffie, and Dosman 1993; Emanuel, Draves, and Nycz 1990).
- The rural elderly report more chronic illness and physical impairment than do their urban counterparts, but they have less access to health services. They are less likely than urban residents to receive formal assistance in every activity of daily living, and a lower proportion use home health services (Manton 1989; Dwyer and Miller 1990; Clark 1992; Lang 1982; Halpert 1988).
- Among rural residents who need mental health services, only one in five is seen by mental health professionals. Few rural hospitals have full-time staff for psychiatric emergencies and many lack qualified psychiatric professionals. Rural areas usually have limited availability of such services as suicide prevention, crisis intervention, and individual counseling. Rural residents fail to obtain psychiatric services they may need because of poverty, low levels of education, stigma associated with mental illness, lack of anonymity in small towns, and geographic and climatic conditions that limit access to health care facilities (Ellis and Gordon 1991; Bachrach 1983; Pothier 1991; Wegenfeld 1990; Runyan and Faria 1992; Thomas 1988; Meyer 1991).
- There is a growing concern about whether rural systems can

provide adequate health care and social services to meet the
needs of people with HIV infection and AIDS. AIDS patients in
rural locations are often victimized by discrimination as well as
shortages of health care personnel and support. Lack of medical
insurance, distances to public clinics, delays in testing, and lack
of adequately trained providers all discourage early medical
intervention for treatment of AIDS in rural areas (Tokarski
1990; Rounds 1988; Alsup and Narramore 1992).

WHAT WE DID

The project's primary goal was to examine access to health care for
people with disabilities living in rural America. We used both quantitative and qualitative methods of inquiry in this component of the
project. Focus group forums and structured telephone interviews
conducted with key informants were the primary sources of data.

We selected five rural counties in Washington state that are representative of diverse rural areas, using criteria such as low population
density and proximity to metropolitan areas, as well as ethnic and
racial diversity, economic characteristics, and distance and geographic barriers between the communities and large (tertiary) health
care centers. We also considered the share of local children living in
poverty, access to timely prenatal care, rates of births to school-age
mothers, and unemployment rates. The sites selected were communities in Ferry, Stevens, and Pend Oreille counties (in northeast
Washington), Yakima County (in south central Washington), and
Skagit County (in northwest Washington).

PRIORITY AREAS

Participants in the forums and interviews were drawn from diverse
backgrounds, income levels, and perspectives, representing different
ages (ranging from 9 to 85 years of age), genders, disability types, and
ethnic and racial groups. In their forum comments and responses to
questions, however, ten central themes emerged repeatedly as "priority areas" affecting access to health care for people with disabilities
in rural communities. What ties these issues together is the desire—
expressed frequently during forums and individual interviews—to
live a secure life, as free as possible from unnecessary external barriers. Following are the ten priority areas illustrated with information
from the interviews and quotations from our forums.

POVERTY, EMPLOYMENT,
AND HEALTH CARE COVERAGE

People with disabilities grapple with unavoidable money issues: poverty, unemployment, and reliance on such public programs as Medicare, Medicaid, and federal disability (SSI). Financial resources are closely connected with health care access. During forums and interviews, people spoke of providers who refuse to accept patients with medical coupons, of low-paid employment without health care benefits, and of inability to pay for costly services. Rural areas tend to be poorer than urban areas, with fewer education opportunities and employment options that provide benefits, and there is a higher prevalence of disability in rural areas. All these factors are associated with high-risk health behaviors.

The majority of informants with disabilities reported annual incomes well below the federal poverty levels, (over two thirds between $5,001 and $15,000, and almost ten percent as less than $5,000). Only one-third of these informants were married, with half reporting being divorced. The annual income levels of the family informants were only slightly higher (less than half between $15,000 and $25,001, and one third at $15,000 and less), reflecting perhaps the higher percentage who were married (70 percent). The majority of the informants had graduated from high school, and half of each group had attended college, though only a few informants earned a bachelor degree or more. Only just over one-quarter of informants with disabilities reported being employed and the majority of these jobs were low-paying and without benefits. Though more than half of the family informants were employed, only a small share had jobs that included benefits. A majority of our family informants were mothers, and many of these were unemployed so that they could stay home to care for their children with disabilities.

> The first thing that everyone starts talking about is what can we eliminate, what can we do without; let's cut this and let's cut that and let's cut mental health, and PT [physical therapy] and OT [occupational therapy] and speech really isn't that important. Let's just dump the kids on the school system, let them pick it up; and then again, who gets the short end of the stick? The clients.
>
> Talking about individuals having their Medicaid dropped as they start employment . . . the jobs available in the community are minimum-wage, part-time jobs. . . . If they're encouraged to be employed, there are no benefits available to them. And there is no stopgap measure there for individuals who are making that transition from Medicaid to employment.

Bureaucratic and System Hassles

People with disabilities, their families, and associates spoke of making their way through confounding and frustrating bureaucracy. Eligibility criteria for public programs are often confusing and contradictory. Program clients often lack information to "work the system" effectively. And they fear cutbacks in services they need.

Almost all of the informants with disabilities and all family informants reported having some type of health care financing—including Medicare, Medicaid, employee benefits, self-pay, private insurance, and others—but only slightly more than half expressed satisfaction with the coverage.

When asked about being refused or rejected by insurance, half of the service and health care providers said this was experienced by their clients and patients, compared with only one-quarter of informants with disabilities and family informants. Reimbursement from insurance was a problem for half of each of the informant groups. A small percentage of informants with disabilities and family informants (one-fifth) said that the lack or type of insurance influenced how often they went to the health care provider, compared to three-quarters of service providers and health care providers who remarked that this was the case with their clients and patients.

> So, you went through everything, all the paperwork, and you filled out everything and went through all the channels and you finally got it, but it took forever—it took a year. This 45-minute interview and 200 pages of paperwork . . . and then this lady says, "Well, I have the final stamp," that's exactly what she told me, I have the final stamp. No services. Whoa.

Inadequate Information, Communication, and Connections

During forums and interviews, individuals spoke of issues such as lack of interpreters for deaf clients and those with limited English proficiency, and of insufficient information networks to inform people with disabilities about availability of programs and services. Many people never hear about existing programs, their eligibility for these programs, or how to access specific services. They remarked on the insufficient public awareness and education regarding the needs of people with disabilities.

We asked the informants to rate their own knowledge of health care services. The informants with disabilities seem less knowledgeable about health care services and available information than the family members we interviewed. The majority of both groups say they have someone to contact for services, but very few feel there is enough information available in the community.

> [Just because you're deaf] doesn't mean you can benefit from an interpreter. You've got to be able to sign and understand what's going on. We have to find alternative methods of communication.

> Getting the information back and forth, that's something doesn't happen on its own. . . . I call him and say I need a report, then he'll send the letter to the primary care physician, which is not a complete documentation of the tests or things that have been done but just is a very brief summary

> The issue is communication. One of the people who I work with is not clearly articulate. . . . Well, in suggesting that maybe an advocate could go with him to help communicate, this was poo-pooed as it's not necessary by the medical staff. The doctor came in the room, initiated a conversation, and didn't understand the response. There needs to be more advocacy and efforts toward active communicating when you have a deficit.

INADEQUATE ACCESS TO PRIMARY CARE PROVIDERS AND SPECIALIZED CARE

Rural areas often have a dearth of physicians and other health care providers, both primary care providers and specialists. Clients face long waiting periods—sometimes several months—for appointments. When they can't wait, they often travel to urban centers to receive care, or they are forced to use emergency room facilities inappropriately.

Though they expressed concern regarding choice and travel issues, the majority of informants with disabilities (91 percent) and family informants (85 percent) report that they have a primary care provider, usually a general practitioner or pediatrician, and the majority of informants expressed satisfaction with their primary care provider. However, 85 percent of service providers and 71 percent of health care providers said there is an inadequate number of primary care providers in their community. While more than twice as many family informants as informants with disabilities use the same care provider for both primary and specialized care, both groups seem to have greater difficulties getting an appointment with their specialists than with their primary care providers. The primary reason for this difficulty was scheduling too far into the future. And almost two thirds of service providers report problems getting appointments with primary care providers for their clients.

In this area, the pediatricians are in one office, and, if for some reason you have a problem with this office, you don't have a pediatrician in [this town].

It's like starting over each time. It's never the same [doctor] and they're really detached because they realize they're only going to spend so long with this person, get them over the worst of this big hurdle and then they're on the their next case.

If you're a physician, if we were to attract a physician, we could guarantee him low pay and a lot of hours, and a necessity to turn down people who need services. . . . It's a high Medicaid population . . . and it just eats the physicians alive.

I'm dealing with the territories north of [here], where it's a real needy area, those areas have to rely on the nurse practitioners who are totally swamped.

PROVIDER LIMITATIONS

People with disabilities often encounter difficulty accessing health care providers who are knowledgeable about low-incidence or rare disabilities and conditions requiring high levels of technology. Some providers are fearful of treating patients with rare and complex conditions, and they may be uninformed. All these problems can become more acute in rural areas with fewer providers. Other problems are lack of coordination of care between local and urban providers treating a rural patient with special needs, and lack of options concerning choices of local physicians.

When asked to rate their primary care providers' knowledge on several issues, informants varied in their perceptions. For example, few seemed confident about the health care providers' knowledge of rehabilitation techniques, though at least half of all four groups of informants felt the providers know about medical equipment. While most of the health care providers claim to know about funding rules (67 percent), fewer informants with disabilities (39 percent), family informants (35 percent), and service providers (30 percent) seem to agree. On the other hand, informants with disabilities (85 percent) and family informants (80 percent) are confident about their care providers' knowledge of their medications, compared with only half of the health care providers themselves.

I took my daughter to [the primary care doctor] when she had her first seizure and I said, "She's doing this and that" and he goes, "Well, I think you're not burping her good enough, or there's something trau-

matic that you're doing at home that is causing her to act that way."
Well, I grabbed her, put her clothes back on, and took her to [the city].
I mean can you imagine how devastating that was.

They panic with an ear infection here. I take my daughter (who has
autism and multiple disabilities) in for an ear infection, and the nurse
has to take the doctor out of the room and explain to him what is going
on [regarding Sara's autistic responses]; [And I say] okay, you know,
she won't hurt you . . . it's like, calm down, it'll be all right—I'm telling
the doctor to calm down. . . . Generally, it's hard to find a primary
provider here, like a family doctor or whatever that will feel comfortable seeing kids [with severe disabilities].

LIMITED ACCESS TO OTHER MEDICAL
AND SOCIAL SERVICES

During forums and interviews, people with disabilities spoke of a
range of health-related services that frequently remain out of their
reach: dental care, routine prevention and screening, substance
abuse treatment, nutrition, exercise, and mental health services. The
problems are few providers, some providers who are reluctant to see
patients with disabilities, and long waiting lists.

Only two thirds of the informants with disabilities report having a
dentist, though 88 percent of these were very satisfied with the care
they received. Of the family informants, three quarters report having
a dentist for their family member, but only half report being very
satisfied.

One of the things we screen for is dental concerns, and unless there is
such severe abscess that we [have] to send them immediately [to the
dentist], we are told to call the dentist staff [in six to seven months]
when there might be an opening. Farm Workers Clinic has 500 on the
waiting list . . . and the other private dentist that's willing to take people on medical coupons said we're booked now, call us in six to seven
months.

Prevention and screening services were used by only 42 percent of
informants with disabilities and by half of family informants.

[No prevention], the only thing [they respond to] is a crisis; but [if] a
crisis [is] coming that I can see, they won't pay a dime until it happens.
It has to be causing him physical deterioration, the vomiting, wetting
the bed, before they will pay . . . nothing to prevent it.

Twice as many informants with disabilities (81 percent) as family
informants (40 percent) claim they are aware of the availability of

alcohol and drug treatment in their communities, though few of both groups (under 10 percent) have sought or used the service. Family knowledge and use may have been low because they were speaking primarily for young children.

> We have exactly the same problem, at least with the deaf community, in drug and alcohol [abuse] rehabilitation, the unavailability of drug and alcohol counselors, and no accessibility to after care [and follow-up].

As with drug and alcohol treatment, twice as many informants with disabilities (81 percent) as family informants (45 percent) are aware of mental health services in their community. Again, the differences between the two groups may be related to age—the majority of the family members with disabilities are children. Still, few access this service, and those who do are only moderately satisfied.

> One of the problems that they have in the mental health services is the per capita [system], which allows no flexibility to the patient. They may need 40 sessions, they may need 15, but you know it's like building a house and stopping halfway through, you can't live in it. You really need to follow through to be able to provide services on a need-based rather than a per capita basis.

> Some of the mental health services that you need aren't covered [by insurance], and oftentimes you don't need someone like a doctor, maybe your needs can be met by a counselor, but because of your insurance you can't go to that person and be reimbursed for that. And plus, you don't get the care that you really need.

Transportation, Remote Location, and Isolation

Many people with disabilities live in rural areas because housing is less expensive, but they face a special set of problems in accessing health care. People spoke of weather problems, remoteness, difficult terrain, inadequate rural transportation systems, insufficient lodgings, and the time, stress, and expense associated with traveling to urban centers for specialized care. There is reluctance by families to move to urban centers for care which would mean moving away from family, friends, and support networks.

Though the same small percentage of informants with disabilities as family informants report problems getting to their primary care provider, more than twice as many family informants (75 percent) as informants with disabilities (33 percent) have difficulty getting to their specialists. The majority of service providers claim that their clients with disabilities struggle to see both primary care providers (70 percent) and specialists (80 percent).

Families are generally dependent on cars to get to both their primary care providers and their specialists. In contrast, informants with disabilities tend to rely on social service staff or vehicles, or public transportation to get to their appointments. Though it takes less than 30 minutes for the majority of informants to get to their primary care providers, 88 percent of family informants require one or more hours to get to their relatives' specialist. Most of these are children being taken to specialized children's hospitals and treatment centers located in urban centers. In addition, 39 percent of informants with disabilities report that it takes one or more hours to get to their specialists. Despite this, when asked if they would prefer to see a specialist rather than a primary care provider for health problems related to their disability even if it meant traveling far, three quarters of informants with disabilities and *all* of family informants said "yes."

> [Our town] has a relatively decent bus service within the town limits, but it only runs during daylight hours and six days a week.

> We have a dial-a-ride transportation system but often they will forget about some individual and not pick them up when there's a call for them, or they'll be an hour or sometimes an hour and a half late . . . and it's required [to give] 24 hours advance notice. So, if you suddenly get sick and need to go to the doctor, you call an ambulance or a taxi, and that's expensive

Social, Emotional, and Long-Term Support

Many noted that social support, whether from a reliable friend, a group of peers with similar problems, or the whole community, is paramount to keeping them and their families healthy. We often expect residents of rural communities to know and help each other, but many forum and interview participants spoke of circumstances that erode the support they need from family, friends, and neighbors. These include distance, remoteness, isolation, and lack of information. It became evident that a side benefit of these forums was their role in bringing people together.

Just over half of the informant groups report being aware of the availability of social support services in their community, but fewer have sought or used support groups. Regardless, the majority of those who do access social support groups report being satisfied. Though

70 percent of family members have sought or used respite care, less than half express satisfaction. This relatively low satisfaction likely reflects people who are either seeking respite and are on large waiting lists, or are those who feel they do not get it provided often enough. Half of the informants with disabilities say they have someone who helps them access community services, and these were primarily friends, family, and social service staff. Only 20 percent of family members say they have someone who helps them, and those who do rely solely on family and friends.

> Some [people I've worked with] have outlived every member of their family. So most of the people I deal with now as adults, the people in their lives when you talk about the social contacts, are paid to be there. And the missing piece is the love, the tenderness that they had at home.

> As the kids get older, you get tireder, you don't have stamina, you're tired of the system. You know by the time they're adults, society [expects] these kids should be independent. But it doesn't happen like that. Our kid's care is increasing all the time; so there's this issue of we're older and more tired, and he's older and needs more services.

> There was no one there who could help us [be caregivers] . . . no one to teach us how to do more care in the home.

REHABILITATION, THERAPY, AND EQUIPMENT

Rural areas generally have few rehabilitation services available locally. People with disabilities often face a lack of physical, occupational, and speech therapists. And as everywhere, they must deal with bureaucratic barriers and excessive costs in obtaining durable medical equipment.

The majority of both groups of informants (85 percent) report that therapies are available in the community, and they reported being used by 69 percent of informants with disabilities and 85 percent of family informants. However, while most of the informants with disabilities expressed satisfaction with their therapeutic services, less than half of family members are happy with their relatives' therapy. The difference may reflect the needs of adults—who seem generally happy with the therapies—versus parents' high expectations for their children's therapies. It is also possible that the parents are not necessarily dissatisfied with the service itself, but the amount of service provided.

> I worked two years in geriatrics and you'll find massive services. I have patients who had both hips and both knees replaced and they were

bedridden and they weren't going anywhere, but yet I can't get a walker for a kid.

[We need to] be staffing the schools with the therapy and personnel that they need, because in a lot of these areas, the school is a central clearinghouse.

A bearing for a wheelchair if you bought it at a medical vendor might be, what, 50 bucks, but if you bought it at a bike shop, [it would cost a few dollars. And] $45 for a caster grind for the front of my son's chair. I bought the same bearing at the Schwinn bike shop for $4.

CHOICE AND QUALITY OF LIFE

Participants in forums and interviews frequently raised quality of life issues, including choice, independence, housing, responsibility, survival . . . and fun.

Nine out of ten informants with disabilities and family members said that they believe that people with disabilities are at greater risk for injury or illness than people who do not have disabilities; this view was shared by three quarters of service providers and half of health care providers. When asked about their own health, the majority of informants with disabilities rated their health as very poor to fair, with only 19 percent rating their health as good. In contrast, 40 percent of family informants rated the health of their relative with disabilities as good. Only 15 percent of both groups rated their health or the health of their relative as excellent.

If you're spending all your energy trying to overcome what average people can do easily—it may take me two hours to do something that takes you 10 minutes to do—what's the rest of my life going to be like? My health is based on how good I feel about myself, just like everybody else, and if I'm so exhausted by doing the simple things what about the things that you do for enjoyment.

I have M.S., and so I know my standard of living is going to drop considerably to the point where it is subhuman . . . so much that all you can do is pay your bills, stay at home, watch the walls grow? Should life be more than that?

You got to have a place to live, have to have some kind of health care, and you got to have friends; but if you're stuck on the top of a mountain because it's free or cheap, then that's where you are, and there aren't very many people out there.

STRATEGIES

People living in rural communities who have disabilities, their families, and the people who work with them are forced to be creative about using available resources and finding solutions to their health care problems. They must grapple with limited resources, services that are in short supply, health care providers who are under-trained or lack understanding of disability and chronic low-incidence conditions, low expectations by the public, confusing regulations, and lack of information.

Within rural communities, individuals and organizations have developed their own strategies to provide health services to people with disabilities. These strategies range from informal collaborations to carefully integrated systems of care. All of these strategies attempt to make the most productive use of limited public and private resources, to provide social and health services as close to home and as conveniently as possible, and to mobilize the best support from their communities. Following is a summary of these strategies and recommendations to improve the quality and availability of health services in rural communities.

REACH OUT WITH SERVICES

Isolation is one of the overriding barriers to health services for people with disabilities living in rural areas, but in every community we visited, we met with people who are addressing the problem by bringing services directly to people in their homes and neighborhoods. The social contact that results is invaluable to health and well-being. These efforts include well-established programs such as Meals on Wheels, satellite clinics and mobile assessments through hospitals and local public health departments, and the promising technology of telemedicine.

CONSIDER THE "ONE-STOP SHOPPING" APPROACH

The benefits of integrated services include a convenient location of multiple services under one roof, reduced transportation barriers for clients and staff, user-friendliness, efficiency, less paperwork, appropriate referrals, streamlined levels of authority, and better continuity of care. "Centralization" of care can be an appropriate program strategy in rural as well as urban areas.

ENCOURAGE LOCAL CONTROL OF SERVICES
AND COMMUNITY OWNERSHIP

Through partnerships, collaboration, and mobilization of the compassion and caring of rural families, local communities can "buy in" and "own" more of their service delivery systems. During our meetings and interviews, we learned about a wide range of efforts to bolster local control of services for people with disabilities, from involving non-disability community organizations in policy making to staging of healing pow-wows.

BUILD INTERAGENCY COMMUNICATION
AND BRING AGENCIES TOGETHER

Local, county, and state agencies that provide health care services to people with disabilities in rural areas often share both clients and funding sources. They benefit from formal and informal mechanisms to communicate about programs, policies, services gaps, and community support. Shared boards, advisory committees, and information systems can also contribute to more effective case management and service delivery for public and private agencies.

ENCOURAGE PUBLIC HEALTH AGENCIES
TO FOCUS MORE ON DISABILITY

The public health system is emerging as a leader in health promotion, education, and assessment in many rural communities. In addition, public health nurses have long provided a critical link between special populations and services. Advocates suggest that public health staff in rural areas should be more proactive in securing services and in developing policies for people with disabilities.

IMPROVE PROVIDER EDUCATION ABOUT DISABILITIES

Recruitment and retention of capable health care providers has always been a problem in rural areas. It is particularly difficult for rural communities to attract providers with adequate training or experience in treating people with disabilities and disability-related health conditions. In addition to more thorough provider education, participants in our study suggested that rural communities explore special incentives for physicians to maintain practices in their communities.

ADVOCATE FOR MORE REIMBURSEMENT FOR SKILLED PREVENTIVE CARE

People with disabilities are no different from other consumers of health care in that preventive services are more effective than treating conditions once they become acute. Several providers informed us that reimbursement for skilled preventive care—particularly through Medicare and Medicaid—continues to be a problem.

DISCOURAGE HOSPITAL "DUMPING"

In some communities we visited, we learned of hospitals discharging people with disabilities from care prematurely to a rural health services delivery system that is unprepared to care for them. Rural communities should develop severe sanctions to discourage dumping, as well as the equally common practice in some rural communities of continuing to hospitalize people with disabilities until their health care financing runs out.

CREATE POINTS OF SERVICE

Even sparsely populated rural communities offer opportunities to provide services and exchange information for residents with disabilities outside of the hospital or the doctor's office. Alternative sites for care and communication include local pharmacies, libraries, beauty salons, barber shops, community colleges, places of worship, coffee shops, and the offices of nontraditional providers.

INSIST ON FAIRLY PRICED EQUIPMENT AND SERVICES

People with disabilities in both rural and urban areas complain frequently about the minimal choice and extraordinary prices they face in purchasing durable medical equipment. Transportation also tends to be prohibitively costly for those who cannot call upon insurance or public programs for reimbursement. The disability community and their advocates must become demanding and outspoken consumers, insisting on reasonable prices for essential equipment and services.

CREATE GATHERING PLACES

One immediate "finding" from the focus group forums was the great benefit of bringing people together to talk. Many participants had to make complicated and time-consuming arrangements to attend the meetings. Some traveled considerable distances. Few participants knew each other before the forums. This was clearly a rare and valued opportunity for people with disabilities, and those working with them, to share experiences and improve their awareness of issues affecting their access to health care. Regardless of the particular issue or priority area on the table, the most effective and important strategy is to establish and support situations for people to gather, to meet, and to network. Providers, agencies, and advocates should seek out and exploit opportunities to bring people together and listen to what they have to say.

CONCLUSION

In recent years both state and federal health system reform efforts are placing greater emphasis on primary care and preventive services. Leaders of rural communities are seeking innovative ways to assure access for their members. In doing so, it is important that local communities understand the multifaceted needs of their members with disabilities. And, it is vital, as health system reform takes shape, that policy makers nationwide have adequate information to guide and support their decisions affecting people with disabilities and their families living in rural America.

Public policies affecting people with disabilities are usually developed by professional researchers, policy makers, and clinicians. People with disabilities rarely help create the programs and service delivery systems they use. This project took a different approach by eliciting views and direct experiences of people with disabilities in their own rural communities. These findings confirmed evidence from the literature that a variety of obstacles to accessing appropriate health care exist for rural residents with disabilities

From our research, we also discovered that a variety of innovative strategies are used in rural communities to improve the quality and availability of health and social services close to home. Among these strategies are encouraging local control of services and community ownership; building interagency communication and bringing agencies together; encouraging public health agencies to focus more on disability; improving provider education; discouraging hospital "dumping"; insisting on fairly priced equipment and services; and creating gathering places and opportunities for people with disabilities and their families to meet, socialize, and network.

In addition to these strategies, the increasing utilization of telemedicine holds great promise for addressing deficits in available health care for this population. This new technology allows local providers to consult with specialist experts in urban centers about complex medical conditions that present. Furthermore, telemedicine is a vehicle for providing continuing medical education to local providers to increase their skills in areas such as treatment for specific disabilities.

This study has a number of unique attributes. We were able to select counties that represented diverse rural populations and characteristics in Washington state, and we were able to include participants representing a wide spectrum of disability, age, income, and multiple perspectives. The study included both quantitative and qualitative procedures, allowing an in-depth analysis of the issues. Most importantly, the study included the "consumers," the people who are directly affected by policy decisions. Finally, while the results may not generalize to the broad population, they provide a rich snapshot of the issues and challenges being met by individuals with diverse disabilities living in a rural communities as they seek health care, community access, and a better quality of life. Indeed, this study puts faces on the data.

NOTE

This chapter is based on a study supported by the federal Agency for Health Care Policy and Research.

REFERENCES

Alsup, P. A., and J. P. Narramore. 1992. "Interdisciplinary care in a rural HIV treatment center." *Journal of the Tennessee Medical Association* 85 (8): 380–81.

Bachrach, L. L. 1983. "Psychiatric services in rural areas: A sociological overview." *Hospital and Community Psychiatry* 34 (3): 215–26.

Brown, L. and W. Vega. 1996. "A protocol for community-based research." *Research Linkages Between Academia and Public Health Practice*, 4–5.

Clark, D. O. 1992. "Residence differences in formal and informal long-term care." *Gerontologist* 32 (2): 227–33.

Clark, J. 1990. "Rural home care for medically fragile children." *CARING Magazine* 9 (12): 32–34.

Donham, K. J., and K. M. Thu. 1993. "Relationships of agricultural and economic policy to the health of farm families, livestock and the environment." *Journal of the American Veterinary Medical Association* 202 (7): 1084–91.

Durch, J. S., L. A. Bailey, and M. A. Stoto, eds. 1997. "Improving health in the community: A role for performance monitoring." Division of Health Promotion and Disease Prevention, Institute of Medicine. Washington, D.C.: National Academy Press.

Dwyer, J. W., and M. K. Miller. 1990. "Determinants of primary caregiver stress and burden: Area of residence and the caregiving networks of frail elders." *Journal of Rural Health* 6 (2): 161–84.

Ellis, J. L., and P. R. Gordon. 1991. "Farm family mental health issues." *State of the Art Reviews: Occupational Medicine* 6 (3): 493–502.

Emanuel, D. A., D. L. Draves, and G. R. Nycz. 1990. "Occupational health services for farmers." *American Journal of Industrial Medicine* 18: 149–52.

Fiene, J. I., and P. A. Taylor. 1993. "Serving rural families of developmentally disabled children: A case management model." *Social Work* 36 (4): 323–27.

Greenwood, J. G. 1985. "Disability dilemmas and rehabilitation tensions: A twentieth century inheritance." *Social Science and Medicine* 20 (12): 1241–52.

Halpert, B. P. 1988. "Volunteer information provider program: A strategy to reach and help rural family caregivers." *Gerontologist* 28 (2): 56–59.

Helge, D. 1984. "Rural transition program needs for students with disabilities." *Rural Special Education Quarterly* 5 (2): 2.

Karasek, R. A., and T. Theorell. 1990. *Health work: stress, productivity and the reconstruction of Working Life.* New York: Basic Books.

Labonte, R. 1988. "Health promotion: From concepts to strategies." *Health Care Management Forum* 1 (3): 24–30.

Lang, R. H. 1982. "Implementation of comprehensive service systems for the elderly and chronically impaired: A conceptual framework and case study." *Journal of Health and Human Resources Administration* 4 (4): 415–50.

Levey, L. M., J. P. Curry, and S. Levey. 1988. "Rural-urban differences in access to Iowa child health services." *Journal of Rural Health* 4 (2): 59–72.

Lishner, D. M., M. Richardson, P. Levine, and D. Patrick. 1996. "Access to primary health care among persons with disabilities in rural areas: A summary of the literature." *Journal of Rural Health* 12 (1): 45–53.

Malach, R. S., and N. Segel. 1990. "Perspectives on health care delivery systems for American Indian families." *Children's Health Care* 19 (4): 219–28.

Manton, K. G. 1989. "Epidemiological, demographic and social correlates of disability among the elderly." *Milbank Quarterly* 67 (2): 13–58.

McManus, M. A., P. W. Newacheck, and R. A. Weader. 1990. "Metropolitan and nonmetropolitan adolescents: Differences in demographic and health characteristics." *Journal of Rural Health* 6 (1): 39–51.

Meyer, H. 1991. "Rural America: Surmounting the obstacles to mental health care." *Minnesota Magazine* 73 (8): 24–31.

Newacheck, P. W. 1989. "Adolescents with special health needs: Prevalence, severity and access to health services." *Pediatrics* 84 (5): 872–81.

Page, C. M., D. M. Bornhoeft, D. F. Barcome, and D. D. Knowlton. 1985. "Providing outreach services in a rural setting utilizing a multidisciplinary team: The CARES project." *Rehabilitation Literature* 46 (9–10): 264–67.

Patrick, D. L., and T. M. Wickizer. 1995. "Community and health." In *Society and Health*, ed. B. C. Amick, S. Levine, A. R. Rarlov, and D. C. Walsh. New York: Oxford University Press.

Pothier, P. C. 1991. "Demythologizing rural mental health." *Archives of Psychiatric Nursing* 5 (3): 119–20.

Rounds, K. A. 1988. "Responding to AIDS: Rural community strategies." *Social Casework* 69 (6): 360–64.

Runyan, C. L., and G. Faria. 1992. "Community support for the long-term mentally ill." *Social Work in Health Care* 16 (4): 39–53.

Thomas, P. 1988. "Misery overwhelms the heartland." *Medical World News* 29 (20): 56.

Tokarski, C. 1990. "Rural areas' AIDS care lacking." *Modern Health* 20 (8): 24.

Wagenfeld, M. O. 1990. "Mental health and rural America: A decade review." *Journal of Rural Health* 6 (4): 507–23.

Washington State Department of Health. 1997. *Public Health Improvement Plan in Action*. Olympia, Wash.: Office of Planning.

Wright, K. A. 1993. "Management of agricultural injuries and illness." *Rural Nursing* 28 (1): 253–66.

Zejda, J. E., H. H. McDuffie, and J. A. Dosman. 1993. "Epidemiology of health and safety risks in agriculture and related industries: Practical applications for rural physicians." *Western Journal of Medicine* 158 (1): 56–63.

Regionalization and Rural Service Delivery

SUSAN MURTY

INTRODUCTION

Consolidation and centralization have changed the face of rural America. We are all familiar with the new rural economy. Local businesses have been replaced by large multi-state or international corporations. The local bank has become a branch office of a large bank based in a distant location. The small family farm is rapidly disappearing, replaced by corporation-owned factory farms. Many traditional rural industries are deteriorating and becoming more dependent on large corporations and the global economy; income levels in rural areas are low and poverty rates high (Coward and Krout 1998; Rowles 1998; American Hospital Association 1993; Agency for Health Care Policy and Research 1991). All this is evidence of the continuing "Great Change" which has been affecting rural communities for many years (Warren 1978).

There is a body of research documenting the negative effects of economic consolidation on rural communities (Goldschmidt 1947, 1978; Appalachian Land Ownership Task Force, 1979; Pellegrin and Coates 1956; Lewis, Johnson, and Askins 1978; Wilkinson 1982). The negative effects of the farm crisis were well documented by research in the 1980s (Mermelstein 1986; Mermelstein and Sundet 1986; Zeller 1986; Jacobsen and Albertson 1987), but the effects have continued through the 1990s.

Similar restructuring and consolidation have been changing the delivery of services in rural areas. The changes are dramatic whether you consider health or social services, whether you look at private or public services, and whether you look at local, state, or federally funded programs. The regionalization of social and health services has resulted in the creation of very large rural service areas covering many counties (U.S. Department of Health, Education, and Welfare 1973; Ginzberg 1977; Foley 1977; Hassinger 1982; Martinez-Brawley 1987; Krout 1998). Although health and social needs are at least as great and sometimes greater for residents of rural areas, rural communities are at a service disadvantage (Krout 1998).

The delivery of health care is an example. Many rural hospitals have closed, resulting not only in a decrease in hospital services, but also adding to the shortage of rural health care professionals and other health care services, and having a negative effect on local economies and communities (Doelker and Bedics 1989; Krout 1998). Many of the surviving rural hospitals have been purchased by large corporations or become part of various regional multi-hospital systems such as consortia, alliances, networks, and coalitions (American Hospital Association, 1993; Rowles, 1998). The Health Care Financing Administration (HCFA) has encouraged consolidations in rural areas, with the 1991 State Rural Health Network/Essential Access Community Hospital (EACH) Grant Program and similar programs under which hospitals participate in rural health networks (Agency for Health Care Policy and Research 1991). Even a local doctor's practice or a nursing home in a rural area may now be operated by a large medical practice, a health maintenance organization, a teaching hospital, or a corporation that operates care facilities. Nursing homes are frequently owned and controlled by large health care corporations unfamiliar with the local community (Rowles 1998). Home nursing is frequently provided by multi-county or multi-state home health care agencies (Krout 1998).

The same pattern is evident in the delivery of other types of health and social services. Rural mental health services are now often provided by a multi-county community mental health center or through a multi-state behavioral health maintenance organization. Services for the elderly are delivered by Area Agencies on Aging; in rural areas, these almost always cover multi-county sevice regions (National Association of Area Agencies on Aging 1996; Krout 1998). Public welfare services may be administered by offices covering multiple counties or from county offices which are administered by multi-county district offices. Special education services for children may be provided by area education agencies or collaboratives that serve multiple school districts. Services for disabled adults may be planned by case management programs that are administered from a state office or from regional offices located in several places in the state. Family preservation services may be contracted to a large corporation covering a region of the state or even many states. Economic development services may be provided from regional offices covering many counties. These are just a few examples of a general trend toward regionalization that has transformed the way rural services are organized.

The changes have been gradual; an early form of regionalization was school consolidation, which replaced the one-room school houses of the past. This trend improved the quality of rural education by bringing students to centrally located schools where more teachers, resources, and special activities could be provided for a larger number of students. However, as the trend has continued, the costs have risen. Further improvements have been brought about at the cost of many hours spent by students on the school bus each day and, in some cases, a loss of local community involvement and sense of identity with the local school district (Sher 1977). In addition, there is evidence that the creation of consolidated schools districts may reduce opportunities for students to participate in school activities and take on leadership roles (Barker 1964; Barker and Associates 1978).

The causes of regionalization are well known. The trend toward centralization in human services has corresponded to a similar trend toward concentration and centralization in business and government throughout the United States. Pressures toward large-scale production, specialization, and efficient use of the time of specialists has pressured programs to provide services in central locations and to improve the productivity and efficiency of service provision (U.S. Department of Health, Education, and Welfare 1973; Bureau of Health Planning and Resource Development 1976; Ginzberg, 1977; Yates, 1980; American Hospital Association, 1993; Martinez-Brawley and Delevan 1993). Regionalization is often described as a process of "rationalization" of resources. Its advocates argue that it is an efficient way to deliver services because large regional organizations take advantage of economies of scale, specialization, and standardized procedures (Lehman, 1975; American Hospital Association, 1977, 1993; Hassinger, 1982; Krout, 1998). The claim has often been made that regionalization can control costs without reducing quality (Dill and Rochefort, 1989) or even improve the quality of services (Ginzberg, 1977).

Inexorably, the process of improving quality and providing a more specialized, more highly trained, "efficient" system has resulted in gradual centralization of more and more services for rural areas. Regional organizations which are common in rural areas are the Area Agencies on Aging (Watkins and Watkins, 1984; Coward and Lee, 1985; Krout, 1998), Community Mental Health Centers (Ginzberg, 1977; Yates, 1980; Keller and Murray, 1982), Regional Economic Development and Planning Commissions, and Community Action Agencies (Wattenberg, 1982). United Way Agencies often cover multi-county regions. Hospitals often function as regional medical centers delivering services to large rural areas (Saward, 1976; Hassinger, 1982; Agency for Health Care Policy and Research, 1991; American Hospital Association, 1993).

This chapter examines the effects of this increasing trend toward regionalization on the delivery of services in rural areas and suggests some ways in which policies can help to ensure that the quality of services to rural communities does not suffer as a result of geographical centralization of services in pursuit of efficiency and cost control.

BACKGROUND

I carried out a study of one rural county in Missouri in relation to disaster planning (Murty 1993; Murty in press). This county has a population of approximately 10,000 and is persistently poor (Cook and Mizer 1994). The population is primarily white and of predominately German descent. Many regional organizations included this county in their service regions. A partial list includes a health district which covers 25 counties; a transportation agency which covers 22 counties; an Area Agency on Aging which covers 18 counties; a highway patrol region, an emergency management region, and a highway region which each cover 14 counties; a community action agency which covers 8 counties; a conservation forestry region which covers 6 counties; a community mental health center which covers 5 counties; and a Division of Aging program which covers 3 counties. Several voluntary organizations and associations also include the county in multi-county regions. For example, it is in an American Red Cross region which covers 50 counties and a region of the Missouri Funeral Directors Association which covers 10 counties. The Salvation Army, with a main office in the nearest population center, includes the county in its service region. There are other regional organizations which serve loosely defined regions which include this county. These include two hospitals and their helicopter ambulance services located in the adjacent county, and several home health agencies which serve large areas in southeast Missouri and Illinois. The headquarters of some other organizations which provide services to the county are located at state offices at the capital or the main campus of the state university. The regional organizations range from government organizations with clearly designated responsibility for a precisely defined geographical area to voluntary and private organizations which are not required to serve a particular area and which have established regions merely as a convenient way to manage the organization.

The research showed that two levels of disaster planning were occurring simultaneously: local community leaders and organizations such as volunteer fire departments, school districts, and the local county health department were actively planning for disaster response in the county. At the same time, state and regional organizations were carrying out a separate planning process with most of the meetings held in the population center in the next county or farther away. These more distant agencies were not familiar with most of the local organizations and community leaders involved in planning for the rural county I studied. No effort was made to integrate the two planning processes and it was evident that the individuals involved in one level of planning had no information about the planning going on at the other level.

Another rural community I studied is located in the northwestern corner of a county in eastern Iowa. The town and its two outlying communities have a total population of approximately 3500. The county has a higher proportion of young people aged 19 or younger than the state as a whole. It also has a higher proportion of families with children in poverty. Per capita income in the county in 1990 was $17,720. The economic base of the county is primarily agricultural, with most farms producing corn, soybeans, and pork. Between 1990 and 1996, the county lost 5.8 percent of its farms, and the average size of the remaining farms increased. Among those employed in the county, the largest segment are in operator, fabricator, and laborer occupations. (Source of data: Web site, Iowa State University, University Extension Service, 1997).

The community is not the county seat and like many rural communities, it is dependent for services on organizations in the county seat, which is located 25 miles away. Additional services are provided in a university town about 15 miles away in another county. These include medical services at a free medical clinic and at two hospitals. In addition, this community receives services from a regional Area Agency on Aging, and a regional Area Education Agency, both with main offices in a metropolitan area located in another county to the west. The community is served by two different Community Action Agencies that cover multiple counties and that have main offices in different towns. A family counseling and domestic violence program has an office in the county seat administered by a private agency located in a nearby metropolitan area. The county is also served by a regional office of Lutheran Social Services which has an outreach office located at the county seat. The Boy Scout and Girl Scout councils cover multiple counties; in fact, the Boy Scout Council covers counties in two states. Several of the regional service providers for the community are located in Illinois.

I soon discovered that few of the residents of the community were aware of the whole range of social and health services available from all these regional programs, whether they were provided in town by traveling service providers or in the county seat, the university town, or elsewhere. After I began to compile information about service providers, the residents of the community suggested that we collaborate on a new resource directory, which is now in preparation.

Residents of this community discussed with me some problems related to regionalized programs. One of these was lack of transportation to service delivery sites in the county seat or the university town. There is no public transportation available to these locations. Therefore people must either provide their own transportation or depend on friends, neighbors, or volunteers. One senior citizen in the town provides a great deal of the volunteer driving for the senior citizens who must travel for health care. I attempted to reach her by phone to arrange a time to meet. Her schedule was so full driving seniors to medical appointments that it was almost impossible to find her at home! Access to services depends on the dedication of volunteers like this; if they become unavailable due to age or illness, services become inaccessible.

Another problem was brought to my attention that related to ownership and control over funds and assets contributed by members of the local community. For example, when the multi-county regional Girl Scout Council took over administration of the local Girl Scout troops, leaders complained that the regional Council closed down the camp which a local contributor had donated and which the local troops had operated for years; they also complained that camping equipment donated to the local troops was appropriated by the regional Council and stored in a warehouse in a central location. In order to use it, the local troops would have had to travel to pick it up and return it; as a result, they felt they did not have access to it anymore. The Girl Scout leaders became increasingly frustrated by what they considered "the attitude" of the Council and decided that as soon as their girls completed the Girl Scout Program, they would no longer support it in the local community.

A similar situation developed in this county with the United Way. The residents decided to organize their own United Way fund separate from the county United Way. They raised money that was to be used only for programs and residents of the local community.

ADVANTAGES AND DISADVANTAGES

Regionalization has had some positive effects on rural service delivery and has always been introduced with the goal of improving services. Some services were never offered in the many rural areas prior to regionalization. In these cases, including rural communities in large multi-county service regions may result in improved access to services even if residents must travel a long way to receive them. Services of any kind, even if they are relatively inaccessible, are an improvement over no services at all. For example, many rural communities had no access to publicly funded local mental health services prior to the establishment of community mental health centers. Many community mental health centers offer services, although they are provided primarily at the population center of the region (Keller and Murray 1982). Access to mental health services at these centers may be a vast improvement over the prior situation where many rural counties had no publicly funded mental health services available to them at all.

Another example is special education services. Many rural school districts had only minimal services for children with special needs prior to regionalization. When regionalized special education programs were established, specialists such as speech therapists, physical therapists, and experts in educational programs for children with particular disabilities were available to travel to provide consultation and services to all the school districts in the region.

The disadvantages of regionalization are most evident when county-level programs are compared with multiple-county programs. Funding for these regional programs is based on the population of all the counties. However, these programs are generally administered from the population center of the multi-county region and most of the staff and most of the services and facilities are located there.

In many cases, service users are expected to travel to the central office in the region if they wish to receive services; considerable research over the years has shown that as travel costs increase, people are less likely to use services (Jehlik and McNamara 1952; Hodges and Dorken 1961; Sohler and Thompson 1970; Cohen 1972; Massam 1975; Shannon and Dever 1974; Sheps and Bechar 1981; Prue et al. 1979; White 1986). Travel and opportunity costs are especially high in rural areas (Smith 1976; Wharf 1985; Martinez-Brawley 1987; Ginsberg 1993; Krout 1998). As a result, rural residents have a service disadvantage (Krout 1998). When the cost effectiveness of programs is evaluated, the criteria used do not generally include the time spent by the client or consumer traveling to receive services.

In some cases, outreach staff from regional programs travel to rural communities on a regular schedule; there may even be a satellite office open a few days a week in some of the rural communities outside the population center. Nevertheless, the "center of gravity" of these regional programs is in the population center of the region. The travel costs are a drain on those programs which transport staff, instead of expecting service users to bear the travel costs (Keller and Murray, 1982). These programs may reimburse staff for mileage or may cover costs of maintenance, upkeep, and depreciation of agency vehicles.

In contrast, county programs are administered from the county seat, and most of the staff work and provide services there. Even if staff and office are not open every day, they are usually located with other county-level programs which can provide information five days a week. The distance to the county seat may present an obstacle to residents of the more remote parts of the county, but the distance is shorter and it is often possible to arrange a ride with neighbors who travel to the county seat to do a variety of errands, to carry out business, or go to work. If staff travel to outlying communities, costs are less because the distances are limited to the area of the county.

Access to services involves more than reducing barriers of distance and transportation. Accessibility is also affected by the financial cost of services, the convenience of the schedule of available services, and the level of comfort which service users experience, which is related to many factors including language, culture, and familiarity (Gillespie and Marten 1978; Krout 1998). Service providers who travel to the community and are not familiar with its customs, culture, and traditions are less likely to be able to enhance these aspects of service accessibility (Keller and Murray 1982; Rowles 1998).

Regionalization can have negative effects on staff as well as consumers and communities. Staff in regional programs are likely to experience the loss of autonomy common in large organizations (Kallenberg and Van Buren 1996). This may be especially important for staff assigned to remote communities in the regions because they may feel hampered by organizational policies. They may be unable to make the necessary decisions on the spot concerning the services that individuals and families should receive (Martinez and Delevan 1993). These staff also tend to feel excluded and neglected by the main office. They may feel that a disproportionate amount of their time is spent traveling to staff meetings held at the central office (Lennox and Murty 1994).

The disadvantages of multi-county service programs versus county level service programs are summarized below. Note that not all regional programs have these characteristics. Some avoid these problems by using methods which are discussed later in this chapter.

1. Regional services are less accessible. Even regional programs which make an effort to provide outreach or satellite offices cannot compare with services provided on a full-time basis in the county seat or the local community.
2. Communication with regional service providers is more difficult. Even telephone calls to make appointments can involve long-

distance telephone charges and frustrations of dealing with a large and unfamiliar agency.

3. Travel costs are not distributed equitably in regional programs. Since public transportation is rarely available in rural areas, the travel is generally by private vehicle or by agency vehicle. The costs are often borne by the residents of the rural counties if they seek services at the main office; the travel costs may be borne by the program if it sends staff out to provide services in the more rural parts of the region or if it provides transportation to clients. The costs include travel time, fuel, and depreciation and upkeep of vehicles.

4. Service providers in the central office of the region do not have an in-depth understanding of the outlying communities and their strengths and resources. For example, they are not able to collaborate as effectively with the local informal social support networks as a county-based service provider can do (Rowles 1998). They do not have an in-depth understanding of the context of each particular rural community and its residents.

5. Rural communities distrust the regional program and its service providers because they are "outsiders." Rural communities are generally slow to accept newcomers and outsiders. Even if the same individuals provide services regularly over a number of years, they are still not seen as members of the local community and trust is slow to develop. The distrust is compounded when the regional service agency is perceived as a large centralized bureaucracy without the human touch (Rowles 1998).

6. Staff who serve outlying rural communities in regional organizations often feel that they are not treated equitably. They resent having to travel to the central office for staff meetings; they believe they are not given sufficient respect and autonomy; they would like to be given the authority to make necessary decisions concerning services to consumers in the rural community they serve (Lennox and Murty 1994).

7. Coordination with other programs that serve particular rural communities is more difficult for regional programs. Since regional service programs rarely share the same geographical territories, collaboration and coordination may involve contacting staff at programs located at various addresses which serve varied populations and areas.

8. Residents of rural counties resent the control which the regional organization has over funds and assets, especially those contributed locally.

9. Residents of rural communities in the multi-county region have fewer opportunities and less influence in planning and improving services for their local community for two reasons:

a. Planning meetings are generally held in the population center where the main office is located; therefore if they wish to have input concerning services, residents of the outlying rural communities must bear the travel costs, including travel time.

b. Planning is carried out on a region-wide basis and rarely incorporates specific adaptations for particular communities in the region; the number of people who advocate for any particular community in the region is small compared to the number of people from other communities at any planning meeting; therefore in any decisions made by majority vote, concerns of members of one community will be outvoted.

The following vignette is provided to illustrate some of the disadvantages of regionalized multi-county service programs. This vignette is based on situations encountered in a number of different rural areas in the United States.

Rural Taylor County has a population of approximately 6000. Average incomes are low and the poverty rate is high. The economic base is logging, mining, and ranching. Like many rural counties, Taylor County has lost many of its young adults to migration. In addition, there has been some inmigration of elders looking for a rural community for retirement. As a result, the county has a high proportion of residents over the age of 60 with fixed incomes. The county is located in rugged terrain and is divided by a mountain range that runs through the center of the county. The population is scattered in small settlements and isolated home sites throughout the county; the county seat is the population center with about 1000 residents. Taylor County is served by a tri-county area agency on aging (AAA). The main office of the AAA is located in the next county to the east, which has a population three times that of Taylor County.

Two seniors represented Taylor County on the AAA Advisory Board. Board meetings were held at 8 P.M. on weekday nights in the central county where the AAA's main office was located. In order to attend, the Taylor County representatives had to travel more than one hour each way over a 6000-foot pass; they often arrived home close to midnight after the meetings. When winter weather was bad, it was dangerous to drive over the pass and travel time was greater. Traveling all the way to the next county was a difficult undertaking for these seniors, especially at night. Nevertheless the Taylor County representatives were faithful in their attendance at the Advisory Board meetings. They asked for mileage reimbursement for travel to board meetings but the AAA staff said that it was against policy to reimburse members of the Board and that there were no funds in the budget to cover mileage reimbursement for Board members.

Although the AAA provided vans in the other two counties to pick up and transport seniors to the congregate meal sites and to medical appointments in the nearest large city, for many years there was no van to serve Taylor County. The Taylor County representatives to the AAA Advisory Board requested van service in Taylor County but their request did not produce results for a long time. Although the needs of the seniors in Taylor County were great, their numbers were small compared to the numbers of seniors in the other two more populated counties in the AAA's region. Finally, after some years, the AAA purchased three new vans. It then agreed to assign one of the used vans to Taylor County and to cover the wages of a part-time van driver. Since this van could not cover the transportation needs of the whole county and was no longer in top condition, it was located at the county seat and provided transportation primarily to seniors who lived in the county seat or the nearby rural area.

Taylor County seniors were interested in setting up a volunteer transportation program to supplement the van service. The service would reimburse local volunteers for their mileage when they picked up seniors and took them to the congregate meal sites and to medical appointments. However, the AAA said that they had a work group looking into this type of program because they were concerned about issues of liability and insurance coverage. They also were doubtful that the costs of coordinating such a volunteer service could be covered, since the transportation funds were completely expended on the van program currently in place. A regional Community Action Program (CAP) had a volunteer driver program but its region covered ten counties and of the three counties covered by the AAA, only Taylor was included in the CAP region. Therefore, the AAA was not interested in arranging a meeting with the CAP to discuss collaborating on a volunteer program. As a result, seniors in Taylor County felt that the AAA was not interested in their needs and concerns.

There are six congregate meal sites in Taylor County, most serving meals three times a week to seniors. The Coordinators of these meal sites in Taylor County are expected to travel to the central county once a month for a Coordinators' Meeting. Although their mileage was reimbursed for these monthly trips, the Coordinators felt that the travel time took up too large a proportion of the hours allocated to their part-time positions and that the information covered in the meetings was not particularly useful to them in Taylor County.

The AAA provides chore services to seniors unable to carry out their own household tasks. In an effort to improve the efficiency of the chore service program, the AAA contracted out the management of the chore service workers throughout the region to a temporary job service. This job service operated from an office located in the central county. Seniors in Taylor County were required to make long-distance calls to the central chore service provider's office and speak to a stranger there if they needed to change hours or days of service, or anything else. This seemed unnecessary to the seniors in Taylor County, especially if they used a neighbor as a chore service worker.

The AAA decided to work with other agencies on a disaster response plan focusing on the needs of the elderly in the aftermath of a disaster. They met with various county, city, and state agency representatives to develop a response plan. However, the health department, volunteer fire departments, and the county and city government programs in Taylor County were not invited to the disaster planning sessions. Congregate meal site coordinators and seniors from Taylor County were invited to attend the planning meetings, but after attending one session, they decided that it was not concerned with Taylor County, and they decided not to attend the other disaster planning meetings that were scheduled.

POLICIES TO IMPROVE REGIONALIZED SERVICES

Although regionalized services are unlikely to disappear in the foreseeable future, a great deal can be done to make sure that these programs offer the best possible services to rural communities (Miller and Ostendorf 1982; Hollister 1982; Lennox and Murty 1992; Martinez-Brawley 1993; Martinez-Brawley and Delevan 1993; Krout 1998). Regional service providers can take specific steps to improve access to services, involve staff in local communities, and ensure rural residents input into planning and evaluation of services. Although some of these steps will increase the cost of delivering services, they are necessary to provide equity in service accessibility and to prevent development of chronic and serious problems among the residents of rural areas as we move into the twenty-first century.

Funding bodies should look for evidence that regional organizations are using appropriate methods to serve the rural communities within their regions. Funding allocation formulas should take into consideration not only the size of the population served but also the costs of providing services to rural areas.

Specific suggestions follow:

1. Regional programs should include residents of each county in the planning process (Rowles 1998) and should make efforts to

reduce the costs to representatives from outlying counties as much as possible. Mileage reimbursement, convenient meeting times, and accessible meeting locations are all factors which may encourage the participation of residents from the more remote communities.

2. Planning meetings should be offered in each county and local agencies and community leaders should be invited and encouraged to participate. Local residents should be consulted about who to invite. The regional plan should be adapted to meet the needs of the particular county. The regional plan should have services that are relevant and appropriate for each of the counties in the region.

3. Services should be provided in each county of the region. If it is not possible to provide services in one or more of the counties, transportation should be provided to those who wish to use the agency's services.

4. Toll-free telephone numbers should be made available to residents of counties in the region if calls to the regional office are long-distance calls.

5. Each regional staff person should develop an in-depth understanding of one of the counties in the region and build relationships with agencies and community leaders in that county. If at all possible, these persons should travel regularly to the county and spend time in the local communities.

6. Satellite offices should be scheduled for regular hours of service in the outlying counties; in addition there should be hours available for drop-in appointments. Staff who are assigned to satellite offices should spend additional time in the county at the local restaurant or café, and making contacts with local residents and programs and with representatives of other regional programs servicing the same county.

7. Staff assigned to outlying offices should be empowered to use discretion and judgment to make decisions about how services are to be delivered in remote areas of the region. They should be encouraged to make decisions based on needs of local residents and the local community.

8. Agency staff meetings should be held in each county in the region at least once a year to distribute the travel costs more equally among staff and to increase knowledge among all the staff of local conditions.

9. Regional staff should determine whether other regional programs provide services to each of the counties in their region and contact them to discuss possible areas of collaboration.

10. Some proportion of funds contributed by local communities

should be allocated for use of the local community rather than pooled with regional funds and assets.

11. Allocation of funds to programs serving rural areas should be based on the costs incurred in delivering services to rural areas. Because distances are great and population density is low, these costs are generally higher in rural areas. Funding formulas should include a factor for rural service delivery (National Association of State Units on Aging, Minority Issues Committee 1992; Coward, Vogel, Duncan, and Uttaro 1995; Krout 1998).

CONCLUSION

Because of increasing corporate ownership and the globalization of the economy, it is the opinion of the author that the economic situation of rural communities of most parts of the United States is unlikely to improve. Although populations in suburban areas and communities within commuting distance of metropolitan areas are increasing, in many parts of the rural United States, populations are decreasing. There continues to be an exodus of young adults from rural communities looking for education and employment opportunities. In addition to the normal increase of people aged 65 and older which we can expect in rural areas, inmigration of retirees will continue to increase the proportion of elderly people in rural communities. In addition, there will continue to be an inmigration of low-income young families looking for low-wage jobs. These will include a growing rural Hispanic population. As a result, the degree of dependency in the rural population is likely to increase due to an increasing proportion of elderly and of children under 18. Based on these projections, needs for social and health are likely to increase rather than decrease in the twenty-first century.

Because of continuing trends toward centralization and large-scale production and reductions in funding for services and pressures to cut costs and reduce taxes, regionalization of service delivery is not likely to disappear from rural America in the twenty-first century. Instead, it is likely that local services will continue to be absorbed into large regional service areas and owned and controlled from metropolitan and urban centers. Of special concern are services to the growing proportion of elderly in rural areas. Isolated from service centers, without public transportation, and experiencing increasing health and social needs as they grow older, these seniors are likely to become our most underserved rural population. A strong stand will need to be taken to guarantee that regional programs provide quality services that are accessible to rural communities as we move into the twenty-first century.

REFERENCES

Agency for Health Care Policy and Research. 1991. *Delivering essential health care services in rural areas: An analysis of alternative models* (AHCPR Pub. No. 91-0017). Rockville, Md.

American Hospital Association. 1993. *Working from within: Integrating rural health care.* Chicago: The Hospital Research and Educational Trust.

American Hospital Association. 1977. *Delivery of health care in rural America.* Chicago: Author.

Appalachian Land Ownership Task Force. 1979. *Who owns Appalachia?* Boone, N.C.: Center for Appalachian Studies, Appalachian State University.

Barker, R. G., and P. V. Gump. 1964. *Big school, small school: High school size and student behavior.* Stanford, Calif.: Stanford University Press.

Barker R. G., and Associates. 1978. *Habitats, environments and human behavior.* San Francisco, Calif.: Jossey-Bass Publishers.

Bureau of Health Planning and Resources Development. 1976. *Health Planning and Resources Development Act of 1974* (DHEW Publication No. [HRA] 77-14015). Washington D.C.: U.S. Government Printing Office.

Cohen, J. 1972. "The effect of distance on use of outpatient services in a rural mental health center." *Hospital and Community Psychiatry* 23 (3): 79–80.

Cook, P. J., and K. L. Mizer. 1994. *The revised ERS county typology: An overview* (Rural Development Research Report 89). Washington, DC: ERS, U.S. Dept. of Agriculture.

Coward, R. T., and G. R. Lee. 1985. *The elderly in rural society: Every fourth elder.* New York: Springer.

Coward, R. T., W. B. Vogel, E. P. Duncan, and R. Uttaro. 1995. "Should intrastate funding formulae for the Older Americans Act include a rural factor?" *The Gerontologist* 35 (1): 24–34.

Dill, A. E. P., and D. Rochefort. 1989. "Coordination, continuity, and centralized control: A policy perspective on service strategies for the chronic mentally ill." *Journal of Social Issues* 45 (3): 145–59.

Doelker, R. E., and B. C. Bedics. 1989. "Impact of rural hospital closings on the community." *Social Work* 34 (6): 541–43.

Foley, H. A. (1977). "Community mental health programming." In *Regionalization and health policy,* ed. E. Ginzberg, U.S. Department Health, Education, and Welfare publication no. (HRA) 77-623, 37–47. Washington, D.C.: U.S. Government Printing Office.

Gillespie, D. F., and S. E. Marten. 1978. "Assessing service accessibility." *Administration in Social Work* 2 (2): 183–97.

Ginsberg, L. 1993. "Introduction: An overview of rural social work." In *Social work in rural communities,* second edition, ed. L. H. Ginsberg, 2–17. Arlington, Va.: Council on Social Work Education.

Ginzberg, E. 1977. "The many meanings of regionalization in health." In *Regionalization and health policy,* ed. E. GInzberg, U.S. Department of Health, Education, and Welfare (publication no. (HRA) 77-623, 1–6. Washington, D.C.: U.S. Government Printing Office.

Glass, J. J. 1976. "Conflict or cooperation: Substate districts and comprehensive health planning agencies." *Growth and Change: A Journal of Regional Development* 7 (4): 18–24.

Goldschmidt, W. 1947. *As you sow.* New York: Harcourt, Brace and Co.

Goldschmidt, W. 1978. "Large-scale farming and the rural social structure." *Rural Sociology* 43 (3): 362–66.

Hassinger, E. W. 1982. *Rural health organization: Social networks and regionalization.* Ames, Iowa: Iowa State University Press.

Hodges, A., and H. Dorken. 1961. "Location and outpatient psychiatric care." *Public Health Reports* 76 (3): 239–41.

Hollister, W. G. 1982. "Principles guiding the development of an innovative, low cost, rural mental health program." In *Handbook of community mental health,* ed. P. A. Keller and J. D. Murray, 86–99. New York: Human Sciences Press.

Iowa State University, University Extension Service. 1997. Web site: http://www.exnet.iastate.edu/.

Jacobsen, G. M., and B. S. Albertson. 1987. "Social and economic change in rural Iowa: The development of rural ghettos." *Human Services in the Rural Environment* 10 (4)/11 (1): 58–65.

Jehlik, P. J. and R. L. McNamara. 1952. "The relation of distance to the differential use of certain health personnel and facilities and to the extent of bed illness." *Rural Sociology* 17 (3): 261–65.

Kalleberg, A. L., and M. E. Van Buren. 1996. "Is bigger better? Explaining the relationship between organization size and job rewards." *American Sociological Review* 61:47–66.

Keller P. A., J. D. and Murray. 1982. "Rural mental health: An overview of issues." In *Handbook of community mental health,* ed. P. A. Keller and J. D. Murray, 3–19. New York: Human Sciences Press.

Krout, J. A., and R. T. Coward. 1998. "Aging in rural environments." In *Aging in rural settings: Life circumstances and distinctive features,* ed. R. T. Coward and J. A. Krout, 3–14. New York: Springer.

Krout, J. A. 1998. "Services and service delivery in rural environments." Ibid., 247–66.

Lehman, E. W. 1975. *Coordinating health care: Explorations in interorganizational relations.* Beverly Hills, Calif.: Sage.

Lennox, N. D., and S. A. Murty. 1994. "Choice, change, and challenge: Managing regional services." In *Fulfilling our mission: Rural social work in the 1990s,* (Proceedings of the 17th National Institute on Social Work and Human Services in Rural Areas, 1992), ed. B. Locke and M. Egan, 150–59. Morgantown, W. Va.: West Virginia University.

Lewis, H., L. Johnson, and D. Askins., eds. 1978 *Colonialism in modern America: The Appalachian case.* Boone, N.C.: Appalachian Consortium Press.

Martinez-Brawley, E. E. 1993. "Community-oriented practice in rural social work." In *Social work in rural communities,* second edition, ed. L. H. Ginsberg, 67–81. Alexandria, Va.: Council on Social Work Education.

Martinez-Brawley, E. E, 1987. "Rural social work." In *Encyclopedia of social work,* 18th edition, ed. A. Minahan, 521–37. Silver Spring, Md.: National Association of Social Work.

Martinez-Brawley, E. E., and S. M. Delevan. 1993. "Centralizing management and decentralizing services: An alternative approach." *Administration in Social Work* 17 (1): 81–102.

Massam, B. 1975. *Location and space in social administration.* New York: John Wiley and Sons.

Mermelstein, J. 1986. "Farm Counseling Services." *Human Services in the Rural Environment* 10 (1): 32–33.

Mermelstein, J., and P. A. Sundet. 1986. "Rural community mental health centers' responses to the Farm Crisis." *Human Services in the Rural Environment* 10 (1): 21–26.

Miller, M. W., and D. G. Ostendorf. 1982. "Administrative, economic, and political considerations in the development of rural mental health services." In *Handbook of rural community mental health,* ed. P. A. Keller and J. D. Murray, 100–9. New York: Human Sciences Press.

Murray, J. D., and P. A. Keller. 1982. "Rural community mental health: Prospects and conclusions." In *Handbook of community mental health,* ed. P. A. Keller and J. D. Murray, 224–29. New York: Human Sciences Press.

Murty, S. 1993. *The effect of regionalization on interorganizational relations in a rural disaster preparedness network.* Doctoral dissertation, Washington University, St. Louis, Mo., 1993.

Murty, S. (in press). "Setting the boundary of an interorganizational network: An application." *Journal of Social Service Research.*

National Association of Area Agencies on Aging. 1996. *National directory for eldercare information and referral: 1996–1997 directory of State and Area Agencies on Aging.* Washington, D.C.: Author.

National Association of State Units on Aging, Minority Issues Committee. 1992. *Description of current and proposed intrastate funding formulas.* Washington, D.C.: Author.

Nelson, G. 1980. "Social services to the urban and rural aged: The experience of Area Agencies on Aging." *The Gerontologist* 20 (2): 200–7.

Norris, J. 1980. "Multipurpose centers in a rural county." In *Rural human services: A book of readings,* ed. H. W. Johnson, 81–85. Itasca, Ill.: Peacock Publishers.

Pellegrin, R. J., and C. H. Coates. 1956. "Absentee-owned corporations and community power structure." *American Journal of Sociology* 61 (5): 413–19.

Perry, B. G. 1976. "Transportation and communication as components of rural health care delivery." In *Rural health services: Organization, delivery, and use,* ed. E. W. Hassinger and L. R. Whiting, 81–94. Ames, Iowa: Iowa State University Press.

Prue, D., T. Keane, J. Cornell, and D. Fos. 1979. "An analysis of distance variables that affect aftercare attendance." *Community Mental Health Journal* 15 (2): 149–54.

Rowles, G. D. 1998. "Community and local environment." In *Aging in rural settings: Life circumstances and distinctive features,* ed. R. T. Coward and J. A. Krout, 105–25). New York: Springer.

Saward, E. W. 1976. *The regionalization of personal health services.* New York: Prodist.

Shannon, G. W., and G. E. A. Dever. 1974. *Health care delivery: Spatial perspectives.* New York: McGraw-Hill.

Sheps, C. G., and M. Bachar. 1981. "Rural areas and personal health services: Current strategies." *American Journal of Public Health* 71: 71–82.

Sher, J. P. 1977. *Education in rural America: A reassessment of conventional wisdom*. Boulder, Colo.: Westview Press.

Smith, J. 1976. "Communities, associations, and the supply of collective goods." *American Journal of Sociology* 82 (2): 291–98.

Sohler, K. B. and J. D. Thompson. 1970. "Jarvis' law and the planning of mental health services: Influence of accessibility, poverty, and urbanization on first admissions to Connecticut state hospitals." *Public Health Reports* 85 (6): 503–10.

U.S. Department of Health, Education, and Welfare. 1973. *Area plan for programs on aging under Title III of the Older Americans Act of 1965 as amended*. Washington, D.C.: U.S. Government Printing Office.

U.S. Department of Health, Education, and Welfare, Administration on Aging. 1977. *Planning for the elderly in natural disaster*. DHEW Publication no. (HHD) 77-20669. Washington, D.C.: U.S. Government Printing Office.

Warren, R. L. 1978. *The community in America*, third edition. Chicago: Rand McNally.

Watkins, J. M., and D. A. Watkins. 1984. *Social policy and the rural setting*. New York: Springer.

Wattenberg, E. 1982. *Competitive tension in delivering social services and programs: The role of CAPs in rural Minnesota*. Minneapolis, Minn.: Center for Urban and Regional Affairs.

Wharf, B. 1985. "Toward a leadership role in human services: The case for rural communities." In *Social work in rural areas: A celebration of rural people, place and struggle, Proceedings of the Ninth National/Second International Institute on Social Work in Rural Areas*, ed. W. H. Whitaker, 9–40. Orono, Me.: Department of Sociology and Social Work, University of Maine.

White, S. L. 1986. "Travel distance as time price and the demand for mental health services." *Community Mental Health Journal* 22 (4): 303–13.

Wilkinson, K. P. 1982. "Changing rural communities." In *Handbook of rural community mental health*, ed. P. A. Keller and J. D. Murray, 20–28. New York: Human Sciences Press.

Yates, B. T. 1980. *Improving effectiveness and reducing costs in mental health*. Springfield, Ill.: Charles C Thomas.

Zeller, S. H. 1986. "Grieving for the family farm." *Human Services in the Rural Environment* 10 (1): 27–29.

III
The People of Rural America

Immigration and the Rural Midwest

ROCHELLE L. DALLA AND SHIRLEY L. BAUGHER

INTRODUCTION

Tranquil portraits of small rural towns, characteristic of Norman Rockwell paintings, no longer represent the reality of many Midwestern communities. Contemporary rural towns are increasingly characterized by poverty, overcrowded schoolrooms, substandard housing, and social upheaval. The rural Midwest, which encompasses hundreds of communities across ten states, is undergoing dramatic social and economic change. Much of the change is attributed to rapid population growth as immigrant and migrant workers flock to rural communities in search of stable employment in the meat-packing industry.

In this chapter, the following issues will be addressed: (1) the changing economy of the rural Midwest; (2) the significant impact of the meat-packing industry on rural Midwestern economics; (3) the immigration and migration of Latinos into rural communities seeking economic viability through employment in the meat-packing industry; and (4) the resulting implications of these dramatic changes for the social, physical, and economic well-being of individuals, families, and rural Midwestern communities.

Investigations of rural communities and their economies have identified two issues significant to the future of the rural Midwest. First, changes in rural Mexico and the rural United States are encouraging settlement of immigrants in rural parts of America. Settlement, in turn, presents the need to provide public and private services to immigrants, migrants and their children. Second, multiple policy responses to immigration exist, ranging from the development of techniques to stop immigration, to discovering ways to successfully integrate immigrants and migrant populations into rural American communities.

A new vision, with new immigration policies, is critical in rural America. The new policies must (1) acknowledge the importance of agriculture and food-processing to local economics; and (2) recognize that the immigrants filling jobs in these local core industries are likely to settle permanently and that services must be available for them and their families as they climb the U.S. job ladder.

MEXICO AND THE UNITED STATES: NATIONAL TRANSFORMATIONS

Observers predict that the sharpest debates in the United States over immigration and integration will shift in the 1990s from Western and Southern states, such as California and Florida, to Midwestern states such as Nebraska, Iowa, and Minnesota (Fitchen 1991). The composition of rural populations is changing at a remarkable rate largely due to *immigration* (movement into a country in which one is not a native) and *migration* (movement from one country, region, or place of abode to settle in another). Between 1980 and 1992, the number of Hispanics in ten Midwestern states (Illinois, Indiana, Iowa, Kansas, Michigan, Minnesota, Missouri, Nebraska, Ohio, and Wisconsin) climbed from 1.2 million to 1.8 million. Over the same period, the Caucasian population in these same states declined by 400,000 (U.S. Bureau of the Census 1996). Simply stated, populations of Hispanic and foreign-born individuals is rapidly increasing, while that of Caucasians is declining precipitously in many areas of the American Midwest. The surge of the Hispanic population has been termed the "browning of the Midwest" ("The heartland's raw deal" 1997). Given the small populations of rural communities, the social fabric can be transformed almost overnight. Conflict is also emerging between immigrants and Midwestern natives, some of whom have seen local Hispanic populations rise by ten to 500 percent since 1990 ("Immigration and the changing face of rural America" 1996).

The magnitude of this geographic and social phenomenon is aptly illustrated through a brief examination of Midwestern communities. Storm Lake, Iowa has grown from a population of 8400 mostly Caucasian residents in 1970 to 10,000 residents in 1990, including 1500 legal Laotian immigrants and 600 Mexican-born residents (300 of whom are unauthorized aliens) (Gouveia and Stull 1995). Similarly, Commerce, Oklahoma, a town of 2500, increased its Hispanic population from 150 in 1990 to 800 in 1996 ("Rural Hispanic" 1996), an increase of 26 percent. And finally, a *Wall Street Journal* profile of Worthington, Minnesota describes how ConAgra (a large meat-processing industry) recruited immigrant Asian and Latino workers for its pork plant, and changed the composition of the town's 10,000 residents (from 2 percent to 20 percent immigrants) ("America's

Heartland" 1995). Census figures from 1992 show that Minnesota's Hispanic population has increased 94 percent since 1980 (from 32,123 to 62,316), the largest statewide percentage increase in Hispanics in the country (U.S. Bureau of the Census 1992). These illustrations are not isolated incidents. Demographic shifts, such as those depicted above, are evident in rural communities across the entire Midwestern section of the United States.

MEXICO

The demography of Mexico is also changing. Families are becoming smaller and the general population is becoming older. The average number of children per woman has declined from six to three in the past 20 years, a decrease of 21 million births (Molina 1995). At the same time, the number of women of reproductive age has doubled, so the annual population growth has remained constant. Significant also is that Mexico's population is aging; the number of people over age 65 was one percent of the Mexican populations in 1960; in 1990, it comprised 4 percent of the population (Molina 1995). Yet, the country's pension system has deteriorated to such an extent that it no longer supports the elderly who have spent their entire lives working and contributing to the fund. Given the present economic crisis in Mexico and current policies of privatization and economic liberalization, which are reducing the role of the protective state, it has become urgent to stress personal family saving schemes.

Anthropologist Soledad González Montes, of the Universidad Nacional Autonoma de Mexico (UNAM), indicates that the national health care program is also deteriorating, with the quality and range of coverage becoming less effective ("Mexico President" 1997). In 1997, President Ernesto Zedillo established a nationwide antipoverty program. He stated, "One in five Mexican families does not receive an income sufficient to buy food that it needs to feed its members; one of every two Mexicans who live in the countryside and one of every nine in the cities lives in extreme poverty" (ibid.). Zedillo has established the National Program of Education, Health and Food, also known as Progressa. Benefits of the program include a monthly food stipend and scholarships conditioned on school attendance for children in grades 3 to 9. (Girls will receive a larger amount to discourage a disproportionately high female dropout rate.) Families will receive an extra 90 pesos (about $11) a month for food, roughly four days of pay for rural workers ("Mexico President" 1997). Despite the newly focused national attention on health and education, the wealth and luxury associated with life in the United States continues to attract Mexican laborers seeking economic stability and a better quality of life for themselves and their families.

IMMIGRATION AND MIGRATION

In many rural Midwestern communities, the arrival of immigrant and U.S.-born migrants has followed a three-step process. Solo men, recruited by employers in border towns or in Mexico, arrived first. Later, their families arrived. They were either Asian refugee families or those of the solo Hispanic male laborers recruited earlier. The Midwest attracted entire families because of the relatively high wages and low living costs. In the final stage, unauthorized immigrants, including friends and relatives of earlier settlers, arrived and often used social networks to find employment (Fitchen 1991; Broadway 1995).

Migrant labor has historically formed the backbone of agriculture in the United States; currently, nearly 27 percent of farm workers in the Central Plains states are migrant workers ("Immigration's other side" 1996). The cover story of the 23 September 1996 *U.S. News and World Report*, "The New Jungle," describes the importance of immigrant workers in Iowa's meat-packing industry by stating, "perhaps no industry is so dependent on this low-wage labor as the nation's meat and poultry companies." Meat-packing, which requires little training or English-language skills, is the primary magnet attracting immigrants to the Midwestern states ("Midwest new hub" 1996).

Significantly, migrational trends are shifting. Migration patterns have been primarily circular in the past, with immigrants and migrants entering a community, securing employment, and leaving after completing the work. The immigrants entering rural Midwestern communities are beginning to stay, however, and new patterns are being established ("America's Heartland" 1995; "Cities must face" 1997).

Research endeavors have increasingly focused on the transfer of poor Mexican laborers to agricultural areas in the United States, where they have little prospect for upward mobility. Subsequently, large pockets of rural poverty are being created. An analysis using the Urban Institute Underclass Database found that the creation of 100 American farm jobs was associated with the influx of 136 immigrants, 139 additional poor residents, and 79 more welfare recipients (Grey 1995). Newly arrived immigrants do not receive welfare, but their presence helps to hold down wages. Farmers and food-processing industries often prefer to hire newly arrived immigrants who provide hard labor at minimum wages; local, unemployed residents receive governmental assistance in the form of welfare benefits. Importantly, the meat-packing industries attracting rural Mexican immigrants are often the core industries within their communities. Thus, local reluctance to drastic labor policy changes that might threaten the local economic viability is understandable.

THE MEAT-PACKING INDUSTRY

The meat-packing industry is a $95 billion per year business dominated by three companies: Iowa Beef Processing (IBP), Cargill's Excel Corporation, and ConAgra's Monfort Incorporated. These companies slaughter and package 80 percent of the feedlot cattle in the United States. In 1995, IBP, the world's largest processor of beef and pork, reported sales of $12 billion and profits exceeding $257 million ("Midwest: meat/poultry" 1998).

Until the farm crisis of the early eighties, meat-packing was largely an urban industry. Given the depressed economic condition of many rural areas during the time, lucrative industries were welcomed, and meat-processing industries often received tax breaks or subsidies to move into agricultural communities ("Farmers" 1996). Industries recognized that production costs could be greatly reduced by packaging meat close to where the cattle and hogs were being raised (Griffith, Broadway, and Stull 1995). A mutually beneficial relationship between rural Midwestern communities and large meat-processing industries thus developed.

In the 1990s, as manufacturing industries have moved into rural communities, rural job growth has been faster than urban job growth. Between 1989 and 1994, rural counties added a net of 167,000 manufacturing jobs, while urban counties lost 1.2 million manufacturing jobs (Broadway 1995). Jobs are being created in rural areas at unprecedented rates. The dominant manufacturer in the Midwestern states is the meat-packing industry. Nonetheless, many of the jobs in the meat-packing industries are labor intensive and unpleasant (i.e., slaughtering and packaging cattle, chickens, and hogs). Immigrant laborers will often work double shifts and overtime at jobs that, according to plant managers, few U.S.-born people would do for comparable wages (Griffith et al. 1995).

In contrast to seasonal farm jobs in California, where migrant and immigrant workers average 1000 hours per year at $5 to $6 per hour ($5000–$6000 annually), workers average 2000 hours in the meat-packing plants of the Midwest, earning $6 to $8 per hour. This equates to $12,000 to $16,000 annually, enough to minimally support a family in the United States (Barkley 1995). Subsequently, larger numbers of families, and fewer solo males, are migrating and immigrating into Midwestern communities. The presence of families raises a number of important community-wide issues including access to housing, education, health care, and welfare ("Sociologists watch the heartland" 1997; "Impact" 1997). On 3 February 1997, *The Nation* ran a story blaming greedy meat-packers and their allies in state and local governments for creating a rural immigrant underclass in the Midwest, referred to as "Mexico on the Missouri" ("Heartland's raw deal" 1997).

Hispanics and Asians dominate the labor forces of Midwestern meat-packing plants. An exceptionally high turnover rate in the industry work force exists, with estimates ranging from 20 to 80 percent annually. Most of the meat-packing plants are continuously hiring new workers to replace those who quit or who are injured on the job. Thus, positions are consistently available for new hires. Some critics of the meat-packing industry argue that the companies encourage high turnover to keep workers at the low end of the wage scale. The companies counter, however, that they spend up to $3000 to recruit and train each production employee and that each worker who leaves represents an investment loss in training and experience ("Latino surge" 1996). Yet, based on turnover rates, it is unclear how much training companies actually provide.

INDUSTRY RECRUITMENT

Midwestern meat-packing companies frequently recruit workers from California, Texas, and Mexico. Many of the workers are recruited along the Texas-Mexican border by "independent recruiters" who receive a finder's fee ($50 to $300) for each new worker they refer who stays on the job for 30 days ("Midwest: meat/poultry" 1998). Recruiters typically promise quality housing, fishing, and other recreation opportunities, and as many hours of work as the laborer wants. After being hired, immigrant workers typically relay information to friends and family in Mexico, setting private labor recruitment networks into motion ("Immigrants are being drawn" 1996).

ILLEGAL IMMIGRANTS

The Immigration and Naturalization Service (INS) district director for Iowa and Nebraska estimates that 25 percent of the 50,000 workers (approximately 12,500) who disassemble animals in the 222 meat-packing plants in the two states are unauthorized aliens ("Meatpackers feel heat" 1996). Industry personnel admit that they can only ask job applicants if they are "legally entitled" to work in the U.S.; close scrutiny of worker documents is avoided for fear of being charged with discrimination. However, the INS estimates that 85 percent of the "documented illegals" are *knowingly hired* by employers (ibid.). U.S. Attorney Stephen Rapp notes that out-of-state-recruitment of workers is a red flag for INS investigators. Nonetheless, he claims, many meat-packers use independent brokers for recruiting purposes, which gives the companies deniability when unauthorized laborers are found (ibid.).

COMMUNITY IMPACTS

The operation and expansion of food-processing industries in rural communities is generating consequences that were not planned and which are now the subject of contention. In many communities, immigrants are perceived by residents as a mixed blessing (Grey 1995). Their arrival stabilizes the population in many counties that were losing residents, thus preserving churches and their pastors, and schools and their teachers ("Melting pot" 1996). And the economic benefits of resident industry is widely evident; meat-packing counties frequently report faster increases in per capita income and retail sales than the states in which those counties are located (General Accounting Office 1998). To illustrate, IBP employs approximately 2500 workers in Lexington, Nebraska (a town with 9000 total population) with an annual payroll of $58 million. Yet, native residents are frustrated at the community-wide changes they observe. At a recent focus group held in one rural Nebraska meatpacking community (Prochaska-Cue and Ziebarth 1997), one participant remarked,

> I can't count how many times I hear English not being spoken at the post office, the grocery store, the bank. . . . I don't think our postmen or grocers or bankers are bilingual. If you're gonna do business, English is the only language here.

Successful integration of immigrant newcomers into small rural communities is clearly thwarted by language and cultural differences.

INTER-ETHNIC RELATIONS

Rapid demographic change often results in heightened racism and discrimination. Not surprisingly, dramatic changes in the ethnic composition of small communities is creating tension, and in some cases, social upheaval. Police in several Midwestern communities report that anti-immigrant literature is circulating ("The human dimension"

1995) and some observers predict that there is potential for violence as economic competition heats up. Long-time residents complain that the influx of immigrants has been associated with increased crime, from drunk driving and driving without insurance, to gang shootings. They report feeling that the quality of life in their communities has deteriorated since the inception of the meat-processing industries ("Melting pot" 1996; "Impact of meatpacking" 1997). And, although native residents admit that the industries bring work and increase local income, they also blame the processing plants for many community-wide problems (Stull and Broadway 1995; Stull, Broadway, and Erickson 1992; Stull 1990).

Immigrant workers and their families are equally frustrated. They report being pleased with their earnings, but also face discrimination (Mueller and Baugher 1996), feel they are denied services, such as housing, due to their large or extended families, and suffer from police harassment (Stull and Broadway 1995). Immigrant laborers further resent community "gringos" who demand that they assimilate into the majority American culture (Mueller and Baugher 1996).

Ethnic tension clearly exists on both sides, and the successful integration of long-time residents and immigrant laborers is not made easier by educational and income-level barricades that exacerbate the isolation of immigrant workers and their families ("The new jungle" 1996). Services that most American citizens take for granted, such as public education, are becoming sources of dire concern in many rural communities experiencing rapid population growth.

EDUCATION AND HOUSING

Housing shortages and crowded schoolrooms fuel the tension between immigrant workers, their families, and long-time rural community residents. To illustrate, Willmar, Minnesota, 95 miles west of the Twin Cities, contains almost 20 percent Hispanics among its 5000 Kindergarten–12th grade students. In March 1996, thirteen Hispanic families sued the school district for providing a "substandard education for Hispanic students," ("Thirteen Hispanic families" 1996). In many communities, teachers lack oral Spanish skills, yet the number of Limited English Proficiency (LEP) children who have entered the school districts has increased dramatically. Many immigrant children are not receiving the full benefits of public education. Community residents, in contrast, complain that the needs of the immigrant children are lowering the quality of the schools for their own children ("More kids" 1996). Educational quality comprises an issue that is not likely to subside in the near future, as rural community industry continues to attract immigrant and migrant workers.

Housing availability, also, has been identified as a significant problem in rural Midwestern meat-packing communities. As described by one participant in a recent investigation (Prochaska-Cue and Ziebarth 1997):

> The men double, triple, quadruple in the rooms. . . . I've been in and done inspections in apartment houses where there's six or eight beds in a one-bedroom apartment. And they're sleeping on the floor and on the couch, too. Then they're bringing their families up. . . . They're not only bringing their wife and their three children, they're bringing their wife's parents and maybe their own parents, and maybe a brother. That's where we end up with ten or twelve people in a house with one or two incomes.

Through their research, Prochaska-Cue and Ziebarth (1997) also found evidence of limited industry support in dealing with the complex issues facing rural communities. Another resident explained:

> The beef and pork companies are not helping. The town and the city are not involved in the situation. They advertise for these people in Texas or wherever they come from and these people think they're going to come up here and they're going to have a house to rent and everything, but the companies don't want to help us find housing or even work with us. They just want the people to work.

Clearly, communities experiencing rapid population growth and an influx of immigrant laborers are forced to grapple with shrinking community-wide resources. Inter-ethnic tension and misunderstanding certainly perpetuate, and may exacerbate, the problems facing many rural Midwestern meat-packing communities.

COMMUNITY RESPONSES

Neither the industries that are attracting the immigrants to the rural Midwest nor the communities that provided subsidies to attract the industries, planned for the migration and immigration of the workers that are being recruited to fill jobs. Fitchen (1991) states that community response to institutional change is random, ranging from vigor (an aggressive and proactive approach), to vulnerability (reactionary responses, or no response, to feelings of helplessness). Lyson and Falk (1993) suggest that a sense of helplessness exists in communities experiencing rapid growth which constrains their capacity to respond to change. Earlier research supports this claim. Social disruption theory asserts that boomtown communities generally enter a period of generalized crisis which disrupts traditional routines and attitudes (England and Albrecht 1984). The ensuing crisis disrupts social networks, the mental health of the residents, and the worldview of the community. At the organizational level, existing businesses and associations struggle to survive the infusion of newcomers. At the community level, the homogeneous culture is fractured and services are often severely taxed. Other studies (Cortese 1982; Cortese and Jones 1997) indicate that the possible economic benefits of rapid growth may be overwhelmed by fiscal distress, disruption of established ways of life, and pathological disorganization. Grey (1995) found that the displacement of traditional workers decreases the social connectedness between processing plants and their communities.

Although many communities feel they cannot sustain the current levels growth, they cannot afford to lose the industries which employ the immigrant and migrant populations, either. An additional concern is that the meat-packing industry may become a mobile industry—one that moves into an area, changes the basic social and economic foundations of the community, and moves on (Broadway 1995). In Tecumseh, Nebraska, the 40 year old Campbell's pork-processing plant closed in 1997. The community is facing dramatic economic (job loss) and social (emigration or transfer of unemployed workers to other communities) transitions which threaten the town's future viability. Community preparation, consisting of developmental plans for the expansion and growth of public and private services, may provide the key to successful adaptation to rapid population surges. Similarly, preparation for out-migration, or emigration, given the mobility of the meat-packing industry, may also protect Midwestern communities from uncertain futures.

PREDICTIONS AND POTENTIAL REMEDIES

The Mexican influx of the past two decades represents the largest sustained mass migration of any one group to the United States and eclipses the earlier arrivals of Irish, Italian, and Jewish settlers. More than seven million Mexican-born people now reside in the United States, and most of them have arrived since 1970 ("American scene" 1998). Gregory Rodriguez, a research associate at Pepperdine University, states "we are assimilating differently than other immigrant groups. . . . We are maintaining our 'Mexican-ness' even as we become American in a way that Italians, Irish, Jews and Greeks could not" ("American scene" 1998, 17). Mexican immigrants, combined with smaller surges from Central America and the Caribbean, are altering American society in ways that are both subtle and profound.

The consequences of rapid growth and demographic shifts are more dramatic and severe in some states (those with fewer people) than in others. The Hispanic population in Nebraska, for instance, soared by 71.2 percent between 1990 and 1996, a rate faster than among any other segment of people in the state ("State's Hispanic numbers" 1997). The state's minority population growth rate was nearly 15 times larger than the non-minority growth rate, according to the U.S. Census Bureau (1997). The state's healthy economy has created the need for more workers, particularly in meat-packing plants and on farms, and this has drawn a large number of Hispanics to the state. Though the total minority population of Nebraska is relatively low (3.8 percent), the trends of minority population growth for the state, as in many Midwestern states, are significant for the future.

Many look at California and predict that other regions of the country will experience similar struggles due to immigration and migration, including worker displacement, poverty, and homelessness. In an effort to prevent similar problems, Americans for an Immigration Moratorium in Northwest Arkansas (AIMNA) was founded to fight immigration to the state. Al Morris, founder of the organization, states "we are being colonized . . . our schools are being impacted, our taxes are up, property values are down and health care is being overburdened" ("American scene" 1998).

To fight animosity, Mexican immigrants are showing signs of political activism. An extraordinary 255,000 people born in Mexico became naturalized citizens in 1997, shattering the previous single-nation record of 106,626 Italians who naturalized in 1944 ("American scene" 1998). Naturalized citizens often turn out in record numbers on election day to exercise their newly conferred right to vote. As this group of new citizens begins to impact the political systems, communities will experience even greater changes. In Grand Island, Nebraska, two local Mexican citizens have developed a Spanish-speaking radio station specifically programmed for Spanish-speaking audiences in the community, including sponsors that advertise in Spanish. Programming includes news of Mexico as well as of the local area. As the number of Spanish programs increases, knowledge about local community issues will also increase. Increased knowledge often encourages citizens and residents to become more politically active.

Native residents of rural communities frequently express ambivalence toward immigrant newcomers and their families. Central to resident concerns are community-wide economic viability, housing availability, and educational quality. Benefits of a thriving economy are felt throughout rural communities, and residents acknowledge the tedious work and long hours immigrant laborers contribute to the growing economic base. Conversely, immigrants are also blamed for taking away jobs from local residents. Nonetheless, the unemployment rate in the Midwest stands at 4.3 percent, a record low throughout the region (Bureau of Labor Statistics 1997).

Significantly, experts agree that education is the largest public cost associated with immigration. Districts face rapid enrollment increases and an influx of non-English-speaking children. If public education is to benefit all children in this country, communication barriers and cultural animosity must be overcome. Yet, access to bilingual education is being contested at local and state levels; policy actions in California, for instance, have recently challenged bilingual education. How can educators provide an optimal learning experience for their students and the next generation of this country if policy makers, administrators, human-service providers, and parents disagree on the basic content of educational curriculum?

Many communities have established diversity committees, working to bridge the cultural chasm between local residents and immigrant newcomers. Effective committees are working with local businesses to ameliorate difficulties arising from population surges. An example is the implementation of annual inspections of rental property in Marshalltown, Iowa. Prior to the inspections, some landlords charged laborers by the head and let them sleep in shifts, or packed immigrant workers into apartments and substandard housing units with rotting floors or broken windows. Such practices have largely diminished in Marshalltown, due to the successful activities of local steering committees.

Illegal immigrants and refugees present additional complexity to issues surrounding rural community change. As long as illegal immigrants work in plants that abuse the labor force, it will be difficult to regulate working conditions. Illegal workers do not report infractions of work place conditions. Communities must assume responsibility, along with local industry, to protect citizen-consumers becoming more political in their actions and eventually making decisions about the quality of life within the community. The IBP plant in Lexington, Nebraska worked closely with community leaders in the mid-eighties and early nineties to establish safe working conditions and conditions that met the needs of their employees. A child care facility is located on the IBP property and the management serves on several community boards to facilitate communication between citizen groups and the company. These examples provide a vision of the collaboration that must occur if the transformations of local communities are to encourage and promote healthy surroundings for their life-long and new residents.

Like most aspects of life in the United States, issues surrounding immigration are complicated and often puzzling, especially in small communities. The challenge to the changing rural landscape is to design strategies to support the new residents, the economy, and the changing face of communities. Transitions will indeed continue to occur in the rural Midwest. The agenda for the future is the identification of 'best practices' within rural communities that have successfully adapted services and markets to the changing population. Lessons learned can inform the work of leadership and guide changing communities into the future.

REFERENCES

"America's Heartland turns into hot location for the melting pot." 1995. *Wall Street Journal,* 31 October, sec. 2, 5.

"American scene." 1998. *Los Angeles Times Newsday,* 7 January, sec. 1, 17.

Barkley, D. L. 1995. "The economic change in rural America." *Journal of Agricultural Economics* 77: 1252–59.

Broadway, M. J. 1995. "On the horns of a dilemma: The U.S. meat and poultry industry." In *Any way you cut it: Meat processing and small-town America,* ed. D. D. Stull, M. J. Broadway, and D. Griffith, 41–60. Lawrence: University Press of Kansas.

Bureau of Labor Statistics. 1997. "Employment rates in the U.S. *Department of Labor.*"

Cortese, A. 1982. "Moral development in Chicano and Anglo children." *Hispanic Journal of Behavioral Sciences* 4 (3): 353–66.

Cortese, C. F., and B. Jones. 1997. "The sociological analysis of boom towns." *Western Sociological Review* 8 (1): 76–90.

"Cities must face immigrant growth." 1997. *Tulsa World,* 24 May, sec. 2, 11.

England, J. L., and S. Albrecht. 1984. "Boomtowns and social disruption." *Rural Sociology* 49 (2): 230–46.

"Farmers, meatpackers, and rural communities." 1996. *Rural Migration News* 2 (2): 3–5.

Fitchen, J. 1991. *Endangered spaces, enduring places: Change, identity and survival in rural America.* Boulder, Colo.: Westview Press.

General Accounting Office. 1998. *Community development: Changes in Nebraska's and Iowa's counties with large meatpacking workforces.* (GAO/RCED-98-62).

Gouveia, L., and D. D. Stull. 1995. "Pork, poultry, and newcomers in Storm Lake, Iowa." In *Any way you cut it: Meat processing and small-town America,* ed. D. D. Stull, M. J. Broadway, and D. Griffith, 109–28. Lawrence: University Press of Kansas.

Grey, M. 1995. "Hay Trabajo: Poultry processing, rural industrialization, and the Latinization of low-wage labor." In *Any way you cut it: Meat processing and small-town America,* ed. D. D. Stull, M. J. Broadway, and D. Griffith, 129–51. Lawrence: University Press of Kansas.

Griffith, D., M. J. Broadway, and D. D. Stull. 1995. "From city to countryside: Recent changes in the structure and location of the meat- and fish- processing industries." In *Any way you cut it: Meat processing and small-town America*, ed. D. D. Stull, M. J. Broadway, and D. Griffith, 17–40. Lawrence: University Press of Kansas.

"The heartland's raw deal: How meat packing is creating a new immigrant underclass." 1997. *The Nation*, 3 February, sec. 1, 3–4.

"The human dimension." 1995. *St. Louis Post-Dispatch*, 17 December, sec. 1, 4.

"Immigrants are being drawn to Midwest." 1996. *Des Moines Register*, 30 June, A1, A3.

"Immigrants Transform Midwest Towns." 1996. *Rural Migration News* 2 (1): 2.

"Immigration's other side: Interdependence." 1996. *USA Today*, 30 September, 19–22.

"Immigration and the changing face of rural America." 1996. Ames, Iowa: Conference Proceedings. Rural Migration News: [http://migration.ucdavis.edu/egi/iHound.acgi] accessed February 2000.

"Impact of meatpacking plants studied." 1997. *Omaha World Herald*. 22 December, sec. B, 1.

"Latinos surge in Midwest." 1996. *Rural Migration News* 2 (3): 1–4.

"Legislators put focus on fences, not jobs." 1997. *San Diego Union-Tribune*, 3 November, sec. B, 2.

Lyson, T., and W. Falk. 1993. *Uneven development in rural America*. Lawrence: University Press of Kansas.

"Meat packers feel heat with INS probe." 1996. *Wall Street Journal*, 27 September, 1.

"Melting pot of perceptions: Hispanics, whites in towns both clash and commingle." 1996. *Omaha World Herald*, 18 February, sec. 1, 3.

"Mexico president hails economic reform anti-poverty program to put human face on a nation's gravest failing." 1997. *Rocky Mountain News*, 16 March, sec. A, 44.

"Midwest: Meat/poultry processing." 1998. *Rural Migration News* 4 (1): 4–6.

"Midwest new hub for Hispanics." 1995. *USA Today*, 15 December, sec. 1, 9–10.

Molina, E. V. 1995. "Mexico-populations: The changing face." *Excelsior*.

"More kids needing English: Immigrants' children swelling Iowa schools." 1996. *Des Moines Register*, 11 October, sec. 1, 1, 3.

Mueller, S., and S. L. Baugher. 1996. "Family functioning of interracially married couples in the Midwest." Paper presented at the American Sociological Association, New York. NEB-92-025 (research supported by U.S. Department of Agriculture).

"The new jungle: Illegal in Iowa.: 1996. *U.S. News & World Report*, 23 September, 33–45.

Prochaska-Cue, K., and A. Ziebarth. 1997. "Growth and locational impacts for housing in small communities." *Rural Sociology* 62 (1): 111–25.

"Rural Hispanic population booms." 1996. *Tulsa World*, 13 October, sec. 1, 5, 7.

"Sociologists watch the heartland adjust to Latino immigrants." 1997. *The Chronicle of Higher Education* 27 June, sec. B, 2.

"State's Hispanic numbers surge." 1997. *Lincoln Star Journal*, 22 December, sec. 2, 1.

Stull, D. D. 1990. "When the packers come to town: Changing ethnic relations in Garden City, Kansas." *Urban Anthropology* 19 (4): 303–20.

Stull, D. D., and M. J. Broadway. 1995. "Dances with cows: Beefpacking's impact on Garden City, Kansas and Lexington, Nebraska." In *Any way you cut it: Meat processing and small-town America*, ed. D. D. Stull, M. J. Broadway, and D. Griffith, 85–108. Lawrence: University Press of Kansas.

Stull, D. D., Broadway, M. J., and K. Erickson. 1992. "The price of a good steak: Beef packing and its consequences for Garden City, Kansas." In *Structuring diversity*, ed. L. Lamphere, 35–64. Chicago: University of Chicago Press.

"Thirteen Hispanic families sue over schools in Willmar." 1996. *Star Tribune*, 8 March, sec. B, 1, 4.

U.S. Census Bureau. 1992. *Hispanic population in the U.S. Department of Commerce, Bureau of the Census.* Washington, D.C.: (No. 502).

U.S. Census Bureau. 1997. *Geographic mobility. Department of Commerce, Bureau of the Census.* Washington, D.C.: (No. 496).

Reframing Rural Education—
Through Slippage and Memory

KAREN ANIJAR

> If you want to have change, of course, the bottom line is that the folk
> for whom the change is meant must be involved in it.
> —Dorothy Cotton, civil rights activist

A cohort of students whom I interviewed in 1994 (with Kathleen Casey[1]) forms the scaffolding of this chapter. Their voices were juxtaposed against, and set in relation to, the narratives of other students, teachers, and administrators interviewed during 1996 and 1997. Narratives from other researchers were added to the polyphonous, oftentimes complex, and contradictory curricular chorus. Spliced between all of the narratives and the surrounding theory are quotations from Southern activists. The bricolage of story fragments woven into the textual tapestry by this methodology seek to highlight the particular exigencies of educational experiences in the contemporary rural South.

LOOKING BACK THROUGH SMOG-CLOUDED VISIONS:
THE AUTOBIOGRAPHICAL IN THE REGIONAL

When I wrote the first draft of this chapter, I was teaching in a school of education in Los Angeles. Often in Southern California I felt like a free-floating signifier wallowing in a contentious semiotic stew of increasing hatred, ennui, anomie, and alienation. The laws passed over the past five years in the "Golden State," reminding me that all that glitters is not gold, did affect me on many levels. My sense of alien-nation may have had much to do with my last name, or may have had much (more) to do with the antagonistic racialized coding embedded in the various propositions passed by California voters (including 187, 209, and 227).

The paradox (for me) being that for a long time I taught Spanish in rural North Carolina. In grades K through 5, the students I taught were in a second-language immersion program. I also received a grant to conduct a dance program in Spanish (as a way of implementing two components of the state's Basic Education Program) for our middle school students (grades 6 to 8). In the evening, on occasion, I would conduct classes at the community college, in Spanish, for law enforcement students. I was called upon to translate, from Spanish to English, for a myriad of people and groups. My second language may have distinguished me somewhat in the county where I resided, but language never prohibited my movement. Speaking both Spanish and English was looked upon as something positive, not otherwise. Pat Mora, a children's book author, writes about her experiences in rural Kentucky:

> Here, I was in a school in which perhaps all teachers and students were Euro-Americans, and the young faces welcomed me with affection and interest. I told them about myself, about the desert I come from, about Mexico, about being Mexican American. As I would tell them about being bilingual and about the pleasures of languages, they would say, "Teach us some Spanish! Teach us some Spanish!" (Mora 1994, 298)

What I experienced in Los Angeles bore no resemblance to what I experienced in North Carolina or what Ms. Mora described in Kentucky. In some ways you could say that I found the "bad ol' South" in Southern California.

MEMORIES ARE ODD

> A mythology exists in which schools are better when remembered than when actually experienced. . . . Many parents think that their education was superb and believe that their children should enjoy the same experience. They want the past improved on or added to, but not changed altogether. (Seals and Harmon 1995, 120)

Memory is a funny thing. Like history it is filtered through selectivities and slippages and silences. The history of the South (whatever that space ultimately is) remains contested, but is always in process. The myth of Southern regional separate-ness often (re)creates the area as an overly determined, monolithic place. The stereotypical constructions, which have continually essentialized and conflated the South (into a singularity), do not account for local conditions, contingencies, and diversity. "Many urban white people" still "have this fantasy that rural people wake up in the morning, feed the cows . . . and go to sleep" (James 1998, 209). A paradox being that in some rural areas, like those in which the interviews took place, agriculture is not the main industry anymore.

Tacit stereotypical assumptions, which are so pervasive, contribute to the aura of oppression, and to oppressiveness. Oppression capital has enormous political and pedagogical consequences. Particularly when generalizations are internalized as a reality. And, especially when culture is still seen as a tangible entity rather than as a process.

PARALLEL PATTERNS AND PERSISTENT FEATURES

Parallel patterns continually emerge in the narratives. Youth is pastoralized as a time of innocence and naiveté, rural areas are pastoralized as places that are naive and unchanging, and so our eyes are directed away from profoundly important themes. When we pastoralize, we trivialize, we don't recognize, and we don't see. We also do not listen.

> The narrators all named their respective communities as both rural and Southern. Which means "that we are not progressive at all," Mary stated flatly. "We are a traditional community."

The areas in which all the interviews took place were predominately white, almost wholly English-speaking, and poor. Most of the population was born in their area of residence. Nevertheless, there has been an influx of people from other regions of the South, from other states, and from other nations to each locale. "It's not unusual today to find a waiter with a Bronx accent in Atlanta. Or a family from Illinois with a passion for grits and a Birmingham, Alabama address" (Spaid 1996, 3). But even with the infusion of other people from other places "things remain pretty much the same." Mary's description is somewhat deceptive, for the more things seem to stay the same the more they change. Nothing is ever static.

THIS SCHOOL IS OUR SCHOOL

The focus on *their* schools (from a very personal perspective) was always present in the narratives. The schools are central to the community. In many rural communities, the school can be the largest economic enterprise. But in areas that are economically oppressed, being the largest may not be enough. "Jobs are what we need here," David stated.

In North Carolina, for example, a group of rural school districts subsidizes both college tuition and books for employees who want to become teachers (Piane 1998, 598). "Well," Priscilla exclaimed "I would not want to teach anywhere but here at ___. I went to school here you know, and so did my parents." Many teachers have expressed "a desire to do something 'more meaningful' with their lives, to 'give back' to their communities" (Piane 1998, 598). "It is a very personable place to work, I know everyone here."

It was not that long ago that the schools in which the interviews took place were considered some of the worst in the nation by traditional standards. There has been dramatic improvement in test scores. Yet, I don't think traditional measures speak to those aspects of curricular and educational experience which represent transformative genres of curriculum. What I found particularly edifying was listening to students who had developed a sense of agency and engaged in a public political pedagogy and praxis concerning their own education and their own lives.

FROM THE HILLS OF BEVERLY

> "Feelings," Eudora Welty wrote, "are bound up in place." Knowing where one started allows one to understand where he or she is. This relationship between place and feeling is central to curriculum theory's study of place. A sense of place sharpens our understanding of the individual and the psychic and social forces that direct him or her. Without place our appreciation of such particularistic forces tends to be fuzzy and depersonalized. Indeed, place particularizes and conveys embedded social forces. (Kincheloe and Pinar 1991, 4)

There is a bit of irony involved in writing a chapter about the rural South in Los Angeles. It has been four years and three thousand miles since I left North Carolina. It has been over five years since I left the rural public school district where I taught. Now I look back on the experience with a form of misty-eyed melancholy that begins in memory.

> (From a phone conversation)
> Karen: So you're telling me nothing has changed.
> David: No, you know policies change and stuff and then they change back, and you just sort of go with the flow, so nothing really changes, its always the same. Except that I am older and tired-er and I bought a house.

I am worried that I am painting a homesick picture existing only in the "Disneyfication"[2] (Fjellman 1992) of my own social construction of nostalgia, of my own highly personal transformation of public memory, through a very distinctive and particularistic lens of selectivities and silences. Yet, knowing that, "burdened by nostalgia," my reflections, my voice, may well be seen as a discourse that could be "prey to sentimentality" by an audience that consigns its melodies to fantasy" (Grumet 1990, 281).

"Southern identity" writes Sears (1990), (perhaps all identity) is an

> elaborate social fiction(s). This dusting of reality by the wings of a fairy seduces us into believing that our differentness is our specialness. But, to borrow a phrase from Bukminister Fuller, differentness is verb—it energizes the journey of our spirit but it is not our spirit. (Sears, 1990: 483–84).

The desert creates mirages, and illusions. The sands shift and swirl creating new configurations, new alliances. One day I was sitting in North Carolina listening to the farm reports. A week later I was Los(t) in Angeles. I had no idea that when I entered the credit-card class in suburban California (which is often labeled as progressive, and post-modern, and forward-looking), that I would look (back) to the voices of students and teachers in a rural Southern county. But I did so con-stantly. I always found there a source of inspiration. I always seemed to encounter possibility, and political praxis. A question still lingers however: why?

> Sherone (a student): __ (town) is a small rural town outside in the mid-dle of nowhere. It's near a big city, but it's probably different that __ (city). Because . . . there's lots of white teachers. And they've been out in the country their whole lives. And their daddy says, "Well, you stay away from them niggers. Don't get near them." And they're just used to hearing that. So that's what they do!

> Sarah (a student): This is a bad place. . . . When I graduate I am going to move!

> James (a student): It is sort of nice here in some ways. . . . Your teach-ers know you, they really know you. Everyone knows you. I think that might mean something.

> Trina (a teacher, interviewed by phone): Why? Be grateful that you got out. You don't realize what is happening to the schools here. I don't know if I am going to teach that much longer. I know I am beginning to get burnout.

INHABIT THE WIND

Given the southern penchant for narrative and for place, political, and cultural histories of the South can usefully and concurrently be situated in the life histories of individual students . . . individual autobiographical work . . . complemented by group processes. (Pinar 1991, 180)

Pinar argues that what the Southern literary renaissance achieved in the early decades of the twentieth century must now be achieved in Southern mass culture, namely a restoration of memory and history of Southern place so that it can be understood as distinctive historically and culturally. (Pinar, Slattery, Reynolds, Taubman 1995, 535)

Home is the space where we act responsibly and with responsibility. It is an expression of collective subjective, interpretive tradition and interpretive community. We frame our lives with the authority and authorship of home. The who, what, where, and how of home is a space where a curricular lens is constructed that transcends schooling. The school in this sense becomes part of a larger public pedagogical practice and can initiate "political action . . . redress[ing] the injustices found in the field site or constructed in the very act of research itself" (McLaren 1994, 140). Home creates and sustains a public political pedagogy. It is in esoteric exigencies, and in particular spaces and places where voices do not merely speak, but are heard. Home is "the how and who [which is] intimately tied to the where" giving a "specific content and a coloration . . . a local habitation and a name . . . a concrete situatedness in a common world. . . . [It is] as social as it is personal. . . . It is also collective in character" (Casey 1993, 23).

I think about all the things we did here when we were just starting out teaching. I doubt if we could have had the opportunity to do it anyplace else. We had a lot of fun, didn't we? But I really think we accomplished a lot. We really did, and the community supported us. That did make a big difference.

Place is crucial to understanding pedagogical practice and educative mechanisms in their broadest definition. Joe Kincheloe (1991), theorizing about the autobiography of William Morris, *Terrains of the Heart,* expressed that "his sensitivity is innocently phenomenological, as he responds poetically to the southern ghosts that haunt his mind and body" (123). Continuing his discussion and use of Morris' autobiography, Kincheloe reminds us that "for the first time in my life, I understood that not all Americans are from somewhere" (132).

> John (a student): Like some teachers. . . . They are different because
> they're from different places. Like this one teacher he's from up North
> and stuff, and he's not teaching racism and stuff, 'cause he gets racism
> too, 'cause the other teachers call him "Yankee" and stuff.

In rural spaces and places where the "self" is so often tied to the land,
to the place, it would be ludicrous to think of the self apart from
place. Identity is bound up in place. We *in*habit home-places, even
though we may well be far away from them (physically, socially,
morally, and ideologically). Mississippi remained in Morris's soul no
matter where he traveled, no matter where he went. He was both part
of it and a part from it, but it was in him and around him and sur-
rounded him much like Hegel's pure being.

> Mrs. Smith (retiring principal): I have been all over the place, but I
> know I will always come back here. This is my home it is where I belong,
> these are my children. . . . I just think it is time to pass the torch on . .
> . but, it is hard not getting up each morning and getting ready to go
> to the school. I have been doing it for so long. . . . It's what I do, it's
> who I am. . . . I got to learn how not to get up so early in the morning
> now. There are other things I can do, other things I enjoy, I just need
> to find out what they are.

Paulo Freire believed education was a process in which ordinary people developed their own language, derived from their own interpretations of social realities. Within the local, within small communities
he saw "the invention of citizenship" where substantive dialogue can
and does open up and transform praxis. It is in small communities
where the public and private spheres blend, where the artificial distinctions between public and private worlds are transgressed. The
cultivation of community localizes caring.

> We're not going to make any changes in what's going on in this coun-
> try until we can make changes in our own community. Not just for us,
> but for everybody. And that's what we're trying to do, make things bet-
> ter for everybody. (Judy Mullins, union member, Newport News, Va.
> [*Southern Exposure*, IX, no. 4: 93])

"We care about places as well as people, so much so that we say that
caring belongs to places. We construct our social worlds in place, we
build upon them, we build with them, and it is from the localized
space of care that we can extend our reaches into larger worlds with
a "unity of mutual implication" (Casey 1993, 113).

> If you left a light on the hill some younger person is gonna' be inspired
> later on to come on and pick this torch up and keep it moving. (Sally
> Mae Hadnott, community organizer and president, Autauga County
> NAACP, Prattville, Ala. [*Southern Exposure*, IV, no. 4: 22])

I would contend that the success of any curriculum innovation is
inexorably intertwined with its direct application to local needs and
particularities.

> There's power in us a-comin' together. (Cordelia Maxwell, nonage-
> narian at Old People's Day, Eighty-Eight, Ark. [*Southern Exposure*, XIII,
> no. 2–3: 15])

Lest we forget, the civil rights movement was ignited in the small
Black Baptist churches that dotted the landscape of the South,
extending into a national movement. The sparks are forgotten in the
fire whose flames have long gone out. Archimedes wrote, "Give me a
place to stand and I will move the world" (quoted in Casey 1993, ix).
"Freedom . . . becomes something that must be won within discourse
(McLaren 1991, 248). But discourse can only happen in spaces where
you can be heard.

> Look, I'm thirteen and I know I can't change the world. I wish I could,
> I am going to make a difference, but I have to start with myself. Then
> I can go on and do other things. Right now nobody is going to listen
> to me, I'm thirteen. But, you know they should listen, I have a lot to
> say. All kids have a lot to say.

As Casey (1995) reminds us, the problem is not with the voices that
speak . . . but with the ears that can not hear" (223).

Framing the Project

> Voice is what enables us to participate in a community. "Finding the
> words, speaking for oneself and feeling heard are all part of the
> process." (Britzman quoted in Connelly and Clandinin 1990, 4)

The students' biggest wishes were for "more freedom" and "more
input." They wanted to be "treated like adults." At three of the four
schools, they complained that administrators never engaged them in
adult dialogue and, therefore, students felt they had no voice in their
own education. The students were fairly knowledgeable about Kentucky's site-based councils and the role they play in school decision-making, but felt that wasn't enough. Students seem to want a voice in their
educational experience (Appalachian Educational Laboratory 1998).

> Maybe people should listen to us for a change . . . I mean we do go to
> school so we know what is happening in schools. (Samantha [student
> narrator])

There has been a proliferation of narrative research in education
with an increased focus on "voice," empowerment, and community.
In theory, this "allows"[3] the voices of the historically silenced to enter
the public arena.

> I found out that if you can talk, you have a lot of power. You can get
> your message across, open the lines of communication and use them
> for yourself. (Donna Bazemore, poultry organizer, Center for
> Women's Economic Alternatives, Ahoskie, N.C. [*Southern Exposure*,
> XVII, no. 2: 33])

> There are a lot of people who think, "what can I do? I don't have a
> voice in what goes on." Well, one person doesn't have a voice. But
> together, a lot of people do. (Foster Strong, financial-reform activist,
> Little Rock, Ark. [*Southern Exposure*, XVII, no. 1: 18])

Nevertheless, despite the rhetoric and hyperbole, there remain
resounding silences in several spheres. Rural voices are usually absent
in discussions surrounding schooling. The prevailing codes in American education speak to and are firmly rooted in a northern suburban experience. Within this nexus, urban becomes other, and rural
becomes other. In the final analysis, the fate of the symbolic other is
to be ignored, marginalized, or declared deviant" (Casey 1992, 2).
Anthropologists and sociolinguists have argued that "schools . . . tend
to value middle-class modes and speech over others, and this privileges white middle class [suburban] students, since the school environment reflects their goals and aspirations" (O'Loughlin 1994, 14).

> I was born in the South and raised in ignorance. I was taught to be a
> good girl and a hard worker—to be nice and polite and obedient. For
> years this cultural conditioning worked and, like a sleepwalker, I
> walked the working-class chalk line unaware of my oppression and its
> true causes. (Brenda Best, educator, activist, union supporter, Char-
> lotte, N.C. [*Southern Exposure*, IX, no. 4: 33])

People are never merely puppets inscribed upon. We all "live in a
world of others' words" and our "entire life is an orientation in this
world, a reaction to others' words" (Bakhtin 1984, 146). Nothing is
ever overly determined. The same words can mean different things
depending on who is speaking and who is listening. Our understandings are contingent on, and forged in, relationship.

BUCOLIC CHILDHOOD

The romantic nostalgia associated with childhood as a construction is a relatively recent phenomena. We construct childhood as a period of innocence and play that deflects significant issues of powerlessness. What we term "childhood" is a period of time that is unstable, contextual, and contingent. Our definition of a traditional childhood is "no more than 150 years old" (Steinberg 1997, 17). Childhood is not, nor was it ever, a universal category.

The shift in the family unit and the work patterns of the family precipitated a change in fundamental understandings of the roles and the composition of the family, and the language of the family. Children were no longer an economic asset or considered useful to the survival of the family. "The child became both economically useless and emotionally priceless" (Skolnick 1991, 35). Young people are not outside historical and cultural formations, even though we present childhood as something that always was, is, and will be irrespective of history, geography or economy. The focus on childhood as a special place, a tabula rasa of innocence and goodness, creates and sustains a scenario where children are not thought of as humans, but as if they were *just like* humans.

Not unsurprisingly, young people are often considered to be "unreliable informants" regarding their own education, just because they are young. While popular psychology continues its celebration of "becoming" for adults, this same process is labeled "unstable," "hormonal," or "a developmental stage" in teenagers. Because young people's education is not "complete," because they have not entered the "real" world of work, because they are not married, because they are not property owners, young people are judged incapable of constructing significant knowledge. Adults continually benefit from their superior position within this relationship in an exploitative exchange. Immature young people require the continual guidance of elders whose authoritative pronouncements must not be questioned. Particularly given that

> [T]he late twentieth century has seen the emergence of a new conception of the period we call youth in extended time, and not only is youth accustomed to its own downward mobility. Where we have a conception of the essential innocence of childhood, we now have another relation: the essential guilt of youth. (Ackland 1994, 146)

Teenagers are denied any authority with respect to their own lives. As Maxine Greene (1993) reminds us, "there are ways of speaking and telling that construct silences" (216). Silenced by adults, young people's particular perspectives are lost; and their own interpretations often remain unheard; as one young woman articulated with tremendous clarity,

> [Teachers] don't listen to your problems. They see it like at their age. They see it as a problem that they would face when they're being in their thirties and forties, but they don't see it as being thirteen years old, and having the same problem.

"The teacher," Greene (1973, 272) protests, "is continually being asked to write a pious and authoritative role for himself and submissive or savage roles for the young people he teaches."

Of course, not all teachers succumb to this temptation. The roles teachers play and the curriculum teachers impart exist in a social context filled with complexities, contingencies, contestations, and contradictions.

ESSENTIALIZING AND ROMANTICIZING THE RURAL CURRICULUM

> My feeling is that if improvement is going to begin anywhere, it will have to begin out in the country and in the country towns. This is not because of any intrinsic virtue that can be ascribed to rural people, but because of their circumstances. Rural people are living, and have lived for a long time, at the site of the trouble. They see all around them, every day, the marks and scars of an exploitive national economy. They have much reason, by now, to know how little real help is to be expected from somewhere else. They still have, moreover, the remnant of local memory and local community. And in rural communities there are still farms and small businesses that can be changed according to the will and desire of individual people. (Theobald and Nachtigal 1995, 113)

Writing about rural Southern youth a West Virginia report stated that typically a student:

- will begin the day with a fairly long bus ride;
- is likely to be from a poor family;
- is more likely than other students (i.e., those from more populous areas) to have parents who are unemployed;
- is more likely than other students to receive special education services;
- is less likely than other students to be classified as gifted;

- is more likely than other students to have parents who did not graduate from high school
- • has a greater chance than other students of becoming a high school dropout. (Seal and Harmon 1995, 119)

The green pastures, rolling hills, clear skies, and sense of rootedness and connectedness to place belie the profound poverty of the rural recesses in the South. Nevertheless, what may "warm the hearts of those who see education as the road to economic well-being for the nation," (ibid., 119) is the notion that "rural communities have precisely the qualities for which the critics of American schools are now looking" (ibid., 119).

In the part of Los Angeles county where I taught for the past four years, a new school called Plaza Azteca (which was once a shopping center[4]) has been built, offering what city officials mistakenly labeled a transformative curriculum genre. The school will house K through 12 classes, vocational classes, university classes, and literacy classes. I laughed a bit, knowing that I had taught for years in a school system much like the new model being proposed.

> A comprehensive report on rural schools found high rates of poverty and low levels of educational attainment. It found that rural schools were staffed by younger, less well-educated faculty members and administrators who earn lower salaries and benefits than their metropolitan counterparts. The report documents persistent problems related to rural school finance, teacher compensation and quality, facilities, curriculum, and student achievement. . . . Rural communities are said to be suffering from a bitter harvest, with the well-educated emigrating to metropolitan areas for better jobs. . . . Rural schools have image problems that stem from long-standing negative attitudes toward country people. (Hertzog and Rittman 1995, 113)

Illiteracy and poverty cannot be merely attributed to image problems. Essentializing imagery betrays the very real material conditions by which people negotiate their lives.

Yet, something is beginning to stir. Even with students who were trained to be docile, trained to say "yes sir" and "no ma'am" and trained via rote methods not to shake things up!

> This is a roar of anger that cannot be silenced and will not be ignored. (Elena Hanggi, financial-reform activist, Little Rock, Ark. [*Southern Exposure*, XVII, no. 1: 17])

> We live in a home my great grandparents built when they arrived here in a covered wagon 125 years ago. Like many of my neighbors and cousins I cannot support my family from the land the way my ances-

tors did. . . . The loss of independent farm culture rocked us out of our
place in he universe. We . . . looked for someone outside of ourselves
to blame. (Wimberly 1996, 27)

A core of dissatisfaction exists which is emblematic of a systemic crisis.

> If I am good enough and if I can only work hard enough, I will live in
> the lap of luxury. If I have not achieved the American dream for myself,
> why not? How come I am such a loser? Our religion reinforces these
> feelings. Christianity tells us we are responsible for the support of our
> families. If we just scrape by, we're to blame for our own misery. Politi-
> cians exploit this sense of loss. (Wimberly 1996, 26)

The future looks economically bleak. And so it is acceptable to blame
someone other than the conditions which brought about the crisis.
"Blaming . . . the substance for . . . a metaphor we have filled with
hate" (Wimberly 1996, 26). A metaphor that does not go unnoticed
by students:

> Lots of whites have different feelings towards blacks because they think
> that "Oh, they don't want to work. They don't want to have a job, and
> stuff like that." That's not right. I lived in a white neighborhood all my
> life, and I felt that, and I've heard it .
>
> Sarah (a student): But, you know . . . I mean . . . I, just one time, went
> out with a black guy. And I suffered a lot of persecution. I found out I
> wasn't strong enough to stand up to that. I feel ashamed of that. But
> it's just kind of hard! I was called "nigger lover" every day. And I know
> it was wrong, but I just couldn't take it.
>   But I think if I ever had the opportunity to go out with another black
> guy . . . well . . . I would do it. Because, I think now I've grown stronger.
> And I feel that anybody who says things like that is just stupid, and they
> don't know what they are talking about, and they are ignorant.
>   You know, I really feel that, now I would go with somebody that was
> of a different race. And I did. But I got so much persecution here in
> this little town. And it's so hard.
>   I understand I am different too. I'm a very different person. My reli-
> gion is different from everybody else. I've gotten picked on always.
>   I'm glad I'm white. Because, I mean, I'm no better than somebody
> that calls somebody a "nigger" or a "pre-human being."
>   I think that you should be happy just who you are. I mean, being a
> white person, perhaps I can get something done in this society .
> Because, if I was black, I probably couldn't. Which is bad. But it's true.
> And I hope I could do something about racism, and things like that.

Many inhabitants of rural communities in the South, which has traditionally been the poorest area of the nation are suffering the consequences of the collapse of the unskilled labor market as many fac-
tories (especially textile plants) have closed. Competition with

third-world countries has contributed to the low wages (Billings 1988; Deaton and Deaton 1988). There were many shortsighted measures that did not consider the effects of globalization or the hyper-reality of postFordist consumption. The ludicrous notion that rural schools existed apart from the postmodern contributed to the huge gap between the type of action instrumented and what was and is really needed, what Jessie Wimberly (1996) calls a combination of neighborly relations and teachable moments, where information is challenged, not belief systems.

Instead, schools (for example) turned to programs of Tech-Prep (as if the factory jobs might someday come back) and Total Quality Management ("yeah, they make us work more hours to pretend we have a say"). And a hegemonic social order is maintained for just a little while longer. But, students are not blind to this. A West Virginia report explains this peculiar problem:

> Two schools had co-op programs in place, and their students spoke well of the "real-life work experiences" they provided, although some of the jobs were described as "not relevant." (Appalachian Educational Laboratory 1998)

As one student explains, "I am learning computer skills on a dinosaur! That's going to get me a job . . . right!" Another student laments: "I got a calculator and the teacher wouldn't let me use it. I asked "why?" She said, in case it broke I wouldn't be able to do math. I said "I would buy another one." She (the teacher) missed the whole point."

Students remain highly conscious of their existence as antagonistic objects in adult discourse ("adults never do see it from your perspective, it is like they have forgotten what it feels like to be kids"). They are also highly conscious of their existence as rural Southerners ("people say we speak "country," it does affect how they see you").

> Students also reflected views typical to small town, rural living: everyone knows everyone and personal relationships with teachers are common. While the students sometimes felt they didn't have a reference point for comparing the quality of their schools to others, they were quick to point out that they had knowledge about "things" outside their community-they were not "isolated and sheltered" from the rest of the world. (Appalachian Educational Laboratory 1998)

The students do understand what the adults do not.

> Sarah: Some of us have got to make a change, but I don't know who could change it. Teachers can't do that because they're not trying hard enough. Some of my teachers this year have been really bad. I mean some of them don't even care that people are racist. And some of them, you know, they support racism.

Readily identifiable motifs appear in student narratives, correspond-
ing in important ways to themes that have been articulated by critical
pedagogues, curriculum theorists, and rural community organizers.

> Here's a dream that comes to mind . . . there's a safe space; folks vent
> their pain, prejudice, and anger. They identify and fully acknowledge a
> long list of wounds. . . . The group's leader brings the men to see how
> these open wounds affect interaction with others. . . . The group is
> encouraged to take a bold new step to invite some newcomers to join
> them for an evening. . . . Ultimately, the[y] work together to create a pos-
> itive and inclusive vision of life in our community. (Wimberly 1996, 27)

"You know, said Katherine "we really need to talk about all of this but
our teachers won't let us. . . . They say if it isn't going to be on the test
and aren't going to do it. But, we need to talk about things like race."

> Sherone (a student): Most of the teachers at the school don't even rec-
> ognize black. . . . February as the national black awareness month.
> They don't make anything to put on the wall. And like . . . on Lincoln's
> birthday, they have some little hats to put on the wall. And George
> Washington's birthday, something about him. And they talk about
> George Bush's birthday, and stuff like that. But they don't ever talk
> about Malcom X.
>
> And every time you ask a teacher about it, they say "Well, it's not in
> the curriculum. We can't teach that!" In the one class that we did do
> it, there was a disturbance. The teacher said: "I'm never doing any-
> thing like that again!" . . . I feel that a lot of white kids want to help
> black kids forget their past, and where they come from, and stuff like
> that. And that black teacher . . . I think a lot of white people have
> helped her forget her past and where she came from.
>
> And that shouldn't be right, because you should always remember
> where you came from. Like white people can walk around with their
> Jewish hats on. Why can't black people walk around with black hats on?
> Malcom X and Martin Luther King hats?

"Narrow" or "essentializing" educational forces have very little significance for these young people. They recognize that green hills and
red barns are betrayed by the rust, dust, and crumbling structures of
a profound economic and social crisis. What remains central to their
educational aspirations are the ethical, political, and economic
dimensions of curriculum, which they see as something sorely missing from their classroom experiences.

THE ETHICAL CURRICULUM

> You can sit around and say it's a shame the way they treat us, but if you
> know darn well something shouldn't exist, you've got a moral respon-

sibility to point in the right direction. The more you know, the more responsibility you have. (Addie Scott Powell, founder, Bethlehem Area Community Association, Bethlehem, S.C. [*Southern Exposure*, 13, (2–3): 25])

We stood up to the Governor and the legislature, and we said, "We will have justice. We will not participate in the demeaning of our profession or of the children and communities we serve." They said, "Accept things as they have always been." We have answered them with strength, unity, and determination to change the system forever. (Alice Harden, president, Mississippi Association of Educators, Jackson, Miss. [*Southern Exposure*, 13 (5): 39])

Sherone: If they're gonna be a teacher, they should at least care about you. They act like they care sometimes . . . and the other times . . . they just want to kill you!

Kimberly: Yeah!

Malika: I mean, some teachers . . . some teachers, they so mean, they need to go to hell!

Kimberly: I mean, sometimes we mess up. But, I mean, they should just help us through those times . . . that we mess up, and make sure we don't do it again. Not yell at us!

Sherone: I mean, when they became teachers, they knew stuff like that was gonna happen. Instead of taking it out on everyone else, they should just go straight to the problem! It's not like we're not saying we're kids !

Katherine (a student): The teacher says she is here for us . . . but, she doesn't bother to listen?

People often have rather prosaic objectives concerning schools. Schools ought to be about reading, writing, history, math, and science. Occasionally, educators may speak to different sorts of values, fostering a democratic spirit, aesthetics, community, and even spirituality. Students, however, place an ethical education as the primary goal for schools and as central to any educative process.

"Kids can be asses and kids are rude. They are unpolite sometimes. Kids are like asses sometimes," but the students distinguish their own culpability from that of teachers: "But teachers don't have to act like asses with them." "I think some teachers are dumbasses," said Sherone, one of the adolescent narrators. His comment is immediately modified by Malika: "They're not . . . they not really dumbasses. They're bitches!" Such a distinction is, in my interpretation, a clear expression of the way in which students hold teachers especially accountable; it is not simply ignorance ("dumbass") which causes some teachers to behave in reprehensible ways; they are conscious and deliberate actors ("bitches") in the eyes of the students." "Bitches" Malika explains "should know better, they aren't stupid!"

What is important is that there is a large gap between word and action, which is seen on a daily basis in school practice. "Just because you are a teacher, doesn't make you smart, there are too many assholes who are teachers." Or as Kimberly explains:

> All teachers say they became teachers because they love kids, but, you know that it is really just easy to say something. Too many people are hypocrites. Too many people say something and then do something completely different. Too many teachers do that.

The language which students use to blame some of their teachers is profoundly ethical. It is within the context of an ethical understanding of education that the student's condemnation of certain teachers' behaviors must be understood.

So, Sherone declares that "some teachers are a pain in the butt!" because they do not show "respect to the students"; some teachers undermine their own authority by dis(respect)ing the students. Elsewhere, Sherone says: "If they're gonna be a teacher, they should at least care about you!" "[Teachers] should be more strict in kindergarten, 'cause then [kids]'ll know not to [be rude] when they are older." Sarah explained,

> If teachers don't start showing them to pay attention and listen well in kindergarten, and in first and second grade, then they'll never do it. They'll always be rowdy, and never pay attention to you, and just always go up and walk in front of the speaker.

The role of the teacher is presented as that of a moral model: "Little kids look at teachers and see 'em and they start doing whatever the teachers are doing."

When the students observed "rude" behavior on the part of some of their teachers ("they would sit there and they wouldn't pay any attention"; "they wouldn't even act like they were serious"; "teachers would snap their fingers at the little kids who were talking"), it is reprehensible on many levels. While their teachers appeared to enforce (in lip service), they actually violated their own stated code of correct behavior. The gaps and slippages did not go unnoticed by the students. As Jennifer described: "students . . . ask the teachers and the teachers wouldn't know because they weren't paying attention." The students would say "The teacher isn't paying attention. Why should I pay attention?" Sherone, responding to Jennifer's comment, retorted: "like, if you're going to do that, why should you want to be a teacher?"

These students are sagacious enough to choose among the variety of available moral mentors. They find mentors whose behavior coincides directly with the stated code of correct behavior, rather than rejecting the code itself. The students have an exceptionally clear criterion for praise or censure of teachers, including the teacher's moral integrity, and her/his capacity to embrace students' own interpretations.

> ___ is the only teacher I met in a long time that'll, like, tell me what the facts are. And she'll speak what she knows and what she thinks. And if you don't agree with it, then you just don't agree with it. She'll side with you if you change her mind, but you have to present the facts to her and things like that.

> I mean there was this one teacher who said we could come to him with our problems, so I did . . . but he was having his own problems . . . so he was too busy to help me at school. What a dick!

> I think it is important to have a teacher that acts like a teacher. I mean somebody who cares about you, somebody who teaches you something and doesn't make you do stupid little worksheets cause they are too busy doing other things.

Is it any wonder why, when the students were given the opportunity to voice their concerns, they censured those teachers who abdicated what they felt was the their ethical responsibility "to teach us something!" The students do want to learn. But, they also recognize filling out worksheets is not learning and "balancing her checkbook" is not teaching. Their concern is one that is communal, for they worry at length about the younger students in their K-8 school. ("Who do you think that second graders learn from, they have to set an example and I don't see them doing it.") They worry about what the future will bring. They worry about how will they survive "when the hosiery factory closed up."

THE POLITICAL CURRICULUM

Pierre Bourdieu referred to "the hegemony of symbolic violence." The students seem to be well aware of the "interrelationship between symbolic violence produced through language" (Bartoleme and Macedo 1997) and the experience of racism, classism, and sexism which also betrays the essentialized constructed genteel patina of innocence in their school experiences, in their experiences as young people, and in their experiences as working-class rural southerners. The students recognize that material conditions are inexorably intertwined with cultural conditions. And that cultural conditions are experienced as material conditions. Speaking about the inclusion of Malcom X, Sherone states:

> And every time you ask a teacher about it, they say "Well, it's not in the curriculum. We can't teach that!" In the one class that we did do it, there was a disturbance. The teacher said: "I'm never doing anything like that again!"

Sarah censures particular teachers' use of racial categorization as a mechanism for reinforcing academic inequality.

> One teacher I have used to have always gave black people bad grades, and white people good grades. I felt . . . I mean . . . it was so stupid! It just outrages me! Like in pre-algebra, there's this one black guy. He's the smartest guy in the class! And the teacher, if he misses something, the teacher doesn't pay any attention to him.
>
> And in social studies, every time the teacher doesn't know something, she'll look at him. And he'll always answer it. But she'll give credit to some little white kid. And so . . . he just stopped answering questions.

Even though Sherone does not use explicitly racial language, we must not forget that it is a young black man who traces his progress through elementary school, in words virtually identical to Sarah's.

> Like when I was little, I made straight As in kindergarten. They still wanted to hold me back, 'cause they said I wasn't ready for first grade. But my mom and them. . . . They argued about it forever.
>
> I went to the first grade, and I had this one teacher, and she kept getting in my face! Even though I was making As in her class! And she said " Well, if you don't understand it, don't come crying to me. I didn't do anything! I can't help you! I don't know!"
>
> And then I went to second grade, and then I went to third. And in fifth grade my real dad was killed in an accident, and then my fifth grade teacher . . . she really was the only teacher to talk to me.
>
> In sixth grade, they taught separately and they didn't talk to anyone. They were just friends among themselves, and they didn't care about students. As long as you go to class, and take a couple of notes, you're OK.
>
> In seventh grade, there's like one teacher. He'll talk to you and stuff. 'Cause I have him for five out of eight periods. And he's the only one that will talk to you. The rest of them are like: "Oh, forty five minutes of you, and then you're gone!" And they're just, like, ready to get rid of you.

Both of these passages speak of perceived racial oppression, and much more. The students are extremely aware of some things that often escape the notice of their teachers and administrators. It is not only issues of race that are paramount to students. They also recognize that issues of class are bound up in place, race, and ethnicity. They recognize that other identifiers such as race often hide the displacement of class in school settings.

According to a report conducted by the Appalachian Educational Laboratory (1998), "Unequal treatment . . . hindered learning, according to students. In a small school where everyone knows everyone else, who your family is can affect the way you're treated and the grades you receive, they thought."

Teachers judge the students by their families, " 'cause they know their families and that isn't fair" (Katherine). "Teachers' kids always do better in school, whether they deserve to or not" (John). "If it was a white kid he wouldn't have gotten in trouble" (Laura). Indeed, "students acknowledged that many "special ed" students aren't really mentally challenged, but simply had "poor home life" (Appalachian Educational Laborabory 1998). "You know what I think about that, don't you?" Sarah queried. "I think it is horrible . . . but it happens, you know, it happens all the time! "

All of the young people who act as narrators for this chapter evidence severe alienation from major parts of their educational experience. But their perspective is not simply existential; it is also political, because this curriculum of anomie is generated by those in positions of power over them.

> Sarah: I don't really like school. I have a few teachers that really get on my nerves! Especially ones that expects us to copy five million tons of notes. And I just can't do it. And, as an eighth grader, I really feel that I don't want to be copying that many notes, and I don't need the responsibility of a high school student. Because I'm not a high school student yet. And I kind of feel, maybe, there's too much expected of kids.
>
> I mean, people don't learn about creativeness and how to be creative and how to explore their feelings and they just don't learn about that. All they learn about is how to do mathematics and science and language arts. And I think maybe some of that needs to be done away with. Maybe we have too much of that. Maybe we need to start showing people how to explore themselves. I mean if you don't know yourself, then you really don't know anything!

Elsewhere Sarah says that middle school "is not a time to be lectured to; it is a time to experience." Speaking to another dimension of this same theme, Sarah contends that, as children grow up, "creativity dies and school does it!" Using a provocative metaphor, she further asserts, "What frightens me so, and continues to upset me, is that I think that the schools try to make us into zombies! I don't want to be a zombie. Do you?"

THE ECONOMIC CURRICULUM

> Teachers are the most resourceful people in the whole world. If our
> government wants to save money, it should put teachers in charge. We
> can get blood out of a turnip. (Loretta Goff, principal of the Agricola
> School, Mississipi [Alan 1995, 19])

What these young people understand is that power and caring
(Noblit 1993) are inexorably intertwined; further, they are able to
distinguish between "power used for its own sake" and "power used
in the moral service of others" (Noblit 1993, 35).

The number of times when these young people mention "paying
attention" is alarmingly significant. "They don't pay any attention to
the kids. If you catch it, you catch it. If you don't, you don't," says one
speaker. In the words of Malika:

> Like, teachers don't care. They don't pay enough attention to the chil-
> dren. If they could get the children off on another teacher, they'll do
> that to get rid of them. And not do what they're supposed to. I know
> a lot of teachers who don't teach their class.

An implicit theory of the political economy of hidden curriculum
emerges from the continual reiteration of such phrases in the narratives. Not only is there a scarcity of attention from teachers; it also
seems as though students do not possess the amounts or kinds of
attention which teachers demand. In this market of social exchange,
some students lack the required assets because of their race; some
because of their religion; others because of their social class. Adolescence, it seems, dispossesses them all.

Because their efforts are neither appreciated nor reciprocated,
these young people perceive their relationship with most teachers to
be largely an exploitative exchange. Many teachers operate in their
own narrow self interest; they work for their own individual profit.
These teachers engage in insider trading, because their publicly
stated ethos does not correspond to the actual transactions in which
they engage. As Katherine says, "They taught separately and they did-
n't talk to anyone. They were just friends among themselves, and they
didn't care about students."

Such an analysis corresponds in important ways to the evidence of
economic antagonism between working-class students and middle-
class teachers which appears throughout the narratives. The perceived self absorption of certain teachers' behavior is criticized in an
economic vocabulary. Instead of paying attention, these (teachers)
"did their paper work; they filled out their income taxes," remarks
Sherone. He continues: "Some people told me that if we ever went
to a year-round school, they'd quit. Because they didn't want to do

that." Referring to the abdicated moral responsibility of teachers to children, Sherone comments elsewhere:

> [Kids]'re not at home six and a half hours out of the day. 'Cause they're at school and teachers should teach them a little something. Instead of being like: "Well, I'm just here. Y'all could do whatever y'all want to. I get my paycheck at the end of the month."
> Or the beginning of the month, or whenever they get it. And they're always complaining: "We don't get paid enough for this." Why did you become a teacher then, dummy? God! I mean, like, I don't get it !

In spite of their apparent dispossession from the official school curriculum, these young people do not see themselves (nor ought they be seen) in culturally deprived terms. These pubescent pedagogues do have solutions: "Keep them in school, and keep them from dropping out. And go on to college and better themselves. . . . That's what we need to do!"

> Then they won't drop out of school, and they will go on to better themselves. Then they won't end up on welfare, and social services, and stuff like that. And they won't tax their tax dollars out of their paychecks. And everybody would be happy, and everything would be peaceful.

Living in an environment of chronic illiteracy, under- and unemployment, what the students hope for and envision is education for economic emancipation. "Some of us have got to do it, we have to," said Sarah.

Indeed, they do! The economic crisis that has fueled the frightening political measures in California has its parallels in the rural recesses of the South. Black churches have been burned as blacks become targets because they "stand in for the real enemy"; it is "protest by proxy" (Nixon on the Southern Exposure Web site 1998).

"That's why these skinhead groups are rising," says Reggie White, associate pastor of the church that burned earlier this year in Knoxville, Tennessee. "Those racist attitudes are still out there, and too often we've forgotten our history. We don't want to think about lynchings; we don't think about the burning churches." (Southern Exposure 1998). And as history and memory are continually effaced by romantic nostalgia and longing for a place to go home to that may never have been, we forget that the past is always a product of the present.

> I think that a lot of white people have helped her forget her past and where she came from. That isn't right, because you should always remember where you came from.

The students can and do historicize notions of identity, race, and class, revealing the partiality and incompleteness of each category. They recognize the limitations of the categorical.

And yet, here in California in the post-proposition 209 world, I do find hope in the voices of rural youth who do recognize the problems that they confront, and who do not forget history.

> It makes me feel ashamed to be white sometimes. Because I know that my race has killed, has hunted down, persecuted and has punished people of a different race, or different at all, for years. It makes me feel guilty.
>
> I hate that my race did that. Does that. I can't help it. I hope that people that were persecuted can look past that. Can look past my skin, and into what a good person I am, or a good person that I try to be.
>
> I hate that our world is built like that. Sometimes when I think about it, I wish I were black. I think that you should be happy just who you are. I hope I can do something about racism and things like that.

But we won't find it "hoping for Tara to return or walking through the wilderness with miles to go before your feet" (a southern arts teacher). What the students look toward are moral mentors who recognize the problems, and seek an ethical curriculum of economic liberation while really naming the historical, political, and material conditions that inscribe themselves on their lived experiences. "After all," says Katherine "you can teach us something or not. But things can't keep going on like this!" Loretta Goff, the principal in Mississippi whose words began this section would agree:

> We discuss among ourselves what is the best thing we can do to get a concept across to the kids. If we conclude we should change the way we're doing something, we change.
>
> Yes, it's hard work, but the children are so responsive. We sense such an improvement in the way they feel about themselves, and the way they feel about learning. (Alan 1995, 19)

NOTES

1. Some of the themes and many of the narratives in this chapter come from research conducted at a multicultural arts festival. The narratives were collected in an earlier work co-authored with Kathleen Casey.

2. Nostalgia (derived from the Greek *nostos*, to return home, and *algia*, a painful condition) literally means a painful yearning to return home. The word presents a peculiar paradoxical conundrum, derived from the pathological and invested into popular vernacular during the 1950s. Fjellman, in *Vinyl Leaves* (1992), makes a powerful argument concerning the Disneyfication of America, which is directly related to the nostalgic mode. Unpleasantness would be dropped from history and stories of the past would be told in a carefully and commercially repackaged form. The world in the Disney version would be a better place if history could be rewritten, leaving only the parts that "should have happened." The transformation of memory that this ideology presents confuses history with nostalgia for a past that never was, or a place that never was. The pastoralization of rural spaces and places falls into this phenomenon.

3. It would be disingenuous and clearly colonizing to assume that anyone can empower or give somebody else voice.

4. The shopping center was donated to the school district by the owner. When the neighborhood changed from a white working-class neighborhood to Latino (Mexican, Mexican-American) many of the merchants fled. It was not given to the community out of benevolence, but as a tax writeoff. The wonderful thing is that the school (courtesy of the Richard Simmons' health club that left) got an Olympic-sized swimming pool.

REFERENCES

Ackland, R. 1995. *Youth, spectacle and violence,* Boulder, Colo.: Westview Press.

Allen, R. 1995 September. "A rural school mobilized the people and miracles happened." *Teaching PreK-8* 26 (1): 52–58.

Anijar, K., and C. Casey. 1997 October. "Adolescent as curriculum theorist." *Journal for a just and caring education* 3 (4): 381–98.

Appalachian Educational Laboratory. 1998. http://www.ael.org.

Bakhtin, M. 1984. *Problems of Dostoevsky's poetics.* Ed. and trans. by C. Emerson. Minneapolis: University of Minnesota Press.

Bartoleme, L., and D. Macedo. 1997. "Dancing with bigotry: The poisoning of racial and ethnic identities." *Harvard Education Review* 67 (2): 222–56.

Beaulieu, L., ed. 1988. *The rural south in crisis* Boulder, Colo.: Westview Press.

Billings, D. 1988. "The rural south in crisis a historical perpsective." In *The rural south in crisis,* ed. L. Beaulieu, 13–29. Boulder, Colo.: Westview Press.

Brtizman, D. 1989. "Who has the floor? Curriculum teaching and the English teachers strugle for voice." *Curriculum Inquiry* 19 (2): 143–62.

Casey, E. 1993. *Getting Back into place: Toward a renewed understanding of the place-world.* Bloomington: University of Indiana Press.

Casey, K. 1992. Unpublished document-notes.

———. 1993. *I answer with my life.* New York: Routledge.

———. 1995. "New narrative research in education." *Review of Research in Education* 21: 211–53.

Connellly, M., and J. Clandinin. 1990. "Narrative Inquiry: storied experience and narrative inquiry." *Educational Researcher* 19 (4): 2–14.

Deaton, B., and A. Deaton. 1988. "Educational reform and regional development." In *The rural south in crisis,* ed. L. Beaulieu, 304–24. Boulder, Colo.: Westview Press.

Fjellman, S. 1992. *Vinyl leaves: Walt Disney World and America.* Boulder, Colo.: Westview Press.

Freire, P. 1982. *Pedagogy of the Oppressed.* New York: Continuum.

Greene, M. 1973. *Teacher as stranger.* New York: Wadsworth.

———. 1994. "Teaching as possibility: a light in dark times." *Journal of Pedagogy, Pluralism and Practice 14.2* http://www.lesley.edu/JAZC

Grumet, M. 1990. "Voice: The search for a feminist rhetoric for educational studies." *Cambridge Journal of Education* 20 (3): 321–26.

———. 1991. "Curriculum and the art of daily life." In *Reflections from the heart of educational inquiry,* ed. G. Willis, and W. Schubert. Albany: State University of New York.

Grumet, M. 1991. "The politics of personal knowledge." In *Stories lives tell: narrative and dialogue in education,* ed. C. Witherell, and N. Noddings, 67–77. New York: Teachers College Press.

Hertzog, M., and M. Rittman. 1995. "Home, family and community: Ingredients in the rural education equation." *Phi Delta Kappan* 77 (2): 113–18.

James, D. 1998. "Pale face, red neck." *Transtion* 7 (1): 204–18.

Kincheloe, J. 1991. "William Morris and the southern curriculum: Emancipating southern ghosts." In *Curriculum as social psychoanalysis: Essays on the significance of place,* ed. J. Kincheloe, and W. Pinar, 123–54. Albany: State University of New York Press.

Kincheloe, J., and W. Pinar. 1991. *Curriculum as social psychoanalysis: The significance of place."* Albany: State University of New York Press.

McLaren, P. *1994. Life in Schools.* New York: Longmann.

———. 1991. "Critical pedagogy: Constructing an arch of social dreaming and a doorway to hope." *Journal of Education* 173 (1): 9–34.

Mora, P. 1994. "A Latina in Kentucky." *Horn Book* 70 (3): 298–301.

Noblit, G. 1993. "Power and caring." *American Educational Research Journal.* 30 (1): 22–38.

O'Loughlin, M. 1995. "Daring the imagination. Unlocking the voices of dissent and possibility in teaching." *Theory into practice* 34 (2): 107–16.

Pinar, W. 1991. "Curriculum as social psychoanalysis: On the significance of place." In *Curriculum as social psychoanalysis: Essays on the significance of place,* ed. J. Kincheloe, and W. Pinar, 167–86. Albany: State University of New York Press.

Piane, B. 1998. *Phi Delta Kappan* 79 (8) (April): 596–602.

Pinar, W., P. Slattery, W. Reynolds, and P. Taubman. 1995. *Understanding curriculum.* New York: Peter Lang.

Seals, K. R., and H. L. Harmon. 1995. "Realities of rural school reform." *Phi Delta Kappan* 77 (2): 119–23.

Sears, J. 1990. *Growing up gay in the south.* New York: Hayworth Press.

Sher, Jonathan P. 1995. "The battle for the soul of rural school reform." *Phi Delta Kappan* 77 (2): 143–49.

Skolnick, A. 1993. *Embattled paradise: The American family in an age of uncertainty.* New York: Basic Books.

Southern Exposure Website. 1998. http://www.southernexposure.org.

Spaid, E. 1996. "In rural Georgia town the twain do meet." *Christian Science Monitor* 88 (219): 3.

Steinberg, S. 1997. "Kinderculture: The cultural studies of childhood." *Cultural Studies* 2: 17–44

Theobald, P., and P. Nachtigal. 1995. "Culture, community and the promise of rural education." *Phi Delta Kappan* 77 (2): 132–36.

Wimberly. 1996. "A bridge not yet built." *Southern Exposure* 24 (1): 25–28.

Winter, W. 1988. "Charting a course for the rural south." In *The rural south in crisis,* ed. L. Beaulieu. Boulder, Colo.: Westview Press.

Corporations and Native Americans in Rural America: Who Wins?

SANDRA FAIMAN-SILVA

RURAL UNITED STATES COMMUNITIES ARE LIKE THEIR COUN-terparts around the globe: reservoirs of opportunity for entrepreneurial development. The U.S. South is particularly appealing with its cheap, exploitable—often ethnic-minority—populations, and its historic resistance to unionization (Colclough 1988, 75–76; Flora et al. 1992, 37–38, 136–37). The rural southeastern Oklahoma Choctaw Nation is just such a strategic hinterland region for two multinational industries, Weyerhaeuser Timber Company and Tyson Foods, Inc., which each entered the region seeking cheap labor, readily available raw materials, and favorable business opportunities. This ten-and-one-half county region was formerly home to the Choctaw tribe, who were relocated from their ancient Mississippi homeland to Indian Territory on the 1830 Trail of Tears. Choctaws settled on a 6.8 million acre estate which they called the Choctaw Nation, an environmentally diverse region bordered by the Arkansas River to the north and Red River to the south. The tribal estate included rich bottomland where some Choctaws developed large homesteads and ranching operations, some using slaves who had accompanied Choctaw settlers on their westward trek. Other Choctaws settled in the hilly Kiamichi Mountains, where they established small subsistence farms, replicating traditional lifestyles brought from Mississippi. In addition to growing corn, beans, sweet potatoes, cotton, and squash, rural Choctaws hunted, fished, raised cattle, and foraged in the abundant Kiamichi hardwood and pine forests.

The new Choctaw homeland by the late nineteenth century was again being overrun by whites, who entered Indian Territory to trade, extract natural resources—mainly coal, stone, and timber—and not infrequently to conduct illegal activities. By 1890 the approximately 10,000 Choctaws were far outnumbered, with more than 28,000 whites and 4400 blacks living in the Choctaw Nation. Choctaws experienced the devastating effects of tribal allotment in the early twentieth century,

259

with passage of the Dawes Severalty or General Allotment Act in 1887. They were soon transformed from a semi-sovereign tribal nation into a rural ethnic minority, their land and tribal sovereignty depleted (Faiman-Silva 1997).

Today, Southeastern Oklahoma's rural main streets in Idabel, Talihina, and Wright City, bear the face of rural poverty: dusty streets and empty storefronts. A century ago the Choctaws numbered 80 percent of the region's population, whereas today they are fewer than 15 percent, with Euro-Americans about 80 percent and African Americans about 5 percent regionally (U.S. Census Bureau 1990).

ECONOMICS OF RURAL DECLINE

Southeast Oklahoma between 1925 and 1970 experienced trends typical of rural America generally: population declines, farm consolidation, and increased welfare and public-sector dependence (see Dillman and Hobbs 1982, 62–63; Snipp and Summers 1991, 82–83; Cornell 1988, 60–62; Flora and Christenson, eds., 1991). The number of farms in Southeast Oklahoma's McCurtain County declined by more than 50 percent and in Pushmataha County by nearly 60 percent between 1929 and 1959 (BIA 1973, 13). Also, like the rest of rural America, the region experienced a noticeable population decline between 1930 and 1960, felt by all sectors, including Choctaws, whose population fell by nearly 40 percent (Dillman and Hobbs 1982, 62–63; BIA 1973, 13).

Depopulation was prompted by a combination of push and pull factors, including declining agricultural employment opportunities, coupled with federally sponsored Indian relocation programs during the 1950s. Since 1960, the trend began to reverse, as many Choctaws returned to take advantage of U.S. Housing and Urban Development-sponsored "mutual help housing" programs, instituted in 1969, which provided low-cost housing to eligible Native American families. Between 1960 and 1980, Southeast Oklahoma's Choctaw population doubled, to about 16,000, about 10 percent of the region's population (Faiman-Silva 1997, 107).

Southeast Oklahoma's economy since the Depression has been typical of hinterland economies globally and the rural U.S. generally: part-time, intermittent employment opportunities, a preponderance of unskilled, low-paid jobs, and ever-increasing state subsidies through public-sector employment, with notable increases in service and government jobs (Coppedge and Davis 1977; Jorgensen 1978; Hall 1995). Overall employment in McCurtain and Pushmataha

Counties declined by nearly 50 percent from 1940 to 1960, mainly due to dramatic declines in agricultural and forestry jobs sectors. During the same period, government jobs—a sector that employed far few workers than did agriculture—increased by 50 percent (Peach and Poole n.d.; Faiman-Silva 1997, 110–11).

Facing more constrained job opportunities, many Choctaws worked for timber companies and in other industries, providing cheap, unskilled and semi-skilled labor, often part-time. Some Choctaw families migrated to Texas to pick cotton during the Depression and World War II, while others did odd jobs for white families or cut and stripped timber posts in the local timber industry. Families supplemented meager cash earnings with gardening, foraging, and the raising of chickens and hogs. Choctaws also weathered hard times by selling allotted land, which by 1960 had been reduced to a mere 144,000 acres. By the early 1980s, most timber region Choctaw families owned fewer than five acres, all that remained of early twentieth-century allotments (Faiman-Silva 1997, 109ff; Debo 1951, 4–5; author's interviews 1980–82).

Southeast Oklahoma's poverty and unemployment woes persisted in the 1980s and 1990s with the highest unemployment rates statewide in 1981, about 10 percent, while the state averaged 4.8 percent unemployed. Local minority unemployment in 1981 was the highest in Oklahoma, 18.6 percent (Oklahoma IMPACT 1981, 31). In 1987, Choctaw timber region unemployment was an alarming 37 percent (*Bishinik* [Durant, Okla.] November 1987, 2). In 1990, Native Americans in both McCurtain and Pushmataha Counties continued to show high unemployment rates, with McCurtain County unemployment 13.3 percent and Pushmataha County, 14 percent. White unemployment was 10.5 and 11 percent respectively in those counties (U.S. Census Bureau 1990; Faiman-Silva 1997, 110–11).

Choctaws and their Euro- and African-American neighbors, many lacking both structures and opportunities for economic self-sufficiency, were exploited in the region's "secondary labor market" as cheap labor for an increasingly hegemonic U.S. economy (Hall 1987, 9, 11–13; 1988; Castile 1993, 273; Flora et al. 1992, 42–43), dominated locally by two multinational giants, Weyerhaeuser Timber Company and Tyson Foods. Choctaws and other minority and unskilled local workers provided substantial value, both in the actual wage work they performed and as *semiproletarians* (Giminez 1990), whose mixed-subsistence production strategy used unpaid household labor to perform essential household maintenance tasks, thereby subsidizing inadequate wages. A study of fifty rural Choctaw households conducted by the author in the early 1980s found that nearly 85 percent of Choctaw householders sampled worked only part-time, mainly in chicken processing and timber work, earning wages that could not sustain their families (Faiman-Silva 1997, 160).

Rural timber region Choctaws, as they did historically, depended on a "mixed subsistence" survival strategy, combining wage labor with hunting, foraging, gardening, craft, and commodity production, resource-sharing, and other extra-wage laboring activities, to meet their livelihood needs. More than 50 percent of households surveyed in the early 1980s participated in some household non-wage subsistence activities, including cutting timber for home heating, fishing, hunting, foraging, quilt-making, and the raising of chickens and hogs (Faiman-Silva 1997, 151). Choctaws also relied on public sector and tribal benefits, particularly food stamps, social security payments, AFDC (Aid to Families with Dependent Children), and tribal assistance programs. Another common subsistence strategy was to share housing space. Younger nuclear families frequently moved in with parents for extended stays, while working as seasonal tree-planters or in the chicken processing industry, relying on parents for child care and other household resources.

Increasingly, Choctaws and their rural neighbors turned to public welfare to subsidize inadequate wages. Between 1950 and 1963 public assistance payments in McCurtain County rose by 60 percent and in Pushmataha County by one-third (Peach and Poole n.d. chart 16). In 1980, nearly half of Pushmataha's population, 45.4 percent, lived below federally established poverty levels, and in McCurtain County the rate was 37.1 percent, while the overall state average was 18.8 percent (Oklahoma IMPACT 1981; Faiman-Silva 1997, 112).

CORPORATE DEVELOPMENT; HINTERLAND UNDERDEVELOPMENT

As in peripheral or hinterland economies globally, corporations like Weyerhaeuser and Tyson Foods, among the top Fortune 500 U.S. companies, find southeast Oklahoma highly attractive both for its cheap labor and its abundant natural resources. Although the region does benefit materially from the multinational corporate presence in jobs, wages, tax revenues, and other corporate "perks," symptoms of economic malaise caused by unemployment, underemployment, and an inadequate tax base—common by products of global hinterland development—are evident in poorly maintained housing, boarded-up urban buildings, and other signs of infrastructure decay. Corporations use shrewd business practices to maximize profits and minimize costs locally, and it is frequently local workers and the communities where they live that bear the hidden costs of entrepreneurial success. As Roberts (1989, 671) noted, "Corporations operating in a world strategy have no strong commitment to place, relocating different divisions according to the most cost-effective strategy—where certain types of labor are cheaper, are more available, or where favorable tax or other concessions are obtained."

Corporate profit-maximizing strategies include vertical and horizontal integration; product diversification; sometimes ruthless management and labor practices; exploitation of cheap, relatively abundant labor; and various forms of corporate "welfare." These strategies constitute the core of corporate entrepreneurial practices, strategies which both Weyerhaeuser and Tyson Foods employ locally and regionally.

For example, Weyerhaeuser, since it entered Southeast Oklahoma in 1969, has increased corporate efficiency and profits through several forms of what Flora et al. (1992, 37–38) call "corporate restructuring." First, Weyerhaeuser in 1969 bought the land holdings of a smaller regionally based company, Dierks Forests, Inc., in what was the largest land purchase in the history of the U.S. timber industry. This purchase of 1.5 million acres eliminated competition and monopolized the regional asset base.

Secondly, the company introduced highly capital-intensive technological innovations to streamline production and reduce labor costs. Weyerhaeuser in 1972 opened a pulp and paper mill in Valliant, Oklahoma, which converts woodchips into paper and paperboard products. This mill requires the labor of only six men who operate the entire mill's sophisticated assembly line from a single control panel (*Pulp and Paper* 1972, 43). Also, the corporation has diversified its production regionally and nationally into other entrepreneurial areas, maximizing product and by-product use. Among its diversified activities are product research and development, acquaculture, home financing, and real estate development enterprises (see Faiman-Silva 1997).

Third, Weyerhaeuser has increasingly relied on cheaper production strategies, such as labor subcontracting, whereby essential timber cutting, maintenance, and harvesting tasks are performed by subcontracted crews. Labor subcontracting, increasingly prevalent in the highly competitive industrial arena of the 1990s, reduces corporate labor force maintenance costs and turns over to the workers themselves many costs to maintain and reproduce the local labor force (Roberts 1989, 678ff; Flora et al. 1992, 42–43).

Weyerhaeuser's subcontracting of timber cutting, harvesting, and tree maintenance tasks, the heart of its local industrial enterprise, epitomizes how the industry exploits and marginalizes laborers to achieve maximum economic advantage and accrue profits while paying little attention to the human costs to workers. This corporate profit-making strategy leaves to the public sector welfare state and workers themselves the task of subsidizing inadequate salaries and benefits. This hidden form of "corporate welfare" is not unique to the Choctaw Nation, but is replicated throughout rural U.S. communities, where underemployed, inadequately paid workers turn to public-assistance programs to subsidize inferior wages.

Labor subcontracting has become big business in Southeast Oklahoma. Currently, only about 12 percent of timber brought to Weyerhaeuser's Wright City Plant is carried by company trucks, the rest by contractors. An estimated 200 men work for independent tree-cutting crews, 100 in chipping operations, and about 40 to 60 in seasonal tree planting. Weyerhaeuser has also contracted road and mill maintenance jobs as well, further eroding its unionized work force (author's interviews, Woodworkers W15 local president, 25 January 1990, 8 June 1993). Throughout the 1980s and 1990s Weyerhaeuser has increased its use of contracted labor to harvest timber, plant, and maintain stands, while slashing its unionized work force dramatically, a strategy designed to reduce corporate costs and increase its competitive edge.

Local Choctaws work as part-time timber cutters, loggers, tree planters, and in tree maintenance crews, hired by labor contractors to perform essential timber-related tasks. The head contractor, or crew boss, obtains work contracts directly from Weyerhaeuser through competitive bidding and then hires his own crew for a particular job. Working as a contractor, crew member, or as an independent logger is a highly competitive, cyclical business dependent on Weyerhaeuser's demand for timber. The head contractor typically supplies all heavy equipment, while timber cutters supply their own chainsaws. Contractors generally provide only legally mandated worker benefits, such as workmens' compensation, and workers often do not receive family health insurance benefits, nor are they paid for layoffs, holidays, or sick days. Non-unionized, subcontracted workers generally receive lower wages and more unstable hours of employment.

Tree planting and tree maintenance, including thinning and insect control, are also performed by part-time crews hired through private contractors. Contractors hiring tree-planting crews afford their workers even less job security and lower pay than do logging contractors, since the tree-planting season is only about four-and-one-half months long, from January through mid-May. Workers reported that they planted from 1000 to 1500 trees per day, with women planting fewer than men and novice workers planting more slowly than experienced workers. Tree planting is physically rigorous, entailing trekking through recently clearcut acreage rough with deep grooves and stumpage where seedlings must be set. Approximately half the tree planters are females and older workers who take advantage of the seasonally available work. Workers are told that if trees are planted too far apart or if the stand does not take, they must return to the site to replant, the cost of which is taken out of their wages (author's interviews, 1981–82, 1993; reported in Faiman-Silva 1997).

Weyerhaeuser's tree harvesting practices have made unionized timbermen a truly dying breed in Southeastern Oklahoma. A single Weyerhaeuser logging crew of twelve men, the last remnants of what in 1978 was a company logging force of 278, has been threatened with elimination if it cannot remain competitive with contracted loggers. This followed corporate field assessments by a management team sent from Tacoma, Washington, which determined that company logging operations were not cost-effective (author's interview, 9 June 1993). This logging crew is also the most ethnically diverse of Weyerhaeuser's work force, with five Native American and seven Euro-American members (reported in Faiman-Silva 1997).

Weyerhaeuser's contract labor system benefits the corporation by substantially reducing or eliminating various production costs which are borne instead by workers and contractors, such as costly equipment like skidders (a truck used to drag logs to transport vehicles) and limbers and worker transport costs to widely scattered work sites on their estimated 890,000 acres of active timberland in the region (which strip extraneous limbs from trees). Also, the company does not bear costs to maintain permanent workers who may not be profitably used throughout the year; nor must it provide costly benefits such as health insurance and vacation pay, further eroding already sub-standard wages. Work force subcontracting and other downsizing measures have reduced Weyerhaeuser's local unionized work force by nearly one-half since the late 1970s, from a high of 2800 to 1525 in 1993 (author's interview, Woodworkers local president, 8 June 1993). "We have had to get lean and mean and competitive, and more profitable," said Weyerhaeuser's Wright City public relations officer (author's interview, 2 June 1982).

The Woodworkers Local W15, representing Weyerhaeuser's unionized workers, has vocally opposed Weyerhaeuser's use of contract labor throughout the 1980s and 1990s not only for its exploitation of local workers but also because it erodes full-time jobs and brings in outside contracting crews, taking jobs away from the local community (author's interviews, McCurtain County, Okla., Grannis, Ark., 5 June 1982, 8–9 June 993). Called by one worker "a snake without a head" for its ruthless treatment of its rank-and-file workers both in the field and at the bargaining table, the company has persistently refused to entertain unionization of its contract workers.

CHICKEN PROCESSING, MINORITIES, AND WOMEN

Like Weyerhaeuser, Tyson Foods, Inc., with a regional work force of approximately 1600, is a fast-growing company, which relies on product diversification, cheap labor, and technological innovations to process locally 1.3 million chickens a week. Tyson Foods, Inc., opened a processing plant in Broken Bow, Oklahoma, in 1969, where its approximately 1200 workers processes 100,000 chickens an hour. Tyson also supports approximately five hundred chicken breeder and broiler houses, some corporate-owned (author's telephone interview, 2 August 1995). The job option is particularly attractive for local unskilled minorities and women. Fifty-seven percent of Tyson's local work force is female, and 70 percent of workers are minorities: 25 percent Native American, 30 percent African American, and 15 percent Hispanic.

Tyson Foods, like its neighbor, Weyerhaeuser, uses a variety of highly successful entrepreneurial strategies to maximize profits and minimize costs. It recently purchased Louis Rich Foods, a Phillip Morris-owned subsidiary. In 1992 it bought Louis Kemp Seafood and Arctic Alaska Fisheries, Inc., to diversify its food production enterprises. Also in 1992, Tyson Foods expanded its operations in Mexico, by linking with Mexican poultry producers, Trasgo S.A. (*Wall Street Journal*, 24 June 1992, B, 4; 28 August 1992, B, 4; 11 June 1993, B, 3; 2 March 1992, B, 4). Tyson, and its predecessor Lane Chicken Company, notorious for their anti-union views and union-busting practices, have persistently resisted unionization efforts throughout the 1970s, 1980s and 1990s. One worker at a local chicken plant related that employee efforts to unionize a shop in Idabel, Oklahoma, in 1978 resulted in termination of about thirty workers. She quit as a result and was rehired only after she pledged to refrain from further unionization activities. She said, "I didn't want to go back there but I had no choice. There was no place else to work" (author's interview, 28 February 1981). Ongoing efforts to unionize the Broken Bow, Oklahoma, plant have met with intimidation and threats by Tyson management, and so far have been unsuccessful. Tyson has not been reluctant to use illegal labor and marketing practices. In 1993 the National Labor Relations Board (NLRB) found Tyson guilty of illegal labor practices at an Arkansas poultry plant; and court decisions in 1992 gave chicken growers rights to organize, efforts Tyson and other chicken processing companies actively resisted (*Wall Street Journal*, 12 August 1992, B, 6; author's interviews, June 1993).

The regional economy dominated by these multinationals has given rise to a racially and gender-stratified job opportunity structure, where women and minorities are over-represented in the more poorly paid, labor-intensive chicken processing and unskilled tree-planting and tree-maintenance occupations, while white males dominate the skilled occupations. Woodworkers Union data show that of its approximately 1500 unionized workers, 1100 are white, 80 are Native American (under 5 percent), 300 African American (20 percent), and 12 Hispanic. Long-time Choctaw workers claim that they have been overlooked in promotions to supervisory jobs for which they were qualified, and no Native Americans worked at the company's Wright City corporate headquarters in the 1980s. Contractors, on the other hand, hire women, minorities, and even illegal aliens, often exploiting them with sub-minimum wages paid under the table to do intermittent and dangerous work, such as insect control and tree limbing (author's interviews, 8–9 June 1993). As earlier noted, women are over-represented in lower-paid chicken-processing and under-represented in better-paid timber industry jobs. Weyerhaeuser's local unionized work force is currently only about 15 percent female, while women comprise 57 percent of Tyson's local non-unionized work force (author's telephone interviews, 2 August 1985, 17 August 1996).

CHOCTAW WORKERS
AND MULTINATIONAL CORPORATIONS

Choctaw workers, unlike fully proletarianized urban workers, are not wholly submerged in the wage sector as landless workers, but are *semi-proletarians* (see Giminez 1990), relying on wage work combined with domestic subsistence activities. By supplementing wages with hunting, fishing, foraging, and craft production, along with public and tribal assistance programs, and otherwise "making do," Choctaw householders shoulder many of the costs to reproduce their own labor force, reducing corporate costs. Furthermore, the community and its workers, rather than Weyerhaeuser or other private employers, bear the costs of low wages and seasonally available work, because workers collect unemployment or public assistance or resort to other subsistence strategies, such as gardening, hunting, odd jobs, even collecting aluminum cans, to compensate for low or erratic wages (Hedley 1993; Collins and Gimenez 1990). In the gender-stratified rural households, women's informal unpaid subsistence activities, commodity production, and resource sharing subsidize underemployed and poorly-paid male timber workers, adding value to household wages (see also Shelton and Agger 1993, 39; Ward 1990; Collins and Gimenez 1990).

These hidden forms of "corporate welfare" bring added profits to corporate owners in this poorly understood and frequently over-looked cycle of underemployment and labor marginalization.

Corporations like Weyerhaeuser and Tyson Foods do benefit local communities through "trickle down" effects of jobs creation, tax payments, and other operating incentives. However, these benefits mask the ways in which local communities subsidize corporate profit-making and are themselves exploited as a cheap, secondary labor force. In the arena of corporate profit-making, publics—both indi-viduals and communities—are subverted, indeed mystified, by entre-preneurial enticements, while they shoulder the effects of peripheral economic exploitation.

Choctaws in the early 1980s were divided in their opinions of Wey-erhaeuser's economic impact on them and their communities. Some noted that young adults could find only the most undesirable jobs, such as seasonal tree planting or chicken processing, which paid only at or slightly above minimum wage. Others, however, argued that Weyerhaeuser had made employment prospects more stable and jobs more reliable, particularly for those willing to travel the 75 or more miles to its Wright City timber processing plants. Tribal and Durant city officials—and Weyerhaeuser spokespersons themselves—touted Weyerhaeuser's contributions to local communities, such as scholar-ships, which amounted to $50,000 annually.

Older retired workers voiced the underlying contradictions of the private enterprise/welfare-subsidized economy, when they pointed out that their own lives actually improved only after they stopped working. Said one man in his mid-sixties,

> Living improved after I stopped working. Now I have a steady income from my VA pension. When I worked I earned six dollars per day on the average doing odd jobs. I was laid off a lot. My kids missed school because I was laid off and I couldn't afford to send them. We went to Texas to pick cotton when we couldn't find work around here. The whole family helped the best they could. It was a harder life for us then. (17 June 1981)

Some recognized that it was not better job opportunities but enhanced public sector benefits which had improved their living con-ditions, along with the so-called "mutual help housing" program, instituted in 1969 under the U.S. Department of Housing and Urban Development (HUD), which provided much-needed low-cost hous-ing to rural Choctaw families. Public Assistance benefits, mutual-help housing, and reliance on domestic subsistence provide most house-holds with sufficient cash and material resources to meet their basic necessities, albeit below federally recognized poverty levels. Several individuals pointed out how the housing program had dramatically changed their lives. One said,

> Life has definitely changed for us for the better. We lived in a two-room house growing up. We had no running water, an outdoor privy. If it weren't for the housing deal, we never would have been able to buy a home. (28 May 1981)

Little more than a decade later, sentiments have changed drastically, particularly for Weyerhaeuser's full-time timber workers, who have seen their comrades disappear into the ranks of non-unionized contract workers with corporate downsizing and the move to contract labor. Fearing the loss of their own jobs, they sullenly talk of Weyerhaeuser production quotas, speed-ups, watchful bosses, and the likelihood that today's pay check will be their last (author's interviews, 8–9 June 1993).

Many workers, however, do not link their strained financial circumstances to corporate production strategies. Individually focused, some value the freedom and independence part-time work affords. Others did not blame Weyerhaeuser for hiring them only part-time or seasonally, since most did not actually work directly for Weyerhaeuser, but for their own kinsmen.

Meillassoux (1981, 128) illuminates why semiproletarian workers like the Choctaws do not perceive themselves as truly exploited. The wage laborer who leaves the domestic sector to participate in wage labor "has access to cash which is scarce and 'dear' in the domestic sector . . . [and] the prospect of a relatively higher income compared to that which is possible for him using the same labour power within the domestic mode of production." Even though the wage laborer in the capitalist sector is underpaid, "his immediate income is nevertheless raised, because, on average, the productivity of his labor has been increased" (1981, 128). The wage earner, however, must contend with exploitation, lack of job security, and inadequate wages (see also McGuire and Woodsong 1990).

THE ENCLAVE POLITICAL ECONOMY:
"CORPORATE WELFARE" IN COUNTY ASSESSMENT AND TAXATION POLICIES

If the more obvious effects of corporate development lie in local labor force exploitation, corporate profit-making strategies also involve indirect methods of bookkeeping, land assessment, and capital investment, which are not readily comprehensible to outside observers. These strategies further deplete local resources and return vast profits to corporate producers, often unbeknown to the communities where production and profit-making occur.

Local communities penetrated by multinationals rely on property and sales tax revenues, which often entice local citizens to welcome corporate development schemes. Property and sales tax and land assessments—the heart of the local revenue base—often favor corporate landowners, undermining revenues returned to local communities (see Flora et al. 1992, 131ff). This process is particularly evident in the Choctaw Nation timber industry at the county level.

Weyerhaeuser is the single largest property-tax payer in Pushmataha and McCurtain Counties, where the majority of its Oklahoma timber land is located. Evidence shows, however, that Weyerhaeuser has not paid its fair share of the county property tax burden, because appraisal methods assure that its property tax rates are extremely low when compared with the land's actual market value. For instance, Weyerhaeuser's timber land in both counties, amounting to about 808,600 acres, is assessed in a category similar to that of agricultural land, to compensate for periods of non-productivity. But in fact, Weyerhaeuser's timber land was assessed at little more than 2 percent of its fair market value (assuming that timber land was worth a mere $300 per acre). Weyerhaeuser acknowledged this shrewd business advantage in its own corporate literature: "This massive asset [approximately 11 billion cubic feet of timber located on nearly 6 million acres] is valued on our books at only $614 million, its historic costs of acquisition, planting and growing, which is only a fraction of current market value" (Weyerhaeuser *Annual Report* 1982, 8).

Since 1969, Weyerhaeuser's average annual timber land growth rates have doubled due to intensive technological innovations in clearcutting and reforestation with genetically improved fast-growing species (Weyerhaeuser *Annual Report* 1988). Weyerhaeuser's own calculations show that their timber and land are worth more than two and one-half times their reported value when the value of assets is adjusted for changes in the purchasing power of the United States dollar (Weyerhaeuser *Annual Report* 1981, 47).

Attempts were made in 1982 to alter Pushmataha County's tax structure to bring in added revenue, because as one local newspaper claimed, "Pushmataha County is going broke" (*Talihina* [Oklahoma] *American* 8 April 1982). One proposed solution was to increase all county land values to a uniform flat rate, a move which would have hit Weyerhaeuser hard. This solution, according to news accounts, "hit a snag called politics," since everyone was related and no one wants a greater share of the tax burden than his neighbor (ibid.). An alternative proposal, a 2 percent sales tax, was more popular, although regressive taxation of this type burdens wage-earners as consumes, while corporate landowners remain largely unaffected.

In 1987 the Pushmataha County tax assessor appealed to County and State Equalization Boards to revise how the county's managed timber is assessed, based on scientifically determined categories of soil type. The tax assessor sought to increase the assessed value of managed timber land to $10.45 per acre. Weyerhaeuser, along with Nakoosa Paper Company, filed suit in District Court in 1990, challenging Pushmataha County's land reassessment effort. An out-of-court settlement was reached, temporarily setting the value of managed timber land at $8.69 per acre. The Court subsequently ruled in Weyerhaeuser's favor when it determined that the asset be classified as "waste timber" rather than in a higher "managed timber" category, a move which county spokespersons describe as "very unfair" (author's telephone interviews, Pushmataha County Tax Assessor, 29 March 1990; 14 August 1996).

Pushmataha County is the only one of five counties where Weyerhaeuser owns managed timber land that is addressing the problem of land assessment equalization based on scientifically determined categories of evaluation, to more equitably distribute tax liabilities. Since 1990, Weyerhaeuser has sold off more than half of its Pushmataha County timber holdings, over 100,000 acres, to John Hancock Mutual Life Insurance Company and a company subsidiary called Forestree, with corporate offices in Birmingham, Alabama (author's telephone interviews 29 March 1990, 14 August 1996). Corporate strategies appear to be to consolidate its local forest base by dispensing with less productive acreage.

These profit-maximizing strategies reflect the power and influence of private entrepreneurs, at the expense not only of the local community's labor force but also of the community at large. Weyerhaeuser can drastically undervalue its timber resources for tax purposes, a practice which is simply one manifestation of the systematic exploitation of satellite economies by metropolitan-based corporations. In the long run, local populations are deprived of revenues from their input both as a labor force and as a supplier of basic raw materials, while the wealth extracted from the community accrues to the corporate owners.

FIGHTING BACK: TRIBAL DEVELOPMENT STRATEGIES AND BINGO

Since the mid-1980s, the Choctaws have devised various economic strategies to solve the tribe's persistent poverty and underemployment woes, in response to Nixon-era "New Federalism" initiatives aimed at increasing tribal self-determined economic development objectives (see Snipp and Summers 1991, 170–71). Under the 1975 Indian Self Determination and Education Assistance Act (PL93-638) and the 1988 Indian Gaming and Regulatory Act (U.S. Title 25, S441), federally recognized tribes including the Choctaws were encouraged to undertake entrepreneurial ventures as a way of building more viable, self-sustaining tribal local economies. The Choctaws, under these so-called New Federalism mandates, developed a variety of economic initiatives. In 1985, the tribe took over administration of the 52-bed Talihina Indian Hospital, renamed the Choctaw Nation Indian Hospital, and three outlying health clinics, which together employed over 200 people. The tribe in 1998 received federal funds to expand the hospital complex. A second tribal initiative was acquisition in 1986 of the 256-acre Arrowhead Lodge, located in the northern Choctaw Nation, which was renovated to provide beach accommodations, amphitheater, and a 12,000-square-foot convention center (*Bishinik* May 1987, 2; February 1992, 1).

The boldest and potentially most controversial tribal undertaking was in 1987, when the Choctaw Indian Bingo Palace opened at Durant, creating about 140 jobs. It is now the centerpiece of an invigorated tribal economic development strategy. The Durant bingo palace attracts approximately 160,000 people per year, 80 percent from Texas. In its second year of operations, bingo netted more than one million dollars in profits. Currently, the tribe operates bingo concessions in four separate Choctaw Nation locations. Since opening the Bingo Palace, the tribe has opened smoke shops in Idabel, Pocala, Hugo, Arrowhead, and Durant, Oklahoma, as well as travel plazas along Highway 69/75 and at other Choctaw Nation locations using bingo concession funds, thereby diversifying the tribal economy (*Bishinik* January 1997, 8). The Choctaw Nation Indian Bingo complex now includes two full-service travel centers, each located on opposite sides of Highway 69/75.

Tribal economic growth, built largely on highly successful bingo and travel plaza enterprises, provided an economic cushion during the 1980s and 1990s when federal entitlement programs were slashed, allowing the tribe to pick up the slack where federal and state monies were unavailable. The Choctaw Nation has become in effect a branch of the U.S. welfare state bureaucracy, channeling substantial profits into what were previously federally and state-mandated programs. Indeed, the tribe's entrepreneurial initiatives have brought significant improvements to the lives of local Choctaws, through a myriad of tribally sponsored subsidy programs, jobs, housing, and health care. The Choctaw Tribe, however, like U.S. subsidy programs generally, serves as another form of "corporate welfare" for the multinationals, subsidizing underpaid and frequently underemployed workers for local extractive and food-processing industries that rely so heavily on unskilled, readily available workers. The rural economy gives rise to diverse forms of "corporate welfare," including tax breaks, labor contracting, part-time labor use, public sector subsidies, and household subsistence. The Choctaw Nation and Southeast Oklahoma generally typify the core/periphery relationship, not only in external control of local strategic resources, particularly timber and natural gas, but also in the peripheral workplace's reliance on unskilled, underpaid, surplus workers, often women and minorities, who subsidize their own inadequate wages through domestic subsistence activities, petty commodity production, and otherwise "making do." The real winners are the multinationals, whose trickle-down benefits mask real corporate exploitation of local communities and their citizens.

Rural non-reservation Native Americans, like the Choctaws, exist in an ambiguous and tenuous relation to this rural hinterland economy, as they seek to retain viability culturally, while working to provide a substantial economic base for their citizens. What hangs in the balance is Native American cultural integrity. As the Choctaws win in the new economic frontier of Indian gaming, entering an economic niche that could enrich them for decades, they face an uneasy future that pits tribal sovereign rights against not only corporate entrepreneurial interests but also U.S. definitions of tribal sovereignty and self-determination. The Choctaws have become in essence another rural ethnic sector vulnerable to the loss of key features that make Native Americans a unique ethnic minority sector, facing formidable challenges to their tribal cultural integrity (Faiman-Silva 1977, 22–25, 205–7, 219–24).

Culturally, the Choctaws face new tribal challenges as they redefine what it means to be Native American in the twenty-first century. They struggle to accommodate to a rural enclave economy dominated by external agents, as they seek to preserve cultural integrity in the face of a tribal life only marginally distinguishable from that in rural communities nationwide. Does tribal sovereignty linked to economic self-sufficiency signal eventual cultural demise for Native Americans such as the Choctaws? Dean Smith (1994) and Cornell and Kalt (1990, 1992a, 1992b) maintain that it is just this mix of effective leadership, shrewd business entrepreneurship, and cultural preservation that spells the formula for Native American cultural and social persistence. Smith (1994, 177), however, notes the inherent tension in the mix: "Only when the individual tribe both controls its own resources and sustains its identity as a distinct civilization does economic development make sense; otherwise the tribe must choose between cultural integrity and economic development." As they enter the twenty-first century, the Choctaws' ability to survive as a cultural entity may serve as a benchmark for an evolving ethnic subcultural reality among Native Americans throughout the United States and indigenous people globally in the context of nation-states, multinational corporations, and global communities.

REFERENCES

Bureau of Indian Affairs. 1973. *The Choctaw Nation: Its Resources and Development Potential.* Planning Support Group Report no. 213. Billings, Mont.: U.S. Department of the Interior.

Castile, George P. 1993. "Native North Americans and the National Question." In *The Political Economy of North American Indians,* ed. John Moore. Norman: University of Oklahoma Press.

Colclough, Glenna. 1988. "Uneven Development and Racial Composition in the Deep South: 1970–1980." *Rural Sociology* 53 (1): 73–86.

Collins, Jane L., and M. Gimenez, eds. 1990. *Work Without Wages: Comparative Studies of Domestic Labor and Self-Employment.* Albany: State University of New York Press.

Coppedge, Robert O., and C. G. Davis. 1977. *Rural Poverty and the Policy Crisis.* Ames: Iowa State University Press.

Cornell, Stephen. 1988. *The Return of the Native: American Indian Political Resurgence.* New York: Oxford University Press.

Cornell, Stephen, and J. P. Kalt. 1990. "Pathways from Poverty: Economic Development and Institution-Building on American Indian Reservations." *American Indian Culture and Research Journal* 14: 89–125.

———. 1992a. "Culture and Institutions and Public Goods: American Indian Economic Development as a Problem of Collective Action." In *Property Rights and Indian Economies,* ed. T. L. Anderson, 215–52. Landham, Md.: Lowman and Littlefield.

———. 1992b. "Reloading the Dice: Improving the Chances for Economic Development on American Indian Reservations." In *What Can Tribes Do?: Strategies and Institutions in American Indian Economic Development,* ed. Stephen Cornell and Joseph P. Kalt, 2–59. American Indian Manual and Handbook Series, no. 4. Los Angeles: UCLA American Indian Studies Center.

Debo, Angie. 1951. *The Five Civilized Tribes of Oklahoma, Report on Social and Economic Conditions.* Philadelphia: Indian Rights Association.

Faiman-Silva, Sandra. 1997. *Choctaws at the Crossroads: The Political Economy of Class and Culture in the Oklahoma Timber Region.* Lincoln: University of Nebraska Press.

Fernández Kelly, M. Patricia. 1989. "Broadening the Scope: Gender and International Economic Development." *Sociological Forum* 4 (4): 611–35.

Flora, Cornelia B., and J. A. Christenson, eds. 1991. *Rural Policies for the 1990s.* Boulder, Colo.: Westview Press.

Flora, Cornelia Butler, J. L. FLora, J. D. Spears, and L. E. Swanson. 1992. *Rural Communities: Legacy and Change.* Boulder, Colo.: Westview Press.

Gimenez, Martha E. 1990. "The Dialectics of Waged and Unwaged Work: Waged Work, Domestic Labor and Household Survival in the United States." In *Work*

Without Wages: Comparative Studies of Domestic Labor and Self-Employment, ed. J. L. Collins and M. Gimenez, 25–45. Albany: State University of New York Press.

Hall, Thomas D. 1987. "Native Americans and Incorporation: Patterns and Problems." *American Indian Culture and Research Journal* 11: 2, 1–30.

———. 1988. "Patterns of Native American Incorporation into State Societies." In *Public Policy Impacts on American Indian Economic Development,* ed. C. M. Snipp. Native American Studies Institute for Native American Development, Development Series #4, 23–38. Albuquerque: University of New Mexico.

———. 1995. "Seeing the Global in the Local: World-Systems Theories and Local Analyses." Paper presented at Social Science History Association meeting, Chicago, Ill., November.

Hedley, Max J. 1993. "Autonomy and Constraint: The Household Economy on a Southern Ontario Reserve." In *The Political Economy of North American Indians,* ed. J. H. Moore, 184–23. Norman: University of Oklahoma Press.

Hernandez, Juan A. 1994. "How the Feds are Pushing Nuclear Waste on Reservations." *Cultural Survival Quarterly* 17 (4): 40–42.

Jorgensen, Joseph. 1978. "A Century of Political Economic Effects on American Indian Society, 1880–1980." *Journal of Ethnic Studies* 6.3: 1–82.

McGuire, Thomas R. 1990. "Federal Indian Policy: A Framework for Evaluation." *Human Organization* 49: 206–16.

McGuire, Randal H., and C. Woodsong. 1990. "Making Ends Meet: Unwaged Work and Domestic Inequality in Broome County, New York, 1930–1980." In *Work Without Wages: Comparative Studies of Domestic Labor and Self-Employment,* ed. Jane L. Collins and M. Gimenez, 168–92. Albany: State University of New York Press.

Meillassoux, Claude. 1975. *Maidens, Meal and Money, Capitalism and the Domestic Community.* Reprinted 1981. Cambridge: Cambridge University Press.

———. 1983. "The Economic Bases of Demographic Reproduction: From the Domestic Mode of Production to Wage-Earning." *Journal of Peasant Studies* 11 (1): 50–61.

Oklahoma IMPACT. 1981. *Profile: Poverty in Oklahoma.* Oklahoma City: Legislative Information Action Network of the Oklahoma Conference of Churches.

Peach, W. N., and R. W. Poole. n.d. *Human and Material Resources of Pushmataha and McCurtain Counties: A Profile for Growth and Development.* Durant: Southeastern Oklahoma State College, Technological Use Studies Center.

Roberts, Brian R. 1989. "Urbanization, Migration, and Development." *Sociological Forum* 4 (4): 665–91.

Shelton, Beth Anne, and B. Agger. "Shotgun Wedding, Unhappy Marriage, No-Fault Divorce? Rethinking the Feminism-Marxism Relationship." In *Theory on Gender/Feminism on Theory,* ed. Paula England, 25–41. New York: Aldine De Gruyter.

Slagle, Allogan. 1994. "Recognized Tribes Must Stay Recognized: Ending the Threat of Administrative Termination of Recognized Indian Tribes." *Indian Affairs* 130: 1.

Smith, Dean. 1994. "Commentary: The Issue of Compatibility Between Cultural Integrity and Economic Development among Native American Tribes." *American Indian Culture and Research Journal* 18: 177–205.

Snipp, C. Matthew, and G. F. Summers. 1991. "American Indian Development Policies." In *Rural Policies for the 1990s,* ed. Cornelia B. FLora and J. A. Christenson. Boulder, Colo.: Westview Press.

Ward, Kathryn, ed. 1990. *Women Workers and Global Restructuring.* School of Industrial and Labor Relations. Ithaca: Cornell University Press.

American Indians in Rural America— Conditions and Concerns

BONNIE JEAN ADAMS

The Unrecognized—The Houma Indians

> Our culture not only exists in time but in space as well. If we
> lose our land we are adrift like a leaf on a lake, which will float
> aimlessly and then dissolve and disappear. . . . We are the
> products of poverty, despair, and discrimination pushed on our
> people from the outside. We are the products of chaos. Chaos in
> our tribes. Chaos in our personal lives. We are also products of a
> rich and ancient culture which supersedes and makes bearable
> any oppressions we are forced to bear. We believe that one's
> basic identity should be with his tribe. We believe in tribalism,
> we believe that tribalism is what has caused us to endure.
> —National Indian Youth Conference, Policy Statement, 1961

AMERICAN INDIANS, ACCUSTOMED TO A LONG HISTORY OF adaptation, have adapted, not assimilated, to non-Indian education, religion, property ownership. Their determination to maintain culture and tradition has made it possible for them to survive, and to continue to face the future with strength and hope. "Practically all wisdom arises as a substitute for what a man would like, but dare not or is not able, to do" (McNickle 1931). More than sixty years ago, D'Arcy McNickle, American Indian author, historian, anthropologist, and activist, wrote in his journal. His words can be a valuable lesson for non-Indians whose limited knowledge and understanding of American Indians precludes their full understanding of the wealth and multiplicity of cultural heritage in existence from before the founding of America. Those who define themselves as Americans can only be enriched by knowing the full story.

If even the best historian is able only to study the past, observe the present, and theorize about the future in the practice of history, what happens to those unseen, unheard? Imagine the scenario: American

276

Indian academic attends a national multicultural conference; presentation in hand, he steps up to the podium and faces—an empty room. The other scholars, historians, writers of history books, and authors of multicultural curricula choose not to hear a report of the latest research about American Indians. This is a true story. And one which Lakota scholar Vine Deloria Jr. states is common, despite the current multicultural rhetoric. "The realities of Indian belief and existence have become so misunderstood and distorted at this point that when a real Indian stands up and speaks the truth at any given moment, he or she is not only unlikely to be believed, but will probably be contradicted and 'corrected' by the citation of some non-Indian and totally inaccurate 'expert.' In this way, the experts are perfecting a system of self-validation in which all semblance of honesty and accuracy is lost. This is not only a travesty of scholarship, but it is absolutely devastating to Indian societies" (Jaimes 1992). How is "multiculturalism" defined? If the word does, indeed, mean many cultures, what about the cultures in our midst?

At the time of this author's visit in 1995, the Houma Indians of Houma, Louisiana, were in the process of making their second application for federal recognition. Formal recognition of the tribe is a prerequisite for federal funding of health, education, and employment initiatives. The Houma Indians, who live along the bayous in Terrebonne and Lafourche parishes (counties), report membership of 5859 on the tribal roll, and are the largest Indian tribe in Louisiana, yet they remain unseen, unheard, unrecognized. Many of the 40,000 current residents of Houma have no knowledge of the existence, or of the history of the Indians from which the town derived its name.

According to historical record, the Houma became demographically invisible early in the eighteenth century because of its traditional movement up and down both sides of the Mississippi River in pursuit of better hunting grounds, and to avoid conflict with other tribes. Conflicting census records concerning tribal location, lack of specific written treaties with colonial powers or with the United States federal government, and reports by government officials who misrepresented the numbers of Indians, led the U.S. government to believe that the Houma Tribe was nearing extinction by the time of the Louisiana Purchase in 1803.

When the United States government denied the land rights granted the Houma by the Spanish, the Houma had to resort to private land ownership. This deprived them of federal protection which is limited to lands held in trust for recognized tribes. It also decreased the likelihood of their retaining a native language, because to survive, the Houma had to live and trade with those who spoke many languages. Increased settlement and agricultural development by non-Indians drove the Indian families further down the bayou. Houma economic life followed a year-round pattern which included hunting, trapping, fishing, and farming. Access to large expanses of undeveloped freshwater and saltwater marshland was essential, but other than a shared understanding that each family would grow crops on the high ground near their own homes along the bayou, there was little concern about personal property boundaries. The Houma have had to struggle not only for land, fishing, and trapping rights, but for formal education to enable them to improve their circumstances.

N. Bruce Duthu, a member of the Houma tribe, describes what it has been like. "Relations between Indians and whites were never easy ... and they became more strained during the mid-twentieth century, when tribal members began aggressively campaigning for basic civil rights, including public education. The first all-Indian public school in Terrebonne Parish opened in the mid-fifties at about the same time the U.S. Supreme Court declared 'separate but equal' school systems unconstitutional." (Garrod and Larimore 1997). Prior to that time, Houma Indian children were not allowed to attend school with white children, and were sent to out-of-state boarding schools. Duthu explains that in the past, "we expected simply to follow in the footsteps of our parents. To think or want otherwise was unrealistic; worse, it might be perceived as a rejection of the traditional way of life" (ibid.).

Many Houma Indians continue to work as farmers, trappers, and fishermen. The Houma Tribe holds no land "in common" on which to build community. Whereas non-Indians define land ownership by legal boundaries, Indians conceive of land in terms of social relations, and community. Tribal members may be scattered, but sense of community remains strong.

N. Bruce Duthu, Dartmouth graduate, recalls coming home. "In the early '80s, the petroleum industry suffered a downturn, which meant people in southern Louisiana had problems finding and keeping jobs. Many close friends from high school were being partly or wholly laid off. Hard times hit many of the families. . . . Talking about law school made me uncomfortable, because it seemed like an indulgence in light of the hardships other family members were experiencing. . . . When I graduated from law school, with honors, literally hundreds of family and friends showed up at my graduation party. . . . It was a community celebration. Family members had cooked and baked all kinds of food. Old friends of mine provided music. The most memorable moment came when an Indian man in his late thirties shook my hand and, with tears in his eyes, told me how proud he was. I cried, too, knowing how my opportunities had come through the coincidence of time and history. What might have been for all those like this generous man, I can scarcely imagine" (ibid.).

Incorporated with the necessary adaptation is the intention to pass on tradition. Duthu speaks about the future. "When I think of my children and my brother's children, I think of the wonderful stories of our youth—the good ol' days when times were bad. I hope the children will all hear these stories. And I hope they will also have the good voices to teach and guide them. And I hope they will listen" (ibid.). The Houma are seeking to become more formally educated because they realize that this will be the only road to future opportunities for their children.

The Houma do have a history of their own. Because the tribe has been recognized by the state of Louisiana, some funding is available to support research, and the writing of this history. Tribal members and non-Indian experts, anthropologists and historians, are researching the genealogies and history of the Houma people. This is part of the process required by the federal government before legal acknowledgment can be granted. Reverend Kirby Verret, tribal council member, explained that the arduous application process had split the tribe. To date, the United Houma Nation remains unrecognized federally.

The power of a recognized tribe lies in its ability to regulate who is a member of the tribe. For a tribe, and for the members of the tribe, unrecognized is synonymous with unrepresented in the legal system of the United States. An Indian is legally defined in terms of his relationship to the legal system of the United States. The fact that all American Indians are American citizens does not erase their dual status as tribal members with loyalties to family and community within their own nations. Membership determines who shares the rights and privileges of community. Tribal membership is defined by each tribe, according to its own determination of descendants, residency, blood, or proof of birth. An Indian does not have to be full-blood to meet tribal or legal definition of Indian.

But even a full-blood Indian who has terminated or abandoned his tribal membership, or who is a member of a tribe not legally recognized, such as the Houma, has no claim to legal benefits of tribal association. There is no access to federal Indian programs. For example, members of unrecognized tribes cannot take advantage of legislation such as the Indian Self-Determination and Educational Assistance Act of 1975, which gave all recognized tribes the right to manage programs and services formerly managed by the BIA.

The power of a recognized tribe lies in its ability to regulate how tribal land is to be used. Whether or not they make their living from it, and aside from the fact that it provides affordable housing, Indians view land as central to their cultural identity. The tribes are legally handicapped from pressing certain claims against the state and federal government. They cannot sue for land in federal court; cannot regulate allotment and use of tribal land. The tribal council, (governing board) of an unrecognized tribe cannot administer justice through its own federally recognized court system (similar to the state system of government); cannot regulate domestic and family relations according to tribal law and custom. The tribe cannot act on its own, or join with other tribes effecting federal legislation in regard to any Indian concerns.

Recognition is federal acknowledgment of a tribe's identity, organization, and rights. The recognized tribe becomes a sovereign nation and political entity. The federal government then becomes obligated to protect the tribal lands and resources of federally recognized tribes and to provide them with health care, education, and economic development assistance.

Treaties, like BIA services and reservation lands, are proof of a tribe's government-to-government relationship with the United States. In his book, *American Indians: Answers to Today's Questions,* Jack Utter states: "As of January 1993, the official BIA count of politically recognized Indian tribes was 515. This number includes 318 'tribal entities' in the lower 48 states, which are described as Indian tribes, bands, villages, communities, and pueblos. The remaining 197 recognized entities are in Alaska" (Utter 1993). In 1978, Federal Acknowledgment Policy (FAP) was enacted to enable unrecognized tribes such as the Houma to petition the federal government for a change in their legal status. Proof of prior relationship between an American Indian tribe and the United States government is one of the requirements of petition.

Many tribes have been unable to secure federal recognition because it is time-consuming, expensive, and a politically charged process rife with congressional politics and budget cutting, BIA bureaucratic delay, and even some Indian opposition. Much can be lost by a tribe in the attempt. Tribal government necessarily becomes overly concerned with the administration of its community, entangled in its own new bureaucracy. Tribal members begin to disagree. Division of even a small tribe is common. The Houma Indians have split into two factions; each has submitted a petition for recognition. Such intertribal competition reduces chance of success for either side.

Federal recognition is not the only solution to American Indian problems. Whatever the advantages gained by recognition are at the price of adaptation; recognition of an assumed authority by non-

Indians, with power to acknowledge tribal sovereignty or not, to allocate funding or not. Those with power enough can daily choose to partner in encouragement of independent enterprise or to complicate daily life with petty bureaucratic details. American Indians recognize the challenges facing them and continue to be fueled by the strength of their own acknowledged tribal identity and community membership. While building a future, basic survival requirements still interfere. In the American Indian Policy Review Commission *Report on Alcohol and Drug Abuse Task Force II* (1976), Reuben Snake wrote: "The streamrolling effort of the 'civilized society' upon the Indian people has wreaked a havoc which extends far beyond that of loss of material possessions. The American Indians . . . are caught in a world wherein they are trying to find out who they are and where they are, and where they get in. The land which was once their 'mother', giving them food and clothing, was taken. Their spiritual strengths were decried as pagan and familial ties broken. Their own form of education, i.e., that of legends, how to live, how to respect themselves and others, were torn asunder by the White society's reading, writing and arithmetic. No culture could, or can be, expected to be thrust into a world different from its own and adapt without problems of cultural shock." (Obrien 1989).

IDENTITY — THE LIMITS OF DEFINITION

[The] Indian has survived, still posing to the white conqueror
a challenge that not all non-Indians, particularly in the United
States, wish happily to tolerate, even, indeed, it they understand
it: acceptance of the right to be Indian. That right suggests, at
heart, the right to be different, which in the United States runs
counter to a traditional drive of the dominant society. Ideally,
the American Dream in the United States offers equal opportunities to all persons; but in practice the opportunities imply a
goal of sameness, and the Indians, clinging to what seems right
and best for them, have instinctively resisted imposed measures
by non-Indians designed to make them give up what they want
to keep and adopt what they have no desire to acquire. That
has been—and continues to be—the core of the so-called
"Indian problem" in the United States, which many Indians
characteristically refer to as "the white man's problem."
—Alvin M. Josephy, Jr. *The Indian Heritage of America*

The American Indian people have not only survived, but their population is increasing. In 1990, under the Census Bureau's system of self-identification, there were 1,959,234 individuals identified as

Indians; 0.8 percent of the total population of the United States. Most Indians live in urban and suburban areas. Jack Utter writes: "At least 50 metropolitan areas in the United States have Indian populations ranging in size from 4000 to nearly 90,000 individuals" (1993).

Some statistics of those who live in rural America: 10 percent of American Indians live within "Tribal Jurisdiction Statistical Areas," which Utter describes as former reservation areas in the state of Oklahoma where tribes retain certain types of tribal jurisdiction; 2.7 percent live in "Tribal Designated Statistical Areas," which are described as those home areas delineated by tribes outside of Oklahoma who do not have reservations, and 22.3 percent live on legally designated reservations or associated trust lands. Modoc Michael Dorris writes:

> Reservations are the residue of North America that, over the past five hundred years of contact with Europeans, Indians never gave up. They are, according to Justice John Marshall's Supreme Court rulings in the early nineteenth century, "domestic dependent nations," subsumed by America but not part of any state. They have complicated rights to internal self-government, to individual judicial systems, to impose their own taxes and make their own laws. They are, in a true legal sense, quasi-sovereign. . . . Their political identity predated that of any other country on the continent; their right to exist and to continue to exist derives from an international recognition of "Aboriginal Claim," the long-term use and occupancy of a territory, theirs by fact rather than because of any written deed certifying ownership. More than three-hundred reservations—so-called "Indian Country"—exist today, and counted together with Alaska Native villages and regional corporations, they comprise just under one hundred million acres, ranging in size from parcels with the dimensions of a generous house lot to the Navajo Nation, roughly as big as West Virginia. (Dorris 1989)

There are about 300 federal Indian reservations located in 33 states. And there are about 12 small state Indian reservations. There are also Indian communities, and colonies where a land base is held in trust by the United States or otherwise protected by the government. A tribe that is federally recognized is not guaranteed reservation land. But such a tribe is required to provide formalized government for its people; one which identifies and responds to member's needs and goals, with respect to culture.

If there seem to be multiple legal interpretation and definition, that is exactly the case. In *American Indians: Answers to Today's Questions,* Utter states: "Legally, no universal definition for the generic term 'tribe' exists in the U.S. Constitution, federal statutes or regulations." [And] no single definition of 'an Indian' exists—socially, administratively, legislatively, or judicially" (Utter 1993). It is how federal laws and regulations define such terms with regard to funding control and distribution, federal benefits and services, and regulation of civil and criminal law that is significant. The Bureau of Indian Affairs (BIA), a branch of the U.S. Department of the Interior, and the Indian Health Service (IHS), a branch of the U.S. Department of Health and Human Services, are the two primary federal agencies which provide services to federally recognized American Indian tribes. Jack Utter explains: "Major benefits and services provided by these agencies include, but are not limited to, the following: medical and dental care, grants and programs for education, housing programs, aid in developing tribal governments and courts, resource management, and other services based upon tribal needs and interests . . . [which can] range from police protection and other law enforcement activities to economic development" (Utter 1993).

Adaptation to others' customs has not been the only accommodation by American Indians; others' laws continue to proscribe legal identity and define rights. In *The Broken Cord*, Michael Dorris writes: "Reservations are more than property for the Indian people who live there. . . . They are the past and the future, the tangible evidence that tribes were once as independent as any peoples in the history of the world, and the hope, if the treaties that recognized them are kept, for a return of self-sufficiency. They are networks of families, of extended interweavings of blood and generations of resentments and forgivenesses, of shared space and time. They are places of historical and contemporary deprivation, of incarceration and religious restriction, of confusing, frustrating social inequities, and of too little cash. But they are also havens, home, where familiar words, be they spoken in the native language or in modern idiomatic English shorthand, are understood, where each ripple in the land has the significance of an old story, where you go when you need to" (Dorris 1989).

Dorris describes the spirituality of community, and he describes physical construction of reservation land: "There is a sameness to these towns that goes beyond common architecture, government-issue paint. They seem somehow temporary, set on the landscape by a child with too few blocks, too little imagination" (Dorris 1989). The reservations, set upon a landscape claimed, can become self-sufficient nations within our own. What about those, like the Houma Indians, who hold no land in common?; those who no longer have a language of their own? American Indians are making a future for themselves; based upon what they imagine, limited only by—proscribed identity, non-recognition of individuals within cultures, those who cannot see, who do not hear.

CURRENT CONCERNS — CULTURAL CONTINUATION

My grandchildren, you are living in a new path. In the future
your business dealings with the whites are going to be very hard.
Try to make a mark for yourselves. Learn all you can.
—Sitting Bull, Sioux Chief
Speech to schoolchildren, 1887

There's no history of my people in the twentieth century.
We don't exist. So I decided through my family to give
an overview that hopefully would inspire Indian scholars
somewhere soon to start doing a definitive history about our
existence in the twentieth century.
—Russell Means, Oglala-Lakota
In reference to his autobiography
Where White Men Fear To Tread

What characterized past relationship between Indian and non-Indian, and continues to do so, is a difference in cultural values, obviously evidenced in definition of terms regarding primary lifestyle determinants: ownership, identity, community, education and religion. American Indians' tribes were communal societies, misunderstood by non-Indians who competed for private ownership. American Indians' culture, which was based upon an oral tradition, began to fade into the background of awareness. History was recorded by non-Indians, those with written language. American Indians became romanticized as a people conquered, part of a past created, and a present controlled by non-Indians. Not surprising, then, that reference is still made to American Indians' cultural regeneration, as though this new awareness on the part of the non-Indian made it fact. Cultural continuation is a more accurate term. American Indians have adapted to non-Indian culture, not been absorbed by it. Throughout history, wherever the tribes dispersed, as much as possible, American Indians have striven to maintain their culture through community. And their strength remains in their identification with community.

The enumerated challenges facing American Indians in rural America may, at first, appear to be similar to those of non-Indians: employment, health, and environmental concerns, but these are compounded by lack of recognition. American Indians remain the unseen people. In the future, social scientists may choose to either propagate a myth, or remove the mystery. It is necessary that a more comprehensive portrayal of the past be realized.

In *American Indians: Answers to Today's Questions*, while Jack Utter provides statistics, he writes that it is important to refrain from making general statements about conditions and concerns because of the great diversity of circumstances nationwide. Facts and figures are easily obtained; knowledge which allows one to maintain a comfortable distance from actual relationship can be found elsewhere. Challenges are being met, changes made. American Indian leaders, those who are making sure that they do not go unheard, who are making a difference, voice their concerns. Who better to do so?

News From Indian Country: The Nations' Native Journal reports that "around the country, American Indians are reclaiming the land their ancestors once inhabited. From the Ojibwa and Chippewa in Minnesota to the Appalachian American Indians in West Virginia, tribes have bought land or are raising money to re-establish their presence in areas they once called home" (Hannah 1997). Hawk Pope, chief of the Shawnee Nation United Remnant Band of Ohio, with his tribe, is buying back ancestral land a bit at a time. The land is used for sharecropping, and to hold council gatherings and ceremonies. Pope plans to utilize tribal manpower to staff the caverns on the land, and to develop a small resort with campgrounds, where festivals and Indian re-enactments can be held. He states: "Why shouldn't it be a gold mine? It's only fitting . . . that the Shawnee profit from the land once taken by white settlers. They did not recognize our claim to the land because we didn't have it in the way they did . . . we never even looked upon it as owning. We looked upon it as someplace we had the right to be, where we had the right to live" (Hannah 1997). Chief for more than 25 years, Pope quit the advertising business to devote more time to tribal affairs. His concerns are about more than business, however. "If we don't do this, our children will have no place where they can know what the land was really like" (Hannah 1997). American Indian leaders learn from their experience "on the outside," in business and in the military, and use this knowledge to better conditions for their own people.

Philip Martin, chief of the Mississippi Band of Choctaw, the tribe which owns the Silver Star Casino and Hotel and a number of other businesses, characterizes himself as the C.E.O. of the operations. When he returned to the reservation after serving in the Air Force, he had no intention of staying: "I knew what the situation was and thought it was beyond my control, so I was going somewhere else. It didn't work out that way" (Torgenson 1997). When he had trouble finding a job, he remembered what he had seen while stationed overseas: "I had seen people eating out of trash cans in Europe. . . . Germany was devastated when I was there. . . . I saw people knocking off bricks and stacking them up and planning on rebuilding. And they did, especially Germany. They built a strong economy in a short time. I said to myself, Why can't we do that? Why can't we start bringing industry in here and employing people?" (Torgerson 1997). And with that idea, he went to work. "I contacted a lot of people in a lot of federal agencies and they didn't believe it could be done. I said, It can be done. . . . We've got everything the city has, I told myself, except water and sewer and roads. That's what I was trying to get—that kind of assistance" (Torgerson 1997). Martin convinced the government to build a small industrial park, which went unused for five years; and he wrote letters to every company listed with Dun & Bradstreet that had an electronics, non-polluting industry—and Packard Electric, a division of General Motors showed an interest. Production of automotive parts began in 1979. When GM moved operations to Mexico, Martin contracted with Ford Motor Company. "With the 2000 jobs at the casino and the 1200 employees of the tribal government, the 8000-member Choctaw Nation now provides 6500 jobs" (Torgerson 1997).

While a number of Indian tribes and communities have businesses and resource-based enterprises that generate income, most reservation tribes have no substantial formal economy of their own to generate operating capital. Their revenues are derived primarily from outside the reservations. Rebecca L. Adamson, an Eastern Cherokee, is one who is meeting needs and facing challenges. She is founder of the nonprofit First Nations Financial Project (FNFP), whose mission is economic self-sufficiency for American Indian tribes. Described by *The New Leader* as one of America's new entrepreneurs, "Adamson and her group are changing the way policy-makers in Washington think about Indians, even the way Indians think about themselves. The notion of 'progress' as applied to life on the reservation is being redefined" (Cleaver 1997). Adamson defines "micro enterprise" as FNFP's tactic to address tribal poverty. "We begin before the beginning. . . . Development is the tedious job that remains after the rhetoric of revolution and independence has been spent." FNFP works with tribes to "take an exotic sounding pipedream and turn it into a dull but successful business" (Cleaver 1997). Small business development engenders income, but more importantly, hope, within the community.

Economic development is of primary concern for most American Indians in rural America. Achievement of independence through self-determination underlies all efforts; as does, the vision of building a future for those who follow. Ray Halbritter, Nation Representative of the Oneida Indian Nation for the American Indian Program, in an address at Cornell University in 1996, stated: "a handful of Indian nations are enjoying a small measure of economic prosperity. We are putting people to work and beginning to secure the future for the generations to come. . . . We have been able to do all of this mostly because Indian nations, during the past thirty years, have been successful in reacquiring lands unlawfully taken from them in prior centuries. Having regained possession of our territories, tribes are reasserting their inherent sovereign powers, including the right to conduct and regulate commercial activities on our lands. . . . It is important to remember that only a small percentage of Indian nations have achieved tangible improvement in their economic welfare over the past twenty years. The vast majority of tribes still find their members living in conditions of poverty. . . . Our people still suffer from higher rates of liver disease, diabetes, alcoholism, suicide, homicide, and accidental death, all signs of a society in stress, a culture endangered and a species nearly extinct. . . . Federal, state and local governments . . . severely underestimate the need that still exists on Indian reservations and the cost of recovery from 200 years of poverty and neglect" (Halbritter 1996).

Former chief of the Oklahoma Cherokee Nation Wilma Mankiller, in an interview for *U.S. News & World Report,* responds to questions about current priorities and future goals for her tribe.

> We provide an awful lot of services—operating clinics, running education programs, building houses—and those services need to be continued. . . . As a matter of necessity, most tribes operate both as government and as a conduit for federal funds and provide needed services to tribal members in a very professional manner. Rarely are there attempts to intervene in the cycle of poverty by organizing Indian communities to resolve problems themselves. . . .
>
> There was a time when tribes had an awful lot of international integrity and controlled their own destiny. They did not have problems such as severe unemployment. We've got to figure out ways to rebuild ourselves as a group of people, and starting at the community level makes the most sense. . . . We're very rarely depicted as real people who have greater tenacity in terms of trying to hang on to our culture and values system than most people. (Mankiller 1986)

In *American Indians: Answers to Today's Questions,* which provides comprehensive statistics, Jack Utter writes: "Policy failures, corruption, bureaucratic incompetence, and politics have gone far toward holding Native Americans back economically since the U.S. became a nation. The many well-educated Native people of today, however, are very familiar with the laws, economics, and government bureaucracies that so thoroughly affect their lives. They and fellow Indians and Alaska Natives appear to be moving in a determined way to take control of their economic destiny. . . . It may take years for some communities, or generations for others, but it is an ongoing trend" (Utter 1993). Utter also quotes Wilma Mankiller: "The best solutions to our problems are within our own communities" (ibid.). American Indians seek self-empowerment; development of partnerships that will move them toward this goal.

In an article in *U.S. News & World Report,* titled "The Worst Federal

Agency: Critics Call the Bureau of Indian Affairs a National Disgrace," Michael Satchell writes: "The Americans who are most dependent on the federal government, the one million Indians who live on reservations, are the most impoverished Americans of all" (Satchell 1994). The Interior Department's Bureau of Indian Affairs (BIA) is the principal federal agency charged with providing social services to reservation tribes. The agency has a reputation for mismanagement among Indians and non-Indians alike. "Many of its problems are the result of good intentions gone awry, but the BIA, which with 13,000 full-time employees is Interior's largest agency, has proved to be remarkably resistant to reform. . . . Remarkably little of the agency's money finds its way to the people who need it. . . . Candid bureau officials estimate that less than 20 cents of each dollar trickles down to the reservations. . . . The BIA has never tried to promote tax incentives, enterprise zones or development banks to attract investment to reservations, where unemployment can run as high as 80 percent" (Satchell 1994).

In *The Broken Cord*, Michael Dorris interviews a health worker on one of the reservations, who stresses the urgency of immediate concerns: "On all the reservations people will say that health is very important, their number one priority, but when you look at what the tribe is doing, all their resources and energy are going into economic development, water rights, land rights, because these are the immediate foreseeable things that they need. We need food, we need resources, we need to have a paycheck. It's hard for these people who are worrying about 'where's my next meal coming from,' or 'am I going to have enough fuel to get through this winter.'. . . It's hard for people to think down the line, twenty years from now, this is what's going to happen. . . . Right now is what's in front of you. The need to survive" (Dorris 1989).

Menominee Ada Deer, BIA chief, lists her accomplishments as freezing cash bonuses, tightening accounting procedures, improving communication with the tribes, and pushing early retirement and buyouts for senior bureaucrats who don't perform. "The mediocrity is as bad as I thought it would be. . . . I feel like I'm carrying 500 years of history on my shoulders" (Satchell 1994). The goal is tribal self-governance, an escape from federal paternalism. Russell Means, Oglala-Lakota activist, author, and actor, currently working to raise funds for a school and addiction treatment center being built on the Pine Ridge Indian Reservation in South Dakota, is one of many who believe that self-sufficiency will not happen until American Indians are able to become entirely independent of the BIA. What Means said in a recent interview, however, best summarizes the sad realization that the BIA is not likely to be abolished; "When has the government ever downsized?" (Lauerman 1997).

Of those who could be referred to as future elders, most American Indian leaders cannot be easily classified by profession. All are required to be part-activist, part-anthropologist, part-historian, and community worker. These are the multiple tasks required of those who seek to recover their own origins and maintain their own traditions, while necessarily adapting to non-Indian society; meeting the daily challenges of a faceless collection of bureaucracies, and acting in the face of disinterest, ignorance, and non-recognition. While economic conditions, basic survival issues, remain most pressing concerns for them, American Indians are working toward building a future, with values instilled and traditions included, for their children. Ernest Dar Dar, of the United Houma Nation, explained to me why it was important for him that his tribe receive federal recognition: "It's not for me . . . I'm too old now . . . it's for my children . . . you know . . . I want them to be something" (Adams 1997).

Joseph Marshall, Lakota author, historian and lecturer, speaking at the twenty-fifth Annual Symposium on the American Indian, quoted his grandfather: "As you walk down the trail you must stop, look back, and remember where you've been so that you won't lose your way." And he added, "History is like that. It is a collective ownership, not just white history and not just Indian history. If we don't want our children to go through the same things, we must help to change attitudes and correct misinformation by becoming aware of ourselves and our history. History is the domain of those who tell it. We need to tell the truth in a way that serves everyone" (Schroeter 1997). American Indians continue to move forward, not only to survive, but to adapt, and progress toward a future of their own making. Non-Indians will choose to play a part; whether it be contribution or indifference. If indifference, it will be non-Indians who will forfeit the possibilities of valuable lessons which could be learned.

MAKING RECOMMENDATIONS
FOR THE TWENTY-FIRST CENTURY

The red man is alone is his misery. We behold him now on
the verge of extinction, standing on his last foothold . . .
and soon he will be talked of as a noble race who once existed
but have passed away.

—George Armstrong Custer, term paper
for his ethics class at West Point

If I should formulate a philosophy at this time . . . I should call
it the Doctrine of Eccentricity: No man may know the truth, for
no truth exists except as that man knows it; no judgement is

> valid . . . there is no longer any chance of catching up and
> entrenching ourselves behind stout lines or dogma or systems,
> we must devote ourselves completely to self-training, objectivity,
> observation, rationalism, experimentalism, selflessness, chaos
> can't be dealt with according to the rules of party government.
> —D'Arcy McNickle, journal entry, 1932
> Cree author, historian, activist

American Indians were not vanquished, but have they vanished? As a non-Indian historian making recommendations for the twenty-first century, I am in agreement with anthropologist Henry F. Dobyns who writes, "The idea that social scientists have of the size of the aboriginal population of the Americas directly affects their interpretation of New World civilization and culture" (Jaimes 1992). Scholars' knowledge of facts and figures is only the beginning. The 1990 federal census reported 1,959,234 Native Americans in the United States, or about 1 percent of the population. The Bureau of the Census projects a population of 2.4 million American Indians by 2000, and 4.6 million, or about 2 percent of the population of the United States by 2050. Yet, American Indians remain an unrecognized minority.

In addition to recognition and respect, what is necessary is a realization and an acceptance of responsibility; not ours for the American Indians; it is not our place to educate and enable others so much as it is to inform ourselves. Memorization of estimated statistics, cursory knowledge of history is not enough. It is important that scholars read what is written by American Indians, history and literature, and to meet and speak with American Indians. Too often, non-Indians continue mistakenly to associate American Indians with ownership of casinos, living on reservations, "out west somewhere"; while occupations vary, and more live in urban than in rural areas. In the midst of cities, there are pockets of vibrant communities keeping Indian cultures alive.

It is not enough that current conditions and concerns of American Indians in rural America or anywhere else be recognized, or immediately addressed. If what is sought is anything more than temporary surcease of social concerns, what is needed is development of the realization that American Indians are a separate and viable people with cultures that have proven to be remarkably flexible over time, and that tribes are nations within our own. With this realization must come respect. There is much to be learned from American Indians on equal terms.

Particularly as scholars, this need to inform ourselves can best be illustrated by this author's own experience with others: An academic recognized for her knowledge of local community colleges, although surprised, remained uninterested after learning that there was such an entity as a Tribal College, just twenty miles from her own campus. And another, a historian, from a town close to Houma, Louisiana, admitted to being unaware that there were any Indians left in the state. It is our responsibility to educate ourselves before we can begin to effectively practice being partners with others for their own empowerment.

More than twenty years ago, D'Arcy McNickle, Cree anthropologist, wrote: "The Indians, for all that has been lost or rendered useless out of their ancient experience, remain a continuing ethnic and cultural enclave with a stake in the future" (McNickle 1973). From American Indians, we can learn community strength and necessary adaptation; perhaps, preservation of our own culture is a lesson we can learn from them. In *The State of Native America: Genocide, Colonization and Resistance,* John Mohawk, Seneca activist and lecturer, writes about what the future could promise. "We are going to have to ask ourselves what our resources are. Our first resource is human compassion, gained through the clear use of our minds, which will allow us to make the best use of the human family. And another of our best resources emerges when we think clearly about the peoples who have alternative answers to the questions that are not being answered by the society we live in. . . . It is possible at last to look at the modern period, not as a process of crisis and decline, but as a wonderful opportunity to amalgamate and pull things together, and to make the world our library. It at last is possible, in other words, not only to finally find the real meaning of Columbus, but to bury it" (Jaimes 1992).

When Mankiller, former chief of the Cherokee Nation, was asked what could be learned from white society, she replied: "As far as values go, I'm not real sure what we can learn. The constant push for financial success, for position, for more money seems like a horrible waste of one's life. There is one thing, however, I do like a lot about everyday American people: that is their willingness to help others" (Mankiller 1986). Will the future choice of the non-Indian be practice of charity or partnership for empowerment? It will take humility and courage to work with and learn from American Indians.

While identification of conditions and concerns may be the beginning of finding temporary solutions to immediate problems, what is needed is a change of attitude, a way of seeing others. Will we make the effort? We are often limited by boundaries of our own making; defined by the lines we choose to cross or to be confined by. Have we courage enough to relinquish the role of expert, to not overtake action, to call the shots, seek the glory? Is the pursuit of a more comprehensive portrayal of the past worth the effort? Is the enrichment of our own culture reward enough? For the future, this question remains unanswered.

References

Adams, Bonnie Jean. 1997. "Sending An American Indian Voice. D'Arcy McNickle—Educator, Anthropologist, Historian—An Intellectual Biography" Ph.D. diss., Loyola University: Chicago, 1997, abstract in *Dissertation Abstracts International.*

Berkhofer, Robert F., Jr. 1979. *The White Man's Indian.* New York: Random House.

Bowman, Greg, and J. Curry-Roper. 1995. "The Houma People of Louisiana—A Story of Indian Survival." Louisiana: Louisiana Indian Heritage Association.

Clark, Thomas. 1994. "Culture and Objectivity." *Humanist* (Sept./Oct.): 38–39.

Clay, Jason W. 1994. "Indigenous Cultures Face Extinction." *The Futurist* (May/June): 54–55.

Cleaver, Joanne. 1997. "She means business." *Chicago Tribune* Section 13 (November 9), 3.

Connor, Walker. 1994. *Ethnonationalism. The Quest for Understanding.* Princeton: Princeton University Press.

DeLoria, Vine, Jr., and C. M. Lytle. 1984. *The Nations Within. The Past and Future of American Indian Sovereignty.* New York: Pantheon Books.

DeLoria, Vine, Jr., ed. 1985. *American Indian Policy in the Twentieth Century.* Tulsa: University of Oklahoma Press.

DeLoria, Vine, Jr. 1983. *Behind the Trail of Broken Treaties. An Indian Declaration of Independence.* Austin: University of Texas Press.

Dorris, Michael. 1989. *The Broken Cord. A Family's Ongoing Struggle with Fetal Alcohol Syndrome.* New York: Harper and Row.

Garrod, Andrew, and C. Larimore. 1997. *First Person—First Peoples. Native American College Graduates Tell Their Life Stories.* Ithaca: Cornell University Press.

Grabowski, Christine Tracey. 1994. "Coiled Intent: Federal Acknowledgment Policy and the Gay Head Wampanoags." Ph.D. Diss., City University of New York, abstract in *Dissertation Abstracts International.*

Guyette, Susan. 1996. *Planning for Balanced Development. A Guide for Native American and Rural Communities.* Santa Fe, N.Mex.: Clear Light Publishers.

Halbritter, Ray. 1996. "Indian economic futures: governance and taxation." *Vital Speeches* 63 (5): 153–59.

Hannah, James. 1997. "Tribal Nations Buying Back Their Lands." *News from Indian Country: The Nations Native Journal* (Mid-June): 5A.

Harmon, Alexandra. 1994. "When Is an Indian Not an Indian? The 'Friends of the Indian' and the Problems of Indian Identity." *Journal of Ethnic Studies* 18 (2): 95–123.

Hauptman, Laurence M. 1995. *Tribes & Tribulations.* New Mexico: University of New Mexico Press.

Hoekstra, Dave. 1997. "Crossing over." *Chicago Sun-Times* Showcase, November 6, section 1, 4.

Jaimes, M. Annette, ed. 1992. *The State of Native America. Genocide, Colonization and Resistance.* Boston: South End Press.

Johnson, Sandy, ed. 1994. *The Book of Elders. The Life Stories and Wisdom of Great American Indians.* New York: HarperCollins.

Lauerman, Connie. 1997. "Means to an end." *Chicago Tribune* November 16, section 1, 4.

Mankiller, Chief. 1986. "People expect me to be more warlike." *U.S. News & World Report* 100 (February): 64.

Margolis, Richard J. 1987. "America's new entrepreneurs." *The New Leader* 70 (18): 11–13.

McNickle, D'Arcy. 1973. *Native American Tribalism.* New York: Oxford University Press.

O'Brien, Sharon. 1989. *American Indian Tribal Governments.* Tulsa: University of Oklahoma Press.

Richardson, Bill. 1994. "The Need to Empower Indian Tribes." *USA Today Magazine* (Nov.): 54–55.

Russell, Cheryl. 1996. "Demo snapshots: Native Americans." *American Demographics* 18 (8): S4.

Satchell, Michael. 1994. "The worst federal agency: critics call the Bureau of Indian Affairs a national disgrace." *U.S. News & World Report* 117 (21): 61–65.

Schoepfle, G. Mark, T. R. Morgan, and P. F. Scott. 1986. "It used to be home." *Technology Review* 89 (July): 52–57.

Schroeter, Elaine. 1997. "Joseph Marshall—Speakers at the 25th Annual Symposium on the American Indian, Northeastern State University at Tahlequah." *News from Indian Country: The Nations Native Journal* (Mid-June): 13A.

Shumway, J. Matthew, and R. H. Jackson. 1995. "Native American Population Patterns." *The Geographical Review* 185–201.

Torgerson, Stan. 1997. "Choctaw succeed in industrial Development." *News from Indian Country: the Nations Native Journal* (Mid-June) 25A.

Utter, Jack. 1993. *American Indians: Answers to Today's Questions.* Lake Ann, Mich.: National Woodlands Publishing Company.

Waldman, Carl. 1985. *Atlas of the North American Indian.* New York: Facts on File.

Waldman, Carl. 1994. *Timelines of Native American History.* New York: Prentice-Hall.

Wilkins, David E. 1994. "Reconsidering the tribal-state compact process." *Policy Studies Journal* 22 (3): 474–89.

Williams, Edith Ellison, and F. Ellison. 1996. "Culturally informed social work practice with American Indian clients: guidelines for non-Indian social workers." *Social Work* 41 (2): 147–51.

African Americans in Appalachia: Intensification of Historical Demographic Patterns

WILBURN HAYDEN JR.

INTRODUCTION

THIS CHAPTER DOCUMENTS AND ANALYZES THE CONTINUED flight of African Americans from rural to urbanized areas in Appalachia. Figures from the U.S. Census reveal an intensification of this traditional demographic trend from 1980 to 1990. Analysis of the 22 "concentrated areas" of African American settlements in Appalachia demonstrated a heavy presence of industrial and mining operations, four-year colleges, cities and towns, and government facilities: all traditional sources and venues of employment for African Americans. It is hypothesized that the recent flight towards the concentrated areas results from the recessions of recent decades and the difficulties of being African American in rural America. Since Appalachia has traditionally been defined as rural, African Americans have been an invisible presence and have lacked the appropriate social services. Thus, during times of economic distress, they become particularly reliant on traditional forms of employment.

CONTINUATION OF TRENDS

African Americans living in Appalachia have tended to settle in the region's more urbanized areas ever since Reconstruction. This historical concentration of the African American population has intensified in recent years: during the 1970s and 1980s, African Americans living outside these relatively urbanized areas moved to them in greater numbers than the population as a whole. Even though the areas where African Americans have traditionally lived have seen a small rise in total population, African Americans have fled to those areas in greater numbers than any other ethnic group. Conversely, the more rural areas of Appalachia, which had always been less heavily populated by African Americans, experienced further decline in the population of African Americans.

This intensification of the historical pattern of African-American demographics in Appalachia has many possible causes. However, clues to this intensification can be found by noting other features of the areas where African Americans tend to live: that is, the presence of (1) government facilities (e.g., the Tennessee Valley Authority), (2) institutions of higher learning, (3) industrial firms, and (4) mining operations. These organizations have often served as sources of employment for African Americans in Appalachia. Although the economic dislocations of the seventies and eighties affected all workers in Appalachia, African Americans were hit the hardest, and—it is hypothesized in this chapter—they became even more reliant on these traditional sources of employment in recent years.

The intensification of the African American's reliance on these sources of employment has not been offset by social services to the poor because of the longstanding conception of Appalachia as predominantly rural. In 1990, 75 percent of African Americans resided within the 63 counties identified in this study as the "concentrated areas" of African American population, while only 37 percent of the white population lived in these same counties. Thus, as a group the African American Appalachians' experience has been geographically different from that of the dominant white population. But it is the rural white experience that has been studied, singled out for governmental resources, and assumed to be the battleground for social-economic power. The African American experience has been marginalized, not solely from racial bias, but from the omission that comes with the rural label that has defined the region.

The connection between Appalachian demographics and the invisibility of African Americans has been discussed in general terms (Cabbell 1980; Hayden 1986a, 1993; Wright 1978). This chapter looks more closely at the characteristics of the urbanized areas within rural Appalachia. This is where African Americans settle. The chapter documents the intensification of African American flight towards these areas in the 1980s. This chapter also puts forth a more specific hypothesis as to why Appalachian African Americans move to urban areas and why they are doing so now in even greater numbers.

POPULATION BY RACE

Twelve years ago the population data by race for the 395 counties covered by the Appalachian Region Commission (ARC) were presented at the Appalachian Studies Conference in Berea, Ky. (Hayden 1986a). The 1980 census provided the data for that paper. Table 1 presents the 1980 and 1990 total population by race for counties covered by the ARC in each of the 13 Appalachian states. The total population in the region grew by 97,501 (0.5 percent). This growth was significantly less when compared to the 1970-to-1980 growth rate, when the total population grew by 2,112,125 (11.6 percent), from 18,256,957 to 20,359,082 (Department of the Interior, 1994b, 1994c). The total Appalachian population was leveling off, with losses in Kentucky (−3 percent), Mississippi (−11 percent), Ohio (−1 percent), Pennsylvania (−5.5 percent), Virginia (−5.7 percent), and West Virginia (−7 percent). The remaining states' growth rates ranged from 0.5 percent in New York to 36.6 percent in Georgia. The white population rose slightly, from 91.6 percent to 91.8 percent of the total. The African American population experienced a decrease from 1,575,348 to 1,475,950, a 6.3 percent loss. At the same time, the African American overall percentage of the total population dropped by 0.5 percent to 7.2 percent. By contrast, the Native American population continued the large growth experienced in the 1970s and 1980s, posting an 81.8 percent increase (24,039). The Native American total was 0.3 percent of the total Appalachian population. The combined other population groups increased by 25,775 (34 percent) for a total of 147,789 (0.7 percent). Asian Pacific was the largest group in the "others" category, which contains three other groups. Despite the large increases for both Native Americans and others, their combined total accounted for only 1 percent of the total population in 1990.

The African American population increased in five of the thirteen states: Alabama, 3.3 percent; Georgia, 31.5 percent; Maryland, 41 percent; New York, 23.6 percent; and North Carolina, 5.5 percent. With the exceptions of Maryland and New York, the white population had similar increases. For Maryland, the white population grew by only 0.6 percent, and in New York it declined by 0.7 percent. Generally speaking, the few states that saw an increase in the African American population also experienced an overall increase in population.

The African American population losses were in Kentucky, −14 percent; Mississippi, −5.6; Ohio, −0.8 percent; Pennsylvania, −30.4 percent; South Carolina, −15.1 percent; Tennessee, −1.4 percent; Virginia, −9.3 percent; and West Virginia, −14.9 percent. Since these

losses were nearly 10 percent of the 1980 African American population, the data signify that the African American exit may be peculiar
to the struggle of being African American in the mountains. For two
of the states, Mississippi and Ohio, the African American losses were
about the same or less than they were from 1970 to 1980. In the
remaining states, the loss differences between the decades ranged
from about 0.4 percent in South Carolina to 26 percent in Pennsylvania (Department of the Interior 1994b, 1994c, 1994d).

It is fair to conclude that African American and white exits are primarily due to the economic climate within the region. Whereas
changes in the nation's economy during the 1980s resulted in
tremendous job loss due to downsizing, the region had already experienced downsizing in the 1970s because of open mining and mech-
anization in the deep mines. Given the perennial weak economic
base in the mountains, the 1980s saw a continuation of the migration
outside the region by African Americans and whites (ARC, 1984). But
for Appalachian African Americans, racism was an added factor that
led to African American departure in numbers. Thus the loss of
African Americans goes beyond the economic condition. It was
pushed along by historical patterns of African Americans being held
back even further when the region's economy experienced difficulties (Hayden 1994; Lewis 1987; Trotter 1990).

METHOD FOR DETERMINING
"CONCENTRATED AREAS"

The mean number of African Americans living in each of the 395
Appalachian counties was close to 4000, according to the 1980 census.
Counties with 4000 or more African Americans in the 1990 census are
identified as "concentrated areas." Contiguous counties with 4000
African Americans each are grouped as a single concentrated area.

Including all counties with a minimum of 4000 African Americans
nets the 22 concentrated areas listed in Table 2. Three new concentrations, one each in New York, Ohio, and Pennsylvania, were
formed. One concentration, in Cabell County, West Virginia, fell
under 4000, so it was dropped. Three other counties in three concentrations dropped below 4000 and were no longer included within
the concentrations. Douglass County in Georgia and Winston County
in Mississippi were added to two of the concentrations. Kentucky and
Virginia did not have any concentrated areas.

Table 3 shows that nineteen of the concentrations had at least one
four-year college or university. In all concentrations, mining or industrial

Table 1 Appalachian Population Totals Within Each State by Race, 1980 and 1990

State	Total Persons			Whites			Blacks			Native American			Others		
	1980	1990	% change	1980	1990	% change	1980	1990	% change	1980	1990	% change	1980	1990	% change
Alabama	2,448,121	2,529,623	3.3%	1,926,125	2,000,348	3.9%	486,438	502,602	3.3%	2,721	10,712	293.7%	32,837	15,961	-51.4%
Georgia	1,104,081	1,508,030	36.6%	1,027,236	1,386,339	35.0%	71,048	93,437	31.5%	2,387	4,399	84.3%	3,410	23,855	599.6%
Kentucky	1,078,076	1,045,357	-3.0%	1,056,048	1,025,449	-2.9%	18,394	15,815	-14.0%	809	1,723	113.0%	2,852	2,370	-16.9%
Maryland	220,132	224,477	2.0%	212,358	213,694	0.6%	6,419	9,049	41.0%	171	288	68.4%	1,184	1,446	22.1%
Mississippi	481,707	428,765	-11.0%	346,080	299,506	-13.5%	133,569	126,098	-5.6%	654	881	34.7%	1,404	2,280	62.4%
New York	1,082,794	1,088,470	0.5%	1,053,887	1,046,727	-0.7%	15,592	19,277	23.6%	3,950	4,318	9.3%	9,365	18,148	93.8%
No. Carolina	1,217,514	1,306,682	7.3%	1,094,682	1,171,545	7.0%	112,137	118,284	5.5%	7,041	9,442	34.1%	3,654	7,411	102.8%
Ohio	1,262,503	1,250,423	-1.0%	1,229,540	1,215,462	-1.1%	26,715	26,491	-0.8%	1,944	3,128	60.9%	4,304	5,342	24.1%
Pennsylvania	6,103,923	5,769,410	-5.5%	5,741,637	5,489,692	-4.4%	332,121	231,039	-30.4%	4,608	7,099	54.1%	25,557	41,580	62.7%
So. Carolina	835,095	888,057	6.3%	654,155	730,531	11.7%	176,481	149,815	-15.1%	675	1,463	116.7%	3,784	6,248	65.1%
Tennessee	2,090,517	2,146,992	2.7%	1,955,618	2,008,904	2.7%	120,755	119,019	-1.4%	2,506	6,315	152.0%	11,618	12,754	9.8%
Virginia	505,480	476,803	-5.7%	493,412	465,195	-5.7%	10,618	9,626	-9.3%	352	545	54.8%	1,098	1,437	30.9%
W. Virginia	1,929,122	1,793,477	-7.0%	1,853,437	1,726,023	-6.9%	65,061	55,398	-14.9%	1,555	3,099	99.3%	9,069	8,957	-1.2%
Totals	20,359,065	20,456,566	0.5%	18,644,215	18,779,415	0.7%	1,573,348	1,475,958	-6.3%	29,373	53,413	81.8%	110,136	147,789	34.2%

Table 2   Counties for the Twenty-two Concentrated Areas by States

ALABAMA	Elmore	Lowndes	*Concentration 13*	Pickens
Concentration 1	*GEORGIA*	Monroe	**Ross**	Spartanburg
Lauderdale	*Concentration 3*	Noxubee	*PENNSYLVANIA*	*TENNESSEE*
Lawrence	Floyd	Otibbeha	*Concentration 14*	*Concentration 19*
Limestone	Bartow	**Winston**	Erie	Knox
Madison	Polk	*NEW YORK*	*Concentration 15*	*Concentration 20*
Morgan	Carroll	*Concentration 7*	**Luzerne**	Hamilton
Colbert	Gwinnett	Chemung	*Concentration 16*	*WEST*
Concentration 2	Hall	*Concentration 8*	Mercer	*VIRGINIA*
Pickens	**Douglass**	**Broome**	*Concentration 17*	*Concentration 21*
Tuscaloosa	*MARYLAND*	*NORTH*	Allegheny	(Fayette)
Walker	*Concentration 4*	*CAROLINA*	Beaver	McDowell
Jefferson	Washington	*Concentration 9*	Fayette	(Mercer)
St. Clair	DC*	Buncombe	Washington	Raleigh
Etowah	*MISSISSIPPI*	*Concentration 10*	Westmoreland	*Concentration 22*
Calhoun	*Concentration 5*	Forsyth	*SOUTH*	Kanawha
Talladega	Marshall	*Concentration 11*	*CAROLINA*	*(Former*
Shelby	*Concentration 6*	Rutherford	*Concentration 18*	*concentration)*
Randolph	Chickasaw	Burke	Anderson	(Cabell)
Tallapoosa	Clay	*OHIO*	Cherokee	
Chambers	Kemper	*Concentration 12*	Greenville	
(Coosa)	Lee	Jefferson	Oconee	

Bold indicates additions since 1980.

Parentheses indicate that a county has dropped below 4000.

*Washington, D.C. is the central city for the Maryland concentration.

sites were found, most of which were small companies. In all but two of the concentrations, there was at least one city or town of 25,000 within the concentration, or there was a large city outside of the concentration to which the concentration was linked.

CITIES AND TOWNS

The total number of cities and towns with 25,000 or more for the entire Appalachian region is 38, 23 of which were within the 22 concentrated areas, as shown in Table 4. Moreover, three of the concentrated areas were linked to a large city outside of the region.

The total number of cities and towns within the concentrations is 23, and the total cities and towns outside the concentrations but linked is 3. As shown in Table 5, the total number of cities and towns over 25,000 but not in the 22 concentrations is 15.

Table 6 shows that the total African American population for the

Table 3 Concentrations by Presence of Three Factors

Concentration #	Mining and Industry	Cities and Towns	Universities
One	x	x	x
Two	x	x	x
Three	x	x	x
Four	x	x	x
Five	x	x	x
Six	x	x	
Seven	x	x	x
Eight	x	x	x
Nine	x	x	x
Ten	x	x	x
Eleven	x	x	x
Twelve	x	x	x
Thirteen	x	x	x
Fourteen	x	x	x
Fifteen	x	x	x
Sixteen	x		
Seventeen	x	x	x
Eighteen	x	x	x
Nineteen	x	x	x
Twenty	x	x	x
Twenty-one	x		
Twenty-two	x	x	x

concentrations was 1,240,673 in 1990 (Department of the Interior, 1994a). In 1980, it was 1,157,986 for the concentrated areas (Hayden 1986b). This increase of 7.1 percent is very significant in light of the 6.3 percent decrease in the overall Appalachian African American population during that same decade. The African American population in the concentrated areas was 13.7 percent of the total population in those areas as opposed to 7.2 percent of the region's population as a whole. The range of African American percent for the concentrations was from 1.2 percent in Concentration 15 (Pennsylvania) to 37 percent in Concentration 5 (Mississippi).

The 22 concentrations made up 84 percent of all African Americans in Appalachia. This is a major increase from the 1980 figure of 73.5 percent (Hayden 1986b). The white population in the concentrations accounted for 41.2 percent of all whites in the region, which is an increase from 36.6 percent. Whereas there was movement among the white population toward the cities and towns, the increase was dramatic for Appalachian African Americans. The increase clearly defines the African American population as urban, with only about 16 percent found in rural areas.

Table 4 Cities and Towns Over 25,000 in the Concentrations

State	Concentration #	Cities and Towns
AL	1	Florence, Huntsville
AL	2	Birmingham, Bessemer, Hoover, Tuscaloosa
GA	3	Rome, Link to Atlanta
MD	4	Hagerstown
MS	5	Link to Memphis, TN
MS	6	Tupelo
NY	7	Elmira
NY	8	Binghamton
NC	10	Winston-Salem
NC	11	Morgantown, Link to Spartanburg, SC
OH	12	Steubenville
OH	13	Between Columbus and Cincinnati
PA	14	Erie
PA	15	Wilkes-Barre, Scranton
PA	16	(Sharon has fewer than 25,000)
PA	17	Pittsburgh
SC	18	Anderson, Spartanburg, Greenville
SC	19	Knoxville
TN	20	Chattanooga
WV	21	Coal Mining
WV	22	Charleston

SUMMARY

This chapter presents the population data for Appalachia from the 1990 Census. The African American population between 1980 and 1990 declined overall and dropped as a percentage of the total Appalachian population. Appalachian African Americans were concentrated into 22 geographic areas. The concentrations were notable for the presence of urban areas, industrial and mining operations, and four-year colleges or universities. The African American population increased in the concentrated areas more than the white population

Table 5 Cities and Towns Not in a Concentration

State	Cities and Towns
MD	Cumberland
NY	Jamestown, Tompkins
OH	Muskinguni
PA	New Castle, Jonestown, State College, Williamsport
TN	Cleveland, Johnson City, Kingsport
WV	Parkersburg, Huntington, Morgantown, Wheeling

Table 6   Twenty-two Concentrations by Race

Conc.	Total Persons	Whites Total	%	Blacks Total	%	Native Amer. Total	%	Others Total	%
One	555,930	459,411	82.6%	86,135	15.5%	4,636	0.8%	5,748	1.0%
Two	1,474,557	1,072,277	72.7%	389,969	26.4%	3,420	0.2%	8,891	0.6%
Three	761,857	677,959	89.0%	63,612	8.3%	1,908	0.3%	18,378	2.4%
Four	121,393	112,764	92.9%	7,375	6.1%	236	0.2%	1,018	0.8%
Five	59,308	36,769	62.0%	22,061	37.2%	67	0.1%	411	0.7%
Six	281,444	177,776	63.2%	101,031	35.9%	712	0.3%	1,925	0.7%
Seven	95,195	88,354	92.8%	5,128	5.4%	301	0.3%	1,412	1.5%
Eight	212,160	203,387	95.9%	3,999	1.9%	438	0.2%	4,336	2.0%
Nine	174,821	159,005	91.0%	14,108	8.1%	526	0.3%	1,182	0.7%
Ten	265,878	197,340	74.2%	65,923	24.8%	453	0.2%	2,162	0.8%
Eleven	132,662	119,921	90.4%	11,610	8.8%	315	0.2%	816	0.6%
Twelve	80,298	75,369	93.9%	4,410	5.5%	253	0.3%	266	0.3%
Thirteen	69,330	64,208	92.6%	4,512	6.5%	148	0.2%	462	0.7%
Fourteen	275,572	258,046	93.6%	14,390	5.2%	379	0.1%	2,757	1.0%
Fifteen	328,149	321,855	98.1%	4,013	1.2%	198	0.1%	2,083	0.6%
Sixteen	121,003	114,531	94.7%	5,810	4.8%	130	0.1%	532	0.4%
Seventeen	2,242,798	2,042,722	91.1%	178,918	8.0%	2,413	0.1%	18,745	0.8%
Eighteen	888,057	730,531	82.3%	149,815	16.9%	1,463	0.2%	6,248	0.7%
Nineteen	335,749	301,788	89.9%	29,299	8.7%	996	0.3%	3,666	1.1%
Twenty	285,536	227,459	79.7%	54,377	19.0%	772	0.3%	2,928	1.0%
Twenty-one	112,052	100,944	90.1%	10,505	9.4%	104	0.1%	499	0.4%
Twenty-two	207,619	192,151	92.5%	13,673	6.6%	233	0.1%	1,562	0.8%
Grand Totals	9,081,368	7,734,567	85.2%	1,240,673	13.7%	20,101	0.2%	86,027	0.9%

did, and the plight of African American people in Appalachia differs from that of whites in the region even more than it has in the past. African Americans' traditional reliance on sources of employment in urbanized areas has intensified, and hence the lack of social services for African Americans has become an even greater problem than it was previously. The historical invisibility of African Americans in Appalachia has worsened in recent years.

With the unsettling of the world global economy, rural America, Appalachia in particular, and Appalachian African Americans specifically are in the midst of further economic hardships. The traditional areas of employment continue to experience job losses, downsizing, outsourcing, and low pay. For African Americans on the bottom of the economic heap, the millennium does not look promising in Appalachia for individuals without education or highly sought skills.

During the eighties there was for all races a noticeable rise in educated and professionals born in the mountains, leaving shortly after high school and returning after years and careers. Many of the returning African Americans had to settle for pay cuts or moved into reduced status and lower-paying careers. This resulted not solely from limited availability of high-status jobs, but even more from racism at the core of the well-established informal system of "white privilege." Dismantling this system is unlikely in Appalachia with the pending economic downfall into the next century. White privilege remains as a final barrier to improved quality of life and life chances for African American Appalachians.

REFERENCES

Appalachian Regional Commission Staff. 1984. "Appalachia: The economic outlook through the eighties." *Appalachia* 16.

Cabbell, Edward J. 1980. "Black invisibility and racism in Appalachia: An informal survey." *Appalachian Journal* 16: 48–54.

Department of the Interior. 1994a. *County and city data book.* Washington, D.C.: U.S. Government Printing Office.

Department of the Interior. 1994b. *U.S. census, 1970.* Washington, D.C.: U.S. Government Printing Office.

Department of the Interior. 1994c. *U.S. census, 1980.* Washington, D.C.: U.S. Government Printing Office.

Department of the Interior. 1994d. *U.S. census, 1990.* Washington, D.C.: U.S. Government Printing Office.

Hayden, Wilburn. 1986a. The Contemporary Appalachian: Urban or Rural. Paper presented at the Ninth Annual Appalachian Studies Conference, Boone, N.C.

Hayden, Wilburn. (1986b). "Blacks an invisible institution in Appalachia?" In *The impact of Institutions in Appalachia: Proceedings of the eighth annual Appalachian studies conference,* ed. Jim Lloyd and Anne Campbell, 128–47. Boone, N.C.: Appalachian Consortium Press.

Hayden, Wilburn. 1993. "Black families: Forgotten people in Appalachia." In *Socio-cultural and service issues in working with rural clients,* ed. Shirley Jones, 21–29. Albany, N.Y.: Nelson A. Rockefeller College of Public Affairs and Policy.

Hayden, Wilburn. 1994. "African-American Appalachians: Barriers to equality." In *Social work in rural communities,* ed. Leon H. Ginsberg. Alexandria, Va.: Council for Social Work Education.

Lewis, Ronald L. 1987. *Black coal miners in America: Race, class and community conflict, 1780–1980.* Lexington: University Press of Kentucky.

Trotter, J. W., Jr. 1990. *Coal, class, and color: Blacks in southern West Virginia, 1915–1932.* Urbana: University of Illinois Press.

Turner, William, and E. J. Cabbell. 1985. *Blacks in Appalachia.* Lexington: University Press of Kentucky.

Wright, Clarence. 1978. "Black Appalachian invisibility—myth or reality?" *Black Appalachian Viewpoints* 1–3.

Economic Development in Rural America

TERRY BUSS

GROWTH AND DECLINE IN RURAL AMERICA

The Federal Reserve Bank of Kansas City recently combined economic use, population, and proximity indicators for rural counties, then looked at economic growth from 1980 to 1993. It analyzed 779 rural counties in 12 states in the Tenth Federal Reserve District) (see Table 1).

Federal Reserve researchers found that winners (high-growth) and losers (decline) were composed of very different county types. Losers were more likely to have larger concentrations of farming and trade-dominated counties, while winners were more likely to boast government, retirement, and mixed-use counties. This likely reflects the remnants of the farm crisis of the late 1980s and early 1990s. Adjacent, larger-population, rural counties tend to grow at greater rates than non-adjacent, smaller-population rural counties. Adjacent counties likely share economic growth factors with urban areas without becoming, as yet, urban areas.

One lesson from Table 1 is that even though it may make sense to talk about differences in prosperity between county types, there are also considerable differences within county categories. From a public policy perspective, this makes targeting federal or state economic development aid or programs problematic: each county should be examined on its own merits. Assistance would be wasted if targeted at all farm-dominated counties, for example, regardless of their economic status.

Another lesson is that, depending on the counties selected for study or how data are presented, rural America can be shown to be prospering or declining overall, or better or worse off than urban America and other regions. This tends to muddy the waters in trying to develop grand strategies for helping rural America, with some arguing that it is in decline (e.g., Barkley 1996) and others that it is in the ascendency (e.g., Gale 1993; Revival of Rural America 1998), depending on their agenda.

**Table 1 Economic Winners and Losers in Rural Counties,
1980–1993, Tenth Federal Reserve District**

County type	Winners		Losers	
	Number	*Percent*	*Number*	*Percent*
Farming	23	15.5	73	30.9
Manufacturing	10	6.8	17	7.2
Mining	1	.7	12	5.1
Government	26	17.6	16	6.8
Retirement	19	12.8	9	3.8
Trade	35	23.6	97	41.1
Other	16	10.8	8	3.4
Mixed	18	12.2	4	1.7
Total	148	100.0	236	100.0

Source: Drabenstott, Mark and Tim R. Smith. "The Changing Economy of the Rural Heartland," in *Economic Forces Shaping the Rural Heartland.*

EVOLVING ECONOMIC DEVELOPMENT: POLICY AND PRACTICE

Federal, state, and local economic development policy and practice have continually evolved over the past three decades to address three epochs in an evolving rural America. The 1970s witnessed the "Rural Renaissance," a period in which rural areas were economically developing and prospering. The 1980s ushered in the farm crisis and decline of many rural places: population loss, declining income, increased poverty, and distress. And the 1990s seem an era of differential prosperity and decline, depending on the region and local circumstances. Economic development strategies evolved from a focus on farming to industrial recruitment to entrepreneurship. In fact, most communities pursue all three simultaneously much as a stock investor diversifies a portfolio (Northern Great Plains Rural Development Commission 1995).

Focus on Farming

Prior to the 1970s, rural programs were devoted to farming needs—credit, subsidies and technical assistance (e.g., Agricultural Extension Service), alleviation of poverty (e.g., Appalachian Regional Commission), and infrastructure improvement (e.g., Economic Development Administration, rural electrification, Corps of Engineers, and Tennessee Valley Authority). Likely as a result of economic restructuring and the crisis in farming, not to mention recession nationally, governments across the country began to take a more proactive role in managing state and local economies; so too did rural policy-makers.

Industrial Recruitment

Following World War II, but especially in the 1970s and 1980s, communities began actively recruiting industry to relocate, branch out, or start up; an activity pejoratively referred to as *smokestack chasing*. Rural places, as do urban ones, promote their amenities and comparative advantages over those of other places. Recruitment activity has become so intense that commentators have come to refer to it as the *war between the states,* or in this case between localities. Communities, in their rush to attract industry, offer every form of incentive imaginable: tax abatement or credits; loans at favorable terms or low interest rates; free or below-market land and buildings; work force or equipment subsidies; regulation relief; technical assistance; and even grants. Many rural places develop industrial parks or rehabbed buildings on speculation, trying to attract tenants.

Rural industrial recruitment strategies tend to focus on attracting branch plants of larger corporations, light manufacturing, distribution centers, and back office functions (e.g., low-skilled data entry for banks), where state and local officials believe they have a comparative advantage. In addition to these, rural policy-makers now chase high-technology companies and service businesses. The eight-county Mount Rogers Planning Commission in Virginia, for example, created a revolving loan fund (see below) to attract high-tech companies, "to target industries that rely on brain power rather than brawn power" (RLFs Promote High-Tech 1998, 4). And officials in the Appalachian Regional Commission boast that every rural and distressed community is covered by a community college (Baldwin 1996). Having access to colleges allows rural policy-makers to replicate high-technology programs common at large, urban universities. In Gadsden, Alabama, Gadsden State Community College set up the Bevill Center for Advanced Manufacturing Technology to offer customized training to employers in the region or those who might be attracted to it.

Public and private initiatives to attract outside industries are now seen by many to be wasted efforts (Barkley 1996). There are just not enough industries willing to relocate or expand operations in rural places to make recruitment worthwhile. And even more importantly, costs of attracting and subsidizing industry often far exceed benefits, and incentive money can often be expended on more productive uses. Most rural places continue to market to outsiders, and just enough are remarkably successful to encourage others to follow suit.

And no public official wants to be accused of not doing everything possible to attract outside business. Nevertheless, no one wants to talk about rural places who went fishing but caught nothing or spend too much.

Entrepreneurship and Business Climate

Rather than devote so much effort to industrial recruitment, many rural places are trying to grow their own economies from within. Indigenous growth requires a focus on starting up new businesses and growing existing ones, with some concern for retention of businesses at risk of closure or flight. In a modest, but illustrative effort, rural communities in North Carolina are redeveloping through the HandMade in America project (Baldwin 1998). Initiative promoters discovered that North Carolina annually contributes $122 million in handmade goods to the regional economy. Local leaders want to increase this many times over through planning and coordination.

Entrepreneurship has ascended as a major rural economic development strategy, especially in places that feel if they do not help themselves, no one else will (Wortman 1996; Hoy 1996). Entrepreneurship has become synonymous with small business development, rather than with development of new products and innovative processes, typically in a high growth context. Interest in rural entrepreneurship developed in the aftermath of the farm crisis of the 1980s. For example, the Council of Governors' Policy Advisors, an affiliate of the National Governors' Association in Washington, D.C., began a series of entrepreneurship studies, sponsored by the U.S. Economic Development Administration, Aspen Institute (through the Ford Foundation), and Northwest Area Foundation, that lead to major policy initiatives by governors in Iowa, North Dakota, Arkansas, and Maine (Buss and Popovich 1988). Then, the Corporation for Enterprise Development, a Washington, D.C.-based think tank, carried the approach further through departments of economic development in Iowa, Montana and Idaho (Horowitz, Levere, and Buss 1994). Individual states, notably Michigan, also supported their own studies (Buss and Gemmel 1994).

Entrepreneurship promotion spawned a host of initiatives, some specialized, some not. Both tend to function in tandem. Specialized ones include:

- *small business incubators,* where entrepreneurs receive business support and advice, and low rents, in the expectation that they will eventually prosper on their own in the local economy;
- *entrepreneurship training,* especially for economically disadvan-

taged groups, displaced workers, or farmers, where "many seeds are planted so that some will grow";

- *technical assistance,* where those who cannot afford help in growing their business or are starting a business receive help;
- *export promotion,* where firms are encouraged to export and occasionally subsidized to export; and
- *financing,* where private capital markets have failed to provided necessary capital for growth and development (see next section).

Studies generally show that entrepreneurs participating in the programs value them, but many entrepreneurs even in the smallest communities are unaware of their existence and many do not seem to need them (e.g., Greenberg and Reeder 1998). In earlier days, in the rush to foster entrepreneurship, organizations with little experience in the field began to work with entrepreneurs. Agricultural extension agents, community colleges, even church groups (this is referred to as faith-based development) began to carve out a role. Although the assistance providers have, over the years, become more sophisticated in their approaches, in the late 1970s and early 1980s, many assistance programs were that in name only. They handed out advice to entrepreneurs that was correct only by accident. Organizations have since become more sophisticated. Now those—public, non-profit and private—offering assistance in some rural places find themselves competing with one another. This has greatly improved quality of services.

Other initiatives focus mostly on improving business climate. This strategy creates a supportive environment for all entrepreneurs. It includes *deregulation*—eliminating needless or counterproductive regulations; *tax reduction*—lowering taxes businesses find oppressive; and *public service provision*—ensuring that education, health, safety, infrastructure, and utilities are effective, efficient and of high quality.

Few analysts argue against this approach, after all this is what government is supposed to do. A new twist has occurred in recent years: reinventing government (Wallace 1997). Even rural economic development programs have come under this reform movement. Whether it will improve practice still remains a point of contention.

Capital

Capital, in the form of debt or equity, drives rural economic development, especially entrepreneurship and local growth generally. There is considerable disagreement about whether sufficient capital exists to serve needs of rural businesses seeking to grow and develop (Capital Formation Steering Committee 1996; Rural Finance Task

Force 1997; Morris and Drabenshott 1991). Those who hold that capital gaps or credit crunches widely exist in rural America, believe any or all of the following.

Concerning debt or credit:

- Rural bankers are inherently conservative (i.e., risk-averse), desiring to lend to longstanding, low- risk customers or to business prospects that have considerable expertise.
- Rural banks lack competitors, so they need not respond to demand for credit even when deals are worthy. Rural banks can charge higher interest rates without facing competition.
- Rural banks are being merged with larger, statewide or interstate banking companies, in the process exporting needed capital.
- Rural banks are closing because they serve very small markets, leaving businesses without credit. Rural banks remaining open do not have sufficient deposits to meet borrower demand.

Concerning equity or venture capital:

- Equity investment does not flow to worthy projects in rural places because investors can make greater profits in areas of concentrated high growth (e.g., Silicon Valley or Route 28 in Massachusetts).
- Equity investors have difficulty finding entrepreneurs, and entrepreneurs in finding equity investors, in rural places.
- Rural places do not have large numbers of venture capitalists or high-net-worth investors willing to acquire equity in companies.
- Rural areas do not have the financial/industrial concentrations and infrastructure—finance experts, professional managers, marketing companies, technicians, skilled labor force, industrial concentrations—to attract or support venture capital investments.

Based on these perceptions, capital markets in rural America have failed. For some, government intervention, either through regulation, direct provision, or subsidy of capital, is appropriate, while for others private reforms are in order (Agricultural and Rural Economy Division 1990; NCARDP 1990; Bonnett 1993; Federal Reserve Bank of Knasas City 1997).

The preponderance of empirical evidence suggests otherwise, however. Studies undertaken by the Federal Reserve Bank (*Financing Rural America* [1997]), USDA's Economic Research Service (*Credit in Rural America* [1997]), Rural Finance Task Force (*The Adequacy of Rural Financial Markets* [1997]), American Bankers Association (*New Tools for Commercial Banks in Rural America* [1994]), Mt. Auburn Associates (*Capital and Credit Needs in the Appalachian Region* [1998]), General Accounting Office (*Rural Development: Availability of Capital for Agriculture, Business and Infrastructure* [1997]), and Gail (1997b) find that rural credit markets effectively serve needs of nearly all businesses in rural areas. In sum, there is no credit gap in rural America.

Consider results of one such study of entrepreneurs seeking bank financing in Idaho, Iowa, and Montana (see Table 2).

Nearly three-fifths of entrepreneurs had bank loans. One in ten was turned down for loans, but only a handful of entrepreneurs were unable eventually to obtain bank financing. These results are replicated in recent studies of entrepreneurs in Appalachia (Mt. Auburn Associates 1998). These and numerous other studies dispel the notion that credit is a problem.

Some analysts believe that as larger banks acquire smaller ones, credit availability in rural places will decrease. Results of studies on the impact of this trend are mixed with respect to rural credit to business (Milkove 1997). Some find that banks will take capital out of rural areas, reallocating it to more productive investments in cities. But others see larger banks, looking for growth, competing for more rural business, not less. Larger banks, having much more capital than small independents actually make more credit available, not less. And banks now use computer credit scoring to evaluate loans, in effect making loans based on merit rather than "good ole boy" networks that characterize rural lending by small banks.

Likewise, the few existing studies suggest that equity investment is widely available in many rural places. Brophy (1997), in a study of equity investment in the form of venture capital and initial public stock offerings (IPOs), found that rural areas do have access to venture capitalists and stock markets, even though these financial institutions may

Table 2 Bank Financing in Rural Idaho, Iowa and Montana, 1993
[percentage of total responses]

Loan Status:	Idaho	Iowa	Montana
Had bank financing	55.2	60.9	57.1
Turned down by bank	10.5	14.7	14.9
Turned down, got loan eventually	7.0	12.2	12.4
Turned down, did not get loan	3.5	2.6	2.5
Did not apply for loan	41.3	36.5	40.4
Seeking loan in future	27.0	23.1	26.5
Seeking loan, turned down in past	5.6	7.6	7.6

Source: Buss, Terry F. and Laura Yancer. "Bank Financing of Entrepreneurs in Rural America," *Public Budgeting, Accounting and Financial Management*.

not be physically located near them. Entrepreneurs have access to equity investors in larger cities that serve rural areas. And, using the Internet, entrepreneurs and investors can link up in ways not possible even a few years ago. So prospects for equity investment in rural areas are good.

Even though there appears to be ample capital flowing to rural America, state and federal credit and equity capital programs abound (Bonnett 1993). State and federal programs offer access to capital where it is otherwise unavailable, and low interest or favorable terms where it is available: USDA's Fund for Rural America, Business and Industry Program, Intermediary Relending Program, Rural Business Enterprise Grants, Rural Technology and Cooperative Development Grants, and Rural Economic Development Grants and Loans; U.S. Small Business Administration's section 7a and 504 Programs; U.S. Economic Development Administration's Economic Adjustment Assistance Program; and Appalachian Regional Commission's programs similar to USDA's (see respective World Wide Web sites for program descriptions; for example: www.ag.ers.gov or www.arc.gov). In vogue at present are revolving loan funds (RLFs) through which a lender receives public monies to lend to business (Mikesell and Wallace 1996). When entrepreneurs repay loans, funds are relent to others. Lenders extract a fee for administering the fund.

Critics of public programs suggest that (1) programs provide capital to those who would have invested private monies anyway—public capital crowds out private, (2) programs transfer monies from those making money to others who are not—robbing Peter to pay Paul, (3) programs subsidize bad businesses ideas or businesses that ought to fail—"lemon economics," (4) programs are inefficient and wasteful, (5) programs although they cost a lot make little difference even in same rural economies, and (6) programs overall lessen economic growth from levels it would have attained without government intervention.

One problem may be that once capital subsidies are created, they are difficult to eliminate. Policy-makers are reluctant to admit that they are bad ideas and program constituents form powerful lobbies to keep them in place.

Another recent trend in public finance of private business is microcredit programs. Micro-businesses employ one or two people, and generally have little growth potential, but they do provide employment for those not employable elsewhere. Public programs provide very small loans at favorable terms. Most are operated as revolving loan funds. Many such programs must be subsidized because they are unable to turn a profit. Because they focus on low-growth micro-businesses, programs do not much affect local economies. For many public officials, they may be more symbolic than economic.

OTHER TRENDS

Networking

Rural economies may not have the same opportunities as cities for growth and development, because they cannot achieve critical mass to bring together financial and technical support, and educational institutions, and most importantly, clusters or concentrations of similar industries that share these institutions (Gibbs and Bernat 1997). Rural places may stimulate this clustering. In the private sector, networking, clustering, and strategic alliances are popular. Firms come together temporarily to exploit economic opportunities that they cannot undertake on their own. Microsoft, a huge corporation, has a cumbersome bureaucracy that cannot develop certain products effectively or efficiently; but partnering with a small company, not so encumbered, can benefit both. Local economic development organizations in rural areas have sensed an opportunity to contribute. They supplement existing networks or create them where none exist. The Appalachian Center for Economic Networks, serving eleven rural Ohio counties, is such an organization (New Directions for Microenterprise Projects 1998). If properly done, these approaches may attract more investment to rural places.

Targeting

Because resources are scarce, rural places like to target resources to those sectors where they may get the most bang for their investment. The latest trend in rural places is to target value-added manufacturing, that is, industries that process food or other natural resource-based products (Gale 1997). The idea is to add value as close to the source of raw materials as possible, in this case farms, mines, forests, and the like. This makes sense as a strategy if the local economies supporting value-added manufactures are the best economically, as opposed to the best politically (see also Buss, forthcoming). This approach is quite new, and not yet studied by economists, so it is unclear how successful targeting will be.

Telecommunications

The telecommunications revolution, stimulated by the Telecommunications Act of 1996 and revised regulations from the Federal Communications Commission in 1997, may lead to greatly increased development opportunities for rural places (Stenberg et al. 1997). Firms can cluster or network (see above) without having to be in the same geographical location. Buying and selling goods and services is greatly enhanced by the Internet. Having access to telecommunications of all kinds leads to innovation and new product development. Rural populations may become part of a work force electronically, staying a home rather than leaving the community for work. The possibilities are endless, yet too new to evaluate adequately.

EZ/ECs and CDFIs

Economic strategies discussed thus far intersect in the new Enterprise Zone/Enterprise Community (EZ/ECs) program and Community Development Financial Institutions (CDFIs). The Clinton Administration designated three rural EZs and thirty rural ECs in 1994 (Reeder 1997). Designation as an EZ or EC makes communities eligible for various types of federal aid, in addition to whatever states may channel to designees. Unlike EZs under past administrations, new ones combine economic development with social services. The three EZs are eligible for $40 million in Social Service Block Grants each, and ECs for nearly $3 million each. USDA also targeted an additional $50 million annually to the EZ/EC areas for infrastructure and business assistance. Each area is eligible for federal tax breaks, relief from government regulation, and other incentives.

In 1997, the Clinton Administration added a program comparable to the EZ/EC initiative, the Rural Economic Area Partnership (REAP), to assist rural places in the Northern Great Plains. Recently, North Dakota received REAP designations for two zones. Funding under REAP is used to develop plans, then implement them. North Dakota created a revolving loan fund.

Earlier in 1996, the Clinton Administration created the Community Development Financial Institutions (CDFI) program for distressed communities, funded at about $50 million annually (Reeder 1997). Selected financial institutions—banks, credit unions, loan or venture capital funds—interested in community development receive subsidies and incentives to invest in distressed areas through first-time home-buyer mortgages, rental housing rehab, start-up business loans, and bank services for low income people. So far, thirty-two CDFIs have been created, ten of which serve rural places.

These programs in turn parallel the 1994 Northwest Economic Adjustment Initiative, a $1.2 billion, five-year finance and technical assistance program for businesses, workers, tribes, and communities hurt by reduced federal timber harvesting in California, Oregon, and Washington. This program also promotes all sorts of partnerships to address revitalization problems.

Although focusing on distressed communities is laudable, the history of similar programs show only isolated instances of success (Fisher and Peters 1997). Evaluations conclude that zones performed no better, and in some cases worse, than comparable areas without zones. Business is not attracted from beyond distressed communities, leading to new jobs and employment. Rather, local businesses simply move into zones to take advantage of incentives. Businesses in the zones tend to hire workers, then take advantage of incentives; in other words, incentives compensate business for what they would have done anyway. Combining economic and social policy has not worked in many places, and early results are not encouraging. Small businesses are jeopardized when forced to hire zone residents who do not want to work, have no work experience, are uneducated, and may have a host of social problems.

RESPONDING TO SHORT-TERM ECONOMIC CRISIS

Most economies, including rural ones, periodically face short-term economic crises, like plant, hospital, or military base closures. In rural places, loss of a major employer can devastate communities with small economies (Knapp et al. 1996; Stenberg 1998; Isserman and Stenberg 1994). Usually, when thinking about rural places, economic crisis often concerns loss of family farms, mine closings, or related industries. Family farms in many rural places are becoming economically redundant as corporate farms gobble them up. Mining ebbs and flows based on energy prices, environmental regulation, competitive pricing, and the like. And farm implement manufacturers, food processors, and distributors suffer when agriculture suffers generally.

But rural places also face crises not resulting from agriculture- or natural resource-based problems. With some manufacturing sectors moving increasingly into rural places, communities are likely to experience the same shocks as urban areas when plants close down. Competition from other regions, either because of free market forces (cheap overseas goods) or public policy like NAFTA (North America Free Trade Agreement) are culprits. Rural hospitals, serving catchment areas dominated by Medicaid- and Medicare-insured or uncompensated care patients, frequently close or greatly cut back operations, not only eliminating jobs, but also denying rural populations needed services. Recently, health maintenance organizations devastated communities with high concentrations of elderly people by dropping them from their health care plans. And military base closures, because of inefficiency or redundancy, not only cost local people jobs, but also take with them military consumers of local products.

Rural places must exert great care not to waste scarce economic resources better invested in responding to short-term economic crisis. Consider military base closings, for example. Some rural places were hard-hit by defense cutbacks, but others were not. Many public officials, encouraged by exaggerated consultant reports, misperceived the nature of the closings. Military bases did not purchase most of their supplies locally. Much employment on bases was taken by wives or husbands of service people. And even though located in rural areas, military bases are part of larger economies able to absorb the shock. So in some places, the crisis was not severe.

Likewise, community leaders misperceived redevelopment opportunities, again, likely influenced by faulty consultant reports. They tried immediately to devise strategies to redevelop closed bases as industrial parks, private airports, tourist attractions, and business incubators and the like. Little thought was given to the viability of these initiatives, and funds were wasted. Rehabbing abandoned military buildings and cleaning up the environment, then marketing them without any notion of whether industry would relocate there, proved foolhardy. It may have been better to do nothing.

PEOPLE, PLACES, AND ECONOMIC DEVELOPMENT

At the heart of rural economic development is the issue of whether to invest scarce resources in places or people. Nearly all rural economic development policy is place-based (GAO 1997). Its intent appears to be to keep people in rural locations, hoping that they can grow their economies, rather than abandon them (e.g., Rowley 1998). The National Commission on Agriculture and Rural Development Policy (1990) makes this explicit. Two goals of rural policy are: "Rural areas and people must be economically self-reliant," and "Rural areas and people must be able to adapt to change" (6). Most rural public investment flows to place, based on the assumption that people living there will benefit. Building industrial parks, recruiting industry, supporting entrepreneurship, developing infrastructure, and improving housing and the like are place-based strategies, because they help only if people reside in rural places where investment are made (Council of State Community Development Agencies 1995). Even training or retraining programs are place-based in the sense that they train people for jobs believed to be needed in the area, but not for better jobs out of town.

Some place-based strategies may work well, to be sure, but others clearly have not. There are still large pockets of rural poverty—poverty counties—in the Mississippi Delta, throughout many states in Appalachia, and on Indian reservations, in spite of the billions spent to make them better places to live (Jaffe 1998). (Needless to say, the same phenomenon applies to urban ghettos, whose problems also seem intractable.) One reason why pockets of poverty remain is that even after continuing heavy public investment, these rural places still lack sustainable competitive advantages over other places. So public subsidies hold many people in place without making their lives better.

People-based programs are quite rare (some might argue non-existent) in rural areas, or urban ones for that matter. These strategies would either build capacity, allowing people more opportunity or choice, or give them the wherewithal to choose. This is the basis of A. Sen's Nobel Prize-winning insight. Allowing people to participate in educational programs that do not hold them to a place builds their capacity to leave it. An engineering degree is portable, opening up opportunities in many places; while training in farm machinery repair is more limiting. Providing displaced rural workers with vouchers to pay for moving expenses allows them to leave town for better opportunities elsewhere; offering subsidized housing on location does not.

It's easy to see why place-based strategies predominate. First, public funding from state and federal government has always flowed to places. This tradition is so long-standing that it would be difficult to conceive of alternative ways to allocate resources. Second, few public officials would be willing to invest in people, only to see them leave (e.g., education, McGranahan 1995). Investments would likely be viewed as wasted. Third, it may be the case that investing in people causes those who are able to leave to go, leaving an increasingly impoverished dependent population in their wake. Fourth, public funding tends to be spent where results are highly visible—a new dam, rehabbed school, expanded park system, or interstate highway connector. Most people-based investments are not so visible. Fifth, government allocation of resources is based not only on efficiency, channeling monies to those places that are economically viable, but also on equity, redistributing resources to places left behind. As long as some places are winners and others losers, government will pursue redistributive strategies.

Perhaps the time has come to invest in people as an economic development strategy. We know how to do this, but have chosen not to.

REFERENCES

Agricultural and Rural Economy Division. 1990. *Financial Market Intervention as a Rural Development Strategy*. Washington, D.C.: Economic Research Service, US Department of Agriculture, #AGES90-70.

American Bankers Association. 1994. *New Tools for Commercial Banks in Rural America.* Washington, D.C.: ABA.

Baldwin, Fred D. 1996. "Appalachia's Best-Kept Secret," *Appalachia* September/ December, 1–9.

———. 1998. "HandMade Communities," *Appalachia,* April/January, 1–7.

Barkley, David L. 1996. "Turmoil in Traditional industry: Prospects for Nonmetropolitan Manufacturing." In *Economic Forces Shaping the Rural Heartland,* 13–38. Kansas City: Federal Reserve Bank of Kansas City.

Bernat, G. Andrew. 1997. "Manufacturing and the Midwest Rural Economy." *Rural Development Perspectives* 12 (2): 2–12.

Besser, Terry L. 1998. "Employment in Small Towns." *Rural Development Perspectives* 13 (2): 31–39.

Bonnett, Thomas W. 1993. *Strategies for Rural Competitiveness: Policy Options for State Government.* Washington, D.C.: Council of Governors' Policy Advisors.

Bowers, Douglas. 1996. "National Growth Continues to Benefit Rural Industries." *Rural Conditions and Trends* 7 (1): 4–6.

Brophy, David J. 1997. "Developing Rural Equity Capital Markets." In Federal Reserve Bank of Kansas City, *Financing Rural America,* 50–65. Kansas City: Federal Reserve Bank of Kansas City.

Buss, Terry F., and M. Popovich. 1988. *Growth From Within Iowa, North Dakota, Arkansas and Maine.* Washington, D.C.: Council of State Planning Agencies.

Buss, Terry F., and D. Gemmel. 1994. *Economic Development of Michigan's Upper Penninsula.* Lansing, Mich.: Department of Commerce.

Buss, Terry F., and S. Dwvedi. 1997. "Military Base Closings and Economic Development: A Review and Update." *Economic Development Commentary* 21: 19–26.

Buss, Terry F., and L. C. Yancer. 1999. "Bank Financing of Entrepreneurs in Rural America." *Public Budgeting, Accounting and Financial Management* (in press).

Buss, Terry F. 1999. "The Case Against Targeting." *Economic Development Review* (forthcoming).

———. 1999. "The State-of-the-Art in Micro-credit Programs." *International Journal of Economic Development* (forthcoming).

Capital Formation Steering Committee. 1996. *The Shortage of Early Stage Capital for Emerging High-Growth Companies in North Carolina.* Chapel Hill, N.C.: Council for Entrepreneurial Development.

Committee on Small Business. 1993. Hearings on the Federal Role in Rural Economic Development. 103rd Congress, 1st Session, July 21, U.S. Senate.

Council of State Community Development Agencies. 1995. Holistic Community Development. www.sso.org/coscda.

Economic Research Service. 1995. *Understanding Rural America.* Economic Research Service, no. 710. Washington, D.C.: U.S. Department of Agriculture.

Economic Research Service. 1997. *Credit in Rural America.* Economic Research Service. Washington, D.C.: U.S. Department of Agriculture.

Federal Reserve Bank of Kansas City. 1996. *Economic Forces Shaping the Rural Heartland.* Kansas City: Federal Reserve Bank of Kansas City.

Federal Reserve Bank of Kansas City. 1997. *Financing Rural America.* Kansas City: Federal Reserve Bank of Kansas City.

Fisher, Peter S., and A. H. Peters. 1997. "Tax and Spending Incentives and Enterprise Zones." New England Economic Review (March–April): 109–31.

Gale, Fred. 1996. "Manufacturing Jobs Continued to Shift to Nonmetro Areas in 1993." *Rural Conditions and Trends* 7 (1): 33–38.

———. 1997. "Value-added Manufacturing," *Rural Conditions and Trends* 8 (3): 4–6.

———. 1997. "Most Value-added Firms Have Access to Needed Capital." *Rural Conditions and Trends* 8 (3): 31–33.

———. 1997. *Is There a Rural-Urban Technology Gap?* Economic Research Service, no. 736-01. Washington, D.C.: U.S. Department of Agriculture.

General Accounting Office. 1994. *Rural Development: Patchwork of Federal Programs Needs to be Reappraised.* GAO, RCED-94-165, July. Washington, D.C.

———. 1995. *Rural Development: Patchwork of Federal Water and Sewer Programs Is Difficult to Use.* GAO, RCED-95-160BR, April. Washington, D.C.

———. 1996. *Economic Development: Limited Information Exists on the Impact of Assistance Provided by Three Agencies.* GAO, RCED-96-103, April. Washington, D.C.

———. 1997a. *Rural Development: Availability of Capital for Agriculture, Business and Infrastructure.* GAO, RCED-97-109, May. Washington, D.C.

———. 1997b *Economic Development Activities.* GAO, RCED-97-193. Washington, D.C.

Gibbs, Robert M. and G. A. Bernat. 1997. "Rural Industry Clusters Raise Local Earnings." *Rural Development Perspectives* 12 (3): 18–25.

Greenberg, Elizabeth and R. J. Reeder. 1998. *Who Benefits from Business Assistance Programs?* Economic Research Service, U.S. Department of Agriculture, no. 736-04. Washington, D.C.

Honadle, B. W. 1993. "Rural Development Policy." *Economic Development Quarterly* 7 (3): 227–36.

Levere, Andrea, M. Horowitz, and T. F. Buss. 1994. *Entrepreneurial Action Handbook. Washington, D.C.: Council for Enterprise Development.*

Hoy, Frank. 1996. *"Entrepreneurship: A Strategy for Rural Development." In* Rural Development Research, ed. Thomas D. Rowley, et al. Westport, Conn.: Greenwood.

Isserman, Andrew, and P. Stenberg. 1994. *The Recovery of Rural Economies from Military Base Closures.* Morgantown: Regional Research Institute, West Virginia University.

Jaffe, Greg. 1998. "Pockets of Decay Are Plaguing the South," *Wall Street Journal,* March 6, A2.

Knapp, Tim, et al. 1996. "A Bumpy Economic Road for Rural Communities," *Small Town* 27, 12–19.

McGranahan, David A. 1998. *Local Problems Facing Manufacturers.* Economic Research Service, US Department of Agriculture, no. 736-03. Washington, D.C.

———. 1998. "Can Manufacturing Reverse Rural Great Plains Depopulation?" *Rural Development Perspectives* 13 (1): 35–45.

———. 1995. "Rural-Urban Migration Patterns Shift." *Rural Conditions and Trends* 6 (1): 14–17.

Mikesell, James J., and G. B. Wallace. 1996. "Are Revolving Loan Funds a Better Way to Finance Rural Development?" Economic Research Service. Washington, D.C.: Department of Agriculture.

Milkove, Daniel. 1997. "Interstate Banking and Rural America," *Rural Conditions and Trends* 7 (1): 43–47.

Morris, Charles, and Mark Drabenstott. 1991. "Rethinking the Rural Credit Gap." *Rural Development Perspectives* 7: 20–25.

Mt. Auburn Associates. 1998. *Capital and Credit Needs in Appalachian Region.* Somerville, Mass: Mt. Auburn.

National Commission on Agriculture and Rural Development Policy. 1990. *Future Directions in Rural Development Policy.* NCARDP. Washington, D.C.

"New Directions for Microenterprise Projects." 1998. Appalachia Center for Economic Networks, Athens, Ohio. www.seorf.ohiou.edu.

Northern Great Plains Rural Development Commission. 1995. Business Development Strategy, www.rrtrade.org/NGP.

Paarlberg, Donald. 1988. "Three Myths About Rural America." *State Legislatures* March, 34–38.

Radin, Beryl A. 1996. "State Rural Development Councils Are Creating Public-Private Partnerships." *Rural Development Perspectives* 11 (2): 2–9.

Reeder, Rick. 1997. "General Assistance Funding Remains Steady." *Rural Conditions and Trends* 8 (1): 9–14.

Rowley, Thomas D. 1997. "The Value of Rural America." *Rural Development Perspectives* 12 (1): 2–4.

———. 1998. "Sustaining the Great Plains." *Rural Development Perspectives* 13 (1): 2–6.

"RLFs Promote High Tech Businesses in Rural Virginia." *Economic Development Digest* 10 (1): 1, 4.

Rural Finance Task Force. 1997. *The Adequacy of Rural Financial Markets.* Columbia: Rural Policy Research Institute, University of Missouri.

Sears, David, W. 1992. *Gearing Up for Success: Organizing a State for Rural Development.* Washington, D.C.: The Aspen Institute.

Stenberg, Peter L. 1997. "Rural Areas in the New Telecommunications Era." *Rural Development Perspectives* 12 (3): 32–38.

———. 1998. "Rural Communities and Military Base Closures." *Rural Development Perspectives* 13 (2): 10–18.

"The Revival of Rural America." 1998. *The Wilson Quarterly* 22 (Spring): 16–41.

Task Force on Rural Development. 1988. *New Alliances for Rural America.* Washington, D.C.: National Governors' Association.

Verhovek, Sam. 1998. "Old and New West Clash in Remote Oregon Area." *New York Times, November 20, A22.*

Wallace, George. 1997. "Reinvented Business Assistance Programs." *Rural Conditions and Trends* 8 (1): 20–25.

Wortman, Max S. 1996. "The Impact of Entrepreneurship upon Rural Development." In *Rural Development Research,* ed. Thomas D. Rowley, et al. Westport, Conn.: Greenwood.

Contributors

BONNIE JEAN ADAMS, Ph.D., is a scholar who does research on rural populations in the South.

KAREN ANIJAR, Ph.D., is Assistant Professor of Curriculum and Instruction, Arizona State University. She is the author of the forthcoming *Teaching Towards the 24th Century: The Social Curriculum of Star Trek in the Schools.*

SHIRLEY L. BAUGHER, Ph.D., is Dean, College of Human Ecology, University of Minnesota.

TERRY BUSS, Ph.D., is Chair of the Department of Public Management, Suffolk University. He is author of *Communicating Social Science Research to Policy Makers.*

KATHERINE L. CASON, Ph.D., is Associate Professor, Department of Food Science and Human Nutrition, Clemson University. She is the South Carolina coordinator for the Expanded Food and Nutrition Educational Program.

LINDA K. CUMMINS is a research consultant who writes and lives in Beaufort, North Carolina. She is co-author of *Social Skills Demonstrated: Beginning Direct Practice.*

ROCHELLE L. DALLA, Ph.D., is Assistant Professor of Family Science, University of Nebraska.

LAURA DeHAAN, Ph.D., is Assistant Professor, Child Development and Family Science, North Dakota State University.

JAMES DEAL, Ph.D., is Associate Professor and Chair, Department of Child Development and Family Science, North Dakota State University.

SANDRA FAIMAN-SILVA, Ph.D., is Professor of Anthropology, Bridgewater State College. She is author of *Choctaws at the Crossroads: The Political Economy of Class and Culture in the Timber Region.*

CAROL K. FEYEN, M.S., is a Ph.D. candidate at the University of Wisconsin.

STEPHEN M. GAVAZZI, Ph.D., is Associate Professor, Human Development and Family Science at Ohio State University.

WILBURN HAYDEN JR., Ph.D., ACSW, CMSW, CSWM, is Associate Professor and Director of the Master of Social Work Program, Social Work and Gerontology Department, California University of Pennsylvania.

DAVID L. KEARNS, Ph.D., is Associate Professor of Clinical Family Medicine at the College of Medicine, University of Iowa. He is author of *Health Promotion: Achieving High-Level Wellness in the Later Years* (with Michael L. Teague and David M. Rosenthal).

PHYLLIS LEVINE, Ph.D., is Assistant Research Professor in the University of Washington Department of Health Services, School of Community Medicine and Public Health, and a Research Coordinator at the Center for Disability Policy and Research in Seattle, Washington.

DENIS LISHNER, M.S.W., is Associate Director of the Washington, Wyoming, Alaska, Montana and Idaho Rural Health Research Center, Department of Family Medicine, at the University of Washington School of Medicine.

PATRICK C. MCKENRY, Ph.D., is a Professor, Human Development and Family Science, at the Ohio Agricultural Research and Developmental Center at Ohio State University.

SUSAN MURTY, Ph.D., is Assistant Professor of Social Work, University of Iowa. She served as the President of the National Rural Social Work Caucus from 1996 to 1998.

ALICE PORTER, M.Sc., is Health Policy Analyst with the University of Washington Center for Disability Policy and Research.

MARY RICHARDSON, Ph.D., is Associate Professor of Health Services, and Director of the University of Washington Graduate Program in Health Services Administration, School of Community Medicine and Public Health, and Director of the Center for Disability Policy and Research.

DAVID ROSENTHAL, Ph.D., is an associate professor and Director of Counseling and Health Promotion Services, Department of Family Medicine, University of Iowa College of Medicine.

TAMMY H. SHEIDEGGER, Ph.D., is an adjunct professor at Ohio State University and in private practice with River Valley Counseling Associates in Fairfield County, Ohio.

ERIK R. STEWART, Ph.D., is Assistant Director of the Ohio State University Survey Research Unit and Adjunct Assistant Professor, Human Development and Family Science.

Index